Reading Instruction in the Secondary School

Reading Instruction in the Secondary School

Betty D. Roe
Tennessee Technological University

Barbara D. Stoodt
University of North Carolina at Greensboro

Paul C. Burns
University of Tennessee at Knoxville

Rand McNally College Publishing Company/Chicago

Rand McNally Education Series
B. Othanel Smith, Advisory Editor

To Mike
and
To Linda and Susan

Preface

Reading Instruction in the Secondary School is committed to the premise that teachers and students should have a balanced approach to the study of reading instruction. To meet this goal, the book's contents include reading theory and practical teaching suggestions. The book provides strategies for teaching reading in the secondary school useful to special reading teachers, content area teachers, and administrators.

This volume contains a comprehensive set of instructional aids. Each chapter begins with a chapter overview designed to provide the student with an appropriate mental set for reading the chapters. Purpose-setting questions follow in each chapter and help to increase comprehension by focusing on important ideas. Assessment questions end each chapter and students determine for themselves their level of mastery of information. Additional self-improvement activities are suggested at the end of each chapter and are useful in ensuring a task-oriented reading of the chapter.

Practical activities for improving students' reading performance are included in abundance in this text. Examples presented include illustrative lesson plans, worksheets, and activity lists. As a result, this text should continue to be a valuable reference book when one begins actual teaching in the schools.

The table of contents suggests the comprehensiveness of the text. All of the major components of a secondary school reading program are treated. In addition, post-secondary reading programs are discussed due to recent increased interest in this area. The introductory chapter presents clearly the need for secondary school reading instruction. The second chapter considers possible causes of reading difficulties of college students. Techniques for adjusting reading assignments to fit all students are discussed in Chapter Three. The three chapters that follow are devoted to basic work recognition skills vocabulary development, and comprehension skills. A more direct application of various skills is presented in the seventh chapter, which discusses reading-study skills. The three subsequent chapters go into detail about reading in different content fields. Due to the importance of individualizing instruction, assessment of pupil progress is treated extensively in Chapter 10. Chapter 11 outlines various plans for reading instruction in the secondary school. Total school reading programs, which involve all of the personnel in a school, are treated in great detail. Further useful material can be found in the Appendices, and extensive cross-referencing is provided within the book. Bibliographies of related readings and sources of instructional materials are found throughout the text.

We, the authors, are indebted to many people for their assistance as our manuscript was being prepared. We would like to acknowledge the many teachers and students whose inspiration was instrumental in making this book possible; it is impossible to name all of them. Appreciation is expressed to those who have granted permission to use sample materials or citations from their respective works. Credit for these contributions has been given in the footnotes. In particular, appreciation is due to reviewers of the first draft of the manuscript: Dr. J. Harvey Littrell, Kansas State University; Dr. Ken L. Dulin, University of Wisconsin–Madison; Dr. Fay F. Bowren, Illinois State University; and Dr. Nicholas A. DiObilda, Glassboro State College.

Grateful acknowledgement is also given to Helen Woodruff for her editorial assistance throughout the production of the book.

Betty D. Roe   Tennessee Technological University
Barbara D. Stoodt   University of North Carolina at Greensboro
Paul C. Burns   University of Tennessee at Knoxville

Contents

1 Reading in the secondary school

Overview 2
  Purpose-setting questions 2
  Key vocabulary 2

The Need for Reading Instruction in the Secondary School 2
  Reading achievement of secondary students 2
  Reading to meet daily needs 6
  Reading as a recreational activity 6
  Reading in various content areas 10

The secondary shool reading program 11
  Phases of the reading program 11
  Some Faulty Assumptions about teaching reading 12
  Persons Involved in a program 13

Self-test 14
Enrichment activities 15
Selected references 15

2 Factors which can cause reading disability

Overview 17
  Purpose-setting questions 17
  Key vocabulary 17

A description of disabled readers in the secondary school 17

Physical causes of reading disability 20
  Vision 21
  Visual perception 25
  Eye movements 25
  Hearing 25
  Auditory perception 26
  General health 27

Factors in reading disability 27
Intellectual factors 28
Emotional factors • *Self-Concept* 29
Language factors 33
Home factors 35

Educational factors in reading disability 36

Concluding comments 37

Self-test 39

Enrichment activities 40

Selected references 41

3 Adjusting reading assignments to fit all students

Overview 42
Purpose-setting questions 42
Key vocabulary 43

Readability of printed materials 43
Factors that influence readability 45
Readability formulas 47

Grouping for motivation and differentiated assignments 49

Approaches for use with content materials 53
Study guides 54
Structural overviews 59
Directed reading approaches 61

Alternate textbooks or supplementary readings 68

Rewritten materials 70
Other adjustments for textbook usage 72

Language experience materials 72

Developing Teaching Units 73
Introduction of the unit 73
Development of the unit 74
Organization of findings 74
Culmination activities 75
Sample unit ideas 75

Media selection sources 76

Self-test 77

Enrichment activities 78

Selected references 79

4 Word recognition in the secondary school program

Overview 81
  Purpose-setting questions 81
  Key vocabulary 81

Sight vocabulary 82
  Activities 84

Word Analysis Skills 86
  Contextual Analysis • *Organization of context clues* • *Assessment of contextual clue usage* • *Instructional strategies* • *Concluding comments* 87
  Structural analysis • *Inflectional endings* • *Affixes and roots* • *Activities* • *Compound words* • *Syllabication/Accent* 91
  Phonic analysis 101
  Dictionary use • *Activities* 106

Balance in word recognition skills 109

Self-test 111

Enrichment activities 112

Selected references 113

5 Concept and vocabulary development

Overview 114
  Purpose-setting questions 114
  Key vocabulary 114

Experience and concept development 115
  Activities 117

A planned vocabulary development program 118
  Assessment 120
  Sensitize and motivate 121
  Word attributes 125
  Preteach and guide 128
  Connectives • *Activities* 130
  Focus upon essential words 133
  Discussion sessions 133
  Systemize strategies 134
  Wide reading 135

Language features related to sentence meaning 135
  Syntax 136
  Punctuation 137
  Figurative expressions • *Activities* 138

Concluding comments 139

6 Comprehension   Self-test   140

Enrichment activities   141

Selected references   142

Overview   143
   Purpose-setting questions   143
   Key vocabulary   143

What is comprehension?   143
   Experience   145

Thinking skills   147
   Organization • *Main ideas* • *Activities* • *Details* • *Paragraph structure*
      • *Whole selections*   147
   Levels of thinking and questioning techniques • *Literal thinking* •
      Activities • *Interpretative thinking* • *Activities* • *Evaluative thinking*
      or critical thinking • *Creative thinking* • *Helping students*
      question   155

Affective dimension   165

Visualization   166

Flexibility   167

Concluding comments   168

Self-test   170

Enrichment activities   171

Selected references   172

7 Reading-study   Overview   174
   skills   Purpose-setting questions   174
      Key vocabulary   175

Study methods   175
   SQ3R   176
   EVOKER   177
   SQRQCQ   177
   REAP   178

Organizational skills   179
   Outlining   179
   Summarizing   182
   Notetaking   183

Location skills 185
 Libraries 185
 Books • *Preface and/or introduction* • *Table of contents* • *Indexes* •
  Appendixes • *Glossaries* • *Footnotes* • *Bibliographies* 188
 Special reference books 190

Report writing 192

Reading to following directions 194
 Activities 195

Graphic aids 197
 Maps • *Activities* 197
 Graphs • *Picture graphs (or pictographs)* • *Circle or pie graph* • *Bar
  graphs* • *Line graphs* • *Reading graphs* 200
 Tables 205
 Charts and diagrams 206
 Pictures 206

Adjusting rate to fit purpose and materials 209
 Factors affecting rate 210
 Techniques of increasing rate and encouraging flexibility • *Machines*
  • *Timed readings* • *Skimming and scanning techniques* •
  Flexibility exercises 210

Retention 213

Test-taking 215

Self-test 217

Enrichment activites 218

Selected references 219

**8 The demands
and common
elements of
content reading**

Overview 221
 Purpose-setting questions 221
 Key vocabulary 221

Need for reading instruction with subject matter 221

The demands of content reading 222
 Basic concepts 225
 Vocabulary 226
 Writing style 226
 Organization style 227
 Readability 227
 Understanding level 227
 Flexible rate 228

Graphic aids   228
Interest   228
Summary statement   228

Common elements within the content areas   229
Abilities and skills   229
Vocabulary   230
Writing patterns   231

Concluding comments   233

Self-test   234

Enrichment activities   235

Selected references   236

9A Reading in the content areas: part 1

Overview   237
Purpose-setting questions   237
Key vocabulary   237

Social sciences   237
Vocabulary, style and organization   238
Writing patterns   240
Additional skills   247
Using newspapers and magazines • *Readability* • *Reading skills* •
Techniques for developing reading skills   248

Science and health   253
Style and vocabulary   253
Writing patterns   254
Additional skills   262
Resource books and magazines   263

Mathematics   264
Words and symbols • *Activities* • *264*
Writing patterns   266
Additional skills   269
Some high interest materials for mathematics   269

English (Language Arts)   270
Types of literature   271
Composition and grammar   275
Individualized reading   276
Other language arts   277

Foreign language   277
Activities   277

Concluding comments   278

Self-test 280

Enrichment activities 281

Selected references 281

9B Reading in the content areas: part 2   Overview 284
Purpose-setting questions 284
Key vocabulary 284

Industrial arts, business education, home economics 284
Common aspects of vocational materials • *Features of reading material • Technical vocabulary • Following directions • Interpreting of graphics • Reading and study of printed materials* 285
Application to specific subjects • *Industrial arts • Business education • Home economics* 293

Other school subjects 305
Physical education 305
Driver eduction • *Activities* 307
Art 316
Music 318

Self-test 320

Enrichment activities 321

Selected references 322

10 Assessment procedures   Overview 323
Purpose-setting questions 323
Key vocabulary 323

Standardized tests of reading achievement 324
Representative standardized reading tests • *Survey • Diagnostic • Oral • Study skills* 326
Other types of standardized tests 330
Selecting and using standardized tests 333

Informal tests of reading achievement 335
Vocabulary • *San Diego Quick Assessment* 335
Group Reading Inventory (G.R.I.) 337
Skill inventories 341
Informal Reading Inventories (I.R.I.) 351
Cloze test procedure 353

Observation checklist 355

Self-assessment 356

Attitude 357

Interests 362

Self-test 363

Enrichment activities 363

Selected references 366

11 Secondary school reading programs

Overview 368
    Purpose-setting qeustions 368
    Key vocabulary 369

Total-school programs 369
    Staff inservice training 370
    Reading committee 371
    Define reading philosophy 372
    Surving student needs 372
    Setting goals 372
    Survey needs for staff and materials 373
    Planning program to meet goals 374
    Initiating program 377
    Evaluating the program • *Student progress* • *Staff utilization* •
       Effectiveness of activities and materials • *Ongoing process* •
       Needs assessment 377

Special "English" classes 379
    Special sections of English 379
    Special units in English 379

Special remedial reading classes 380
    Identifying remedial readers 380
    Working with remedial readers 380
    Reading improvement classes 381

Reading laboratories 382

Combination programs 383

Responsibilities for reading instruction 383
    Principal or administrator 383
    Reading consultant 388
    Special reading teacher 389
    Summary statement 389

Self-test 389

Enrichment activities   391

Selected references   391

12 Post secondary reading programs

Overview   393
   Purpose-setting questions   393
   Key vocabulary   393

Need for such programs   393

Types of programs   395
   Developmental programs • Lectures • Workbook/worktexts •
    Mechanical equipment   395
   Remedial programs   399
   Combination programs   400

Approaches to organization   401
   Regular classroom organization   401
   Open laboratory   401
   Combination approaches   402

Approaches to instruction   402
   Lecture classes   402
   Project packages   403
   Strictly individual assignments   406
   Standardized tests   407

Three post-secondary programs   407
   Program 1   407
   Program 2   408
   Program 3   408

Self-test   408

Enrichment activities   409

Selected references   410

Appendices

Appendix A: Additional Materials for Teaching Reading in Secondary Schools   413

Appendix B: Additional Materials for Supplementary Reading in Secondary Schools   416

Appendix C: Sources of Free and Inexpensive Teaching Materials   419

Appendix D: Reading/Study Skills Tests   420

Appendix E: Publisher's Addresses   423

Appendix F: Answers to "Self-Tests"   430

1 Reading in the secondary school

This chapter focuses upon two main topics: the need for reading instruction of secondary students, and the responsibilities of various school personnel for a reading instructional program.

Purpose-setting questions

As you read this chapter, try to answer these questions:
1. What are several justifications for reading instruction in the secondary school?
2. What responsibilities for reading instruction in secondary schools belong to the content area teacher?

Key vocabulary

As you read this chapter, check your understanding of these terms:

readability levels
uninterrupted
  sustained reading
  periods
narrative prose
expository prose

developmental
  reading
corrective/remedial
  reading
recreational reading

content area
  reading
capacity level
comprehensive
  reading program

The need for reading instruction in the secondary school

In this section, reading achievement of high school students, reading to meet daily needs, reading as a recreational activity, and reading in various content (subject) areas will each be discussed in turn.

Reading achievement of secondary students

The need for providing well-conceived secondary school reading programs has grown in recent years as the population in secondary schools has increased and the importance of comprehensive curricula has been recognized.

2

The wide range in reading ability among junior and senior high school students presents secondary school teachers with one of their most vexing problems. In a group classified as seventh graders, for example, there may be boys and girls equal in reading skill to tenth or eleventh graders. Some twelfth graders may have fifth- or sixth-grade reading ability, while others read at the level of college seniors.

The reading ability of students in classes above the sixth grade commonly has a range of at least eight school years. Complicating the problem is the large extent of retardation in reading among secondary school students. Up to 20 percent of all junior and senior high school students may be in need of small group or individual remedial work to correct specific reading disabilities. Teachers in secondary schools should know that grade placement may mean nothing in terms of reading ability.

Wallace Ramsey[1] has studied the reading achievement of Kentucky children at fourth-grade and eighth-grade levels. His evidence indicates that although the fourth-grade children were reading satisfactorily compared to national norms, there was a substantial lag among the eighth-graders studied.

In her doctoral dissertation, Ruth Penty found that more than three times as many poor readers as good readers dropped out of high school before graduation. Of the students in the lowest quarter of their class, measured by reading ability, 49.9 percent left school before the twelfth grade while only 14.5 percent of those in the highest quarter left school before completing their senior year. The time in which the majority of drop-outs left school was during the tenth grade. Penty's study also revealed that a very large percentage of the young people who dropped out of school (or of the poor readers who remained in school but who experienced difficulty in reading) had reading potential. With proper help, these students could have shown marked improvement in reading ability, which would probably have contributed to better scholastic achievement and personal adjustment.[2]

A study in the city of New York that compared the reading achievement of freshmen and sophomore high school students with their mental ability revealed that 15.6 percent of the students were reading at least one year above the expectancy level determined by their mental ability, 42.1 percent were achieving at a level commensurate with expectancy, while 42.3 percent were reading below expectancy.[3]

1. Wallace Ramsey, "The Kentucky Reading Study," *The Reading Teacher* 16 (December 1962), 178–81.
2. Ruth Penty, *Reading Ability and High School Drop-Outs* (New York: Bureau of Publications, Teachers College, Columbia University, 1956).
3. Bernard E. Donovan, *Survey of Abilities of Pupils Entering the Academic High Schools in September 1955* (New York: New York Board of Education, 1955), p. 3.

It has been found that approximately 25 percent of college freshmen lack the reading skills to do their work successfully.[4] Obviously these students could have benefited from a secondary school reading program. (Many colleges today maintain extensive developmental reading programs to help students who do not read well enough to pursue a college program.)

William Gray and Bernice Rogers applied a reading maturity scale to fifty-nine adults representing various educational and social levels and several occupational and vocational groups; their study presented three conclusions:

1. Those adults in the study who had completed high school were superior in reading only to a limited extent to those who had terminated their education experience at the end of grade school.

2. The abilities to understand and interpret meanings from reading and to react to and use the ideas gained from reading were low in the adult reader.

3. The immature reader did not see reading as a source of pleasure, understanding, and insight.[5]

The data in the preceding paragraphs have admittedly been cited from reports of 15 or 20 years ago. But has the situation changed? The *Survival Literacy Study* of 1972 showed, among other findings, that 34 percent of its subjects encountered difficulties in completing a Medicaid application.[6] Another 1972 study[7] indicated that many men in military jobs lacked adequate skills to read instructional manuals for their jobs and that a lack of reading skills often had a negative effect on job proficiency. The U.S. Department of Health, Education, and Welfare has supplied data which indicate that approximately one million teenagers cannot read most of the material in newspapers, job application forms, and directions for performing various tasks.[8]

The National Assessment of Education Progress is a study to determine competence in a number of learning areas. The subpopulations that formed the basis for the first reports were students of ages 9, 13, and 17, and adults between the ages of 26 and 35. Findings included the following:

1. Relatively few young Americans could read and interpret graphs, maps, or tables.

---

4. Ruth Strang, Constance M. McCullough, and Arthur E. Traxler, *The Improvement of Reading*, 3rd ed. (New York: McGraw-Hill, 1961), p. 27.

5. William S. Gray and Bernice Rogers. *Maturity in Reading—Its Nature and Appraisal* (Chicago: University of Chicago Press, 1956).

6. *Survival Literacy Study* (Washington, D.C.: Government Printing Office, 1972).

7. T. G. Sticht et al., "Project REALISTIC: Determination of Adult Functional Literacy Skills Levels", *Reading Research Quarterly* 7 (Spring 1972), 424–65.

8. *Literacy Among Youth 12–17 Years* (Washington, D.C.: U.S. Government Printing Office, 1973).

2. Less than half of the nation's seventeen-year-olds and young adults could accurately read all parts of a ballot.[9]

In spite of acknowledged inadequacies of assessment tests, a fair-minded interpretation of the data surely should give teachers reason to be concerned. And while these data may not be true for all secondary schools of the country as a whole, the facts are fairly representative. About 20 percent of the students in a typical middle-class suburban high school are likely to read below their grade level; in a typical inner-city high school, at least 50 percent of the students read below grade level.

Perhaps the most recent development stemming from the failure to teach minimum reading competencies is the requirement by some State Boards of Education that students acquire certain abilities before they are awarded a diploma certifying that they have graduated from high school. California, Oregon and other states have now published minimum requirements for graduation. The state of Maryland has developed pilot programs to test reading guidelines that they wish to establish for students at varying grade levels. The guidelines include such statements as these:

1. All sixth graders in Maryland should be able to read road signs, telephone books, cash register slips, and directions on medicine bottles.
2. All tenth-grade students should be able to read first-aid directions, want ads, hotel reservations, and application forms.
3. All high school graduates should be able to use indices and read directions on voting machines, income tax forms, and bank statements.[10]

At the same time, a recent study revealed the following possibly typical facts about the secondary schools of one state:

1. On the secondary level, only three percent of the schools indicated that reading skills are taught as part of the pre-scribed curriculum.
2. In 36 percent, little emphasis is placed on reading skill instruction in content subjects.
3. Another 32 percent responded that reading skills are taught "as the need arises."
4. About one-third of the secondary schools do not provide content teachers with any formal help in the teaching of reading.[11]

9. J. Stanley Ahmann, "A Report on National Assessment in Seven Learning Areas," *Today's Education*, 64 (January–February 1975), 63–64.

10. *Reading in Maryland* (Baltimore, Md.: Maryland State Department of Education, 1974 75) p 11

11. Edward B. Fry and Lillian R. Putnam, "Should All Teachers Take More Reading Courses?" *Journal of Reading* 19 (May 1976), 614–16.

Such data serve as strong justification for the need for reading instruction in the secondary school.

Reading to meet daily needs

Good reading skills are necessary for an adult if he or she is to function successfully in career and personal life. Adults with poor reading skills often have negative self-images (poor views of themselves as persons). Everyone needs to read in order to function adequately. We read street signs, precautions, instructions on medicine bottles, advertisements, and menus. The shopper reads labels describing the content of items; the gardener reads directions for using insecticides or fertilizers; the architect reads blueprints; the traveler reads maps; the electrician reads wiring diagrams; the job-hunter reads want ads; and the voter reads propositions and names of candidates and parties.

Americans read for assistance in dealing with the vital concerns of everyday life. Books on baby care sell millions of copies; sets of instructions for making items are sold daily; thousands of people grow plants from printed directions; books of favorite recipes are sold by the thousand each week; music is studied from printed directions of various kinds; travel agents respond to hundreds of requests for travel booklets on where to go and what to see on one's vacation; pamphlets on learning to perform other activities are sent out by the thousands each year. Through books, people learn how to keep accounts, repair machines, build houses, till the soil, and lose or gain weight. The importance of reading in the adult life of persons in professions such as medicine, law, and teaching is so obvious that it scarcely needs to be stated. Almost all adult Americans engage in a multitude of specialized reading activities, such as reading timetables, newspapers, magazines, mail, menus, and movie bills.

Young adults (secondary school students) also read such materials as those cited in the preceding paragraph, but they have even more daily reading activities since they must read material for their classes at school. Reading and understanding written directions are skills called for in almost every secondary school classroom. Other commonly-needed skills include reading to discover main ideas, details, and inferences. Of even more importance than the vast quantity of printed material that daily confronts us is the need for critical reading skills—the need to sort out fact from opinion, truth from half-truth, information from emotion. Students should learn to do this before leaving secondary school.

Reading as a recreational activity

If literacy is a practical necessity inside and outside the school, it is also a wellspring of pleasure; it enables those who have acquired it to unlock unknown worlds of adventure in print. High school students (as well as others) love to live vicariously—witness the popularity of television, movies, and the like. Reading calls for even greater creativity of the mind than such visual dramatizations. Being able to see in the mind's eye the Tara of *Gone With The Wind* and the monster of *Jaws* and to feel the emotions in *Captains and the Kings* and the shocks of *Helter-Skelter* involves a magical vision that only the reader can create. Books bring quiet hours of relaxation when the reader scales the Himalayas with Hillary and Tensing, follows the German paratroopers closing in on their target in *The Eagle Has Landed*, or laughs for an hour with Gilbreath's *Cheaper by the Dozen*.

A young person is surrounded by a multitude of problems associated with approaching maturity. Identifying with characters in similar situations can sometimes help with the struggle. Sometimes a person's whole life may be influenced for the better by the characters and precepts he or she has found in literature. Satisfaction from such literature may account for the popularity of such stories as *Eric* (Doris Lund), *Outsider* (S. E. Hinton), or *Then Again Maybe I Won't* (Judy Blum).

Adolescents are not very different from the adult population and, like them, are not given to much outside reading. Assuming that the development of reading as a leisure-time activity is desirable, some provision for its nourishment must be made in the secondary school curriculum. So many demands are made on the time of teen-agers that the school must provide time for reading within the school day.

Perhaps one of the most difficult tasks is to convince the content area teacher of the need for motivating students to read more widely for pleasure. While an English teacher or a reading specialist has a unique responsibility for motivating reading for pleasure, this responsibility also belongs to the content area teacher. There are three major reasons that this is so:

1. A teacher of a content area may have a special rapport with several students who do not like to read and with whom no other secondary teacher has this special relationship.
2. A particular content area may be the only one in which a student is interested at any particular time. (For example, a physical education teacher may be able to motivate a particular boy or girl to read some books on sports.)
3. Particular subject matter appears more real as events are experienced in imaginative literature. (For example, the American Revolution may take up only Chapter 3 in a social studies textbook and may seem more meaningful after reading Esther Forbes' *Johnny Tremain*, where Johnny experiences the political intrigue of the times and the preparations for war.)

Science teachers can enrich their own programs as well as encourage individual reading interests through the use of science fiction (such as Ray Bradbury's *R is for Rocket*) and non-fiction (such as *Your Trip into Space* by Lynn Poole). In classes in such areas as industrial arts and agriculture, often considered remote from the realm of literature, opportunities abound for acquainting adolescents with literary materials (such as Henry Lent's *O-K for Drive Away*, a book on automobiles and automobile makers, or Billings' *All Down the Valley*, the story of T.V.A.). Such efforts may lead to enduring reading habits and tastes.

What do secondary students want to read? Many boys like to read mystery, sports, science fiction, adventure, animal, and sea stories; many girls like to read romance, mystery, career, and comedy stories. Many teenagers like to read about leading characters who are young (15 to 25 years old), attractive, kind, intelligent, physically strong, good-natured, with a sense of humor, and popular. George Norvel investigated reading interests of students in grades seven through twelve over a period of 25 years. Among his conclusions were the following:

1. Age and intelligence are not significant factors in the selection of materials for a given age.
2. Differences in sex are a highly significant factor in the reading choices of boys and girls.
3. Girls like many books chosen by boys, but boys dislike many of those chosen by girls.
4. Boys like stories that include adventure, sports, mystery, humor, animals, and male characters.
5. Girls like stories that include adventure (without too much violence), patriotism, love, family life, school life, humor, animals, and both male and female characters.[12]

G. R. Carlsen attributes the distinction in interests by sex to acculturation. Regarding age, he states:

chronological age is more important than is mental age in determining what a child will enjoy reading. The average and the above-average thirteen year old will be interested in reading the same kinds of books.[13]

Carlsen lists the types of stories enjoyed most by early, middle, and late adolescents as follows:

Early Adolescence (Ages 11–14)
    Animal stories
        Boys tend to prefer stories about animals in the wild.

---

12. George Norvell, *The Reading Interests of Young People* (Boston: D. C. Heath, 1950).
13. G. Robert Carlsen, *Books and the Teenage Reader* (New York: Harper and Row, 1971), p. 3.

Girls tend to prefer stories about animals dependent upon humans.

Adventure stories
   Preferred by boys.

Mystery stories
   Boys like the stories in wild and unusual spots.
   Girls like the stories set in familiar locations.

Tales of the supernatural

Sport stories

Growing up around the world
   Girls are particularly interested in adolescent life in various countries.

Home and family-life stories
   Preferred by girls.

Broad bold slapstick

Settings in the past
   Girls prefer stories—not historical fiction—which use the setting and life-style of times past.

Middle Adolescence (Ages 15–16)
   Non-fiction accounts of adventure
      Boys prefer first hand accounts.

   War Stories
      Preferred by boys.

   Historical novels
      Preferred by girls.

   Mystical romance
      Preferred by girls.

   Stories of adolescent life—contemporary stories of adolescents
      Both sexes like these.

Late Adolescence (Ages 16–18)
   The search for personal value
   Books of social significance
   Strange and unusual human experience.
   The transition into adult life.[14]

Regardless of the general likes of high school students, a teacher must learn about the individual tastes of students through some means—such as through the use of interest inventories (see Chapter 10, pages 362–63), pupil records, or personal observation of students. It should be pointed out that the research cited previously on the differing reading interests of boys and girls probably reflects cultural biases which there is no reason to perpetuate.

---

14. G. Robert Carlsen, *Books and the Teen-Age Reader* (New York: Bantam Books, 1967), pp. 25–30.

In the process of developing and extending reading interests, many opportunities exist to instill a love of reading. A few are listed below:

1. *Teacher enthusiasm.* The influence of a teacher who is a lover of good books is very great. The teacher must set an example. If he or she wants students to read more, he or she must enjoy reading and be acquainted with books.

2. *Booklists and librarians.* A teacher can learn much from prepared booklists. (Some booklists are cited in Chapter 3, pages 76–77, and also in Appendix B). School and public librarians and media specialists also can be very helpful in suggesting books and supplementary materials of various readability levels (or levels of difficulty) on a topic for study. The reading specialist in the secondary school can suggest reading materials for disabled readers in the content area classes. (See the selected resources for the various content areas in Chapter 9A and Chapter 9B.)

3. *Motivational devices.* A classroom atmosphere that will encourage reading can be created in several ways. First, surrounding the students with a wide variety of interesting books heightens the probability that they will pick them up and read. Second, setting up a browsing area where books are displayed attractively is a good device. Be sure to include many types: paperback books, tradebooks (library books), high interest–low readability books, reference books, subject matter textbooks, and the like.

4. *Magazines and newspapers.* Provide journals and newspapers in abundance within the classroom. Teenagers tend to like *People*, *Mad*, *Sports Illustrated*, *Hot Rod*, *Ebony*, *TV Guide*, *Seventeen*, *Reader's Digest*, and *Time*. Many students like magazines dealing with science and mechanics, and many others like magazines dealing with photography.

5. *Uninterrupted sustained reading periods.* Provide time for letting students select their own reading material and time during which everyone in the class reads for pleasure from the wide selection of materials.

Reading in various content areas   Reading is the common denominator of learning in the secondary school classroom. The secondary school relies largely on the printed page in the daily work of the classroom. Lectures, demonstrations, discussions, and learning by doing are, of course, part of a good secondary school instructional program; however, textbooks, along with supplementary materials, are the major sources of information.

As learners enter junior high school, the demands of subject matter impose upon them the necessity of applying reading and study skills already mastered, of sharpening other reading skills not previously used, and of learning new reading techniques. More advanced specialized reading material will demand new reading and study techniques.

As indicated earlier, there are wide individual differences in student reading ability, and this must be taken into consideration when choosing content reading material. Robert Karlin reviewed research related to content reading and concluded that 25 percent of the U.S. high school population lacks the reading skills necessary to read required materials with the comprehension expected.[15] An important factor to consider is whether the readability of textbooks and supplementary reading materials will enhance or diminish the reader's comprehension of the material.

Furthermore, there is little relation between a student's general reading ability and ability to read content area material. Many students who can read ably in narrative prose (or stories) need special help in learning to read in expository (or informative) prose such as social studies material. Content area reading is built on both general reading skills and specialized reading skills. Each content area demands unique reading skills, as each has its own specialized vocabulary, conceptual load, style of writing, and the like.

Comprehensive programs for reading instruction at the secondary school level are described in Chapter 11. Here, we merely offer a brief overview of the phases of reading, point out several faulty assumptions about roles and responsibilities of teachers, and suggest key individuals and other team members for a school-wide reading program.

The secondary school reading program

The total or comprehensive reading program should be composed of at least four interrelated phases.

Phases of the reading program

1. The basic or developmental phase. This program is for average and good readers who elect to enroll in it. Such students usually can improve their interpretive comprehension ability, critical reading ability, creative reading ability, vocabulary knowledge, rate of reading, and study skills. (Each of these is discussed in detail in later chapters.)

15. Robert Karlin, "What Does Educational Research Reveal About Reading and the High School Student?" *The English Journal* 58 (March 1969):368–95.

2. The corrective or remedial phase. This program is for disabled readers, those students who read one or more years below their capacity (or potential reading) level. Such students usually need to devote attention to basic word recognition and comprehension skills. As these improve, the students will need to learn how to apply general study skills.

3. The content area phase. This program is for all students enrolled in a content area course. Here the student is helped to comprehend the specific subject matter. The special reading skills required for effective reading of the content area material are considered. Within each content area—English, mathematics, social studies, science, etc.—material must be provided with which students can experience reading success.

4. The recreational phase. Since the ultimate goal of all reading instruction is to develop lifetime reading habits, this program is an important, though frequently neglected, aspect of the comprehensive reading program.

Some faulty assumptions about teaching reading

The following faulty assumptions should be addressed briefly:

1. *Teaching reading is a concern only in the elementary school.* The idea that a youngster, at the completion of the sixth grade, should have mastered the complex process of reading fails to take into account the fact that learning to read is a continuing process. Children learn to read over a long period of time, attempting more advanced reading skills as earlier prerequisite skills are mastered. Even after all reading skills have been encountered, the reader continues to refine them. No matter how old a person is or how long he or she has been out of school, that person can continue to improve his or her reading skills.

2. *Teaching reading is separate and distinct from teaching subject matter.* Teaching reading and study skills is an integral part of teaching any subject in which reading is a tool of learning. Teaching reading and teaching subject matter are not two separate processes. The teacher has the obligation to teach students how to read the printed materials that are assigned. Anytime a teacher uses printed materials to teach a content area, he or she is using reading as a teaching and learning aid. When reading is used as an aid to learning, the teachers must see that it is used at its maximum effectiveness. Putting it another way, teaching reading in subject matter areas is a complementary learning process, inseparable from subject matter. The efforts of teachers to teach

reading in the various content areas are important for the success of any junior or senior high school reading program.

3. *Reading problems in the secondary school can be solved through remedial work alone.* Some schools fail to make an essential distinction between "developmental" or general reading, which is directed to meet the needs of all students, and "corrective" or "remedial" reading, which provides specific assistance to the disabled readers.

4. *A reading specialist or an English teacher should be responsible for the teaching of reading.* While the reading specialist has distinct responsibilities in a secondary reading program, his or her efforts will be negligible if classroom teachers take no responsibility. It is true that English teachers often have greater background and interest in the field of reading, but reading is no more important a tool for learning in the English class than in most others. Responsibility for teaching reading cannot be delegated solely to English teachers any more than to teachers of social studies or science.

5. *The teaching of reading and teaching of literature are one and the same.* Reading skills are important to the study of literature, as they are to the study of any other content area. The study of literature, even in the junior high school, should not be reduced to having students read stories and then to giving vocabulary drills, exercises in finding details or main ideas, and the like. It is dangerous to assume that one improves content reading skills only by practicing with selections of literature.

Persons involved in a program

Four types of individuals within the secondary school should play a part in providing appropriate reading instruction. These include the principal or administrator, the reading consultant, the special reading teacher, and the content area teacher. The specific roles of the first three types are detailed in Chapter 11; the role of the last is detailed in Chapters 8, 9A, and 9B. Other important team members for a school-wide reading program include such personnel as the director of the learning materials center, the departmental chairperson, guidance counselors, and the school nurse.

It is crucial to involve content area teachers in a comprehensive secondary reading program. This does not mean they have responsibility for the total reading development of the students they instruct, but it does mean they must guide their students' reading of required printed material. Even youngsters who read well require preparation for those concepts and vocabulary terms that are unique to the subject matter, as well as for the organizational arrangements commonly used and the study skills frequently needed in the content area material. To assist all their students, the content area teachers need to know:

1. Factors that can cause reading difficulties (see Chapter 2).
2. The entry level achievement of students (see Chapter 10, pages 324–31).
3. The ability of students to handle content material (see Chapter 10, pages 331–33).
4. Attitudes and interests of students (see Chapter 10, pages 357–62).
5. The level of difficulty of material used in teaching (see Chapter 3, pages 43–49).
6. Ways of assigning students to groups (see Chapter 3, pages 49–53).
7. Uses of teaching outlines or guides (see Chapter 3, pages 53–61).
8. How to adapt and select materials for varying levels of reading ability (see Chapter 3, pages 68–72).
9. Word recognition skills, vocabulary and concepts, comprehension skills, and reading-study skills (see Chapters 4, 5, 6, and 7).
10. Difficulties in content area reading (see Chapter 8).
11. Ways to develop reading skills in content classes (see Chapters 8, 9A and 9B).

Finally, content area teachers can contribute through serving on school-wide reading committees for a well-balanced, articulated reading program (see Chapter 11) that should extend to post-secondary years (see Chapter 12) and beyond.

Researchers who explored the problems of teaching content reading have presented a rather bleak picture of the situation. They generally conclude that many subject area teachers possess a very limited understanding of the reading skills required by content area materials. But in defense of content area teachers, only recently has attention been provided to preparing such teachers for recognizing and alleviating the problems of content area reading. Hopefully, study of this book will help.

Self-test   (Check your knowledge of information in this chapter. Answers are located in Appendix F)
1. What range of reading ability commonly appears in classes above the sixth grade? (a) 2 years (b) 4 years (c) 6 years (d) 8 years
2. What percent of secondary school students may be in need of corrective/remedial reading instruction? (a) 5% (b) 15% (c) 20% (d) 25%

3. To whom does responsibility for encouragement of recreational reading belong? (a) English teacher (b) special teacher of reading (c) content area teacher (d) all of these
4. What is a significant factor in the reading choices of students? (a) mental age (b) chronological age (c) sex (d) none of these
5. What percent of secondary school students may lack the reading skills needed to read content area materials (a) 10% (b) 15% (c) 25% (d) 30%
6. Which is a true statement? (a) Reading instruction is the concern of only the elementary school. (b) Teaching reading is an integral part of teaching any subject. (c) Only a remedial reading program is needed in secondary schools. (d) Reading and literature instruction should be considered synonymous.
7. What type of reading program reflects the fact that learning to read is a continuing process? (a) developmental (b) corrective/remedial (c) content area (d) recreational
8. Which personnel are primarily responsible for finding subject matter materials appropriate to varying levels of reading ability? (a) administrators (b) reading consultant (c) special reading teacher (d) content area teacher

---

1. Visit a secondary classroom. Try to identify the range of reading abilities. Compare your impressions with those of the teacher.

*2. Interview a student of each of the following types: (a) accelerated reader, (b) average reader, and (c) disabled reader. Try to get each student's prospective as to the effect of his or her reading ability in terms of school achievement, self-image, and life goals. Share your findings with the class.

3. Keep a log of your reading activities for a week. What do your findings suggest about reading to meet the daily needs of young adults?

*4. Interview students of various ages (11–14, 15–16, and 16–18) about types of stories they like. Compare your findings with those cited by Carlsen on pages 8–9.

*5. What do you think are the most important things about reading that a content area teacher should know? Interview a content area teacher on the same question. Compare the findings.

Enrichment activities

Aukerman, Robert. *Reading in the Secondary School Classroom.* New York: McGraw-Hill, 1972. Chapters 1 and 15.
Burmeister, Lou E. *Reading Strategies for Secondary School Teachers.* New York: Addison-Wesley, 1974. Chapter 12.

Selected References

---

* Starred activities are designed for inservice teachers, student teachers, and practicum students.

Dillner, Martha H. and Joanne P. Olson. *Personalizing Reading Instruction in Middle, Junior, and Senior High Schools: Utilizing a Competency-Based Instructional System.* New York: Macmillan Company, 1977. Chapter I.

Duffy, Gerald, ed. *Reading in the Middle School, Perspective in Reading.* No. 18. International Reading Association, 1974. Chapters 4, 5, and 7.

Hafner, Lawrence. *Improving Reading in Middle and Secondary Schools.* 2nd ed. New York: Macmillan Company, 1974. Sections I and II.

_____. *Developmental Reading in Middle and Secondary Schools.* New York: Macmillan Co., 1977. Chapter 1.

Karlin, Robert. *Teaching Reading in High School.* 2nd ed. Bobbs-Merrill, 1972. Chapters 1, 11, and 14.

_____. *Teaching Reading in High Schools: Selected Articles.* Indianapolis, Ind.: Bobbs-Merrill, 1969. Sections I and II.

Miller, Wilma H. *Teaching Reading in the Secondary School.* Springfield, Ill.: Charles C. Thomas, 1974. Chapters 2 and 8.

Robinson, H. Alan. *Teaching Reading and Study Strategies.* Boston, Mass.: Allyn and Bacon, 1975. Chapter 12.

Shepherd, David. *Comprehensive High School Reading Methods.* Columbus, Ohio: Charles E. Merrill, 1973. Chapter 13.

Factors that can cause reading disability

2

This chapter describes disabled readers in secondary schools and discusses the factors related to reading disabilities of students at this level.

As you read this chapter, try to answer these questions:
1. Why are adolescent reading problems more significant than reading problems that occur at earlier stages of development?
2. What causal factors are likely to be related to adolescent reading disability?

Purpose-setting questions

As you read this chapter, check your understanding of these terms:

reading disability
multiple causation
etiological factors
visual acuity
aniseikonia
astigmatism
convergence

fusion
hyperopia
myopia
visual perception
auditory
   perception
auditory
   discrimination

auditory acuity
emotional
   maladjustment
self-concept
divergent dialect
standard English

Key vocabulary

"What went wrong?" is a common question now that so many students who appear capable of meeting secondary school reading requirements fail to do so. Wilma Miller has reported that 50 percent of the secondary students in inner-city schools read below their expectancy

A description of disabled readers in the secondary school

levels.[1] Having developed only minimal reading skills, these students are years behind the reading level required by the materials they are expected to read.

The disabled reader at the secondary level presents a very unhappy picture. He or she is likely to be frustrated and discouraged, with little or no interest in reading. The reading skills of such a high school student may be those of a second- or third-grade child; he or she may lack knowledge of basic sight words, phonics skills, ability to use context clues, and structural analysis skills. Without these skills, the student is unable to read enough to understand required textbooks. A limited meaning vocabulary and poor comprehension skills contribute to the unhappy situation. Adolescent disabled readers have low achievement in the majority of school subjects because they cannot read well enough to comprehend the meaning and to develop the concepts presented in their textbooks.

The problems of disabled readers in the secondary school are not limited to academic areas; they frequently suffer problems in other areas of development as well. Their personal adjustment may be inadequate; they may have poor self-concepts and poor social adjustment. Apparently, reading disability can result in severe behavior problems. William Amos and Charles Wellford[2] point out that there is a high correlation between behavior problems, delinquency, and the inability to read.

The inability to read prevents many adolescents from achieving, which is a fundamental need of human beings.[3] The ego and self-concept of a person are seriously, perhaps irreparably, damaged by failure at the adolescent stage of development. According to Elizabeth Hurlock, "at no other age in the entire life span is failure so serious and its effects so long-lasting and far-reaching as at adolescence."[4] This is true because it is a time in an individual's life when he or she attempts to tackle problems alone. If these attempts result in failure, the adolescent will conclude that he or she cannot be successful without the aid of others. He or she may develop a failure complex that will destroy the motivation needed for future success.

Adolescents are constantly confronted with failure; they cannot escape situations that threaten them with failure. They must stay in school and take certain subjects that require reading skills. As adults they will make their own choices; as children they had parental assistance; but as adolescents, they are faced with a threatening

1. Wilma H. Miller, *Diagnosis and Correction of Reading Difficulties in Secondary School Students* (New York: Center for Applied Research in Education, 1973), p. 30.

2. William E. Amos, and Charles F. Wellford, "The Culturally Disadvantaged Adolescent," in *Understanding Adolescence*, James F. Adams, ed. (Boston: Allyn and Bacon, 1973), p. 411.

3. Elizabeth B. Hurlock, *Adolescent Development.* (New York: McGraw Hill, 1965), p. 312.

4. *Ibid.*, p. 323.

situation from which there is no escape. A student may withdraw or may strike out through undesirable behavior, but either alternative is unacceptable to the adults in his or her environment. Furthermore, the adolescent usually cannot hide failures from parents, peers, and siblings. These others' awareness of his or her failures occurs at a time when the opinions of others have the most profound influence on the adolescent's opinion of him- or herself.[5]

The adolescent disabled reader must be helped to achieve, become independent, and earn a living. Given assistance, the disabled reader may learn that reading can be a source of satisfaction. He or she can develop and maintain self-confidence. Reading enables such students to engage in productive work related to their capabilities and their interests.

The classroom teacher can help some secondary students with their reading problems while students with more severe problems require the assistance of a reading specialist. Example 2.1 contains the profiles of two secondary reading disability cases; one student can be helped by the classroom teacher; the other requires specialized diagnosis and treatment.

Example 2.1

Sample reading disability cases

Case One

John is a tenth-grade student. He is passing with the minimum grade all of his subjects that require reading. Intelligence tests indicate that John's intelligence range is 110 to 120. Teacher observation supports this evaluation of his intelligence. Scores on reading achievement tests show that he is reading at the eighth-grade level. John's written assignments are poorly organized and poorly written. His spoken and written vocabulary are limited, and his scores on the vocabulary section of reading achievement tests are low.

John appears to require assistance in vocabulary, organization of content, and study skills. These skills can be handled best by the various content teachers because they know the particular needs of their content areas. Moreover, John can be helped by classroom teachers because he is quite capable of learning and because his reading difficulties seem to relate to lack of experiences promoting concept and vocabulary development. Research-study skills and organization skills are discrete and specific and can be learned with systematic instruction. These are the kinds of assistance a teacher can provide.

---

5. *Ibid.*, p. 324.

Case Two

Mary is a tenth-grade student. She is unable to pass any of the courses that require reading skills. She is unable to read any of her textbooks above the frustration level. Intelligence tests indicate that she has an intelligence range of 90 to 100. Reading achievement test scores show that Mary is reading at a third-grade level.

Mary must have assistance from a remedial reading teacher because she is unable to progress in school. A classroom teacher could not provide adequate assistance in this case. Mary reads far below her grade level. A classroom teacher would not have the time (or perhaps the expertise) to provide the extensive diagnosis and help sorely needed by her.

A study of the factors that cause reading disability in adolescents is appropriate if teachers are to prevent and correct reading problems. Reading problems are the result of multiple causes, and the existence of multiple problems may mask the retarding effect of any single problem. Stanley Krippner[6] studied etiological (or causal) factors of reading disability and concluded: "Rarely is one etiological factor responsible for a reading problem. . . . Isolating the major factor was extremely subjective in many instances and the multifactor causation of reading disabilities became apparent to the clinicians involved in this study." Causes of reading disability can generally be classified in the following categories, each of which is discussed in turn.

Physical factors   Language factors
Intellectual factors   Home factors
Emotional factors   Educational factors

Physical causes of reading disability

Much of all that is learned is first experienced through the sense organs. Sensory experience forms the basis of perception. Through sensory experience the individual perceives and interprets information. Cognition (thinking) is based upon perception. It should be apparent that impairment of sense organs may reduce reading efficiency because sensory information is not reaching the brain. Fortunately, a reduction in the sensory input from one source does not usually disable a reader because other sources of sensory information can compensate for the weakness. A deficiency in any single sense organ rarely causes reading disability.

---

6. Stanley Krippner, "Etiological Factors in Reading Disability of the Academically Talented in Comparison to Pupils of Average and Slow Learning Ability," *The Journal of Educational Research* 61 (February 1968): 275–79.

Vision is a significant factor in reading difficulty because the reading process begins with seeing. The two eyes must coordinate, move along the lines of print, and send perceptual messages to the brain. Clear, accurate images of letters and words are necessary to the reader; otherwise, letters and words that have similar configuration may be confused and the reading process impaired. Perceiving letters, words, and sentences with the eyes is basic to the reading process.

Vision

Visual acuity, the ability to see clearly, is a mechanical or physical process. The role played by visual acuity problems in reading problems has not been clearly delineated by research although Helen Robinson's[7] classic study of reading failure produced the conclusion that approximately 50 percent of the disabled readers in the study had visual or visual-perceptual problems. The study also indicated that no single factor was the cause of a reading problem. Apparently, though vision may be one of several factors causing a reading problem, with the exception of total blindness, vision is not generally the single cause of a reading problem.

Although research is not decisive regarding the relationship between vision and reading disability, certain vision problems occur more frequently among disabled readers. Hyperopia (farsightedness) appears to be related to reading difficulties, while myopia (nearsightedness) does not. Binocular difficulties, those problems connected with the lack of ability to coordinate the eyes, occur more frequently in disabled readers than in average readers. Fusion problems, or difficulties in focusing the eyes to see a clear image, occur more frequently in disabled readers. Following are listed the basic types of vision problems that relate to reading problems in the adolescent.

1. *Aniseikonia* results from the fact that the physical size of the two eyeballs is different. Thus the images seen by the eyes differ in size, and the reader has difficulty fusing the images into one picture.

2. *Astigmatism* is a result of the uneven curvature of the lens of an eye and causes print to appear blurred. Astigmatism also causes eye fatigue.

3. *Fusion* problems occur when the eyes do not coordinate or work together in vision to make images fall on the proper corresponding points of the retina. Lack of fusion causes cross-eyedness when the eyes turn in too far and wall-eyedness when the eyes turn out too far. Fusion problems cause difficulty in seeing clear images.

---

7. Helen M. Robinson, *Why Pupils Fail in Reading* (Chicago: University of Chicago Press, 1946), p. 223.

4. *Convergence* problems occur when the eyes do not turn inward properly as they come closer to a given point. The eyes must converge to insure a centering of the image. (The centering is a kind of fusion, so convergence is a fusion problem.) Adjusting the eyes to perceive type at a normal reading distance requires convergence of the eyes.

5. *Hyperopia* is farsightedness, which is a result of a defect in focusing of the eye where rays of light are focused behind the retina. The eye may compensate for this problem by straining. Hyperopia results in blurring, eye fatigue, and headache and is one of the vision problems most closely related to reading disability.

The first step in diagnosing vision problems involves careful, knowledgeable observation of the student by the teacher. A checklist[8] such as the one in Example 2.2 may be used to aid the teacher in observing students and recording observations. There is no statistical evidence to show how many of these conditions must exist in order to signify that a student needs special help. If 50 percent or more of the listed symptoms exist, there is little doubt that the subject should be referred for further examination. If fewer of these symptoms are evidenced, the teacher should use his or her judgment. Where there is reasonable doubt, the subject should be referred for further screening and examination.

Example 2.2   *Educator's Checklist*
Observable Clues to Classroom Vision Problems
Student's
Name _____ **Date** _____

1. APPEARANCE OF EYES:
    One eye turns in or out at any time   _____
    Reddened eyes or lids   _____
    Eyes tear excessively   _____
    Encrusted eyelids   _____
    Frequent styes on lids   _____
2. COMPLAINTS WHEN USING EYES AT DESK:
    Headaches in forehead or temples   _____
    Burning or itching after reading or desk work   _____
    Nausea or dizziness   _____
    Print blurs after reading a short time   _____
3. BEHAVIORAL SIGNS OF VISUAL PROBLEMS:
    A. *Eye Movement Abilities (Ocular Motility)*
        Head turns as reads across page   _____
        Loses place often during reading   _____
        Needs finger or marker to keep place   _____

8. *Educator's Checklist Observable Clues to Classroom Vision Problems* (Duncan, Okla.: Optometric Extension Program Foundation, 1968.)

Displays short attention span in reading or copying   _____

Too frequently omits words   _____

Repeatedly omits "small" words   _____

Writes up or down hill on paper   _____

Rereads or skips lines unknowingly   _____

Orients drawings poorly on page   _____

B. *Eye Teaming Abilities (Binocularity)*

Complains of seeing double (diplopia)   _____

Repeats letters within words   _____

Omits letters, numbers or phrases   _____

Misaligns digits in number columns   _____

Squints, closes or covers one eye   _____

Tilts head extremely while working at desk   _____

Consistently shows gross postural deviations at all desk
activities   _____

C. *Eye-Hand Coordination Abilities*

Must feel of things to assist in any interpretation
required

Eyes not used to "steer" hand movements (extreme lack
of orientation, placement of words or drawings on
page)   _____

Writes crookedly, poorly spaced: cannot stay on ruled
lines   _____

Misaligns both horizontal and vertical series of
numbers   _____

Uses his hand or fingers to keep his place on the page   _____

Uses other hand as "spacer" to control spacing and
alignment on page   _____

Repeatedly confuses left-right directions   _____

D. *Visual Form Perception (Visual Comparison, Visual
Imagery, Visualization)*

Mistakes words with same or similar beginnings   _____

Fails to recognize same word in next sentence   _____

Reverses letters and/or words in writing and copying   _____

Confuses likenesses and minor differences   _____

Confuses same word in same sentence   _____

Repeatedly confuses similar beginnings and endings
of words   _____

Fails to visualize what is read either silently or orally   _____

Whispers to self for reinforcement while reading silently   _____

Returns to "drawing with fingers" to decide likes and
differences   _____

E. *Refractive Status (Nearsightedness, Farsightedness,
Focus Problems, etc.)*

Comprehension reduces as reading continued; loses
interest too quickly

Mispronounces similar words as continues reading   _____

Blinks excessively at desk tasks and/or reading; not
elsewhere   _____

Holds book too closely; face too close to desk surface   ———
Avoids all possible near-centered tasks   ———
Complains of discomfort in tasks that demand visual
interpretation   ———
Closes or covers one eye when reading or doing
desk work   ———
Makes errors in copying from chalkboard to paper
on desk   ———
Makes errors in copying from reference book to
notebook   ———
Squints to see chalkboard, or requests to move nearer   ———
Rubs eyes during or after short periods of visual
activity   ———
Fatigues easily; blinks to make chalkboard clear up
after desk task   ———

OBSERVER'S SUGGESTIONS:

Signed _____

(Encircle): Teacher; Nurse; Remedial Teacher; Psychologist; Vision
Consultant; Other.

Address _____

_____

Additional screening may be conducted using the following
instruments:

1. Keystone Visual Survey Telebinocular, 2212 E. 12th Street,
   Davenport, Iowa 52803.
2. Ortho-Rater, Bausch and Lomb Optical Company, Rochester,
   New York.
3. Professional Vision Tester, Titmus Optical Company, Petersburg, Virginia.
4. Titmus Biopter, Titmus Optical Company, Petersburg, Virginia.

Any vision screening conducted by teachers should be followed
by referral of the student to an optometrist or an ophthalmologist for
examination if possible problems are discovered. Any concerns regarding a student's vision should be checked by a trained specialist.

Visual perception

Those concerned with the reading problems of adolescents should realize that visual perception is as important as visual acuity in reading. Visual perception refers to the ability to correctly interpret visual symbols. Visual perception is a mental process in which the reader processes visual information in relation to location, memory, and intersensory relationships. An element of visual perception is visual discrimination, which is the skill of seeing likenesses and differences in the physical characteristics of letters and words. Visual perception also relates past experiences to the word being seen.

Visual perception is a significant factor in beginning reading because many letters and words look very much alike in English; for example, *b* and *d* or *was* and *saw*. There are a large number of commercial materials and tests available for diagnosing and developing this skill, but most of these materials are designed for the primary school child. While visual perception skills correlate positively with reading achievement at the primary levels, as a youngster grows older, the relationship between visual perception and reading achievement diminishes. Thus visual perception is not the most significant factor in the reading achievement of secondary students.

Eye movements

Some years ago, reading researchers turned to the study of eye movements as a key to improving reading skills. Studies of eye movements are concerned with the left to right progression of the eyes across the page. Good readers move their eyes more efficiently across the page and have fewer regressions (backward movements) and fewer fixations (pauses) than disabled readers. It has been found that inefficient eye movements are *symptoms* of reading difficulty rather than *causes* of reading disability. Any effort to treat eye movements is not likely to result in improved reading skills. When reading skills are improved, the eye movements become more efficient.

Hearing

Hearing influences reading achievement because readers often make an association between the oral pronunciation of a word and the printed word. Such associations are inhibited by hearing problems. Speech development is also dependent on hearing acuity and is also closely related to reading skill. Youngsters who are deaf or hard of hearing show definite difficulty in acquiring reading skills.

Auditory acuity is the physical ability to hear both the loudness of sound and the pitch of sound. Impaired hearing may be the result of physical damage to the inner ear, the middle ear, or the ear drum. Loss of hearing may be caused by a collection of wax in the ear canal or by brain damage. Research indicates that there are more cases of impaired auditory acuity among disabled readers than among average readers. The ability to hear sounds pitched at different levels and at varying degrees of loudness is related to reading skills.

Teachers can screen students for auditory acuity by noting the following symptoms in the classroom behavior of their students:

1. Frequent requests that information be repeated.
2. Poor articulation.
3. Opening the mouth when listening.
4. Tilting the head when listening.
5. Poor spelling.
6. Poor phonics skills.
7. Apparent inattentiveness.
8. Complaints of noises in the ears.
9. Drainage or discharge from the ears.
10. Frequent colds.
11. Unnatural voice in oral reading.

If observation suggests the likelihood of a hearing problem, the student should have an audiometer test administered by trained personnel. The audiometer is the only valid means of determining auditory acuity.

Auditory perception

While auditory acuity is physical, auditory perception is a mental process. This process enables the listener to screen out unimportant sounds and to attach meaning to the sounds he hears. In order to achieve good auditory perception, the listener must separate important sounds from background noise and properly sequence the sounds heard. Auditory discrimination is an element of auditory perception and refers to the ability to hear likenesses and differences in the sounds of letters and of words. This is an important skill because many words in the English language sound somewhat alike. For example, the listener must discriminate carefully to hear the difference between *run* and *fun*.

Experts vary in the weight of importance they place on auditory perception in relation to reading achievement. However, two factors related to auditory discrimination are important. First, the older the student, the less likely it is that poor auditory discrimination is a significant cause of reading disability. Second, auditory discrimination is more important when the student is placed in an instructional program that relies heavily on phonics or oral reading.

Auditory discrimination may be evaluated with a variety of available instruments. Most of these tests require that the subject listen to pairs of words and indicate whether the words are the same or different. This type of testing is called for when the student is involved in a phonics-oriented or an oral reading program. *The Wepman Auditory Discrimination Test*[9] or the more recent *Goldman-Fristoe-Woodcock Test of Auditory Discrimination*[10] can be used for this testing.

Reading is a complex and often arduous task; therefore, good general health is important for the reader. Good general health enables the reader to be alert, to concentrate, and to participate in classroom activities. Any physical condition which decreases the student's vitality creates fatigue and makes it difficult for the student to be attentive. Poor health also may interfere with school attendance. The student may be absent when important skills are taught and thus may miss presentation of the skills required for subsequent learning, causing him or her to fall farther and farther behind in reading.

General health

Teachers may rely on observation, parent interviews, and permanent records to provide information regarding general health. Information should be sought regarding chronic illnesses, allergies, stamina, medication, eating habits, sleep habits, school absence, and extended illness.

Classroom observations may focus on the following factors:

1. Many colds and/or respiratory infections.
2. High absenteeism.
3. General fatigue.
4. Headaches.
5. Irritability.
6. Stomachache.
7. Overweight or underweight.
8. Difficulty concentrating.

The presence of several of these symptoms would indicate that the student should be referred to a physician for a thorough physical examination.

Research shows that intellectual, emotional, language and home factors can interact to cause reading disability. This section will present a discussion of each of these factors in turn.

Factors in reading disability

9. Joseph M. Wepman, *The Auditory Discrimination Test*, Rev. Ed. (Chicago: Language Research Associates, 1973).

10. Ronald Goldman, Macalyne Fristoe, and Richard W. Woodcock, *Goldman-Fristoe-Woodcock Test of Auditory Discrimination* (Circle Pines, Minn.: American Guidance Service, 1975.)

Intellectual factors   The level of a person's intelligence is related to his or her reading progress at all academic levels. G. L. Bond and E. B. Wagner[11] have found that the correlation between intelligence and reading success is closer at the higher grade levels than at lower levels. This closer relationship may be the result of the nature of the reading skills required by the more sophisticated reading materials used in the upper grades. Reading at the higher levels is a complex act requiring reasoning, abstract analysis, synthesis, and various comprehension skills that are related to higher levels of mental ability.

Skepticism regarding the value of intelligence testing has been increasing recently throughout the United States. Intelligence tests measure only a small portion of that complex entity, intelligence, and can only attempt to measure an individual's innate ability. A person's innate ability is developed through experience with the environment, and an important dimension of experience is reading. Reading provides much of an individual's vicarious experience and expands his or her store of information. An important source of intellectual development is cut off by lack of reading skill, sometimes causing the poor reader to have a low score on an intelligence test.

Intelligence tests also measure vocabulary in order to assess level of intelligence. The vocabulary of the poor reader is limited by his or her lack of reading skill, which prevents scoring well on traditional intelligence tests.

Poor readers often experience problems in the testing situation. An intelligence-testing experience may be influenced by general health, emotional outlook, fear of the testing situation, and cultural factors. Intelligence tests have a particular cultural bias because most are designed for middle-class students. Children of lower socio-economic levels tend to be less verbal, less confident, less conforming, less motivated to academic achievement, less inclined to follow directions, and less interested in pleasing teachers by putting forth their best efforts than their middle-class peers. Such factors make children of low socio-economic classes appear to have lower intelligence. Accepting test scores alone as the authoritative measurement of intellectual potential is unwise. A large number of students are frightened of tests and become very tense while taking tests. This is particularly true of secondary students who have experienced testing situations that have resulted in undesirable attitudes that inhibit test performances.

Among the problems related to intelligence testing is the attitude of teachers toward test scores. Teachers tend to view intelligence test scores as static and tend to have high expectations for students with high intelligence test scores and lower expectations for students

---

11. G. L. Bond and E. B. Wagner, *Teaching the Child to Read,* 4th ed. (New York: Macmillan, 1966), p. 63.

with lower scores. Thus the intelligence test score may become a self-fulfilling prophecy for the student, as students tend to achieve in accordance with teacher expectation.

Intelligence may be measured by group intelligence tests or individual intelligence tests; however, group tests are not recommended for the poor reader because they are primarily tests of reading skill. The best instruments for measuring the intelligence of secondary students are individual tests such as the *Wechsler Intelligence Scale for Children*, Revised (WISC-R). This test should be used with students up to the age of 15; after the age of 15 the *Wechsler Adult Intelligence Scale* (WAIS) should be used. Both of these tests are available from the Psychological Corporation, 304 East 45th Street, New York, New York. The *Stanford-Binet Intelligence Scale* is a widely used individual test. This test is available from Houghton-Mifflin Company, 110 Tremont Street, Boston; Massachusetts. The WISC-R, the WAIS, and the Stanford-Binet must be administered by psychologists. The *Peabody Picture Vocabulary Test* is an individual intelligence test that can be administered and interpreted by classroom teachers. This test may be used with students from the age of 2½ years through the age of 18 years. It is available from American Guidance Service, Publishers Building, Circle Pines, Minnesota.

Any evaluation of a student's intellectual level should include teacher observation of the student in a variety of situations. Ruth Strang recommends that teachers observe "the student's ability to remember and to see relations, his use of words, and his quickness to learn, to follow directions and to solve practical and theoretical problems."[12] Combining teacher observation with test scores permits a more valid evaluation of student intelligence.

Emotional factors

There is no question that a student's emotions are a significant factor in learning to read or in failing to learn to read. Since reading is a highly valued skill in this literate society, failure to develop reading skill has strong emotional impact on the student. The precise relationship between emotions and reading is difficult to ascertain, but it is apparent that emotional maladjustment may be a cause, a result, or an accompaniment of reading disability. Furthermore, the relationship between emotions and academic achievement is circular—each affects the other. A person's self-concept, which is one of the most important dimensions of emotional development, is very significant in reading success or failure.

---

12. Ruth Strang, *Diagnostic Teaching of Reading* (New York: McGraw Hill, 1964), p. 217.

Stanley Krippner studied causal factors of reading disability and found that "almost all children with reading disability have some degree of emotional disturbance, generally as a result of academic frustration."[13] Albert Harris[14] reported similar findings in a 15 year study of disabled readers in which he found that nearly 100 percent of the disabled readers exhibited some kind of emotional maladjustment.

A large percentage of poor readers manifest symptoms of emotional maladjustment that indicate poor personal and social adjustment, as well as failure to deal with the demands of school life. The emotional symptoms exhibited by disabled readers range from aggression to the opposite extreme of passive withdrawal. Emotional maladjustment as it is related to reading is manifested in characteristics such as the following:

poor self-concept	lack of motivation
self-consciousness	timidity
anxiety	aggression
disorganization	nervousness
social isolation	apathy
impulsiveness	immaturity
instability	withdrawal
inattention	hypertension

The above characteristics may function either as causes or effects of reading problems; whatever the relationship, they function to impede progress in learning to read.

Emotional maladjustment of secondary students is often the result of their inability to learn to read successfully in elementary school. Failure to learn to read at an acceptable level creates a vicious cycle of overall failure and having negative self-concepts; this cycle must be broken by a remedial reading program. Many students will become better adjusted as they experience success in reading; however, some secondary students may need special counseling from a guidance counselor, school psychologist, or a psychiatrist in order to achieve emotional health.

In Example 2.3, John is an example of a student who made successful progress in reading due to the solution of an emotional problem.

In addition to the emotional problems that accumulate for maladjusted students, young people are frequently rejected by teachers who react negatively to their emotional problems. Obviously, teacher

---

13. Stanley Krippner, "Etiological Factors in Reading Disability of the Academically Talented in Comparison to Pupils of Average and Slow Learning Ability," *The Journal of Educational Research* 61 (February 1968): 275-79.
14. Albert J. Harris and Edward Sipay, *How to Increase Reading Ability*, 6th ed, (New York: David McKay, 1975), p. 300.

Example 2.3

Sample reading disability case

Case One

John was an eighth grade student in a private school located in a Midwestern city. He deeply resented his family's move from another Midwestern city, but this did not seem to be the root of his reading problem. John's family provided an excellent home environment of background experience and family interest. His intelligence quotient of 120 indicated that he was capable of learning to read. John was enrolled in a university reading clinic where it was discovered that he resented both his father, who gave him too little attention, and his mother, who smothered him with attention. His clinic teacher was able to counsel both parents and John over an extended period of time. Through counseling, the emotional blocks to learning were removed so that John could benefit from reading instruction, which he also received in the clinic.

rejection further complicates a reading problem. James Hake[15] studied both good and poor readers and found that negative teacher reaction was a factor in the emotional problems of disabled readers.

Poor relationships with teachers increase student anxiety. Teachers of disabled readers should realize that anxiety has specific side effects in a reading situation. For example, anxiety causes disorganized behavior, thus hindering the student from concentrating on the task at hand. Anxiety also decreases the ability to understand and to operate in new situations. If a reading task is unfamiliar or ambiguous in its structure, the disabled reader becomes anxious and is unable to function at his best in the situation. The disabled reader should be provided reading experiences set in a friendly, relaxed atmosphere that helps reduce anxiety. Teacher acceptance adds to this proper atmosphere and is an important element in the reading situation for disabled readers.

Self-Concept Self-concept is the most important single aspect in the emotional development of human beings. The self-concept is the set of attitudes and beliefs that an individual holds about him or herself. Self-concept is defined by Paul Berg as "the individual's understanding of the expectations of society and his peers; and the kind of behavior which the individual selects as a style of life."[16] A self-concept is the product of an individual's interactions with family, friends, and teachers. The actions of others toward an individual tell

---

15. James M. Hake, "Covert Motivations of Good and Poor Readers," *Reading Teacher* 22 (May 1969): 731–38.
16. Paul C. Berg, "Reading: The Learner's Needs and Self-Concepts," *Florida Reading Quarterly* 4 (June 1968): 2–8.

that person what he or she is like. Experiencing success and failure causes the student to see himself as a success or a failure and to act accordingly. The student who continually fails to please the adults in the environment will begin to feel inferior and subsequently will develop a poor self-concept. Interaction with the people in a student's environment provides him or her with a view of self and a base for self-appraisal.

Students with poor self-concepts believe that they cannot succeed in difficult tasks, and they tend to give up easily. Many of these students lack the motivation to start a task or to persist until the task is completed. A student's level of aspiration is based on his or her self-concept; and if he or she does not aspire to learn, he or she will be unable to learn. Unfortunately, some students do not learn to read because they believe they cannot learn to read.

Research has established that self-concept is an important factor in reading achievement. Studies by William Padelford,[17] and by Maxine Cohn and Donald Kornelly[18] show that a positive relationship exists between reading achievement and self-concept. William Wattenberg and Clifford Clare[19] found that kindergarten measures of self-concept were predictive of reading achievement of the students 2½ years later. E. Zimmerman and G. W. Allebrand[20] studied the personalities of good and poor readers and found that good readers possessed more feelings of personal worth, belonging, personal freedom, and self-reliance.

Denis Lawrence[21] reports three experiments that are related to counseling retarded readers, providing reading assistance for these students. In each of the three experiments the students who received counseling showed significantly greater improvement in reading achievement than the students who received reading instruction only. The following factors were found to be important in counseling:

1. Total acceptance of the child's personality.
2. Respect for the individual.
3. Respect for privacy.
4. Enjoying the child's company.

Self-concept and learning are related in a circular fashion. Self-concept influences success in learning, and success in learning

17. William Padelford, *The Influence of Socio-economic Level, Sex and Ethnic Background Upon the Relationship Between Reading Achievement and Self-Concept,* Los Angeles: Unpublished Doctoral Dissertation, University of California, 1969.

18. Maxine Cohn, and Donald Kornelly, "For Better Reading—A More Positive Self-Image," *The Elementary School Journal* 70 (January 1970): 199–201.

19. William W. Wattenberg and Clifford Clare, "Relation of Self-Concepts to Beginning Achievement in Reading," *Child Development* 35 (June 1964): 461–64.

20. E. Zimmerman and G. W. Allebrand, "Personality Characteristics and Attitudes Toward Achievement of Good and Poor Readers," *Journal of Educational Research* 50 (September 1965): 29–31.

21. Denis Lawrence, "An Experimental Investigation into the Effects of Counseling Retarded Readers," in *New Horizons in Reading* (Newark, Del.: International Reading Association, 1976), pp. 434–41.

influences self-concept. When students are helped to improve their reading skills, their self-concepts will frequently improve along with the improved skills in reading. Counseling that improves self-concept can result in improved reading skill.

Although teachers are not trained in psychoanalysis, they can effectively study the emotional reactions of their students. Teacher observation can be useful in assessing emotional maladjustment because teachers have daily contact with students over extended periods of time. Interviews with students can aid in diagnosis of emotional problems. The teacher can use such questions as: What do you think about your reading problem? What caused your reading problems? What can we do about your reading problems? The reading autobiography suggested in Chapter 10 is a useful tool for gathering information. Rating scales such as the one developed by Larry Kennedy and Ronald Halinski[22] can be used to help evaluate attitudes.

Teachers should be as sensitive to the emotional difficulties of their students as they are to word recognition problems. Poor readers often exhibit negative self-concepts, anxiety, aggression, withdrawal, negative feelings about home and school, and extreme distaste for reading. When teachers understand these factors they can better adapt instruction to meet the needs of pupils. One way teachers can understand and accept pupils is by respecting students' language, because language is closely related to self-concept.

Language factors

Language is an intellectual factor and is the basic medium for communication. Language is necessary for obtaining knowledge and skills. Written language is the content of reading; an author attempts to communicate with the reader through language, and the reader uses his or her own language to reconstruct the author's meaning. If the discrepancy between the writer's language and the reader's language is too large, communication may be inhibited.

Language interference with reading can come from two sources. The first source is the existence of a developmental lag in, or a delay in maturation of, language. Since listening and speaking precede reading, the student whose language maturity lags is likely to experience difficulty in reading. The second source of language interference is an individual's dialect. The impact of speaking divergent dialects on the acquisition of reading skills has not been fully explored, but it is obvious that speakers of divergent dialects must experience problems in a world where the mainstream of written communication is standard English.

---

22. Larry D. Kennedy and Ronald S. Halinski, "Measuring Attitudes: An Extra Dimension," *Journal of Reading* 18 (April 1975): 518–22.

Some researchers believe that dialect interference in learning to read is such a severe problem that students should be taught to read in their own dialect with special "dialect materials." Other researchers believe that such factors as teacher attitudes toward language are more important than the actual dialect spoken by the student.

Joan Baratz[23] has discovered a significant correlation between learning to read and facility with standard English. She concludes from her data that children speaking nonstandard English do not learn to read traditional materials as well as children who speak standard English.

Lloyd Leaverton[24] takes a different point of view based on his study in Chicago with a language arts instructional model for teaching reading to students who spoke nonstandard English. An experimental group read stories written in "everyday talk," while a control group read stories written in "school talk." The data indicate that the "everyday talk" stories were effective in reading instruction. This was particularly true for boys. Leaverton points out that a significant factor in his research was the attitude and behavior of teachers toward children's oral language. The fact that this study allowed stories written in "everyday talk" encouraged teachers to respect and accept children's language. Leaverton believes that this factor may be more important than teaching students to read a dialect. Richard Rystrom who also researched the relationship between dialect and reading disability, states on the basis of his study that "speaking a black dialect does not cause reading failure."[25]

Richard Venezky and Robin Chapman examined dialect interference in learning to read and concluded that there is "little direct interference of dialect with reading but an enormous potential for indirect interference."[26] They found that dialect interference could arise either through the failure of the teacher to understand various dialects or through the failure of textbook authors to limit the semantics and syntax of their materials. These researchers suggest limiting the semantics and syntax of textbooks to a common core of language which could be taught orally within a reasonable period of time prior to initiating reading instruction.[27]

The most disabled readers at the secondary level can comprehend standard English, although they have missed an important

23. Joan C. Baratz, *Relationship of Negro Non-Standard English Dialect Speech to Reading Achievement*, Washington, D.C.: Center for Applied Linguistics, Unpublished paper, 1970.

24. Lloyd Leaverton, "Dialectual Readers: Rationale, Use and Value," in *Language Differences Do They Interfere?* James Laffey and Roger Shuy, eds. (Newark, Del.: International Reading Association, 1973), pp. 114–25.

25. Richard Rystrom, "Reading, Language and Nonstandard Dialects," in *Language Differences, Do They Interfere?* James Laffey and Roger Shuy, eds. (Newark, Del.: International Reading Association, 1973), pp. 114–25.

26. Richard L. Venezky, and Robin S. Chapman, "Is Learning to Read Dialect Bound?" in *Language Differences Do They Interfere?* (Newark, Del.: International Reading Association, 1973), p. 69.

27. *Ibid.*

source of language learning through the reading of standard English. Although the secondary student is older and more experienced, he or she continues to need opportunities for oral language development.

Observation is one of the best ways to diagnose the level of language development attained by individual students. A cloze procedure (see Chapter 10) can also be used to analyze knowledge of semantics and syntax; the words a student uses to complete a cloze test can be analyzed to determine his or her understanding of syntax and semantics in standard English.

Language is largely a product of the home in which the student grew up. However, language is only one of the factors influenced by the home.

One of the most important influences on a student's reading development is his home environment. Although it is difficult to establish a causal relationship between the home and reading disability, many characteristics closely related to reading success are influenced by the home environment. A home that provides love, understanding, and a feeling of security provides the best possible background for a student. In contrast, neglect by parents makes the student feel that he is unloved. Parental indifference to a student's learning problems can create anxiety in the student.

Home factors

Research regarding the relationship of home factors to reading disability is more limited than that involving the relationship of other factors to reading disability. Bruce Peck and Thomas Stackhouse[28] studied families of problem readers and of those who had no problems. They found that the families of problem readers had an atmosphere of closed communication and had taught the children how not to learn. Byron Callaway, Bob Jerrolds, and Wayne Gwaltney[29] found that students who rated highest in reading and language achievement also had homes with the greatest amounts of reading material.

Students who come from homes where parents provide good nutrition, opportunities for adequate rest, and a stable environment will have advantages in a learning situation. Students from homes where reading materials are available and reading skills are valued by the parents also have an advantage in school. Parents who provide a broad experiental background for their children help to enable students to read textual materials with understanding. Unfortunately, many youths tend to experience environments that deter rather than

---

28. Bruce B. Peck and Thomas Stackhouse, "Reading Problems and Family Dynamics," *Journal of Reading Disabilities* (October 1973): 506–11.

29. Byron Callaway, Bob Jerrolds, and Wayne Gwaltney, "The Relationship Between Reading and Language Achievement and Certain Sociological and Adjustment Factors," *Reading Improvement* 11 (Spring 1974): 19–26.

enhance development of reading skills. Students from these homes tend to:

1. Move more frequently.
2. Have background experiences different from that reflected in the textbooks.
3. Speak nonstandard English.
4. Have fewer magazines and newspapers in the home.
5. Not value reading.
6. View reading as a feminine activity.
7. Have poor nutrition.
8. Have less rest.

An important deficit in the background of many students from lower socioeconomic homes is the lack of experience needed to read and understand textbooks. Experience is necessary for conceptual development; students who lack basic experience also lack the basic concepts necessary for reading comprehension. The experience that a student brings to the written page is as important in successful reading as what is written on the page.

Educational factors in reading disability

Unfortunately, schools, teachers, and instructional materials can and do contribute to reading problems. Any school policy or instructional practice that prevents adjustment of instruction to individual needs will hinder student progress in acquiring reading skills. Regard for individual differences is a necessary concern in secondary schools.

School policy in many school systems today supports promotion by age rather than achievement (this is sometimes called social promotion). When this policy is combined with rigid curriculum policies, it contributes greatly to the reading disability of secondary students. Students are passed from grade to grade without achieving adequate reading skills, but the curriculum is not adjusted to the lower reading skill levels of the students. Furthermore, many teachers mistakenly feel that a student whose grade placement is eighth-grade should read eighth-grade materials.

Reading curricula and reading materials are generally not designed for students whose maturation lags behind that of the average student. Basic reading skills are introduced in the primary grades and reinforced in the intermediate grades, but the student who does not grasp basic skills at the appropriate levels often does not have another chance at them unless he receives remedial instruction.

The reading curricula in many schools are deficient in providing for the development of study skills and content reading skills. The reading materials used to develop reading in elementary schools may be largely composed of story materials instead of the nonfiction materials necessary for developing study and content reading skills. This lack in curricula and materials results in students who are expected to use reading skills that they have not been taught.

To add to the problem, the reading curriculum of a school often ends at the sixth-grade level even though many students have not attained reading maturity by the sixth grade. Some students referred to reading clinics could make progress in public schools if secondary reading programs were provided. The lack of such programs forces secondary students to seek help outside the public school system.

Some school systems attempt to meet individual needs by using test scores as a basis for assigning instructional materials to students. Unfortunately, this is not always a viable approach because test scores may reflect the frustration rather than the instructional level of the student. Instructional materials assigned on the basis of test scores may be too advanced for the reader. Furthermore most tests are based on narrative materials, while secondary students must read content books as well to complete their assigned work.

One of the greatest problems in secondary schools is the lack of teacher preparation for teaching reading. The colleges, universities and state departments of education have failed to provide adequate preparation of teachers in the area of reading. Most elementary teachers have a three- to five-quarter-hour course in reading, while most secondary teachers have had no course work in reading. Teachers at all levels need basic reading courses, diagnostic reading courses, and content reading courses if they are to meet student needs.

Due to lack of preparation, many secondary teachers do not realize that they should provide instruction in the specialized reading skills required by the disciplines they are teaching. Indeed, some teachers take reading for granted; they are not aware of the skills needed by their students. Teachers have a responsibility to prepare students for their reading assignments and to give a clear purpose for each assignment. Education of secondary teachers that draws attention to factors such as those cited in this chapter should help eliminate some of the educational factors that increase reading disability.

Concluding comments

The checklist in Example 2.4 is a tool for soliciting detailed information regarding the factors related to reading disability. The classroom teacher completes one checklist for each pupil who has reading problems. The information then can be analyzed by the reading specialist to determine whether the student requires specialized assistance in reading.

Example 2.4 _____

Checklist of factors related to reading

Name _____ Sex _____

Age (years and months) _____ IQ _____

Reading Achievement Test Score (most recent) _____

1. Physical Development
    a. Visual acuity good   _____
    b. Auditory acuity good   _____
    c. No refractive errors   _____
    d. Good general health   _____
    e. No diagnosed brain damage   _____
    f. No allergies   _____
    g. Appropriate weight   _____

2. Intellectual Development
    a. Attention span appropriate for age   _____
    b. Memory span appropriate for age   _____
    c. Sees relationships   _____
    d. Associates symbols, pictures, objects, facts   _____
    e. Follows directions   _____
    f. Solves abstract problems   _____
    g. Solves practical problems   _____
    h. Thinks clearly   _____
    i. Thinks sequentially   _____
    j. Expresses his thoughts in his own words   _____

3. Emotional Development
    a. Normal degree of self-confidence   _____
    b. Good self-concept   _____
    c. Good attitude toward school   _____
    d. Interested in reading   _____
    e. Good peer group relations   _____
    f. Works well in a group   _____
    g. Can tolerate failure   _____
    h. Good attitude toward home   _____

4. Language Development
    a. Vocabulary appropriate for age   _____
    b. Articulation clear   _____
    c. Pronounces words accurately   _____
    d. Expresses self clearly to others   _____
    e. Uses good sentence structure in oral language   _____
    f. Speaks standard dialect   _____
    g. Understands the oral language of others   _____

5. Home Background
    a. Average socioeconomic level   _____
    b. Has attended few different schools   _____
    c. English language spoken in the home   _____

d.	Standard dialect spoken in the home
e.	Parents have average educational level
f.	Regular school attendance

———————————————————————————————

We wish to caution that study of the material in this chapter is not sufficient for the classroom teacher to make a formal diagnosis of students. Throughout, we have referred to various specialists who should be utilized—the optometrist or opthalmologist, the specialist trained in hearing problems, the physician, the psychologist, the guidance counselor, the psychiatrist, the reading teacher, and others. But we do believe that the classroom teacher can become sensitive to the items suggested in the preceding checklist and can keep them in mind when working with students, particularly those who have difficulty in reading. The classroom teacher can make a major contribution by being a concerned part of an interdisciplinary team and by providing information based on close observation of the student's performance in content area classes—of his physical functioning, his abilities to handle thought problems, his interest and attitudes, his communication abilities, and pertinent home background information.

Finally, in addition to referral and consultative efforts, the teacher should make adaptations in the instructional program, including such aspects as the following:

1. Special seating arrangements, use of large-type books or cassettes, and time adjustment when doing close reading and writing work.
2. Use of many visual materials, first hand experiences, concrete objects, and simplified (lower reading level) materials.
3. Differentiation of assignments according to interests and abilities. Utilization of a variety of classroom activities (as simulation, role playing, resource persons, discussion, etc.).
4. Oral tests and information provided on cassettes, by other readers, etc.
5. Praise for good ideas and good effort. Listening and conferring with a student to provide needed encouragement.

For more information on this area, read Chapter 3, which focuses entirely upon "Adjusting Reading Assignments to Fit All Students."

———————————————————————————————

Self-test

1. What percentage of secondary students in the inner-city are reading below their expectancy level? (a) 25% (b) 75% (c) 50% (d) 40%
2. Which is a true phrase about the adolescent disabled reader? (a) Low achievement in reading only (b) Low achievement in the majority of school

subjects (c) Possibly average achievement in spite of his problem (d) Above average achievement

3. Reading problems at the secondary level are especially significant due to which of the following factors? (a) They may damage self-concept. (b) They may prevent vocational development. (c) They may cause behavior problems. (d) All of the above

4. Which is true about the factors that cause reading disability? (a) They can be isolated easily. (b) They are multiple. (c) They are due to the lack of phonics instruction. (d) They are due to incompetent first-grade teachers.

5. What physical factors relate to reading disability? (a) Vision (b) Hearing (c) General health (d) All of these

6. What effect will training the eye movements of disabled readers achieve? (a) Improve reading achievement (b) Confuse the student (c) Improve visual perception (d) Treat a symptom of reading disability

7. What is auditory perception? (a) Ability to hear (b) Ability to hear likenesses and differences in sounds (c) Ability to hear high and low sounds (d) Ability to interpret the sounds one hears

8. For which students are visual perception skills related to reading achievement? (a) Elementary students (b) Secondary students (c) Students at all levels (d) No students

9. How should level of intelligence be evaluated? (a) Individual tests (b) Group tests (c) Tests plus observation (d) None of these

10. How are emotions related to reading disability? (a) They are a cause of reading disability. (b) They are a result of reading disability. (c) Neither of the above. (d) Both *a* and *b*.

11. What percent of disabled readers have emotional problems, according to Harris? (a) 100% (b) 75% (c) 50% (d) 65%

12. Some students do not learn to read because they believe they cannot learn to read. This statement: (a) Is untrue (b) Reflects the relationship of self-concept to reading (c) Reflects a bad attitude (d) Reflects a condition that can only be cured by a psychiatrist

13. How do parents influence their children's reading achievement? (a) By providing a rich background of experience (b) By genetic planning (c) By making their children go to school (d) Not at all

14. What educational factors influence reading achievement? (a) Teachers (b) Reading materials (c) Instructional practices (d) All of these

---

Enrichment activities

1. Obtain an auditory discrimination test and administer it to at least two students and compare the responses of the students.

2. Administer a *Peabody Picture Vocabulary Test* to a student and compare the results of this test with your observation of the student to evaluate the intellectual level of the student.

3. Administer an attitude scale such as the Kennedy-Halinski Scale to a group of secondary students and analyze the results.

4. Interview disabled readers at the secondary level; ask them what their reading problems are and why they think they have reading problems.
5. Interview the parents of a disabled reader regarding the development of his reading problems and the possible causes of the reading problems.
6. Use the reading checklist in Example 2.4 to guide your observations of several students and briefly summarize the reading problems of each student.
7. Discuss the reading problems of students with teachers of various content areas. How are the reading problems of their students alike and how are they different?

Selected references

Aukerman, Robert. *Reading in the Secondary School Classroom.* New York: McGraw-Hill, 1972. Chapter 14.

Burmeister, Lou E. *Reading Strategies for Secondary School Teachers.* New York: Addison-Wesley, 1974. Chapter 1.

Cushenberry, Don. *Remedial Reading in the Secondary School.* West Nyack, N.Y.: Parker Publishing Company, 1972.

Dechant, Emerald. *Reading Improvement in the Secondary School.* Englewood Cliffs, N.J.: Prentice Hall, 1973. Chapters 2 and 3.

Dillner, Martha H. and Joanne P. Olson. *Personalizing Reading Instruction in Middle, Junior, and Senior High Schools.* New York: Macmillan Co., 1977. Chapter 9.

Forgan, Harry W. and Charles T. Mangrum. *Teaching Content Area Reading Skills.* Columbus, Ohio: Charles E. Merrill, 1976. Modules 9 and 10.

Hafner, Lawrence E. *Developmental Reading in Middle and Secondary Schools.* New York: Macmillan Co., 1977. Chapters 20, 21.

————. *Improving Reading in Middle and Secondary Schools.* 2nd ed. New York: Macmillan Co., 1974. Section 12.

Karlin, Robert. *Teaching Reading in High School.* 2nd ed. New York: Bobbs-Merrill Publishing Company, 1972, Chapter 2.

————. *Teaching Reading in High Schools: Selected Articles.* Indianapolis, Ind.: Bobbs-Merrill Company, 1969. Chapter 2.

Robinson, H. Alan and Rauch, Sidney J., ed. *Corrective Reading in the High School Classroom.* Newark, Del.: International Reading Association, 1966.

Strang, Ruth. *Diagnostic Teaching of Reading.* 2nd ed. New York: McGraw-Hill, 1969.

3 Adjusting reading assignments to fit all students

This chapter deals with the effect of readability of content area materials on achievement of students in content classes. Factors that influence readability are discussed and readability formulas for determining the difficulty of materials are suggested and described.

Grouping and motivating students for differentiated assignments are discussed. Means of differentiating assignments through use of study guides, directed reading approaches, alternate textbooks, rewritten material, and language experience materials are explored. Attention is given to development of teaching units. Media selection sources are suggested.

Purpose-setting questions

As you read this chapter, try to answer these questions:
1. How is an understanding of the readability levels of textbook materials important to a teacher?
2. What are some types of groups that a teacher might wish to form within a classroom?
3. What is the purpose of a study guide?
4. Under what circumstances would a teacher wish to locate alternate textbooks or printed materials for use in his or her classroom?
5. Is it possible for classroom teachers to rewrite textbook materials at lower readability levels?
6. How can a teacher use language experience materials at the secondary level?
7. What four basic types of activities are a part of a teaching unit?
8. What selection aids are available to help secondary school teachers locate appropriate books for the readers in their classes?

As you read this chapter, check your understanding of these terms:

directed reading
   approach
high interest, low
   vocabulary
   materials
multi-level textbooks

language experience
   materials
readability
readability formula
structured overview

student-tutorial
   groups
study guide
teaching units
trade books

When educators refer to the readability of printed materials that students are asked to read, they mean the reading difficulty of these materials. Selections that are very difficult to read are said to have high readability levels; those that are easy to read are said to have low readability levels. Unfortunately, studies have shown that secondary level textbooks in various curriculum areas tend to have high readability levels in relation to the reading abilities of the students who are expected to read them. Evidence also indicates that there is a wide variability of difficulty within single texts and that many texts do not have a gradation of difficulty from the beginning to the end. Following are listed some representative studies that illustrate the problem:

Readability of printed materials

1.   Joyce Bryant studied the readability of science, social studies, English, and literature textbooks using the Flesch Readability Formula. The readability of these textbooks was compared to the reading levels of 900 students in grades 10, 11, and 12. More than half of the students were assigned content books that were too difficult.[1]

2.   Calfrey Calhoun and Barbara Horner compared the readability of first-year bookkeeping texts with the reading levels of the students enrolled in the bookkeeping classes. The Flesch Readability Formula and the Nelson-Denny Reading Test were used. Of the seventy-three students who participated in the study, twenty-four read below tenth-grade level and sixteen read above twelfth-grade level. The difficulty levels for the texts were as follows: thirteenth- to sixteenth-grade for two texts and tenth- to twelfth-grade for two texts. A significant number of the chapters in all of the textbooks had a readability level above the expected reading range of the students.[2]

1. Joyce Elaine Peaden Bryant, "An Investigation of the Reading Levels of High School Students with the Readability Levels of Certain Content Textbooks with Their Costs," in *Dissertation Abstracts* 33, Part A (September-October 1972):887A.

2. Calfrey C. Calhoun and Barbara Horner, "Readability of First-Year Bookkeeping Texts Compared with Students' Reading Level," *Business Education Forum* 30 (October 1975):20–21.

3. Donald Daugs and Fred Daugs used the cloze procedure to determine whether a biology text designed for use with tenth graders was written at a level the students could comprehend. The study involved 285 tenth-grade biology students. The difficulty score for the texts was 43.9%, which is equivalent to a 75% comprehension score.[3] This means that the students should be able to read the texts with teacher guidance but probably not independently.

4. Dean Miller, Karen Miller, and Judy Scheer studied the readability of four series of junior high school health textbooks. The eighth-grade books all had readability levels below the assigned grade level. The seventh-grade books all had readability levels below or on grade level.[4]

5. Robert Aukerman studied the difficulty of junior and senior high school literature anthologies and decided that secondary school students in the bottom 26 percent of their class would be unable to read most, if not all, available literature anthologies.[5]

6. Regis Wiegand investigated the readability of nine mathematics texts for grades eight through twelve. He discovered that the predicted readability levels were consistently higher than the reading levels of most of the students who were expected to use the texts.[6]

7. Loren Kline examined five eighth-grade science books adopted by Texas. Of the five, two had a readability of ninth to tenth grade, two had a readability level of eleventh to twelfth grade, and one had a readability level of seventh to eighth grade.[7]

More recent studies of individual textbooks done by graduate students as a part of their coursework have generally shown that textbooks have difficulty levels higher than their grade placements. In these studies only social studies textbooks have tended to show lower readability levels than the grade levels at which they were placed.

Why does this situation exist? Why are most textbooks used in grade nine written at a tenth-grade readability level or above? The answer is fairly simple. Many textbook authors are subject matter

3. Donald Daugs and Fred Daugs. "Readability of High School Biology Materials," *Science Education* 58 (October 1974):471–82.

4. Dean Miller, Karen Miller, and Judy Scheer, "Readability of Junior High Health Textbooks," *Journal of School Health* 44 (September 1974): 382–85.

5. Robert C. Aukerman, "Readability of Secondary School Literature Textbooks: A First Report," *English Journal* 54 (September 1964): 533–40.

6. Regis B. Wiegand. "Pittsburgh Looks at the Readability of Mathematics Textbooks," *Journal of Reading* 11 (December 1967): 201–04.

7. Loren E. Kline, Jr., "Textbook Readability and Other Factors Which Could Influence the Success of Eighth-Grade, Earth Science Course in the Texas Public Schools," *Dissertation Abstracts* 27 (February 1967): 2283A.

specialists in a specific field, not reading specialists. As a result, these authors often know little about factors that influence readability, nor do they know how to adjust the readability of materials they are writing. Because of this situation, the materials they produce may be of extremely high readability or may be uneven in readability throughout the work. Literature anthologies, which contain material written by a number of different authors, often vary widely in readability from selection to selection since editors have not attempted to place selections of the same, or similar, readability levels together.

Even if textbooks are properly labeled as to the intended grade placement (that is, the text says grade nine and is written on a ninth-grade difficulty level), many students in that grade will be unable to benefit from them. Many students in the ninth grade are unable to read with understanding material written on that level. Many ninth-grade students read anywhere from one to five grade levels below their placement, and a few are even further behind than that! This situation obviously presents a difficult problem for the teacher working with this variety of abilities. Furthermore, the teacher will have some students who are reading one to five (and possibly more) grades above their ninth-grade placement. A textbook may be adequate for teaching subject-matter concepts to these better students, but it may seem so elementary that more challenging supplementary materials will need to be provided to avoid boredom on the part of the gifted students.

Finding challenging materials for gifted students is generally not a difficult task. Difficulty often does arise, however, when teachers are confronted with textbooks that are too difficult for their students. Available materials at lower readability levels are often designed for younger children and may, therefore, seem childish to older students. Some possible solutions are to use alternate textbooks written on an appropriate maturity level, to find trade books that cover the material at a lower readability level, or to rewrite the text material at a lower readability level. These solutions and several others are discussed later in this section.

Many factors influence the difficulty of printed materials. Some of these are vocabulary, sentence length, sentence complexity, abstract concepts, idea organization, reader interest, reader background, size and style of print, and format. Although all of the factors mentioned obviously have some effect on difficulty, vocabulary and sentence length have been found by researchers to be the most important ones to use in predicting readability.

Of the factors identified, two are not possible to control when producing printed materials: reader interest and reader background.

Factors that influence readability

A piece of literature may be of great interest to one student and yet have little appeal for another. A reader's areas of interest may be related to his background of experience. This background enables a reader to understand easily that material for which vocabulary and concepts have been experienced directly or vicariously by the individual.

Those who are writing materials for secondary school students would do well to consider all of the controllable factors that affect readability and make the material understandable for the young people intended to use it. Use of easier synonyms for difficult vocabulary words, short sentences instead of lengthy ones, simple sentences instead of compound and complex ones, concepts that are as concrete

Table 3.1

Formula	Characteristics Measured	
	Vocabulary difficulty	Sentence difficulty
Dale-Chall Readability Formula[a]	Percentage of "hard words"	Average sentence length
Flesch "Reading Ease" Formula[b]	Average number syllables per 100 words	Average sentence length
SMOG Grading Formula[c]	Polysyllabic word count for 30 sentences	
Fry Readability Graph Formula[d]	Average number of syllables per 100 words	Average number of sentences per 100 words

[a] Edgar Dale and Jeanne S. Chall, "A Formula for Predicting Readability," *Educational Research Bulletin* 27 (January 21, 1948): 11–20, 28; also Edgar Dale and Jeanne S. Chall, "A Formula for Predicting Readability: Instructions," *Educational Research Bulletin* 27 (February 18, 1948): 37–54.

[b] Rudolf Flesch, *The Art of Readable Writing* (New York: Harper & Row, 1949).

[c] Harry G. McLaughlin, "SMOG Grading—A New Readability Formula," *Journal of Reading* 12 (May 1969): 639–46.

[d] Edward Fry, "A Readability Formula that Saves Time," *Journal of Reading* 11 (April 1968): 513–16, 575–78.

as possible, and a clear organizational pattern will enhance the readability of the material. Size and style of print and format must also be considered in material that is to be published.

Readability formulas   Various formulas have been developed to measure the readability of printed materials. Most contain measures of vocabulary and sentence difficulty. Some of the most frequently used formulas are listed in Table 3.1.

The Dale-Chall Readability Formula, although one of the most well-validated formulas, is relatively difficult and time-consuming to use. A number of samples of approximately 100 words each are used for computation of readability. A word from a sample that is on the 3,000 word Dale-Chall list or is an acceptable variation of a word on the list is considered easy; if the sample word is not on the list, it is considered hard. The Dale score is computed by determining the percentage of hard words in the sample. The average sentence length for the sample is then computed, and the Dale score and the average sentence length are inserted into a formula. This procedure is followed for each sample chosen. A sample is usually taken every tenth page for books or four samples per 2,000 words for articles. The sample scores are averaged, and a correction table is provided with which to determine the grade score for a selection. Powers, Sumner, and Kearl have revised the formula in order to modernize it.[8]

The Flesch "Reading Ease" formula is also somewhat complex. When using the Flesch formula, it is necessary to count the number of sentences in the sample and to compute the average sentence length. Flesch says to count each grammatically independent unit of thought as a sentence "if its end is marked by a period, question mark, exclamation point, semicolon, or colon."[9] Sentence fragments are treated as sentences also. Once having determined the "Words per Sentence" and "Syllables per 100 Words" figures, a chart prepared by Flesch can be used to determine the "Reading Ease" score.[10] Usually 25 to 30 samples are taken per book. The Flesch "Reading Ease" Formula was recalculated at the same time that the Dale-Chall formula was recalculated.[11] This formula is obviously time-consuming for teachers to use.

The SMOG Grading Formula requires the user to count each word of three or more syllables in each of three 10-word samples. The approximate square root of the number of polysyllabic words is calculated; to which figure the number three is added to give the SMOG Grade. This formula takes less time to calculate than do the Dale-Chall and Flesch formulas.

The Fry Readability Graph is another relatively quick readability measure. To use the graph, it is necessary to select three 100-word samples and to determine the average number of sentences and the average number of syllables per 100 words. (The number of sentences in a 100-word sample is determined to the nearest tenth of a sen-

---

8. R. D. Powers, W. A. Sumner, and B. E. Kearl, "A Recalculation of Four Adult Readability Formulas," *The Journal of Educational Psychology* 49 (April 1958): 99–105.

9. Rudolph Flesch, *How to Test Readability* (New York: Harper & Row, 1951), p. 3.

10. Rudolph Flesch, *The Art of Readable Writing,* (New York: Harper & Row, 1951), p. 5.

11. Powers, Sumner, and Kearl, "Four Adult Readability Formulas."

tence.)[12] Using these figures, it is possible to enter the graph and determine the approximate grade level of the selection. Fry's Graph and the instructions for using it are reprinted in Figure 3.1.

Some educators prefer to use the more lengthy formulas because they feel that they are more accurate. Considering the number of

Figure 3.1   *Graph for estimating readability*

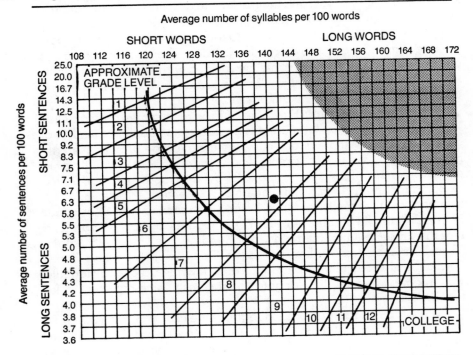

DIRECTIONS: Randomly select 3 one hundred word passages from a book or an article. Plot average number of syllables and average number of sentences per 100 words on graph to determine the grade level of the material. Choose more passages per book if great variability is observed and conclude that the book has uneven readability. Few books will fall in gray area but when they do grade level scores are invalid.

EXAMPLE:	Syllables	Sentences
1st Hundred Words	124	6.6
2nd Hundred Words	141	5.5
3rd Hundred Words	158	6.8
AVERAGE	141	6.3

READABILITY 7th GRADE (See Dot Plotted on Graph)

Source: Edward Fry, reprinted from the *Journal of Reading*, April 1968, and *Reading Teacher*, March 1969. Reproduction permitted; no copyright.

12. Edward Fry, *Reading Instruction for Classroom and Clinic* (New York: McGraw-Hill, 1972), p. 231.

factors that formulas fail to take into account, however, none can provide more than an approximation of level of difficulty. For this reason, the quick formulas should not be scorned. Determination of the relative difficulty levels of textbooks and other printed materials can be extremely valuable to a teacher. It has been demonstrated that estimating reading difficulty by using a formula produces much more consistent results than estimating without the aid of a formula.

All teachers should be familiar with at least one formula so that they can check the printed materials used in their classes. Then perhaps students will not be asked to read textbooks or supplementary materials that are too difficult for them to comprehend.

Teachers who know the results of reading tests administered to their students (see Chapter 10 for a discussion of testing) and know the readability levels of the textbooks to be used can readily determine if the textbooks are appropriate, too easy, or too difficult for each student in the class. Two examples of grouping procedures with regard to such information are given in Example 3.1.

Grouping for motivation, and differentiated assignments

Example 3.1

Case 1

Mrs. Jones is a ninth-grade science teacher. The science textbook assigned to her class has a readability level of ninth-grade. Examination of reading test results for the students in her class reveals this information:

Reading grade level (Instructional)	Number of students
11	3
10	5
9	10
8	9
7	4
6	2
5	1
	34

In order to have optimum utilization of the textbook, it would seem necessary to divide Mrs. Jones' class into instructional groups. Group *A* would include the eight students with instructional reading levels of grades 10 and 11. These students would be able to read the textbook independently, without the teacher's constant supervision. They could probably set their own purposes for reading most of the time, or at least work cooperatively with the teacher on purpose-setting.

Example 3.1 (cont.)   Group *B* would include the ten students reading at a ninth-grade level, who could profit from the textbook with the aid of the teacher. The teacher would need to prepare them carefully for the reading, setting purposes for them or helping them set their own purposes. As they proceeded with the reading, the teacher would need to be available to help them with any difficulties they might have.

Group *C* would include the 16 students reading at levels ranging from grade five to grade eight. These students would be frustrated by the reading demands of the textbook and would need to have alternate reading material of some type. There could be rewritten material prepared by the teacher, alternate textbooks, or supplementary library books. Obviously, the span of reading levels within Group *C* is too great for all of the students to use identical materials all of the time. Rewritten text material at the fifth-grade level could be utilized by the entire group. Alternate texts, if available, should be more nearly fitted to each student's reading level, as should supplementary library books. The things learned by each individual from the various sources could be synthesized through group discussion and individual presentations of summary statements. These statements could be elicited by the teacher through the use of the language experience approach discussed later in this chapter.

Group *C* may be able to utilize the textbook to a limited degree. For instance, all members of the group could study the graphic aids offered in the textual material. In addition, at times the 9 students reading on the eight-grade level could use a limited portion of the written text with extensive help from the teacher.

Whole class discussion could follow the study of a topic by the three individual groups. The poorer readers would be able to contribute to the discussion, having studied the subject from material that they could understand. They would probably learn more from the whole class discussion because the better readers could have gained more insights into the overall subject through their superior ability to do critical reading. As the better readers discuss the concepts presented in the material, these concepts will be clarified for others in the class.

Case 2
If a group reading inventory or a cloze test has been administered to Mrs. Jones' class, three similar groups can be formed. Group *A* would include the students for whom the textbook is on an independent level. Group *B* would consist of students for whom the textbook is on an instructional level. Group *C* would be made up of students for whom the textbook is on a frustration level. These tests and levels are thoroughly discussed in Chapter 10.

The two illustrations of grouping procedure discussed in Example 3.1 are both examples of *achievement grouping*, or grouping students on the basis of their general (achieved) ability to read material of certain levels with understanding.

There are other types of grouping within a class which may facilitate differentiation of assignments or provide motivation for completing assignments. These include *needs groups, student tutorial groups, partnerships, interest groups, research groups,* and *friendship groups.* Each type is discussed below:

1. Needs groups—Some students in a class may have trouble with basic reading skills; this may impede their understanding of the content of the subject area textbook. For example: Some students may have difficulty determining main ideas. This will make study of any subject area difficult. Some students may not be able to read to follow directions. Work in science, mathematics, art, and vocational subjects will suffer greatly from this problem. Some students may be unable to read maps adequately. Social studies and, possibly, science classes often require students to be able to handle map-reading tasks in order to completely understand the material. Some students may not be able to recognize common prefixes and suffixes. This skill is very important in many science and mathematics classes. The examples could go on and on.

A teacher may form needs groups, each consisting of students who lack a particular skill. The needs group members may not all be from the same achievement group (or at the same reading level) because many of the best students have gaps in their reading skill development corresponding to those of poorer students. The teacher can use materials specially designed to aid students in applying needed skills to the content area involved. A needs group can be assembled when the remainder of the class is involved in other purposeful activity, such as doing research, working on a study guide, or doing supplementary reading from library books.

Needs groups are formed when a need becomes apparent to the teacher and are disbanded when that need has been met. Some students will require only one or two meetings to achieve the desired goal. Others will need more time. No student should be retained in a needs group after he or she has mastered his or her needed skill.

2. Student tutorial groups—While the teacher is busy working with one group of students (either an achievement group or a needs group), another group of students can be assisted by a classmate who has achieved mastery in the area in which they need help. Student tutors must be given explicit instructions as to their responsibilities. They must know exactly what they should and should not do to help classmates. (For example, if a tutor merely tells other students answers, which might be considered help by the classmates, he or she would not bring about the results desired by the teacher.) Student tutors can be particularly helpful in supervising the completion of study guide assignments, which are discussed later in this chapter.

Student tutorial groups generally prove beneficial to both the tutor and the "clients." The student tutor often achieves a more complete understanding of the material in attempting to explain it to classmates or in attempting to clarify students' incomplete concepts or to correct their misconceptions. Being placed in the position of student tutor is also an ego-satisfying situation. While the tutor benefits from his or her experience, classmates generally improve their skills. Some of them may be able to express their difficulties more easily to a fellow student than to a teacher, and the student tutor may be able to explain ideas in the students' own language more adeptly than the teacher.

When student tutorial groups are used, the teacher must be careful to choose students who can work together. Some students tend to be more disruptive when in the presence of certain other classmates. Such combinations should be avoided for they cannot possibly result in the desired outcomes. It should be clearly understood by all of the group members that any disruptive behavior will result in immediate termination of the group engaged in such behavior.

Roles in student tutorial groups should not be static; that is, one or two students should not always be tutors while the others are always in the role of clients. As many different students as possible should be allowed to function in the role of tutor. There should, of course, be the limitation that no student act as tutor in a situation where he or she is not competent.

3. Partnerships—When two (or possibly more) students have nearly attained mastery of a skill or when they have marginal competence to complete an assigned task, the teacher may decide to set up a partnership grouping. In such a grouping, the students are presented a task (for example, a study guide) to be completed and are allowed to pool their resources in order to successfully complete it. Each individual is more likely to be successful in a partnership than working alone at a task, and success is a strong positive reinforcement for the activity or skill involved. Being successful also tends to motivate the students to continue to try in successive reading tasks.

Teachers must be as careful in choosing students for partnerships as in choosing students for tutorial groups. Disruptive partnerships should be immediately dissolved. Setting a very specific task and a time limit for the partners to complete it may help a partnership remain task oriented. Partners may work together while the teacher is involved with other groups.

4. Interest groups—When units are being taught in the content areas, many possibilities for additional student reading are available, often more than the teacher wishes to utilize. In such cases the teacher may allow class members to choose areas of interest for supplementary reading. The students who choose the same area may be formed into an interest group, asked to read individually in the area of interest, and brought together to discuss with the other group members the material read. The group may be charged with the responsibility of reporting its findings to the whole class through a formal report, a panel discussion, a dramatization, or some other means. Individual

group members may be on different achievement levels in reading since they can read materials designed for their own individual levels and then can contribute their findings to the group as a whole.

Interest groups are motivational because the students are allowed to pick their own subjects for reading. They help to avoid the stigma that is sometimes attached to members of low achievement groups because they provide an opportunity for these students to be mixed with students from other groups.

5. Research groups—Research groups are similar to interest groups in that a group of students read independently about a particular topic, discuss it together, and share their findings with the class as a whole. These groups are different from interest groups in that the topics and group members are assigned by the teacher. The teacher may deliberately mix students with varying strengths and weaknesses to capitalize upon each group member's strengths and to enable students with specific weaknesses to learn from those with corresponding strengths. The groups may need to be closely monitored to ensure that these results are achieved. Research groups do not have the built-in motivation for reading content that interest groups do. They do, however, provide an intermingling of students from varying achievement levels.

6. Friendship groups—At times, class members can be allowed to work on certain assignments with friends of their choice. This type of grouping is motivational and may be highly beneficial for some students. Other students may be unable to conduct themselves properly under such conditions. Friendship groups should be used with discretion.

All teacher-assigned groups should be flexible. In achievement groups, for example, some students may experience sudden spurts in attaining reading skills warranting transfer to higher groups. Other students, because of extensive absences, emotional difficulties, or other reasons, may fall behind the group in which they have been placed. These students should be moved to a lower group, at least temporarily. In needs groups, students are included and dismissed as their needs are detected and met. Student tutorial groups, partnerships, and research groups last only until the assigned task is completed.

Reading approaches for use with content materials

After grouping is accomplished, the teacher has to develop ways to work with different groups. Three effective ways to guide reading assignments are using study guides, structured overviews, and directed reading approaches. These techniques may be used separately or, at times, concurrently.

Study guides   Robert Karlin suggests two types of study guides that may be helpful for students: process guides and content guides.[13] A process guide gives students ideas about reading content material to gain information. It points out the skills necessary to understanding the material. A content guide helps students focus on particular information by offering purpose questions.

Actually, these two types of guides can be synthesized into a single study guide which sets purposes for reading and provides aids for interpretation of the material. These guides are particularly valuable when the teacher employs grouping in the content class. They can be designed in such a way that the different groups have differentiated assignments, or separate guides can be prepared for different groups and can call for use of different skills and different levels of sophistication in handling the material. Each small group of students can sit together, work through the study guide individually, and then discuss their answers with each other. During the discussion, the group members will try to reconcile any differences in answers they discover. A whole class discussion may follow the small group sessions. All class members will have something to contribute from their learning during the guided reading or during their ensuing group discussion. Since each group has a different focus, the contributions from all groups (not just those from the high groups) are valuable.

Handling material this way causes the students to think about the material that they are reading; critical thinking is necessary when small groups try to reach a consensus about certain answers. Thinking is also necessary later when the different groups perceive how all of their findings fit together. Retention of material is aided by the act of critically thinking about it.

Example 3.2 shows a social studies selection from a four-book series entitled Scholastic World History Program followed by a study guide.

Example 3.2   *Sample social studies selection and study guide*

K'ang-hsi was a talented writer, who left thousands of pages of documents. What would K'ang-hsi's diary show us about the China of his day? We've created an imaginary diary based on his actual writings. Let's take a look.

THE FORBIDDEN CITY, PEKING; MAY 13, 1700. I spent some time this morning talking to my old servants, the Manchu Ushi [OOSH-ee] and the Chinese Ts'un Chu [ts'un-choo]. The Son of Heaven has no equals, so you would think he has

---

13. Robert Karlin, *Teaching Reading in the High School*, 2nd ed. (Indianapolis: Bobbs Merrill Company, 1972), 307–10.

no friends. But these two are truly friends. I have ruled for almost 40 years. These two have been close to me since my boyhood, when I came to the throne.

We often talk about the old days, when we spent months hunting on the northern plains. We shot deer and geese with the crossbow. Then we roasted the game over a fire in the open air. When we were not hunting game, we were on military campaigns. We added Mongolia and Tibet to the empire. Now we must keep the entire empire at peace.

I travel to every part of the Middle Kingdom. That's the only way to find out what is really happening. If officials are stealing money, I have to uncover it. If the flood dikes on the Yellow River are broken, I must know. If grain isn't reaching the capital by canal, I must find out why. And if the army lacks supplies, the empire is in danger.

It's not always easy to learn the truth. On the one hand, people are afraid to speak to the emperor. On the other hand, they cover me with flattery. I have to dig for the truth in their fancy words.

I insist that my high officials and governors send their reports directly to me. I write my comments myself and send them back. That way they know I have read the reports personally.

Reading these reports takes a great deal of time. I am up at sunrise, and work into the night. My ministers marvel that I am able to work such long hours. But I have my duty to perform.

Some of the Ming emperors were lazy. They turned their work over to others. Their officials lied and stole, and the empire suffered. I must set a better example.

I must also make sure that artists and writers are cared for. Here I have tried to set an example of a different kind. I learned to write Chinese as a boy. Now I think my literary works are worthy as models for other writers.

Anyone with talent is welcome at my court. That is why I have allowed some Westerners to be included among my advisers. These Westerners are Roman Catholic priests called Jesuits [JEZH-uh-wuts]. They have much to teach even the Middle Kingdom in mathematics and the study of the stars. I use their star charts to tell the time while I am camping out on journeys.

These foreigners have been useful. They have reformed our ancient calendar. And they have been helpful in making cannon to use against invaders. The Chinese have feared the horsemen of the north for hundreds of years. Now they have nothing to fear. Firearms have ended the threat of the horsemen. A few shots can scatter any group on horseback.

The people who need watching are those from Europe. More and more of them reach our shores with every passing year. The Portuguese have had a colony in our southern port of Macao [muh-COW] for more than a century. They pose no dangers that I can see. But the other Western traders do. They must be strictly limited to the city of Canton [kan-TAHN]. The power of China is greater than that of any Western kingdom. But we must watch to make sure the Westerners do not use their trade to weaken our empire.

Our reign is, I believe, a successful one. I will die leaving a strong empire to those who come after me.

Source: Francis Plotkin, Diana Reische, Edwin Sparn, Robert Stine, *Empires Beyond Europe* (New York: Scholastic Book Services, 1976), pp. 92–93. Reprinted with permission from Scholastic Magazines, Inc.

Study guide

Overview Questions: What were the differences between the Ming emperors and the Manchu emperor who might have written this diary entry? What kind of person was the Manchu emperor?

*1. Read the italicized paragraph at the beginning to find out if K'ang-hsi really wrote the selection you are about to read. What word gives you the answer? What does "based on his actual writings" mean?

2. In the first paragraph of the diary entry, who is meant when the word "I" is used? Who is the Son of Heaven?

** 3. Why might you think that the Son of Heaven has no friends?

4. The second paragraph of the diary entry mentions a crossbow. What is a crossbow? In the same paragraph, what does the word "game" mean? Is the "military campaign" mentioned like the political campaign? If not, how is it different?

** 5. How can the lack of supplies for the army endanger the empire?

6. In the third paragraph of the diary entry, note that the main idea is stated in the first two sentences. The other sentences are details related to the main idea.

*7. What is flattery? Can flattery give you wrong ideas about things?

*8. In paragraph six the word "marvel" is used. What does it mean?

** 9. Does K'ang-hsi want to be like the Ming emperors? What facts support your answer?

10. How does the writer of the diary feel about artists and writers?

**11. Does K'ang-hsi think he is a good writer? What statement makes you believe this?

12. Which Westerners does K'ang-hsi include among his advisors?

**13. Why does K'ang-hsi allow these Westerners at his court?

14. Look for two cause and effect relationships in paragraph ten of the diary.

**15. Does K'ang-hsi trust Europeans? Why, or why not?

16. What does the word "But" in paragraph eleven signal for you?

The study guide in Example 3.2 is designed to be used with two groups, one of which can handle the textbook material independently and one with the teacher's help. The items without asterisks by the number are for students in both groups. The items with a single asterisk are for the group that needs the teacher's help with the material. The items with a double asterisk are for the students who can handle the text independently. A group that cannot handle the text material should be given another reading assignment in order to learn the content or related content. This group should have its own study guide, geared to its assignment. The whole class discussion that should follow the small group sessions with the guides would help all of the students clarify their concepts and see relationships between ideas.

Study guides are extremely helpful with science materials. Example 3.3 shows a sample science study guide for a selection from a science program designed specifically for nonacademic students.

Sample science selection and study guide   **Example 3.3**

What Goes on in There?

We are now at the point at which scientists studying matter made one of their most important breakthroughs. They had collected enough data to decide that matter was made of tiny, invisible particles, the atoms.

There are about 100 kinds of matter, the elements. Each element is composed of large numbers of its own kind of atom. Each element's atoms are different from the other 99 or so kinds of atoms. You already know many of the elements. The element iron is the metal that tools, machines, cars, and a million other things are made of. The element aluminum is used for making wrapping foil and pots and pans. Copper is the shiny red metal in wire and pennies. Oxygen, the important gas you breathe for life, is an element. Carbon is the element in coal—and diamonds.

You can probably name about a dozen or so more without half trying. All metals are elements. Phosphorus, sulfur, iodine, silicon are all elements. The 100 or so different kinds of atoms of the elements represent the building bricks of matter. It takes two different kinds of atoms to make water. It takes three kinds of atoms to make sugar. It takes about 20 kinds of atoms to make you!

So now we come down to the question: What is there about different atoms that makes the differences among the elements? Why are the atoms of one element different from those of another? Maybe atoms are not the end of the line. How could information be gathered to solve the problem of what an atom is like? Help came from an unexpected direction. Scientists working in electricity came up with information that provided clues to this problem.

Source: Melvin S. Domatz and Harry K. Wong, *Ideas and Investigations in Science: Physical Science*, p. 71. Copyright by Prentice Hall, Inc. Englewood Cliffs, N.J. Reprinted by permission.

Study guide

Overview question: What is the relationship between atoms and elements?

*1. What is a breakthrough? Do the two parts of this compound word help you understand the meaning? (First paragraph)

2. What are atoms? (Use the context clues in the first paragraph to decide.)

3. What are elements made up of? (Notice in the context another word meaning "made up.")

**4. Is gold an element? What sentence provides you with the clue to this answer?

**5. What kinds of experiments does the selection imply that you will perform to find out about atoms?

The items marked with a single asterisk are designed to be used with students for whom the material is at an instructional level. The questions with double asterisks are designed for the students reading on their independent levels. Unmarked questions are for both groups.

A three-level study guide is one in which the student is guided toward comprehension at the literal level (or understanding ideas that are directly stated), the interpretive level (or reading between the lines), and the applied level (or reading to use information to solve problems). Such a guide can be especially useful with literature selections. The guide in Example 3.4 is designed for use with the short story, "The Man Without a Country" by Edward Everett Hale.

Example 3.4   *Three-level study guide*

Directions: Check the statement or statements under each level that answer the question.

Level 1—What did the author say about Phillip Nolan?

☐ a. Phillip Nolan said, "I wish I may never hear of the United States again!"

☐ b. Phillip Nolan never actually met Aaron Burr.

☐ c. The court decided that Nolan should never hear the name of the United States again.

☐ d. Nolan was placed on board a ship and never allowed to return to the United States.

☐ e. Nolan was often permitted to go on shore.

☐ f. Nolan did not intentionally make it difficult for the people who were supposed to keep him from knowing about his country.

Level 2—What did the author mean by his story?

☐ Nolan never seriously regretted having denied his country.

☐ Nolan spoke against his country without realizing how much it had meant to him.

☐ Nolan never really missed hearing about his country.

Level 3—How can the meaning be applied to our lives?

☐ People should consider the consequences of their actions before they act.

☐ People can live comfortably away from home.

☐ Punishment is not always physical; it may be mental.

Another technique for guiding reading is use of structured overviews. Richard Barron[14] developed this technique; it involves using a graphic arrangment of terms that apply to the important concepts in the passage. The six steps in developing a structured overview are:

1. List the vocabulary words that the students need to understand.
2. Arrange the vocabulary words in a manner that shows the interrelationships among the concepts that they represent.
3. Add any vocabulary terms that the students understand and that will help show relationships between the current assignment and the general discipline.
4. Evaluate the graphic presentation. Consider possibilities for simplification.
5. As an introduction to the assignments, show the students the overview and explain why the terms are arranged in the order you have chosen. Encourage them to participate in the discussion and to contribute any information they have.
6. As the assignment is carried out, continue to relate new information to the overview.

Figure 3.2 shows an example of a structured overview in the area of atomic structure.

Structural overviews   Figure 3.2

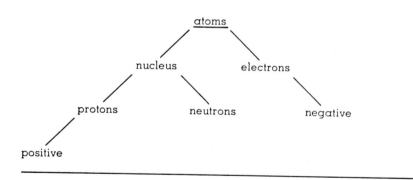

Samples of two structured overviews in the field of literature are shown in Examples 3.5 and 3.6.

14. Richard F. Barron, "The Use of Vocabulary as an Advance Organizer," in *Research in Reading in the Content Areas: First Year Report*, Harold Herber and Peter Sanders, eds. (Syracuse, N.Y.: Syracuse University Press, 1969), pp. 29–39.

Example 3.5   *Sample structured overview for Split Cherry Tree by Jesse Stuart*

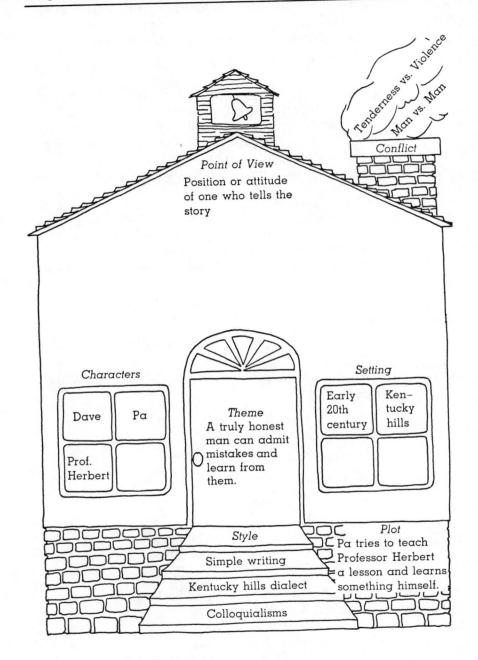

Source: *Reading Effectiveness Program for Middle, Junior and Secondary Schools,* Indiana Department of Instruction 1975 p 84

Sample structured overview for *The Scarlet Letter* by Nathaniel Hawthorne   Example 3.6

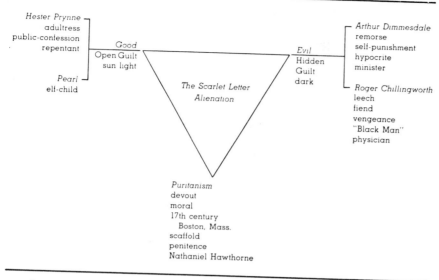

Source: *Reading Effectiveness Program for Middle Junior, and Secondary Schools,* Indiana Department of Instruction 1975 p 86

Other examples of structured overviews may be found in *Teaching Reading and Mathematics* by Richard A. Earle (Newark, Del.: International Reading Association, 1976) and *Improving Reading in Science* by Judith Thelan (Newark, Del.: International Reading Association, 1976). Both are part of the IRA Reading Aids Series, Peter B. Messmore, review editor.

Students are more likely to benefit from structured overviews if they are allowed to actively participate in the construction. For example, the youngsters can be given vocabulary terms on slips of paper and can be encouraged to place them in a logical arrangement, showing relationships. The teacher can then see what initial information the students have and can correct any erroneous impressions. The activity could be repeated after the assignment has been studied to assess the comprehension of the interrelated concepts presented.

Directed reading approaches

A directed reading approach is a method for guiding students through the reading of a textbook selection. It is most often used with basal reader selections, but it can be adapted for use with content area selections. Directed reading approaches vary from source to source in the number of steps involved, but the following components are present in all of the plans:

1. Motivation and building background.
2. Guided reading of the story.
   a. Silent.
   b. Oral.
3. Skill development activities.
4. Follow-up activities.

The *first step*—motivation and building background—consists of a discussion of background concepts needed to understand the selection and of the relationship of the content to the background experiences of the students, some discussion of difficult vocabulary in the material, and a preview of the selection to see what type of information will be presented. The teacher may wish to help build background by using films, filmstrips, slides, still pictures, models, or other visual aids. These aids ordinarily generate some motivation to study the passage to follow. Discussion of the way the content relates to their lives can also be motivational for the students.

Difficult vocabulary words that are not clearly explained by the context may need to be presented prior to the lesson. Vocabulary words that have appropriate context clues should *not* be presented before the reading. The student should be expected to use his reading skills to determine the meanings of these words. Students should also be alerted to the glossaries present in many content area textbooks and encouraged to use them when needed.

A preview of the selection—including reading the title, the introduction, the bold-face headings, and the summary—will give the student a framework into which the ideas gained through reading can fit. A brief examination of graphic aids to reading such as pictures, maps, graphs, and diagrams may also be helpful.

The *second step*—guided reading of the selection—includes setting purposes for reading and actual reading. Purposes for reading may be developed in different ways. They may be in the form of questions constructed by the teacher. (In this case, a study guide might be used to guide the reading.) They may be questions that have been formulated by the students themselves, perhaps based upon the bold-face headings observed during the preview of the selection. Or they may be predictions about what the selection will offer, based upon the clues from the title and illustrations. In the latter case, the students would read to confirm or deny the earlier-formed hypotheses (predictions). Russell Stauffer believes that this last type of purpose setting is likely to encourage students to think as they read.[15]

Once the purposes have been set, the students read to fulfill them. The initial reading should be silent. Silent reading always precedes oral reading unless testing for word recognition skills is taking place. There are several reasons:

---

15. Russell G. Stauffer, *Teaching Reading as a Thinking Process* (New York: Harper & Row), 1969.

1. Silent reading allows the reader an opportunity to decode an unfamiliar word without being subject to embarrassment in front of his or her peers.
2. Silent reading allows the reader the chance to become familiar with the phrasing patterns before having to read orally.
3. More of the reading at the secondary level should be silent than oral because silent reading is more prevalent in every-day situations.

After the silent reading, the students may discuss the answers to the purpose questions, perhaps reading orally to verify some of them. Any oral rereading that is done should be purposeful. Purposeful oral rereading would include reading to prove a point, reading to appreciate the beauty of the language (especially in poetry), and reading to interpret characterization (when reading a play with different readers assuming various parts). Not all directed reading lessons at the secondary level will include an oral reading component.

The *third step*—skill development activities—would include any direct teaching of vocabulary, word recognition skills, comprehension skills, or study skills. A skill taught may be one that caused some difficulty to the students as they read the selection; for example, if the students had trouble reading a map in the story, a map-reading lesson might be in order.

The *fourth step*—follow-up activities—would include enrichment activities related to the lesson. Examples might be reading additional books on the same topic or by the same author, illustrating an event or concept from the story, constructing a model, or writing a story related to the content.

Movement through a sequence of steps such as those described above may sound time consuming, but in actuality will probably involve no more time than a teacher typically spends on a section of a content text. Furthermore, after the students have been led through the above steps, they will be more likely to understand the material. They will also be more likely to retain the material because they have had adequate preparation for the lesson and have read the material with a purpose in mind.

Example 3.7 shows a directed reading approach used with a section of a mathematics textbook.

Directed reading lesson (mathematics)   **Example 3.7**

THE LANGUAGE OF SETS

1–1 Representing Sets

In this course you will be working with various geometric figures such as lines, planes, angles, and circles. Since every geometric figure will be regarded as a set of points, it would be well to start by refreshing your knowledge of sets.

Example 3.7 (cont.)   A *set* is any collection of objects that are clearly identified. The objects in a set are called its *members* or *elements* and are said to belong to or to be contained in the set.

To specify a set you must identify its members. One way to do this is to list its members within braces { }. For example, you write $A = \{2, 4, 6\}$ which is read

"A is the set whose members are 2, 4, and 6"

or

"A is the set that contains 2, 4, and 6."

In this case Set *A* is said to be specified *by roster*. The order in which the members are listed is not significant. Thus, you could specify *A* by writing $A = \{4, 2, 6\}$.

Often it is inconvenient or impossible to specify a set by roster. For example, you cannot list all the members of the set of real numbers between 0 and 1. However, you can specify this set by writing a description or rule within braces.

$B = \{$the real numbers between 0 and 1$\}$,

which is read

"B is the set of the real numbers between 0 and 1."

A set may contain any number of elements. If the elements of a set can be counted with the counting process coming to an end, the set is said to be a finite set (*fy*-nite). Otherwise, it is an *infinite set* (*in*-fi-nit). Thus, the set of light bulbs in Florida is a finite set even though an exact count of the members of the set would be difficult to make. However, the set of all odd integers is an infinite set since a count of the elements would never end.

It is possible to have a set that contains no members. For example, the set of odd integers whose squares are even integers contains no members. A set that contains no members is called the *empty set* or the *null set* and is designated by the symbol $\varnothing$. We agree to classify the empty set as a finite set with a count of zero elements.

Two sets are said to be *equal sets* if and only if they contain the same members. Thus if *A* and *B* are sets and $A = B$, *A* and *B* are simply different designations for the same set.

The following will help you recall the meaning of other symbols used in working with sets.

Notation	How Read
$x \in A$	x is a member of A. (or) x belongs to A.
$x \notin A$	x is not a member of A. (or) x does not belong to A.
$\{3, 4, 5, \ldots, 25\}$	The set whose members are 3, 4, 5, and so on through 25.

$\{1, 2, 3, \ldots\}$	The set whose members are 1, 2, 3, and so on indefinitely.
$\{x : x \in A\}$	The set of all x such that x belongs to A.
$\{x : 2x + 8 = 12\}$	The set of all x such that the sum of twice x and 8 is equal to 12.
$x \in R$	x belongs to the set of **real** numbers.

Source: R. C. Jurgensen et al., *Modern Mathematics: Geometry*, pp. 1–3. Copyright 1972 by Houghton Mifflin Co. Reprinted by permission.

1. Motivation and building background
   a. Refresh the students' memories of what sets are. Have them give examples of sets.
   b. Discuss the meanings of the terms "finite" and "infinite."
2. Guided reading
   a. Silent—Have the students read the section silently to discover the meanings of the following terms: set, element, finite set, infinite set, null set, equal sets.
   b. Oral—Have various students read aloud the portions of the section that define the terms specified by the teacher in 2a.
3. Skill development activities
   Study the pronunciations given in parentheses for "finite" and "infinite." Discuss the way the accent is indicated and the way long and short vowel sounds can be determined.
4. Follow-up activities
   Have students use what they have learned from reading the selection by doing exercises that follow it.

Example 3.8 shows another directed reading lesson based on pages 143–144 of *Modern Chemistry* by H. Clark Metcalfe *et al.*

Directed reading lesson (science)

Example 3.8

CHEMICAL EQUATIONS

Formula equations:
A simple way to represent chemical change is by the use of *word equations*. Such equations enable us to state briefly our observations of chemical reactions. Word equations give the names of the substances that enter into chemical reactions and the names of the substances that are produced. Thus, word equations have only *qualitative* significance.

Example 3.8 (cont.)   From experiments, chemists know that water is formed by the combustion of hydrogen in the oxygen of the air. The word equation for this reaction is

$$hydrogen + oxygen \rightarrow water$$

We read, hydrogen and oxygen react and yield water. This equation signifies that when hydrogen and oxygen react as indicated, water is the only product. Thus, it briefly states an experimental fact. It does not tell us the circumstances under which the reaction occurs, or the quantities involved.

In our discussion of the law of conservation of matter and energy, we recognize a very useful generalization: *In ordinary chemical changes, the total mass of the reacting substances is equal to the total mass of the products.* This may be thought of in terms of the *law of conservation of atoms.*

Suppose we replace the names of the *reactants,* hydrogen and oxygen, and the name of the *product,* water, with their respective formulas. We can now write the equation as a *balanced formula equation* which agrees with the law of conservation of atoms.

$$2H_2 + O_2 \rightarrow 2H_2O$$

This agreement is verified by comparing the total number of atoms of hydrogen and oxygen on the left side of the reaction sign ($\rightarrow$) to their respective totals on the right. Two molecules of hydrogen contain 4 atoms of hydrogen; two molecules of water also contain 4 hydrogen atoms. One molecule of oxygen contains 2 atoms of oxygen; two molecules of water also contain 2 oxygen atoms. Thus a chemical equation is similar to an algebraic equation. *They both express an equality. Until it is balanced a chemical equation cannot express an equality and is not a true equation.* The yields sign ($\rightarrow$) has the meaning of an equals sign ($=$). In addition the yields sign indicates the direction in which the reaction proceeds.

Our formula equation now signifies much more than the word equation.

1. It tells us the relative proportions of the reactants, hydrogen and oxygen, and the product, water.
2. It tells us that *2 molecules* of hydrogen react with *1 molecule* of oxygen and *2 molecules* of water are formed.

And since there is an Avogadro number of molecules in each mole of a molecular substance, most importantly,

3. *It tells us that 2 moles of hydrogen molecules react with 1 mole of oxygen molecules and 2 moles of water are formed.*
   The mass of a mole of a molecular substance is its grammolecular weight.
4. It tells us that *4 g* of hydrogen reacts with *32 g* of oxygen and *36 g* of water is formed.
   Furthermore, these masses are only relative masses. Hence,
5. *It tells us that any masses of hydrogen and oxygen which are in the ratio of 1:8 respectively and which react and form only water will yield a mass of water which is related to the masses of hydrogen and oxygen as 1:8:9.*

Finally, in any equation, the equality exists in both directions. If $x + y = z$, then $z = x + y$. So our formula equation

6. Tells us that *2 moles* of water, if decomposed, yield *2 moles* of hydrogen molecules and *1 mole* of oxygen molecules.

From these six statements, it is clear that formula equations have *quantitative* significance. Formula equations represent facts concerning reactions which have been established by experiments or other means. They indicate the nature and relative masses of reactants and products. But equations reveal nothing about the mechanism by which the reactants are converted into the products. Important reaction conditions are sometimes written near the yields sign.

It is possible to write an equation for a reaction which does not occur. Gold and oxygen do not combine directly to form gold (III) oxide, Au_2O_3. But we can write a word equation which says gold and oxygen react and yield gold (III) oxide. The corresponding formula equation can even be balanced to conform to the law of conservation of atoms. However, these would be false equations, since they are contrary to known facts.

Source: H. Clark Metcalfe, et al. *Modern Chemistry*, pp. 143–44. Copyright 1974 by Holt, Rinehart and Winston.

Directed reading lesson

1. Motivation and building background
    a. Discuss the meaning of an equation as it has been presented to students in mathematics.
    b. Refresh their memories of what chemical formulas are. (This has been covered in the previous chapter of the textbook.)
    c. Discuss the meanings of the following words: qualitative, quantitative, reactants, product (of a chemical reaction), equality, molecule, mole, decomposed.
2. Guided reading
    a. Silent—Have students read the selection silently to discover the meaning of the term "balanced formula equation." Ask them to decide from the selection what a balanced formula equation tells them that a word equation does not tell them.
    b. Oral—Have chosen students read aloud the parts that answer the questions provided for the silent reading.
3. Skill development activities
    a. Remind students that italicized words and sentences are italicized for emphasis. Have students refer to the italicized words and sentences in the selection and state the reason that italics were used in each instance.
    b. Have them examine the following words: qualitative, quantitative, reactants, equality, and decomposed. Ask them to decide what the root word is for each listed word. Talk about the meanings of the root words and about the formation of the new words by adding affixes.

4. Follow-up activities

> Have them write word equations for several well-known substances (salt, water, etc.). Let them attempt to write balanced formula equations for the reactions that produce these substances. Have them save these papers to check for accuracy after reading subsequent sections that provide further information on equation writing.

Alternate textbooks or supplementary readings

If a teacher finds that a segment of the students in a class is unable to benefit from the textbook designated for the class because of its readability, an obvious solution would be to locate alternate textbooks or supplementary reading materials with lower readability levels. Sometimes this is a practical solution. In some situations, it may be difficult to secure an adequate supply of alternate materials. Many times, however, teachers overlook the possibilities of such materials even when they are readily available.

An ideal situation, of course, would be to have several textbooks that cover identical content but that are written on varying difficulty levels. Science Research Associates has produced material of this type on the subject of career education. The New Rochester Occupational Reading Series[16] includes books written at three levels of reading difficulty but which all cover the same material. The information is presented in a story format and, therefore, is probably likely to appeal to poorer readers. A teacher's manual accompanies the textbooks, and there are workbooks also designed for three different reading levels. The skills covered in the workbooks are all practical ones related to the stories and to real life needs of teenagers. Unfortunately such multi-level materials are not at present popular items with publishers. Requests from knowledgeable secondary school teachers might change this attitude and start a trend in this direction.

Although multi-level textbooks covering identical material with identical formats may not be available, teachers should not discard the idea of using textbooks at different levels. Many textbooks on the same subject (biology, chemistry, plane geometry, algebra, American history, civics, health, etc.) are produced by various publishers. One publisher may include in a health text designed for eighth graders many of the same topics that another publisher includes in the health text designed for seniors in high school. A teacher assigned to use the health textbook from the second publisher might acquire some health textbooks from the first publisher to use with the students who cannot

---

16. Herman R. Goldberg and Winifred T. Brumber, eds., *The Job Ahead*, New Rochester Occupational Reading Series (Chicago: Science Research Associates, 1963).

read the textbook designated for the course. This possibility becomes even more appealing if the lower-level textbook does not have "eighth grade" printed on it to label it as material for younger students. (Many textbooks have ceased to carry such designations in recent years.) Where there are common topics in the two textbooks, part of the class could be assigned reading in one text and part in another. The reading, which of course would have been done for specified purposes, could then be followed by class discussion with both groups taking an active part.

Another possibility which should not escape the teacher's consideration is use of material from different publishers but designed for the same grade. As has already been mentioned in this chapter, a textbook for a particular grade may not really be written on that grade level. By checking the readability of various publishers' products, a teacher may find a considerably easier textbook than the one being used, although written for the same grade level and subject.

Some attempts are being made to provide high interest, low difficulty materials for use as regular basal materials in some content fields. The Scholastic World History Program[17] is an example of a move in this direction. This program is a four-book series on world history written at a sixth- to eighth-grade level of difficulty, but designed for use in secondary school world history programs at any grade level.

If alternate textbook materials are unavailable, a teacher can still find supplementary material for those who cannot manage the reading in the textbook. Trade books (library books) on various levels are available on almost any topic covered in the school curriculum. Some publishers (for example, Follett) have available information on the readability levels of many of the trade books that they produce. If such information is not readily available, the teacher can apply readability measures, following the procedures discussed earlier in this chapter.

Trade books are not the only available useful materials. Pamphlets produced by government agencies; newspaper articles, editorials, and other features; copies of political platforms of candidates; popular magazines; and a variety of other materials can be used. The teacher should probably check the readability of the portion of this supplementary material earmarked for the poorer readers. He or she should keep in mind that material that carries a high enough interest factor for the students may be readable even if it is on a slightly more difficult reading level than students can ordinarily manage.

The supplementary materials suggested above should not be limited to use with poorer readers. On the contrary, better readers will benefit greatly from having exposure to different points of view,

---

17. *Scholastic World History Program* (New York: Scholastic Book Services, 1976).

different methods of presentation, and additional information, even though they may use the textbook as the basis for their studies.

Teachers need to be aware that all reading difficulties in content areas will not necessarily disappear magically simply because the student has a book "on his level." Regardless of the reading level of the book, guidance in approaching content area reading tasks is needed.

Rewritten materials   If teachers find that there is insufficient supplementary reading material available in their content areas, they should not assume that poorer readers have to suffer through use of the assigned textbook. Secondary school teachers *can* and *have* rewritten materials from their assigned textbooks to lower difficulty levels when many of their students were unable to read the original text. One of the authors of this text has experimented with this activity in a course entitled "Teaching Reading in the Secondary School."[18] All participants were inservice classroom teachers. The results were excellent. Not only did the classroom teachers manage to lower from two to four grade levels the reading difficulty of selections from history, English, literature, and science textbooks, but most of the teachers said that the experience was eye-opening and enjoyable. Several continued rewriting activities after the class ended. The entire experience was so successful that the author has continued to use this assignment each time she has taught the class.

In an earlier portion of this chapter, mention was made of the fact that vocabulary and sentence difficulty are the two most significant indicators of readability. Rewriting a selection to a lower readability level primarily involves simplifying the vocabulary and sentence structure contained in the material. Easier synonyms can be substituted for difficult words, and sentences can be simplified by shortening them or by changing compound and complex sentences into simple sentences. An example of how this can be accomplished follows.

Original sentence: The ancient Phoenicians were the undisputed masters of the sea; they were also adept at business matters, keeping scrupulous records of all transactions that took place during their extensive excursions.

Rewritten material: The Phoenicians who lived in the year 1000 B.C. were the best sailors of their time. People from other nations did not doubt that Phoenicians were masters of the sea. They were also good at the business deals that took place during their long trips over the seas. They kept careful records of those deals.

18. Betty D. Roe, "Teacher Prepared Material for Slow Readers," *Journal of Reading* 15 (January 1972): 277–79.

Although the rewritten material contains more words, the vocabulary and sentence structure have been simplified. Easier synonyms or explanations were substituted for words that might have offered problems for poor readers: ancient, undisputed, adept, scrupulous, transactions, extensive, excursions. A thirty-one word sentence was simplified by breaking it down into four sections, ranging from seven to eighteen words in length.

Example 3.9 shows a selection rewritten by an education student, Paula King. The bracketed material indicates the readability sample taken from the passage. The italicized words within the brackets are the unfamiliar words in the passage. The bracketed passage from the original is 100 words long; the bracketed passage from the rewritten material is 108 words long. When the Dale-Chall Readability Formula was applied to the two samples, the original selection was found to be written on a ninth- to tenth-grade level, while the rewritten selection was found to be on a fifth- to sixth-grade difficulty level.

Rewriting a selection at a lower readability level   **Example 3.9**

Original: HOW ARE FAIR TRIALS GUARANTEED?
No distant place for trial. [The *Constitution* protects the *individual* in that it forbids a *trial* to be held at a great *distance* from the *scene* of the *crime*. Unless the *accused* person asks for a *trial* in another *judicial district*, he cannot be removed from the *community* where the *crime* was *alleged* to have been committed.
No treason trial for politics. The people in the United States are free from *unreasonable prosecution* for *treason*. In a *dictator-ruled* country, the *dictator* can charge his *opponents* with *treason* if they do not agree with him. At times *dictators* have ordered large numbers of people to be put to death without *trial*.] Our Constitution prevents the bringing of a charge of treason merely for political purposes by this provision: "Treason against the United States, shall consist only in levying War against them, or in adhering to their Enemies giving Aid and Comfort."

Citizens of the United States cannot be convicted of treason without positive proof. The Constitution provides that no person can be convicted of treason without at least two witnesses to the same treasonable act, or unless the person confesses in open court.

Source: Robert Carter and John M. Richards, *Of, By, and For The People* (Westchester, Illinois: Benefic Press), pp. 205–206.

Rewritten: HOW ARE FAIR TRIALS GUARANTEED?
No distant place for a trial

[The *Constitution* of the United States protects the *individual*. It does not allow a *trial* to be held too far away from the *scene* of the *crime*. Sometimes the person charged with the *crime* asks to be tried in another place. If not, he cannot be removed from the *community* where the *crime* was supposed to have taken place.

Example 3.9 (cont.)

No treason trial for politics

The people of the United States are free from unfair *prosecution* for *treason. Treason* is the act of trying to overthrow the government. Some countries are ruled by an all-powerful ruler or *dictator.* At times these rulers have ordered large numbers of people to death without a fair hearing.] Our Constitution does not allow this to happen. The Constitution states two acts considered to be treason. One is going to war against the United States. The other is giving aid or comfort to the enemy.

Citizens of the United States cannot be convicted of treason unless there is no question about the act. Two persons must actually see the person commit treason or the person must admit the act in an open court.

---

*Note: Subheadings were not counted in word count.

Other adjustments for textbook usage

If the teacher feels that certain textbook material is essential in its unchanged form (for example: a poem or a beautifully worded essay), he or she may wish to tape the passage and set up a listening station for students who cannot read it for themselves. The teacher or a particularly good reader from the class may be the reader on the tapes. (If a class member makes the tapes, it would be wise for the teacher to preview the tapes before releasing them for general use.) If students who are unable to read the text for themselves follow along in the book as they listen to the tapes, they may pick up some sight vocabulary as they absorb the content.

Sometimes the tapes of textbook selections may be used by students who can handle the textbook reading assignments, but who learn best through the auditory mode, rather than the visual mode. These tapes can also be an alternate way of studying for tests on material previously read.

Language experience materials

In earlier sections of this chapter, it was suggested that the teacher make differentiated assignments for students who have different levels of reading ability, following these assignments with class discussions to which all groups contribute. This class or large group discussion period offers an excellent opportunity for use of language experience materials that can be beneficial to all students, but especially to the poorer students.

Language experience materials are materials written in the students' own words. In the elementary school, language experience stories are often developed by a group of students who have had a special experience in common. In the secondary school, experience materials may be written by a group of students who have read about a common topic and wish to summarize their findings. The teacher can record all significant contributions on the chalkboard as they are offered. At the conclusion of the discussion, the teacher and students together can organize the contributions in a logical order (chronological, cause-effect, etc.). The teacher can then have duplicates of the group-composed material made and can give them to the students on the following day.

The members of the groups who are able to handle the textbook with ease may file the experience material to use for review for subsequent tests. A group that is unable to handle the textbook presentation may use the material more extensively. For example, the teacher may meet with this group and guide the members through the reading of the material by using purpose questions. The students are likely to succeed in reading this material because they have seen the content written on the board in the words of fellow students. Having heard a discussion of the contents, the students will find it easier to apply context clues as they read. Any technical vocabulary or multiple-meaning words can be located and thoroughly discussed. These words may be written in a special notebook with accompanying pronunciations and definitions and a reference to the experience material in which they occurred. A booklet made up of experience material can serve as a reference source for these words when they are encountered again. Needless to say, the booklet is also used by this group in studying for tests on the material.

Experience materials may also be developed by individuals and groups who wish to record the results of scientific experiments or the periodic observation of some natural phenomena. These materials may be shared by the rest of the class in oral or written form. Such activities are extremely valuable for students who are not able to gain much information from a textbook that is too difficult.

A teaching unit is a series of interrelated lessons or class activities organized around a theme, a literary form, or a skill. A unit generally involves four basic types of activities:

Developing teaching units

1. Introduction of the Unit.
2. Development of the Unit.
3. Organization of Findings.
4. Culmination Activities.

Each of these activities is explained below.

The students are introduced to the unit's theme or central idea, the literary form to be explored, or the skill to be developed. Through class discussion and/or pretests, the teacher determines the extent to which

Introduction of the unit

the students' background of experience in the area can contribute to the unit. The teacher discusses with the students what they already know about the area of consideration and helps them to evolve questions that they need to answer or areas in which they need clarification. During this discussion the teacher helps the students relate the area of study to their own personal experiences or needs. Motivation for participating in the unit activities may be supplied by showing a film or filmstrip or by playing records or tapes related to the area to arouse curiosity and give a preview of possible future activities.

Development of the unit

The teacher assigns areas of concern to the students or allows them to choose areas in which they have particular interest. The result is several small groups attempting to answer specific questions or clarify specific areas of concern. The teacher may meet with each group to discuss reference sources available to the members as they pursue their research. Textbooks, library books (fiction and nonfiction), encyclopedias, other reference books, magazines, newspapers, original documents (such as *The Declaration of Independence*), films, filmstrips, and a variety of other audiovisual aids should be included among the possible sources. The teacher must be alert to the variety of reading abilities within the group and must help the group members to expend their effort in ways most likely to be fruitful. Books and reference aids on a number of different levels should be available. A review of such study skills as use of the card catalog, use of encyclopedias, outlining, notetaking, skimming, and scanning may be helpful for some members of each research group. Needs groups encompassing members from all of the research groups may be formed for these purposes.

Each member of each research group will have a responsibility for collecting data for the group. Differentiated assignments within the groups may be developed by the teacher or a skillful group leader who is under the teacher's watchful eye.

Organization of findings

The research groups meet after ample time has been allowed individual members for data collection. The group then discusses the information collected from the various sources, resolves differences of opinion through discussion, and welds the findings into a coherent report. The report may be oral or written. It may be accompanied by audiovisual aids such as charts, tables, maps, graphs, pictures, filmstrips, or tapes. It may be in the form of an oral report, a panel discussion, a skit, a more complete dramatization, a mural, etc.

At the end of the unit study, the various research groups present their findings in a variety of ways. The class critically examines the information presented and determines if the purposes of the unit have been met. If the class feels that not all of the original purposes have been met, the members may regroup to attempt to remedy the situation.

The teacher should help the students to see how the findings relate to their individual lives. An activity that immediately applies the findings would be beneficial by emphasizing the relevance of the unit.

Culmination
activities

A unit in health might be arranged around a theme such as "The Basic Four Food Groups." A discussion of the theme could make apparent the background knowledge that the group has concerning the theme. A film or filmstrip on the topic could clarify the composition of each of the basic four food groups. Four research groups could be set up, one for each food group. Additional groups might be formed to study fad diets.

Sample unit ideas

Each group studying a basic food group could investigate the importance of the foods in its group, setting out to answer the questions: What are the benefits from eating these foods? What are the problems that could result from not eating them? Groups on fad diets could weigh the benefits and dangers of these diets. A variety of sources should be available, including current paperbacks, newspaper articles, and magazine articles concerned with nutrition and dieting. Textbooks and reference books, such as encyclopedias, should also be utilized.

The group reports could take a variety of forms; one possibility would be to have a student describe what happened when he or she went on a fad diet. In the whole-class discussion following the group reports, relationships among the reports should be emphasized. For example, the fad diets that sometimes have bad results often leave out some of the basic food groups.

A unit in literature might be developed around a type of literature, such as "Tall Tales of the United States." The opening discussion could include an attempt to define "tall tales" and opportunities for the students to name tall tales with which they are familiar. The teacher might use a film, filmstrip, or tape during the introductory stage to clarify the nature of tall tales. Different groups could be formed to read tall tales about different superhuman individuals, for example, Old Stormalong, Paul Bunyon, Mike Fink, and Pecos Bill. Other groups could concentrate on tall tales of other types such as Washington Irving's "Rip Van Winkle" and "The Legend of Sleepy Hollow" or Mark Twain's "The Celebrated Jumping Frog of Calaveras County." As a culminating activity each student could write a tall tale of the general type that he read. The tales could be shared in oral or written form with the rest of the class.

Media selection sources

There are a number of selection aids that can help secondary school teachers locate appropriate books for the variety of readers in their classes. Some of the especially useful ones follow:

American Association for the Advancement of Science, *The AAAS Science Book List*, 3rd. ed. (Washington, D.C.: American Association for the Advancement of Science, 1970).

American Library Association, *Doors to More Mature Reading: Detailed Notes on Adult Books for Use with Young People* (Chicago: American Library Association, 1964).

George J. Becker, "Offbeat Paperbacks for Your Classroom," *Journal of Reading* 10 (November 1971):127-29.

Toby M. Berger, ed., *Senior High School Library Catalogue*, 10th ed. (New York: H. W. Wilson Company, 1972).

G. Robert Carlesen, *Books and the Teenage Reader: A Guide for Teachers, Librarians, and Parents*, 2nd. ed. (New York: Harper & Row, 1972).

Anita E. Dunn et al., *Fare for the Reluctant Reader* (Albany, N.Y.: Capitol Area School Development Association, 1964).

Raymond Emery, and Margaret Houshower, *High Interest—Easy Reading for Junior and Senior High School Reluctant Readers* (Champaign, Ill.: National Council of Teachers of English, 1965).

Daniel Fader, and Elton McNeil, *Hooked on Books: Program and Proof* (New York: Putnam, 1968).

Kathryn A. Haebich, *Vocations in Biography and Fiction: An Annotated List of Books for Young People* (Chicago: American Library Association [ALA], 1962).

National Council for the Social Studies, *World Civilization Booklist: Supplementary Reading for Secondary Schools* (Washington, D.C.: National Council for the Social Studies, 1968).

National Council of Teachers of Mathematics, *The High School Mathematics Library*, 3rd ed. (Washington, D.C.: National Council of Teachers of Mathematics, 1967).

New York Public Library, *Books for the Teenager* (New York: New York Public Library, 1975).

Virginia M. Reid, ed., *Reading Ladders for Human Relations*, 5th ed. (Washington, D.C.: American Council of Education, 1972).

George Spache, *Good Reading for Disadvantaged Readers* (Chicago, Ill.: Garrard, 1972).

George Spache, *Good Reading for Poor Readers*, rev. ed. (Champaign, Ill.: Garrard, 1968).

George Spache, *Sources of Good Books for Poor Readers* (Newark, Del.: International Reading Association, 1969).

Ruth Strang, Ethlyne Phelps, and Dorothy Withrow, *Gateways to Readable Books*, 4th ed. (Bronx, N.Y.: H. W. Wilson, 1966).

Elinor Walker, ed., *Book Bait*, 2nd ed. (Chicago: American Library Association, 1968).

Elinor Walker, ed., *Your Reading: A Booklist for Senior High School*, 5th. ed. (Champaign, Ill.: National Council of Teachers of English, 1975).

Marian E. White, ed., *High Interest-Easy Reading for Junior and Senior High School Students* (New York: Citation Press, 1972).

Jean A. Wilson, *Books for You*, rev. ed. (New York: Washington Square Press, 1971).

John E. Wiltz, *Books in American History* (Bloomington, Ind.: Indiana University Press, 1964).

Teachers who wish to locate appropriate periodicals for their students may consult one or both of the following:

Bill Katz, *Magazines for Libraries* (New York: R. R. Bowker Co., 1969).

Marian H. Scott, *Periodicals for School Libraries* (Chicago: American Library Association, 1969).

Some periodicals contain information that can help teachers choose audiovisual materials. Several useful ones are the following:

Audiovisual Instruction, National Education Association, Department of Audiovisual Instruction, 1201 16th Street N.W., Washington, D.C.

The Booklist, Chicago: American Library Association.

School Library Journal, New York: R. R. Bowker Co.

Self-test

1. Which statement is incorrect? (a) Textbooks placed at grade nine often are written at a tenth-grade readability level or above. (b) Content textbooks tend to be written by reading specialists. (c) Literature anthologies often vary widely in readability from selection to selection. (d) Many students in any given grade are unable to read at grade level.

2. Readability of printed material is influenced by which factors? (a) Vocabulary. (b) Sentence length. (c) Sentence complexity. (d) All of the above.

3. What are the two factors that researchers have found to be the most useful in predicting readability? (a) Vocabulary and sentence length. (b) Vocab-

ulary and reader background. (c) Sentence length and abstract concepts. (d) Idea organization and format.

4. Achievement grouping in reading refers to which arrangement? (a) Grouping students on the basis of their general ability to read material of certain levels with understanding. (b) Grouping students on the basis of the skills they lack. (c) Grouping students on the basis of a common interest. (d) None of the above.

5. What is true of student-tutorial groups? (a) The tutor is allowed to plan his or her own lessons. (b) The tutor does not benefit from the activity, although the "clients" do. (c) One or two especially good students should always act as tutors. (d) None of the above.

6. What should teachers who use groups within their classes remember? (a) Needs groups should continue for a minimum time period of a semester. (b) All groups should be flexible. (c) Both a and b. (d) Neither a nor b.

7. Which statement is true of study guides? (a) They are not helpful for poor readers. (b) They are useful when the teacher is employing grouping with the content class. (c) They can be designed to help students focus on particular information by offering purpose questions. (d) Both b and c.

8. Which statement is true of structured overviews? (a) They involve a graphic arrangement of terms that apply to the important concepts in the passages. (b) They contain a list of purpose questions. (c) They cannot be used with mathematics materials. (d) All of the above.

9. Which one of the following is *not* a step in a directed reading approach? (a) Motivation and building background. (b) Oral reading, paragraph by paragraph, without specific purposes. (c) Skill development activities. (d) Guided reading of the story, silent and oral.

10. If secondary school students cannot read the textbooks assigned for their classes, what can the teacher do? (a) The teacher can rewrite the material to a lower difficulty level. (b) The teacher can find an alternate textbook or other alternate printed material. (c) The teacher can tape portions of the textbook for student use. (d) All of the above are possibilities.

11. Which statement is true of language experience materials? (a) They consist of the students' own words. (b) They are inappropriate for use above ninth grade. (c) They must be developed in small groups. (d) All of the above.

12. Which statement is true if teaching units are utilized? (a) Separate lessons are unrelated. (b) Research groups can be profitably employed. (c) All students engage in identical activities. (d) None of the above.

Enrichment activities

1. Apply the Fry Readability Graph Formula to a 100-word sample from the social studies textbook selection in Example 3.2. Start counting your 100 word sample with the third paragraph, which begins "We often talk . . ." After you have completed the formula application, check your answer by referring to Appendix F.

2. Construct a study guide that could be used with the mathematics selection found in Example 3.7 or the science selection located in Example 3.3. Discuss your guide with your classmates.

*3. Construct a study guide for a secondary level textbook that you are currently using. Try it with your students and report to the class concerning the results.

4. Write out a plan for a directed reading lesson for the social studies selection in Example 3.2 or the science selection in Example 3.3 of this chapter. Discuss your results with your classmates.

*5. Write out a plan for a directed reading lesson for a section of a textbook that you are currently using. Try it with your students and report to the class concerning the results.

6. Choose a topic and locate printed materials, both textbook and nontextbook, on a variety of difficulty levels which could be used by your students when studying this topic.

7. Take a selection of about 500 words from a secondary level textbook of your choice and rewrite it to a lower difficulty level by simplifying vocabulary and sentence structure. Use the Fry Readability Graph Formula to test the original passage and rewritten passage.

8. Learn to use a readability formula other than Fry's formula. Test a passage of a secondary level textbook of your choice using this formula, and then test the passage using the Fry formula. Discuss with your classmates the results of your activity.

*9. Try using a language experience activity with students in one of your secondary classes. Report the results to your college class.

*10. Plan a unit from your chosen subject area. Try it with students in your class. Decide how you could improve the unit if you were to teach it again.

11. Arrange the vocabulary terms at the beginning of the chapter in the form of a structured overview. You may need to add some terms. Explain your arrangement to the class.

Selected references

Artley, A. Sterl. *Trends and Practices in Secondary School Reading.* Newark, Del.: International Reading Association, 1968.

Aukerman, Robert. *Reading in the Secondary School Classroom.* New York: McGraw-Hill, 1972.

Burmeister, Lou E. *Reading Strategies for Secondary School Teachers.* New York: Addison-Wesley, 1974.

Burron, Arnold and Amos Claybaugh. *Using Reading to Teach Subject Matter.* Columbus, Ohio: Charles E. Merrill, 1973.

Dechant, Emerald. *Reading Improvement in the Secondary School.* Englewood Cliffs, N.J.: Prentice-Hall, 1973.

Dillner, Martha H. and Joanne P. Olson. *Personalizing Reading Instruction in Middle, Junior, and Senior High Schools: Utilizing a Competency-Based Instructional System.* New York: Macmillan Company, 1977. Chapter 8.

---

* These activities are designed for inservice teachers, student teachers, or practicum students.

Duggins, James. *Teaching Reading for Human Values in High School.* Columbus, Ohio: Charles E. Merrill, 1972.

Earle, Richard A. and Peter L. Sanders, "Individualizing Reading Assignments." *Journal of Reading* 16 (April 1973): 550–55.

Forgan, Harry W. and Charles T. Mangrum. *Teaching Content Area Reading Skills.* Columbus, Ohio: Charles E. Merrill, 1972.

Hafner, Lawrence E. *Developmental Reading in Middle and Secondary Schools.* New York: Macmillan Company, 1977. Chapters 20 and 21.

Herber, Harold L. *Teaching Reading in Content Areas.* Englewood Cliffs, N.J.: Prentice-Hall, 1970.

International Reading Association. *Reading Instruction in Secondary Schools.* Newark, Del.: International Reading Association, 1974.

Karlin, Robert. *Teaching Reading in High School.* 2nd ed. Indianapolis: Bobbs-Merrill, 1972.

————. *Teaching Reading in High School: Selected Articles.* Indianapolis: Bobbs-Merrill, 1969.

Shepard, David. *Comprehensive High School Reading Methods.* Columbus, Ohio: Charles E. Merrill, 1973.

Smith, Richard J., and Thomas C. Barrett. *Teaching Reading in the Middle Grades.* Reading, Mass.: Addison-Wesley, 1974.

Stauffer, Russell G. *Reading as a Thinking Process.* New York: Harper & Row, 1969.

Tutolo, Daniel J. "The Study Guide—Types, Purpose and Value." *Journal of Reading* 20 (March 1977): 503–7.

Word recognition in the secondary school program

4

This chapter is devoted to ways of helping youngsters read independently using a variety of methods of word recognition. These methods include 1) sight vocabulary, particularly knowledge of specialized vocabulary terms met in content area reading, and 2) word analysis skills, such as context clues, phonics, structural analysis, and use of the dictionary. Two ideas permeate the chapter: the reader must be flexible in his or her approach to an unfamiliar word and must realize that two or more word recognition skills can be used together to help in arriving at the pronunciation and meaning of a word.

As you read this chapter, try to answer these questions:

1. How can important content area words become recognizable at sight?
2. How can word analysis skills be developed by the content area teacher?
3. What is meant by "establishing balances in word recognition skills"?

Purpose-setting questions

As you read this chapter, check your understanding of these terms:

sight vocabulary	structural analysis	grapheme
tachistoscope	morpheme	consonant blend
word analysis skills	derivative	consonant digraph
meaning clues	affixes	vowel digraph
contextual analysis	inflectional endings	diphthong

Key vocabulary

semantic clue   variants   schwa

syntactic clue   phonics   glossary

Sight vocabulary

Words that a reader can recognize immediately on sight are frequently called "sight words." Developing a store of sight words is important to a reader since the larger the store of sight words a person has, the more rapidly and fluently he or she can read a selection. Comprehension of a passage and reading speed suffer if a person has to pause too often to analyze unfamiliar words. The more mature and experienced a reader becomes, the larger that person's store of sight words becomes. One goal of reading instruction is to turn into sight words all of the words that students continually must recognize in print. In the elementary school, the emphasis of reading instruction is upon developing such words as of, *through, two, know, give, come,* and *once* as sight words; at the middle, junior, and senior high school levels, the focus of sight vocabulary instuction should usually be upon the technical words that appear in content area reading material.

What words should a teacher choose to teach as sight words? How should the teacher work with potential sight words? These questions are the focus of the following discussion.

In Chapter 10, some basic sight word lists used at the elementary school level are mentioned. Such lists are appropriate for some disabled readers in the secondary school, but most students who need to master these words are (or should be) in a remedial reading program with a special teacher of reading. The secondary school teacher is seldom equipped to deal with these students' reading problems.

A list of basic sight words for disabled readers who are older is given in Example 4.1. Secondary school content teachers might find this listing helpful since the words, which are of a general and nontechnical nature, are high frequency words in secondary level reading materials.

Example 4.1   *A corpus list of basic sight words for older disabled readers*

1. more	22. last	43. course
2. than	23. might	44. war
3. other	24. great	45. until
4. such	25. year	46. something
5. even	26. since	47. fact
6. most	27. against	48. though
7. also	28. himself	49. less

8. through	29. few	50. public
9. should	30. during	51. almost
10. each	31. without	52. enough
11. people	32. place	53. took
12. Mr.	33. American	54. yet
13. state	34. however	55. government
14. world	35. Mrs.	56. system
15. still	36. thought	57. set
16. between	37. part	58. told
17. life	38. general	59. nothing
18. being	39. high	60. end
19. same	40. united	61. didn't
20. another	41. left	62. later
21. while	42. number	63. knew

Source: Jerry Johns, "A List of Basic Sight Words for Older Disabled Readers," *English Journal* 61 (October 1972): 1057–59. Copyright © 1972 by the National Council of Teachers of English. Reprinted by permission.

An older publication[1] dealing with technical vocabulary is also worthy of study by content area teachers as at least a start toward developing their own basic lists of specialized terms important for mastery of their content area.

The content area teacher should always carefully peruse the unit or chapter about to be presented to the class. During such study, the teacher could extract approximately ten specialized terms that could be important for the study and understanding of that unit or chapter. In preparing the students for the study, attention would be focused upon these terms.

For example, suppose a unit or chapter on the study of light (in a science class) includes these words:

concave	retina
convex	sensory
gland	translucent
membrane	opaque
optical	diffuse
refract	transparent

The teacher would write the words, each in the context of a sentence, on the chalkboard, in a chart, or using an overhead projector. The words would be pronounced, by either students or the teacher, and discussed considering the context. Some attention may be given to certain parts of a word; for example, the prefixes *con, trans,*

---

1. Luella Cole, *The Teacher's Handbook of Technical Vocabulary* (Bloomington, Ill.: Public School Publishing Co., 1940).

and *di*. Comparison and contrast may be used; that is, the pronunciation or meaning of a new word can be compared to a similar known word or contrasted with a dissimilar known word as *translucent* and *transparent*. Where appropriate, real objects or pictures of objects may provide a useful context for presenting a word; for example, *opaque* and *transparent* may be demonstrated through use of appropriate materials. Later, after the students have read the related material, the words could be presented again for further clarification and explanation. During the course of study of the material, the teacher may feel that it is important to isolate certain words for additional practice. There are several ways in which this may be done. A few are listed below.

Activities

1. Use flash cards. Print words or phrases on individual cards and have students take turns checking each other. The word

Figure 4.1   *Teacher-made tachistoscope*

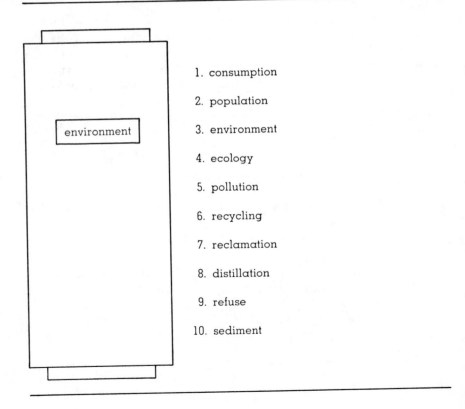

1. consumption
2. population
3. environment
4. ecology
5. pollution
6. recycling
7. reclamation
8. distillation
9. refuse
10. sediment

or phrase cards can be flashed quickly, with known ones in one stack and unknown ones in another. Further study of unknown words can be provided for those who need it.

2. Use mechanical devices. One common mechanical device is a tachistoscope, which reveals printed material on a screen for brief periods of time. If a tachistoscope is not available, teachers or students can make their own for use with vocabulary terms. An illustration of this device is shown in Figure 4.1. A strip of cardboard with the words on it is pulled through an opening cut in the holder. As a word is exposed, the student pronounces it.

   Another device designed to teach vocabulary is the *Language Master Machine* (N.Y.: Bell and Howell). It can be particularly helpful if the teacher prepares the cards to be used by the students.

3. Use games. Games such as word bingo games can be used for practice with sight words. The teacher or a leader calls out a word, and the students who recognize that word on their cards may cover it. When a student covers his entire card, he or she says, "cover," and the teacher or leader checks the card to see if all the covered words were called. A sample is provided in Figure 4.2.

Bingo Card   Figure 4.2

congruent	chord	tangent
diameter	free	equidistant
radius	segment	intersect

Other card games in which students accumulate "books" of matching cards can be developed into word recognition games. (An original deck is formed by printing the sight words on blank cards.) The rules of a familiar game such as "Go Fish" could be used, except that to claim a book the student must name the word on the matching cards.

4. Encourage wide reading. Providing students with a wide variety of easy reading material on the topic under consideration and encouraging voluntary reading of such books, magazines, and newspapers is one of the most effective ways of developing a store of sight words. Since a number of repetitions of a word are generally necessary before that word actually becomes a sight word, the most useful practice

with potential sight words presents the words in context. It is only in context that words can be pronounced or understood with certainty (especially with words like *desert*).

5. Employ other activities. Some activities that can be used to provide reinforcement include matching words to definitions or pictures, completing sentences with new sight words, having vocabulary check tests, doing creative work to portray new words. These varied ways are illustrated in Example 4.2.

Example 4.2   *Sample sight word activity*

---

1. Match the terms in column 1 with the appropriate meaning from column 2.

Column 1		*Column 2*	
1.	decimeter	a.	1000 grams
2.	kilogram	b.	$\frac{1}{10}$ meter
3.	hectoliter	c.	10 millimeter
4.	centimeter	d.	$\frac{1}{10}$ kiloliter

2. A dekagram is (a) 10 grams (b) 1000 grams (c) $\frac{1}{20}$ g.
3. A gram is the weight of a _____ of water.
4. If ☐ represents 100 sq meters or 1 are, then draw a square to represent a hectare.

Word analysis skills   A sight vocabulary alone is not the answer to independent reading on an adult level. The reader needs to acquire a variety of methods for analyzing words in order to continue to grow in word knowledge. The teacher should help students develop and maintain this sort of independence through providing frequent guided opportunities to use word analysis techniques. Some things that a reader does in analyzing and identifying strange words are:

1. Anticipating the meaning to come.
2. Guessing a word from context.
3. Studying the word from the point of view of sound or structure.
4. Consulting the dictionary.
   Each of these will be discussed in turn.

Learning to use meaning clues basically consists of developing a mind set or an attitude. It is important to develop an attitude of expectancy about what is being read. For example, consider the following sentences: *Billy looked at his toy airplane and put his hands on the wings. As he lifted it off the airstrip, a new pilot was born.* The words *airplane* and *wings* in the first sentence allow the reader to anticipate the meanings and use of *airstrip* and *pilot* in the second sentence. If the words in the first sentence were familiar to the reader and the words in the second were not, identification of the latter would be facilitated by anticipation based on meaning clues.

Use of meaning clues and contextual analysis are quite similar, but the latter involves rereading or prereading. Contextual analysis means identifying unfamiliar words or phrases by examining their *semantic* and/or *syntactic* environment or context.

Example of semantic clue: The harshness in his voice and the scowl on his face told that father was in a *captious* mood.

Example of syntactic clue: His *truculent* criticism of the article revealed his deepest feelings.

In the first example, the meaning of *captious* is suggested by some accompanying semantic indications: *Harshness in his voice* and *scowl on his face*. In the second example, the reader to whom *truculent* is unfamiliar can tell that the word is not a noun or a verb by its position in the sentence. Its position shows that it describes a type of criticism; that is, it is an adjective.

Many students do not use context clues for reasons such as the following.

1. They stop when they meet an unknown word, forgetting that clues may be provided by succeeding words in the sentence or even by succeeding sentences.
2. They rely too much on other ways of analyzing words, such as looking at configuration (shape of the word) or beginning or ending sounds.
3. They wait for the teacher to provide the contextual signals.

Students need to be encouraged to keep reading backward and forward to where clues may be, to generate hypotheses, to test alternate possibilities, to demand sense, and to recognize a wide variety of language clues.

Organization of context clues Table 4.1 suggests different types of contextual aids to understanding word meanings. These kinds of aids are often encountered by students who should be given extensive practice in using them if contextual analysis is to become an important means of word analysis.

Table 4.1   Types of Contextual Aids

Type	Example
1. Definition	A *micrometer* is an instrument used with a telescope or microscope for measuring minute distances.
2. Restatement	A cockroach has two *antennae*, or feelers, at its head.
3. Example	"The ship plows the sea" is an example of a *metaphor*.
4. Comparison/contrast	A *machete*, like a sword, can be very dangerous. In bright light, the pupils of the eyes contract; in the dark, they *dilate*.
5. Description	A *ginkgo* is a tree of eastern China with fan-shaped leaves, providing much shade.
6. Synonyms/antonyms	The *mercury* in the thermometer was dropping—the *quicksilver* was getting heavier. The *acid* was reacting with a *base* to redden the litmus.
7. Familiar experience of language	*Artificial respiration* was applied to the nearly drowned man.
8. Association	He ate as *ravenously* as a bear.
9. Reflection of mood	All alone, Jim heard the creaking sound of the opening door and saw a shadowy figure standing suddenly before him. Jim was literally *stupefied*.
10. Summary	Even though he was 65 years old, he continued to love sports. He played a skillful game of tennis, and seldom missed his daily swim. He was very *athletic*.

Context clues are rarely used in isolation from other word analysis techniques. When used in combination with the other techniques cited in this chapter, context clue usage becomes highly important. Using context clues is not wild guessing but very calculated guessing as to what word makes good sense in a specific sentence. It is the word recognition skill most frequently used by the mature reader.

Assessment of contextual clue usage A cloze procedure (somewhat similar to the one described in Chapter 10) may be useful for determining student skill in use of context clues. Using this procedure, a passage is selected and prepared that does not have too many unknown words in it. Using a textbook selection that is written on a level below the instructional reading level of the group being assessed is recommended. The following procedures are followed:

1. First, students read the entire passage silently.
2. Then, they reread, writing in missing words that seem to fit.
3. Next, the teacher discusses with the students their reasons for choosing the replacement words.
4. Finally, students compare their finished product with the original.

In this assessment, synonyms are acceptable as well as the actual word (only the latter is considered correct when checking for reading levels). A score of 75 percent or better on filling-in the omitted words indicates satisfactory performance of contextual clue usage.

Instructional strategies Several procedures are useful for providing instruction in contextual clue usage.

1. Bring to the attention of students the values of context clues and some techniques for using them, using sentence and paragraph examples from the students' content materials. The teacher and students cooperatively can circle unknown words and discuss how they might arrive at the meanings and pronunciation of the strange words. The purpose of such study is to help students become aware of clues that are present, to learn to search for these, and to synthesize the clues to get the meanings and pronunciations of the words. From such discussion, summary charts can be cooperatively developed to provide ideas for systematic context analysis. An example is suggested below:

   a. Read the entire sentence or paragraph.
   b. Try to think of a word that would make sense in place of the strange word.
   c. Listen to your pronunciation of the unknown word. Does it match a word you know?
   d. See if there are other words that give you an idea about or clue to this strange word.
   e. Use other word analysis skills to help you unlock the word.

2. Encourage students to find in their text materials examples of the types of contextual aids presented in Table 4.1.
3. Present exercises like the following to groups of students who need them.

    a.   Partial indication of word

An agreement was impossible; an im—as—e had been reached. (part spelling)

An agreement was impossible; an i—————e had been reached. (first/last letter)

An agreement was impossible; an i————— had been reached. (first letter)

An agreement was impossible; an ——————had been reached. (number of letters)

An agreement was impossible; an _____ had been reached. (space)

    b.   Multiple-choice

The vase was _____ (fractious, fragile, fragment).

    c.   Scrambled sentences

germs. us the protects epidermis from

    d.   Nonsense words

Betty's *dreb* expression showed she was not cheerful today.

4.   Encourage students to compose exercises for others to answer. Individual students (or groups of two or three) can make up sets of sentences, the teacher can compile and ditto them, and other students can then work together in small groups to solve them. References to specific classroom activities or classmates can personalize and add some zest to otherwise drab and humorless exercises.

5.   Prepare and use cloze exercises. (Details for the preparation and administration of cloze exercises are given in Chapter 10.) One way of presenting the cloze technique is to play a tape recording with key words omitted. Provide a copy of the script to the students and have them fill in the blanks as they listen to the tape.

6.   Relate contextual clue usage to special types of words that need attention; these types include homonyms (That is the only *course* he could take. The dress was made from *coarse* material); synonyms (*drill—bore*) antonyms (*talkative—taciturn*) and homographs. Homographs are words that look alike but have different meanings and pronunciations. (Did you *record* the science experiment? Jim broke Tom's *record* for the most interceptions in one game.) Multiple meanings of words can cause confusion. The word *base* may appear in mathematics class, but the student may know the word as used in "the *base* of the lamp" or "Jim is stationed at the air *base.*" Figurative language (similes, metaphors, personification, hyperbole, euphemism) abounds in literature, both prose and poetry, and will also require special attention. These types of

problems are discussed in detail in Chapter 5 in terms of their effect upon comprehension.

Concluding comments As suggested throughout this section on context clue usage, certain factors appear to be operating within context reading:

1. Reasoning ability. The student must utilize a series of reasoning steps when meeting a strange word. Certain questions must be considered: What else has been said that might reveal the word? What words might fit here? Why?

2. Store of word meanings. As knowledge of word meanings expands, use of context clues becomes more helpful. Attention to the special types of words suggested in the preceding section is one way to develop a larger vocabulary.

3. Extent of information about a topic. To encourage best utilization of context clues, teachers must build background before students read about topics with which they have had little experience. A reader who knows a great deal about the topic of cars, for example, will be better able to determine both the pronunciation and meaning of words like *generator, transmission, chassis, accelerator, gasket, lubrication, ignition system*, and even more technical terms like *fore, stroke, displacement, valve, compression, drive shafts, axle, distributor, plug thread, exhaust system*, than a reader wtih less background.

4. Knowledge of other words in the selection. Teachers must choose reading material carefully; they must "match" student and material. A student cannot be expected to use context clues effectively if his or her word recognition for a selection is less than 95 percent—or the student finds more than one unknown word in twenty running words.

Structural analysis skills enable students to decode unfamilar words by using units of meaning called *morphemes*. Structural analysis is sometimes called morphemic analysis. Morpheme is a linguistic term denoting the smallest meaningful unit of language. For example, *cat* is one morpheme; the word *cats* has two morphemes, *cat* plus *s*, which means plural. There are two classes of morphemes—*free* and *bound*. Free morphemes are those that can stand alone; bound morphemes must be affixed to a free morpheme. A word that results from affixing a bound morpheme to a root or base morpheme is called a derivative or a variant. Combinations of free morphemes—such as *book* and *store* (*bookstore*)—are called *compound words*. Structural analysis is the procedure of examining meaningful elements within a word. (One

Structural analysis

exception to this statement is syllabication. Although syllabication is considered to be part of structural analysis, syllables are not always meaningful elements or morphemes.)

Instruction on the most common affixes and roots, on compound words, and on syllabication and accent can add greatly to a student's strategies for identifying and pronouncing unfamiliar words.

Before providing instruction on structural analysis, a worthy procedure is to assess the student's abilities and skills in this area. One good way to assess structural analytic ability is through the use of nonsense (synthetic) words. If real words are used on an assessment, the teacher can never really be sure whether the students possess the ability to analyze or whether they just happen to know the words on the test. A possible assessment inventory is suggested in Example 4.3.

Example 4.3   *Informal structural analysis inventory*

Affixes and roots:
   Directions: Complete the chart appropriately.

Root word	Prefix	Suffix

   untoe
   prehand
   orangement
   locktion
   stomachness

Compound words:
   Directions: Complete the chart appropriately.

Root word one	Root word two

   basketstring
   suppermeet
   weaveplayer
   enactclaim
   chambersail

Syllabication
   Directions: Divide each word into syllables. Pronounce the word to the
              teacher.
   abtenfab
   fabsotion
   gehleetol
   cokatsuming
   boledorable

Students who do poorly on diagnostic pretests of structural analysis skills may be provided special instruction in unlocking the meanings and pronunciations of unknown words in a content area.

Inflectional endings　Inflectional endings denote tense, number, and degree (as *ask—asked, asking; boy—boys; speech—speeches; green—greener, greenest*). Inflectional endings also indicate gender (*host—hostess*), and possession (*Bill—Bill's*). Inflectional endings may change the part of speech of a word (*happy—happily*). The words that result when inflectional endings are added to root words are called *variants*.

Through continual practice, the student will probably realize such generalizations as the following:

1. When a root word ends in a final e, the e is usually dropped before an ending that begins with a vowel. (Example: *pro-duce—produced*) However, when a root word ends in ce or ge, the e is usually retained when the ending begins with a or o. (Examples: *change—changeable; notice—noticeable*)
2. If a syllable or root word ends in a single consonant preceded by a vowel, the consonant is usually doubled when an ending is added. (Example: *ship—shipping; map—mapped*)
3. Words ending in f or fe usually form their plurals by changing the f to v and adding the plural ending. (Example: *half—halves*).
4. When a word ends with y preceded by a consonant, the y is usually changed to an i before an ending is added. (Example: *century—centuries*).

Affixes and roots　Prefixes and suffixes are affixes or sequences of letters that are added to root words to change their meanings and/or parts of speech. A prefix is placed before a root word and a suffix is placed after a root word. Prefixes simply change the meanings of the root words, but suffixes may change the parts of speech of root words in addition to modifying the meanings.

Of the 20,000 most commonly used words in English, 4,000—or 25 percent—have prefixes. Fifteen prefixes make up 82 percent of the total usage of all prefixes. They are listed below.

ab (from)—abnormal
ad (to)—adhesion
be (by)—belittle
com, con, co, col (with)—conjunction
de (from)—decentralize
dis; di (apart)—dissect
en (in)—enact
ex (out)—extract
in; (il, un, ir) (not)—inadequate
pre (before)—predict
pro (in front of)—proceed
re (back)—rebuttal
sub (under)—subway
un (not)—unannounced

Other common prefixes and their meanings include:

ante (before) — antedate	non (not) — non-union
anti (against) — antidote	out (beyond) — outweigh
auto (self) — autobiography	peri (around) — perimeter
bi (two) — bisect	poly (many) — polygon
bene (well) — benefactor	post (after) — postscript
circum (around) — circumnavigate	retro (backwards) — retrogressive
contra (against) — contradict	semi (half) — semicircle
equi (equal) — equilateral	super (above) — superimpose
fore (before) — forepayment	syn, sym (with) — synthesis
inter (between) — interurban	trans (across) — transform
mono (one) — monologue	tele (afar) — telescope

The more common suffixes and their functions are listed below. The most common suffixes are starred.

Noun Suffixes

-ness* (state of being) — arbitrariness
-ment* (agency or instrument) — government
-ance* (quality, state of being) — disturbance
-tion* (state of being) — irrigation
-ant* (person or thing acting as agent) — descendant
-ion (results of) — fusion
-sion (the act, quality, result of) — explosion
-ation (the act of) — formation
-ity or -ty (state or condition) — electricity, unity
-ence (quality, state of being) — congruence
-hood (condition, state of being) — neighborhood
-ship (condition, state of being) — hardship
-or (state, quality, agent, doer) — elector
-ism (state of being) — nationalism
-ist (state, agent, doer) — scientist

Adjective Suffixes

-able* or -ible* (capacity, fitness tending to, able to) — serviceable, divisible
-al* or ial* (belonging to, pertaining to) — coastal, remedial
-ful* (full of) — fearful
-ive* (having nature or quality of) — productive
-ous* (abounding in, having) — mountainous
-ic (of, relating to) — volcanic
-ish (of the nature of) — mannish
-less (without, free from) — selfless
-ary (pertaining to, place for) — tributary

Verb Suffixes
-ize (to acquire, become like)—Americanize
-fy (to make, add to, form into)—magnify
-ate (acted upon, function, affected)—emancipate
-en (made of or belonging, cause to be)—soften
Adverb Suffixes
-ly (in manner of)—rapidly
-wise (with regard or respect to)—lengthwise
-ways (course, direction, manner)—sideways
-ward (toward, position)—southward

To the content area teacher, the most important affixes and roots to be considered are those that are important to the particular subject. For example, a science instructor might find the following affixes occurring commonly in the reading material:

homo- (same or like) homochromatic
hetero- (other or different) heterogeneous
hydro- (water) hydrocarbon
equi- (equal) equidistant
aqua- (water) aqualung
pro- (forth) progenitor
inter- (between or among) intercellular
bi- (two) biped
-ology (study of) biology
-ism (state or condition) alcoholism

On the other hand, a mathematics instructor might well find the following list of affixes more appropriate to develop:

hemi-, demi- (half) hemisphere, demitasse
uni-, mono- (one) unitary, monologue
bi- (two) bisect
tri- (three) triangle
quadra-, tetra- (four) quadrilateral, tetrameter
penta-, quin- (five) pentagon, quintet
hex-, hexa- (six) hexagonal
sept-, hepta- (seven) septuagenarian, heptameter
octa- (eight) octagon
nona- (nine) nonary
dec- (ten) decade
centi- (hundred) centimeter

One source of important morphemes in the content areas of English, social studies, science, and mathematics may be found in Appendix C of Lou E. Burmeister's, *Reading Strategies for Secondary School Teachers* (Reading, Mass.: Addison-Wesley, 1974).

Some attention to structural analysis of words should be given by the content teacher in assignment-readiness lessons or during the structured overview. (See Chapter 3.) During a course of study, a teacher may find it helpful to isolate particular skills for additional practice. Several ways in which this may be done are listed below.

Activities

1. From a list of words, have students cite prefixes, the meanings of the prefixes, and the meanings of the words.

	Prefix	Prefix meaning	Word meaning
bisect			
circumference			
encircle			
enclose			
perimeter			
polygon			
semicircle			

2. Develop cards for sets of words that use a particular prefix, suffix, or root word.

photo	graphy

    bio-
    biblio-
    ortho-
    carto-
    geo-
    steno-

3. Have students build new words, making as many new words as possible by adding various prefixes and suffixes to the given root word.

    construct

construction	reconstruct
constructing	reconstruction
constructed	reconstructing

4. Have students divide words into structural components. Use words from the content area textbook.

Prefix	*Root*	*Suffix*
in	sol	uble

5. Consider content area words in terms of Greek or Latin word roots. A sheet such as the following might be developed in a science class.

Directions: The parts of each word have basic meanings. From the basic meanings, try to define the words. Then check with your dictionary.

a. If *thermos* means hot, what is a *thermostat?* a *thermometer?*

b. If *hydro* means water, what do these words mean: *dehydrate? hydrophobia?*

c. How is *hydroplane* related to *hydrant?*

d. If *tele* means far, what is the meaning of these words: *telescope? television?*

e. If *zoo* means animal, what is the meaning of *zoology?* Who is a *zoologist?*

f. If *tome* is the act of cutting, what is an *appendectomy?*

g. If *micro* means "small", what is a *microscope?*

h. Why would you call *dynamite* and a *dynamo* first cousins?

i. What do a *pedagogue* and an *orthopedic* hospital have in common?

6. Similar exercises (presenting words in sentence context) can be prepared about the following sets of words:

centum- (one hundred)
    centenarian
    centennial
    bicentenary
    centuplicate
    centesimal

circum- (around)
    circumlocutions
    circumspect
    circumambulate
    circumvent

demi-semi-hemi- (half)
    demigod
    demivolt
    hemiolgia
    hemicycle

multi- (many)
    multiplicity
    multivocal

Compound words Compound words consist of two (or occasionally three) free morphemes that have been joined together to form a new word. The original pronunciations of the component words are usually maintained and the meanings of the original words are connected to form the meaning of the new word. An example, in industrial arts, is the word *hammerhead* (striking part of a hammer). Students can be asked to define selected compound words whose component words are part of their vocabularies. Examples from a physical education class might include: *hammerlock, armdrag,* and *bootleg* (play). Students can also be asked to underline or circle component parts of compound words, as: <u>whip</u> <u>stich</u>. Or they may become more aware of compound words if they are given an opportunity to put together familiar compound words. For example: For each of the words in Column 1, find a word in Column 2 which when combined with the word in Column 1 will form a compound word. Connect the words you form as shown.

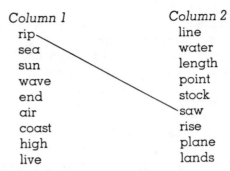

Column 1	Column 2
rip	line
sea	water
sun	length
wave	point
end	stock
air	saw
coast	rise
high	plane
live	lands

Syllabication/Accent. Syllabication/accent are extremely important when students are reading multisyllabic words. A pretest is appropriate to determine the ability of the student to utilize this analysis technique for pronouncing words. The use of nonsense words may be best in order to see if students possess the ability to determine the words. A sample pretest—and the particular technique that is being probed—might include such items as the following:

a. prenabing (use of prefix)
b. exstraimable (use of suffix)
c. subpeetly (use of stem or root)
d. depatsuming (consonant-vowel-consonant/consonant-vowel-consonant or CVC/CVC pattern)
e. desimenable (consonant-vowel/consonant-vowel or CV/CV pattern)

In (a) the prefix *pre* should be noted; in (b) the suffix *able;* in (c) the stem, *peet;* in (d) the CVC/CVC application, as in *can/cel;* and in (e) the CV/CV application, such as in the *fi/nite.*

As teachers observe a student's attempt to pronounce words, they should note whether the student looks for prefixes, suffixes, and roots, and whether the student divides stems into syllables.

Students must understand that a syllable is a word or a part of a word in which there is just one vowel sound, plus any consonant sounds that go with it. While high school students are likely to know the difference between a consonant and a vowel, many students may confuse a *vowel* with a *vowel sound.* The vowel in the word *bent* stands alone and contains the vowel sound, while the vowel sound in *beam* is derived from two vowels, e and a. A vowel sound may form a syllable by itself (*a/mong*). Only in a syllable that contains a diphthong (such as *oi, oy, ou, ow*) is there more than one vowel sound (*oil, boy, house,* cow) since diphthongs are treated as single units, although they are actually vowel blends. Students must also be familiar with the ways in which consonants combine to form a single sound or a consonant digraph, as the *sh* in *shot* or the *ph* in *photograph*.

Such syllabic generalizations as the following are useful. They are, of course, more meaningful if formulated by the learner than if simply presented to him or her.

Guide to Syllabication

1. Divide between the two words in compound words, as well as between syllables within the component words. (Example: *thun/der / storm*)

2. Divide between a prefix or a suffix and the rest of the word. (Example: *sub/merge, sky/ward*) Note: When er, est, ing, and ish, are added to a word, a separate syllable is always formed. (Example: *fool/ish*) When ed is added to a word ending in *t* or *d*, a separate syllable is usually formed. (Example: *weight/ed*)

3. When two consonants come between two sounded vowels, you usually divide between the two consonants. (Example: *ad/dend*)

4. When one consonant or consonant digraph (*ch, th, sh, ph, ng, ck*) comes between two sounded vowels, you usually divide before the consonant if the first vowel is long. (Example: *re/check, so/lo*) You usually divide after the consonant if the sound of the first vowel is short. (Example: *rock/et*)

5. Consonant blends (*st, br, sk, gl, bl, cl, dr, fr, pr, sp, str, spl*) and consonant digraphs are treated as units and are not divided. (Example: *spec/trum*)

6. If a word of more than one syllable ends in *-le*, the consonant directly before the *l* begins the last syllable. (Example: *cir/cle*)

Practice may take several forms. Note that the following ideas begin with using auditory discrimination.

Activities

1. Present words of one syllable, pronounce them, and ask students to underline the sounded vowel.

2. Read a list of words of two syllables and see how many separate vowel sounds the student hears in each of the words. Then words of three or four syllables may be similarly presented.

3. Provide opportunity for practice in dividing compound words into syllables (as *steam/ship*).

4. Provide practice for dividing words with prefixes and suffixes (as *dis/solve* and *com/bus/tion*).

5. Provide practice for dividing words where two consonants come between two sounded vowels (CVC-CVC pattern, as *mag/net*) and where one consonant comes between two sounded vowels, with the first vowel long (CV-CV pattern, as *tro/pism*).

6. Provide practice with words where consonant blends, consonant digraphs, and the ending consonant plus *-le* are *not* divided (as *vi/brate*, *chem/o/ther/a/py*; and *tri/an/gle*).

7. Following such practice, a list of words may be given to students with the directions to use the correct rule from the *Guide to Syllabication* for dividing the words. Have students write the number of the rule that pertains to each word. Sometimes two rules are used for the word.

cargo	car/go	rule 3
rainfall		
recoverable		
cactus		
vaporing		
telephone		
needle		
limestone		
machine		
alcohol		
hunted		

8. Hypothetical word structures may be presented for which the student decides upon the number of syllables.

VCVCVC	_____	VCVVCV	_____
CCVCCVC	_____	VCCV	_____
VCCVCCVV	_____	VCV	_____
VVC	_____	VCV	_____
CCCVC	_____		

9. Nonsense words may be presented for the student to determine the number of syllables.

Through application, the student should become familiar with the following principles of accent:

1. Words of two or three syllables are usually accented on the first syllable. (Example: SUL-*fur*) Multisyllabic words have

primary and secondary accents (*BOOK'-keep'-er*) and even tertiary (third strongest) accents.

2. When one or more affixes is added to a root word, the accent is usually on the root word. (Example: *dis'-ap-POINT-ment*)
3. Words ending with the suffix *-sion* or *-tion* are usually accented on the syllable preceding the suffix. (Example: *di-MEN-sion*)
4. When the last syllable of a word ends in *le*, the syllable is unaccented. (Example: *TUM-ble*)
5. Some words are accented differently in accordance with their function in a sentence. (Example: *CON-tract* [noun], *con-TRACT* [verb]) That is, first syllable is accented for nouns and second syllable for verbs.

When a real word is to be presented in a content area, such as *liability* in a business class, a step-by-step procedure such as the following may be used:

1. Write the word on the board (in a sentence context).
2. Ask the students to try to pronounce it.
3. Ask how many syllables the word has and where the syllabic divisions should be made. Mark them. Then ask students to pronounce it.
4. Reinforce appropriate syllabication and accent generalizations.
5. Ask again for the pronunciation. Ask students to define the word or use it in a sentence.

Phonic analysis

Phonics is the relationship that exists between letters and sounds. The English language (depending on dialect) utilizes about 45 phonemes or distinctive sound units (there are 14 to 20 vowel phonemes and 26 consonant phonemes). These sounds are represented by the 26 graphemes in our alphabet. In all, there are more than 200 letter-sound relationships in English. For example, an *f* sound can be spelled as *f, ph, ff,* or *gh*. On the other hand, the letter *f* can represent the *f* sound as in *foot* or the *v* sound heard in *of*. Some letter-sound correspondences are consistent (*m* always represents the phoneme heard in *man*), while other letters and letter clusters have more than one correspondence (*c* can be either *k* or *s*), and others have varying but unpredictable correspondences (as *s* in *sea, sugar, pleasure, isle,* and *has*). And some consonants may be silent (*k*nee, and bom*b*).

Following are some commonly used terms in phonic analysis:

1. *Vowels.* The letters *a, e, i, o,* and *u* represent vowel sounds. The letters *w* and *y* take on the characteristics of vowels when

they appear in the final position in a word or syllable. (Examples: *brow, body*) The letter *y* also has the characteristics of a vowel in the medial (or middle) position in a word or syllable. (Example: *myth*)

2. *Consonants.* Letters other than *a, e, i, o,* and *u* generally represent consonant sounds. *W* and *y* have the characteristics of consonants when they appear in the initial position in a word or syllable. (Examples: *work, yard*)

3. *Consonant blends.* Two or more adjacent consonant sounds blended together with each individual sound retaining its identity constitute a consonant blend. For example, although the first three sounds in the word *strike* are blended together smoothly, it is possible to detect the separate sounds of *s, t* and *r* being produced in rapid succession.

4. *Consonant digraphs.* Two adjacent consonant letters that represent a single speech sound constitute a consonant digraph. For example, *sh* is a consonant digraph in the word *shoe. Sh* represents one sound and not a blend of the sounds of *s* and *h*.

5. *Vowel digraphs.* Two adjacent vowel letters that represent a single speech sound constitute a vowel digraph. In the word *foot, oo* is a vowel digraph.

6. *Diphthongs.* Vowel sounds that are so closely blended that they can be treated as single vowel units for the purposes of word identification are called diphthongs. An example of a diphthong is the *ou* in *out*.

As noted in Chapter 10, there are standardized tests for checking the ability of a secondary school student in the area of phonics (for example, *The California Phonics Survey*). Where deficiencies are evident, some instruction is appropriate, for it cannot be assumed that phonics skills have been learned in the elementary school years.

When a teacher wishes to use an informal measure of ability, a phonics inventory such as in Example 4.4 would be helpful. The first two parts would probably not be needed for administration to most students.

Example 4.4   *Informal phonics inventory*

---

1. Consonant Sounds (initial)
   Directions: Write the beginning letter of each word I say.

1. dog	9. rob	17. top
2. now	10. hope	18. jump
3. lamp	11. kiss	19. water

4. me   12. you   20. zoo
5. boy   13. sat   21. quit
6. put   14. has   22. got
7. fat   15. cat   23. grant
8. vine   16. city

2. Consonant Sounds (final)
   Directions: Write the last letter of each word I say.
   1. has   4. hoop   7. dog
   2. tax   5. chalk   8. head
   3. chief   6. pen   9. glass

3. Consonant Digraphs
   Write the first two letters of each word I say.
   1. shoe   4. chin
   2. this   5. chorus
   3. thin   6. photo
   Write the last two letters of each word I say.
   1. sang   3. dish
   2. sick   4. cloth

4. Consonant Blends
   Directions: Write the first two letters of each word I say.
   1. step   4. skate   7. claw   10. proud   13. splash
   2. bright 5. glum   8. draw   11. speed
   3. slate   6. black   9. frown   12. string

5. Directions: Write the double consonants of each word I say.
   1. pass   4. better 7. coffee 10. ladder 13. rubber
   2. hello   5. summer 8. happy   11. egg   14. puzzle
   3. narrow 6. manner 9. success 12. suggest

6. Long and Short Vowels and Schwa Sound
   Directions: If the vowel is short as I say a word, write short and the vowel.
   If it is long, write long and the vowel. If a soft "uh" sound, write schwa and
   the vowel.
   1. if   5. of   9. bug
   2. mild   6. note   10. bed
   3. act   7. odd   11. blaze
   4. hot   8. tube   12. he

7. Vowel Combinations, Digraphs, and Diphthongs
   Directions: Write the two vowels that go together to form a unit in each
   word I say.
   Digraphs   *Diphthongs*
   1. meat   7. because   12. coin
   2. bread   8. blew   13. boy
   3. bleed   9. soon   14. ounce
   4. maid   10. good   15. now
   5. day   11. awful
   6. boat

8. Nonsense Words
   Directions: Pronounce the following words, written on the board.
   1. protabing
   2. unsprimance

Example 4.4 (cont.)
3. comsolitly
4. badnabsoling
5. metumalful

___

Important phonic generalizations suggested by the informal phonics inventory include:

1. When c or g is followed by e, i, or y, each usually has its soft sound. When c or g is followed by o, a, u, each usually has its hard sound. (See Part 1 of the inventory.) The soft sound of c is heard in the word cent. The hard sound is heard in the word cake. The soft sound of g is heard in the word gym. The hard sound is heard in the word go.
2. In some words that contain two consonants together (such as sh, wh, th, ch, ng, ph), the consonant digraph produces a single sound. (See Part 3 of the inventory.)
3. Some words have a blend of two or more consonants, each of which retains its own sound. (See Part 4 of the inventory.)
4. In words that contain double vowel combinations (such as ai, ay, oa, ee, ea), usually the first vowel is long and the second one is silent. (See Part 7 in the inventory.)
5. In some words that contain two vowels together (special vowel digraphs such as au, aw, ew, oo), the vowel letters have a special sound unlike either of the vowels. (See Part 7 of the inventory.)
6. Some words have a blend of two vowels (diphthongs) that produce a blended sound (such as oi, oy, ou, and ow). Note: These letter combinations are not always diphthongs (as in snow, routine). (See Part 7 of the inventory.)

In relation to previous knowledge about syllabication and accentuation, the following additional generalizations may be derived:

1. The vowel in a syllable that ends with one or more consonants (termed closed syllable) generally has a short sound. (Example: mĭll)
2. A vowel that is the final letter of an accented syllable (syllables ending in vowels are called open syllables) is usually long. (Example: hē)
3. A syllable having two vowels, one of which is a final e, usually contains the long sound of the first vowel with the final e being silent. (Example: blāze)
4. An unaccented syllable of a word may contain the schwa sound—designated by the inverted e (ə). (Example: about)

The teacher should be sure to caution that there are many irregular symbol-sound relationships. This again supports the need for increasing a sight word vocabulary, as discussed earlier in this chapter. All words cannot be analyzed by phonic principles. Some exceptions to the generalizations are noted below to emphasize this caution.

1. In words beginning with *rh*, the *h* is silent following *r*. (Example: *rhombus*) In words beginning with *kn* and *wr*, the *k* and *w* are silent. (Examples: *knight, wrong*)
2. Only one of a set of double consonants is usually sounded. (Example: *common*)
3. Since *q* has no sound of its own, *qu* usually takes the sound of *kw*. (Example: *equivalent*)
4. The letter *x* most often stands for sound of *ks*, although at times it stands for sound of *gz* or that of *z*. (Examples: *box, exact, xylophone*). The digraph *ch* has the sound heard in *church*, but at times sounds like *sh* or *k*. (Examples: *chef, chemistry*)
5. For the digraph *ph*, neither consonant is sounded—the sound of *f* is used. (Example: *graph*)
6. The sound of a vowel preceding *r* is neither long nor short. (Examples: *car, fir*)
7. Borrowed words are often non-phonetic. (Example: *concerto*)

A secondary school content teacher can demonstrate the use of phonics analysis during the vocabulary presentation in an assignment overview. By previewing a unit or chapter that is being used in the class, the teacher can select about ten of the most significant vocabulary terms and decide which of the terms lend themselves to phonic analysis. As the vocabulary terms are analyzed on the chalkboard, the teacher can present the relevant phonic generalizations to the students. The teacher should also provide guidance to students if the textbook offers phonetic pronunciations of specialized vocabulary terms.

From a unit in biology, such terms as the following might be analyzed in terms of consonant digraphs, consonant blends, double consonants, long vowels, short vowels, silent vowels, schwa sounds, vowel digraphs, and diphthongs. Of course, other analysis tools may also be used; for example, structural analysis of roots, affixes, compounds, syllabication, and accent.

chromatin	contractile
cytoplasm	ribosomes
cellulose	chlorophyll
protoplasm	mitochondria

For readers who wish to learn more about phonics and word analysis, such programmed textbooks as the following may be useful:

John M. Equing, *Word Analysis for Teachers* (Danville, Ill.: Interstate Publishing Co., 1974).

Marion A. Hull, *Phonics for the Teacher of Reading*, 2nd ed. (Columbus: Charles E. Merrill, 1976).

Leo M. Schell, *Fundamentals of Decoding for Teachers* (Chicago: Rand McNally College Publishing Co., 1975).

Robert Wilson and Maryanne Hall, *Programmed Word Attack for Teachers* (Columbus: Charles E. Merrill, 1968).

Phonics skill is a means to an end, not an end in itself. If a word can be recognized without resorting to letter-by-letter sounding, it will be recognized more quickly and will interfere less with the reader's train of thought. When the words to be recognized are seen in context, as they are in most normal reading activities, the sound of the first letter alone may elicit recognition of the whole word. Context clues can provide the reader with an idea about the word's identity, and the initial sound can be used to verify an educated guess. This procedure is efficient and is a good way of quickly identifying unfamiliar words found in connected discourse.

Dictionary use   Most secondary school students occasionally find themselves consulting a dictionary in search of the meaning of an unfamiliar word. In addition to providing definitions, dictionaries are valuable aids to pronunciation and spelling. Though many secondary school students have a knowledge of the alphabet, an understanding of alphabetization, and a familiarity with glossaries and dictionaries, continued instruction and practice are needed by some.

As recommended frequently in this text, only those students who need additional help should be provided with it. A diagnostic pretest of dictionary skills may be accomplished through a set of questions for students who can read the content area textbook successfully. Example 4.5 is a sample taken from a social studies textbook.

Example 4.5   *Diagnostic pretest of dictionary skills*

1. *Look up the word delinquent.* What are the two guide words found on the page on which the word was found?
2. What does the word *incorrigibility* mean?
3. In the dictionary, on what page are the pronunciation and meaning of the word *exigency* found?
4. What synonyms are provided for the term *indeterminate?*

5. What is the derivation of the word *psychological?*
6. What part of speech is the term *adjudicated?*
7. What diacritical marks are used in the phonetic spelling of *arbitrariness?*
8. What is the dictionary entry for the word *interrogation?*
9. How many syllables does this word have: *ungovernability?*
10. Which syllable of *omnibus* receives a secondary emphasis?
11. What vowel sounds are given for each accented syllable in the word *formulation?*
12. Which syllable of the word *juvenile* receives a schwa sound?

Words selected from: Allen Schick and A. Pfister, *American Government: Continuity and Change* (Boston: Houghton Mifflin, 1972), pp. 292–96, Unit on Interpreting Federal Law: Case Analysis 5.

As students do required reading in the content areas, consultation of a dictionary may be necessary for word identification. Certainly the following skills are necessary for locating and pronouncing words in the dictionary:

1. Knowledge of alphabetical order.
2. Ability to use guide words.
3. Ability to locate variants and derivatives in the dictionary by locating root words.
4. Ability to interpret phonetic spellings used in the dictionary through use of the pronunciation key and knowledge of sounds ordinarily associated with single consonants.
5. Ability to interpret the accent marks found in the dictionary.

For those who need it, practice, application, and refinement may be centered upon locational skills, pronunciation skills, and definition selection. An example of each type of activity follows.

Activities.

1. *Alphabetizing:* Number the words in the order in which you would find them in a dictionary.

    negative
    nuclei
    neutron
    neuron
    nuclear

2. *Using Guide Words.* Underline the word(s) in *Column B* which would be on the pages indicated by the guide words in *Column A.*

Column A	Column B
confound-conjugate	congruent, conic, conjunct

irony-isinglass   irruption, irrigate, isthmus
poll-pompom   plastic, pollen, pollute

3. *Derivation.* Read the information between the brackets in the dictionary entry for each word to determine the derivations of the following words:

radius
perimeter
quadratic
factor
trapezoid

4. *Dictionary Entry.* Write the entry word under which each of the following words would be found in the dictionary.

fumigating
sterilizing
exhalation
chlorinated
liquefier

5. *Pronunciation.* As mentioned in the section on syllabication and accent, numerous exercises are possible to note the division of words into syllables, accented syllables, the vowel sounds of accented syllables, and which, if any, of the syllables contain the schwa sound.

6. *Correct Definition.* A most practical exercise involves determining which meaning from the dictionary fits the context in which the word is used in a content area textbook.

Many secondary content texts contain glossaries where students may find pronunciations and meanings of the unknown words they meet. A glossary adds greatly to a student's use of a textbook, having the advantage of providing a definition that exactly fits the requirement of the unknown word in that content area textbook.

There is little value in preparing a list of specialized vocabulary terms in the content area and then requiring students to look up their pronunciations and meanings. This kind of exercise contributes little to effective dictionary or glossary usage. The most important point that should be stressed during instruction is to use a dictionary or glossary when it is necessary, rather than skip over unknown terms. Students should use the dictionary to locate the pronunciation and meaning of unknown terms that they meet in their content reading. In brief, dictionary or glossary usage should be practiced in meaningful, rather than contrived, situations.

Some simplified dictionaries that can be used to span the broad range in reading achievement among students include the following:

Harcourt Brace School Dictionary (New York: Harcourt Brace
Jovanovich, 1972), Grades 4–8.

Macmillan School Dictionary (New York: Macmillan Co., 1974),
Grades 4–6.

Macmillan Dictionary (New York: Macmillan Co., 1973), Grades
7–12.

Thorndike-Barnhart Intermediate Dictionary, 2nd ed. (Chicago:
Scott, Foresman, 1974), Grades 4–8.

Thorndike-Barnhart Advanced Dictionary, 2nd ed. (Chicago:
Scott, Foresman, 1974), Grades 9–12.

Webster's Intermediate Dictionary (New York: American Book Co.,
1972), Grades 4–8.

Webster's New Student's Dictionary (New York: American Book
Co., 1974), Grades 9–12.

This chapter has discussed various strategies for decoding unknown words. While all of these strategies are important for efficient, mature, and independent reading, they cannot and must not develop in isolation. Consideration must be given to relationships that exist between the various skills.

Balance in word recognition skills

1. There should be a balance between refinement of word recognition techniques and the development of a large meaning vocabulary (see Chapter 5). Because sound alone is without meaning, the student who does not know a word's meaning may not realize he has arrived at a correct pronunciation. Teaching solely analytical techniques with no development of meaning vocabulary may well reach a point of diminishing returns. On the other hand, if meaning is emphasized and word analysis skills are neglected, the student may not be able to decode words.

2. There should be a balance between sight vocabulary and word analysis skills. Although it is important to be able to analyze words, continued practice with these words is necessary to elevate them to the sight recognition level. The student who has adequate analysis skills but a limited sight vocabulary is often a slow, laborious reader. He lacks the ability to read fluently and concentrate on gaining meaning. On the other hand, the student who commits all words to his sight vocabulary and fails to develop skills in contextual, structural, and phonic analysis will find that memory fails fairly quickly.

3. There should be a balance between using meaning clues and analytical aids. Proper decoding requires the use of

clues within words as well as clues among words. The student who is over-reliant on context may deviate from the printed text to the point that he strays from the meaning intended by the author. The student who depends too greatly on analytical aids—forgetting to use context as a check for meaning—may have poor comprehension of what he has read.

4. There should be a balance among the analytical techniques. Some words are more readily decoded by one technique of word analysis than another. For example, the following words and types of decoding suggest this need for flexibility with polysyllabic words: *carpetbagger* (compounds), *reforestation* (structural analysis), *mutation* (syllabication), and *ichneum* (dictionary). The student needs to have mastered several techniques in order to be most efficient. Sometimes context clues provide enough information to determine the pronunciation and meaning of an unknown word; however, a phonics clue in addition to context will often be extremely useful. Students need to develop all the decoding skills and use them in combination, not independently of each other.

In summary, it is helpful if students know a procedure for decoding unfamiliar words. At any point in the following procedure the reader may discover the word; the student should stop the procedure at that point and continue reading. Sometimes it is necessary to try all of the steps.

Step 1. Apply context clues.
Step 2. Try sound of initial consonant, vowel, or blend along with context clues.
Step 3. Check for structure clues (prefixes, suffixes, inflectional endings, compound words, or familiar syllables).
Step 4. Begin sounding out the word using known phonic generalizations. (Go only as far as necessary to determine the word).
Step 5. Consult the dictionary.

There are some useful books for word analysis practice for the serious secondary school student who wishes to study independently on this topic. A few are suggested below. Others may be cited by the reading teacher in your building.

Richard A. Boning, *Working With Sounds*, Adv. (New York: Barnell Loft).
Richard A. Boning, *Syllabication*, Adv. 1, 2, 3, (New York: Dexter and Westbrook, Ltd.)

Richard A. Boning, *Compounds*, Adv.; *Endings / Suffixes*, Adv. 1, 2, 3,; *Prefixes*, Adv. 1, 2, and 3; and *Roots / Stems*, Adv. 1, 2, 3, 4, 5, and 6 (New York: Dexter and Westbrook).

Olive Niles, *Tactics in Reading* (Chicago: Scott-Foresman).

---

1. What are sight words? (a) Those recognized by context clues (b) Those recognized without resort to analysis (c) Those words of regular sound-symbol relationship (d) Those words that are useful and meaningful   **Self-test**

2. What is the best statement about word recognition techniques? (a) It is wise to teach a single approach to word analysis. (b) Phonics is the single best word recognition skill to teach. (c) A balance of word recognition techniques should be acquired. (d) Not given

3. Using which type of clue represents anticipation on the reader's part? (a) Meaning clues (b) Structural clues (c) Phonic clues (d) Not given

4. What is a useful pretest form for determining student skill in context clue usage? (a) Context clues inventory (b) Test, using nonsense words (c) Modified cloze procedure (d) All of the above

5. What type of words are best to use on an informal structural analysis inventory? (a) Synthetic words (b) Difficult words (c) Real words (d) None of the above

6. Which is a false statement? (a) Consonant letters are more consistent in the sounds they represent than are vowel letters. (b) Phonic generalizations often have numerous exceptions. (c) There is a vowel sound in every syllable. (d) Not given

7. What are homographs? (a) Words that are spelled differently. (b) Words that sound alike (c) Words that have identical meanings. (d) Not given

8. Which of the following is not an aspect of structural analysis? (a) Prefixes (b) Context (c) Compound words (d) Syllabication

9. What term is applied to words that result from adding inflectional endings to root words? (a) Derivations (b) Compound words (c) Variants (d) All of the above

10. Which of the following is true about prefixes and suffixes? (a) They usually form separate syllables. (b) They are usually not accented. (c) Both a and b (d) Neither a nor b

11. In what form may context clues exist? (a) In definitions (b) In comparisons (c) In associations (d) All of the above

12. What does every syllable contain? (a) A consonant sound (b) A vowel sound (c) A digraph (d) A diphthong

13. Which is a true syllabication statement? (a) There is only one vowel letter in each syllable. (b) Schwa sound is often found in accented syllables. (c) Consonant blends and consonant digraphs are treated as units and are not divided. (d) Prefixes and suffixes are usually accented.

14. Which type of accent mark indicates the heaviest emphasis? (a) Primary (b) Secondary (c) Tertiary (d) Not given

15. The word *sheep* is made up of how many sounds? (a) Three sounds (b) Four sounds (c) Five sounds (d) None of the above

16. Which of the following words contains a soft *c* sound? (a) cent (b) cannon (c) cat (d) cute

17. In the word *strong*, the letters *str* (a) Represent consonant sounds (b) Are silent (c) Represent a single sound (d) Not given

18. When does the letter *y* have the characteristic of a vowel? (a) In initial position in a word or syllable (b) In final position in the word or syllable (c) Both *a* and *b* (d) neither *a* nor *b*

19. What are two or more adjacent consonants sounded together, with each individual sound retaining its identity, called? (a) Consonant blend (b) Consonant digraph (c) Diphthong (d) Not given

20. What is usually true about the first vowel in a word when there are two vowels and one is a final *e*? (a) The first vowel is long. (b) The first vowel is short. (c) The first vowel is a schwa. (d) The first vowel is silent.

21. Where is the schwa sound ordinarily found? (a) In accented syllables (b) In unaccented syllables (c) In one-syllable words (d) Not given

22. Which is the most important statement about dictionary use regarding pronunciation of unfamiliar words? (a) Dictionary should be consulted first. (b) Dictionary is useless. (c) Dictionary should be used only as a last resort. (d) Not given.

23. What is true of consonant digraphs? (a) They represent two blended speech sounds. (b) They represent a single speech sound. (c) They are always silent. (d) Not given.

24. What term is applied to *oa* in word *boat*? (a) A vowel digraph (b) A diphthong (c) A blend (d) Not given

25. What is contained in the word *diphthong*? (a) Three consonant blends (b) Three consonant digraphs (c) A consonant digraph and two consonant blends (c) Not given

26. What skills are needed when using the dictionary? (a) Locational skills (b) Pronunciation skills (c) Definition selection skills (d) All of the above

---

Enrichment activities

1. If feasible, administer a standardized test to check the word recognition skill of a student.

2. Prepare a mini-lesson to present instructional strategies to peers on each of the following items. (Use words from a content area.)
   a. sight words
   b. context clues
   c. structural clues
   d. phonic clues
   e. dictionary or glossary

*3. Develop an informal procedure (such as the cloze procedure described earlier) to assess context clue usage. Use with a student and report results to the class.

---

* These activities are designed for inservice teachers, student teachers, and practicum students.

*4. Administer an Informal Structural Analysis Inventory to a student. Analyze and share results with the class.

5. Study a chapter or unit in a content area textbook. What affixes and roots appear to be the most important ones?

6. List examples of compound words commonly found in a particular content area.

*7. Supply a secondary school student with a list of words such as found on page 100. Check the student's use of syllabic generalizations that appear in the Guide to Syllabication.

*8. Administer an Informal Phonics Inventory to a secondary school student. Analyze and share results with the class.

*9. Administer a Diagnostic Pretest of Dictionary Skills to a secondary school student. Analyze and share results with the class.

10. Gather the material needed and construct a skill development game or activity for some aspect of word recognition.

11. Locate examples of the different kinds of contextual clues (see Table 4.1) appearing in a content area textbook. Write the examples and bring them to class for discussion.

Selected references

Burmeister, Lou E. *Reading Strategies for Secondary School Teachers.* New York: Addison-Wesley, 1974. Chapter 6.

Dechant, Emerald. *Reading Improvement in the Secondary School.* Englewood Cliffs, N.J.: Prentice Hall, 1973. Chapter 6.

Dillner, Martha H. and Joanne P. Olson. *Personalizing Reading Instruction in Middle, Junior, and Senior High Schools: Utilizing a Competency-Based Instructional System.* New York: Macmillan Company, 1977. Chapters 2 and 10.

Duffy, Gerald, ed. *Reading in the Middle School, Perspectives in Reading.* No. 18. International Reading Association, 1974. Chapter 12.

Forgan, Harry W. and Charles T. Mangrum. *Teaching Content Area Reading Skills.* Columbus, Ohio; Charles E. Merrill, 1976. Modules 5 and 8.

Hafner, Lawrence. *Improving Reading in Middle and Secondary Schools.* 2nd. ed. New York: Macmillan, 1974. Section 3.

Karlin, Robert. *Teaching Reading in High School.* 2nd. ed. Bobbs-Merrill, 1972. Chapter 5.

———. *Teaching Reading in High Schools: Selected Articles.* Indianapolis, Ind.: Bobbs-Merrill Company, 1969. Chapter 5.

Miller, Wilma H. *Teaching Reading in the Secondary School.* Springfield, Ill.: Charles C. Thomas, 1974. Chapter 3.

Olson, Arthur and Wilbur S. Ames. *Teaching Reading in Secondary Schools: Readings.* Scranton, Pa.: International Textbook Co., 1970. Chapter 5.

Robinson, H. Alan. *Teaching Reading and Study Strategies.* Boston, Mass.: Allyn and Bacon, 1975. Chapter 4.

Shepherd, David. *Comprehensive High School Reading Methods.* Columbus, Ohio: Charles E. Merrill, 1973. Chapter 3.

Smith, Richard J. and Thomas C. Barrett. *Teaching Reading in the Middle Grades.* Reading, Mass.: Addison-Wesley, 1974. Chapter 2.

5 Concept and vocabulary development

This chapter focuses upon vocabulary and deals especially with word units and sentence units. (Paragraphs and larger units are treated when general comprehension is discussed in Chapter 6.) This chapter and Chapter 6 are related since comprehension is dependent to a great degree on understanding the meanings of words. At the same time, Chapter 7, "Reading Study Skills," is an extension of the discussion on comprehension in Chapter 6. The topics discussed in Chapter 7 are important to reading comprehension, particularly in content area reading.

Purpose-setting questions

As you read this chapter, try to answer these questions:
1. What associations have experience and concept development. with word, sentence, and general meaning?
2. What are the features of a planned vocabulary development program?
3. What language features are related to sentence meaning?

Key Vocabulary

As you read this chapter, check your understanding of these terms:

concept
semantics
categorization
direct vocabulary
  instruction
euphemism
hyperbole

oxymorons
homonyms
heteronyms
analogy
connotative
denotative
vocabulary study
  guide
acronyms

connectives
syntax
sentence patterns
kernel sentence
transform sentence
figurative
  expressions

Comprehension depends upon having a large store of available information regarding the world. This store of information is derived from experience. As the reader reads symbols, they trigger related experiences stored in the brain and comprehension results. For example, if Linda reads about the term *intersect* in her mathematics book, she will understand better if she has seen a street intersection. There will be very little comprehension if the topic considered is entirely removed from a reader's experience. Direct experience with every subject about which a student reads is not possible, but the teacher can help students relate experiences to the content of reading materials and thus aid comprehension. When the reader has not had experiences related to topics about which he is reading, the teacher can build experience through field trips, films, filmstrips, resource persons, and pictures.

At times, students who have had experiences related to a topic are unaware of how their experiences are related. For example, in the earlier discussion of *intersect*, Linda might not have recognized that a street intersection is related to the mathematics word *intersect*. Students cannot benefit from experience unless the teacher helps them find a point of contact between their experience and the concept being developed.

Experience is essential for building concepts. Concept development is one of the basic goals of reading for secondary students. Each content field has key concepts that the reader must learn in order to read with understanding. Knowledge of concepts such as *add* and *subtract* is essential for reading mathematics, while knowledge of concepts such as *atom* and *molecule* is essential for reading science.

A concept is a generalized idea about a class of objects. Every learner categorizes objects and events. In the process of conceptualization, the learner looks for properties that are common to a number of similar objects or events. Conceptualizing is a process of abstracting into a generalization the common features or attributes that specify a category. The categories thus specified are concepts. Concepts provide the learner with a mental filing system that helps sort out and organize information. Concepts provide for economy in learning because a learner can distinguish the class or category of many objects for which he or she does not know the name; thus one can know something about these objects before one knows precisely what they are called. For example, a learner may recognize an object to be a tree without knowing the specific kind of tree being observed.

Growth in concept development comes not only through experience, but through relating new experiences to previous experiences. Teachers can help students with this process by providing experiences related to the readers' previous experiences and by asking questions that help students compare and contrast experiences. Discussion

Experience and concept development

questions can also lead students to relate new experiences with previous experiences.

Teachers should examine reading assignments carefully to determine whether the author of the textbook has assumed that students know concepts they do not know. The teacher should be particularly careful to determine which concepts are necessary for student comprehension of the selection. If the author has incorrectly assumed knowledge of concepts on the part of the students then the teacher must make provision for developing those concepts before expecting students to read with comprehension.

The teacher's task in conceptual development is to select materials and experiences that will help students recognize patterns in their experiences. Conceptual development is enhanced by reading activities that help students think of connections, likenesses, and differences; these are the bases for categorizing information acquired from reading. Information can be categorized in a variety of ways. For example, likenesses in form and function can be used to categorize information. Categorization by form is concerned with sense perceptions of objects or experiences, such as the look, feel, taste, sound, and smell. Categorization by function is concerned with the question, "What does it do?" Christian Gerhard provides suggestions for using categorizing as a part of reading comprehension in a recent publication entitled *Making Sense: Reading Comprehension Improved Through Categorizing* (Newark, Del.: International Reading Association, 1975).

A classroom example using some of Gerhard's ideas might involve the use of a worksheet such as the one in Example 5.1, which focuses upon science content (geology).

Example 5.1.   *Categorizing worksheet*

Directions: Place the words at the bottom of this sheet under the proper categories.

Seismology   *Diastrophism*

Petrology   *Minerology*

Words: earthquake, crust, quartz, rocks, salt, fracture, sedimentary, seismograph, fault, metamorphic, fold, Richter scale, gypsum, dolomite, Marcolli scale, seismograph, joints, igneous, foliation, Newman-Wood scale, calcite, joints, minerals, slate.

Other examples of classroom activities utilizing categorization are listed below.

Activities

1. Divide the class into groups of five students and provide each group with three to five objects. These objects may be found in a variety store and may include plastic toys as well as functional objects. Ask the students to categorize the objects on the basis of common characteristics such as form, function, color, or texture.

    a. Objects and suggested categories:
        Objects: rubber ball, frisbee, balloon.
        Common characteristics: round (shape), red (color), smooth (texture), toys (function).
    b. Objects and suggested categories:
        Objects: wash cloth, towel, wash and dry towelette.
        Common characteristics: soft (texture), cotton (composition), bathing (function), blue (color).

2. Provide a category and ask students to supply related concepts. For example, if the category of *football* is suggested, students might suggest words such as: fans, stadium, half-back, full-back, penalty, yards, touchdown and field-goal.

Conceptual development is also enhanced by reading units that help students think of connections, likenesses, and differences. For example, students may read *No Promises in the Wind* by Irene Hunt, which presents a story set during the depression years. This book, set in industrial areas and large cities, helps the reader acquire an understanding of the depression in the factories and cities. *The Grapes of Wrath* by John Steinbeck portrays a rural family during the depression years. Students who read both these selections can achieve a more complete concept of the depression than either book alone would provide. Students may compare and contrast these books to achieve an understanding of the economic setting and the social setting of the depression. They will find points where the readings are related, points of agreement, and points of disagreement. George Henry[1] describes this kind of teaching in great depth in his book, *Teaching Reading as Concept Development.*

---

1. George H. Henry, *Teaching Reading as Concept Development: Emphasis on Affective Thinking* (Newark, Del.: International Reading Association, 1974).

Concept development is closely related to semantic (vocabulary) development because many of the words in one's vocabulary are labels for the concepts one has formed. Since concepts are a vehicle for intellectual organization, they facilitate thinking. Through words one can communicate one's concepts, and through the words of others one can expand one's knowledge.

A planned vocabulary development program

It would be difficult to overestimate the value of semantics in reading comprehension. A rich vocabulary is necessary for effective communication; the reader must understand the words of authors and speakers in order to comprehend their ideas. Writers and speakers must have words to communicate their ideas to others. The business of life is carried on in words, and human beings do their thinking with words. Readers gain knowledge through words. A person can increase his store of information by listening to and reading the words of others. Words symbolize the key concepts that reside in the intellect. People are more comfortable when they can attach a verbal symbol to an experience. For example, a patient feels more confident when told that he or she has a virus than when told that the doctor does not know what is making the patient ill. Human beings work, play, and think with words.

The words in one's vocabulary are influenced by one's sex, age, socioeconomic status, and geographic factors. The words an individual knows are the product of his or her experiences. A male student would not discuss his new dress, but a female student might. First graders do not discuss fall quarter classes, but college students are well acquainted with this terminology. City students may not have a concept for the word *heifer*, while farm students would be familiar with the term. If the reader's experiences have been varied, and if he or she has been interested in the ideas and activities experienced, he or she will probably have a rich vocabulary. The importance of expanding vocabulary cannot be overstated because word understanding is crucially related to reading comprehension.

There are three methods of building vocabulary that are most commonly mentioned in research and by experts in the field of reading. These methods are direct vocabulary instruction, incidental attention to building word meaning, and wide reading as a vehicle for expanding vocabulary. Although each of these methods for building vocabulary contributes to expanding vocabulary, direct instruction is most effective in significantly increasing student vocabulary.

The structure, planning, and scheduling involved in a direct vocabulary instruction program make this type of program more effective than the less structured planning in a program of incidental vocabulary building or wide reading. The goal of a direct vocabulary program is attaining word power, the power to find the meanings of unfamiliar words and to make them a part of one's working vocabulary. This kind of vocabulary program uses a combination of methods for vocabulary development because a combination of methods produces greater expansion of vocabulary than any one method alone. The program is based on words for which the students have immediate need rather than words drawn from sources unrelated to current tasks. Because most vocabulary programs fail to produce results in a short period of time, this program is a daily, year-long-approach to building vocabulary. A period of evaluation and consolidation should be provided each week for the students; during this period, words and principles of learning words are reviewed. Principles of a program of planned, direct vocabulary development include the following.

1. Evaluate the vocabulary development of pupils to determine the status of their achievement and needs.
2. Sensitize and motivate students to develop larger vocabularies. Provide both direct and vicarious experiences for students.
3. Alert students to the unique attributes of words; tell them that words may name, words may show action, words may describe, words may have multiple meanings, different words may have similar meanings, and words may have denotative and connotative meanings.
4. Preteach difficult words that occur in content reading materials. Teach students to focus on words that are repeated frequently in content that is being read because these words are usually important to understanding.
5. Teach students connectives, as well as substantive words, because connectives show relationships that are important to understanding.
6. Recognize that all unknown words cannot be taught, due to the constraints of time. The reader does not have to understand every word in order to comprehend what he is reading.
7. Plan vocabulary discussion sessions that center around specific topics that are relevant to the students.
8. Help students develop a system for expanding vocabulary.
9. Encourage students to engage in wide reading.
10. Instruct students in the use of context clues as an aid to solving the meaning of unknown words. (See Chapter 4.)
11. Teach only frequently recurring prefixes and suffixes that have invariant meanings as aids to solving the meaning of unknown words. (See Chapter 4.)

12. Utilize the dictionary wisely. (See Chapter 4.)

The first nine points above will be discussed below.

Assessment   Evaluation of student vocabulary development is necessary for planning vocabulary instruction. It is important to evaluate the growth of meaning vocabulary. Edgar Dale suggests four methods of testing vocabulary:

1. Identification—the student responds orally or in writing by identifying a word according to its definition or use.
2. Multiple choice—the student selects the correct meaning of the tested word from three or four definitions.
3. Matching—the tested words are presented in one column and the matching definitions are presented out of order in another column.
4. Checking—the student checks the words he knows or doesn't know.[2]

When testing students with the first method, identification, the student responds orally or in writing to a list of words supplied by the teacher. The list should be organized from easy to difficult. The student may self-check his or her responses in this testing situation, thereby getting immediate feedback. This technique is particularly useful for alerting students to their own vocabulary strengths and weaknesses. The following example of an identification vocabulary test uses words that are drawn from a science book.

_____observe   _____substance

_____describe   _____interact

_____hypothesis   _____chemical change

_____molecules   _____element

_____atoms   _____compound

The second method of testing vocabulary, multiple choice, presents words in context and provides several answers from which the student selects the best response. After completion of the exercise the responses should be discussed with the students. Following is an example of a multiple-choice exercise.

Susan broke a window. "You're a big help," her mother said. Susan's mother was being _____. (appreciative, sarcastic, ironic).

---

2. Edgar Dale, Joseph O'Rourke, and Henry Bamman, *Techniques of Teaching Vocabulary* (Palo Alto, Calif.: Field Educational Publications, 1971), p. 20.

The third method of evaluating vocabulary development is the use of matching exercises such as the following set of words from a social studies textbook.

1. Census
2. Human geography
3. Suburb
4. Urban
5. Population distribution

a. A town near a large city
b. The study of where people live and carry on their activities
c. A count of people
d. Areas where people live close together in villages, towns and cities
e. Where people live on the surface of the earth

The fourth method of vocabulary evaluation is self-checking by the student and is useful for alerting both students and teachers to vocabulary strengths and weaknesses. Dale suggests the following code for self-checking.

+ means "I know it well, I use it."
✔ means "I know it somewhat."
− means "I've seen it or heard it."
O means "I've never heard of it."[3]

The following list of words for self-checking were taken from a mathematics book.

commutative _____
metric   _____
symmetrical _____
pentagon   _____ .
hexagon   _____

Sensitize and motivate

Once the state of the students' vocabulary development has been assessed, the next step in any vocabulary building program is sensitizing students to words. This is probably the most important step for ensuring success in a vocabulary building program. A sense of excitement about words, a sense of wonder about words, and a feeling of pleasure related to words are essential ingredients in vocabulary development. As the students become word sensitized they are motivated to expand their vocabularies and are rewarded by the recognition that their vocabularies are expanding.

Word consciousness begins with activities related to words and results in an alertness to new words in one's environment. Resource

3. *Ibid.*, pp. 20–26.

books such as *A Hog on Ice*,[4] *Horsefeathers*,[5] and others in a series by Charles E. Funk provide interesting stories related to words and their meanings. Through books like these, students learn how the meanings of words have changed over the years. For example, the word *nice* once meant ignorant; it was no compliment to be called nice in those days. As a result of being used daily over a period of years, the words in a living language gradually change in predictable ways. A dead language, such as Latin, which is no longer spoken does not change. Following is a list of the ways in which words change.

1. *Amelioration*—The meaning of the word has changed so that the word means something better than it once did. For example, a person who was called *enthusiastic* was once considered a fanatic. Currently, enthusiasm is considered a desirable quality.

2. *Pejoration*—Pejoration indicates that the word has a lower meaning than it did earlier in history. For example, a *villain* once was a feudal serf or a servant from a villa. Currently, a villain is considered to be a depraved scoundrel.

3. *Generalization*—Some words become more generalized in meaning. When generalization operates, the meaning of words is broadened. Once upon a time, a *picture* was a painting, but now a picture may be a print, a photograph, or a drawing. In fact a picture may not be a picture at all, because in modern art a picture may not have a distinct form.

4. *Specialization*—The opposite of generalization is specialization. In this case, word meanings become more specific than they were in the past. At one time, *meat* was any food, not just mutton, pork, or beef. The Chinese used the word *pork* to mean any kind of meat earlier in their history.

5. *Euphemism*—This term is assigned to an affectation used to achieve elegance. For example, a *janitor* is often called a custodian or maintenance engineer, and a person does not die, but "passes away."

6. *Hyperbole*—This is an extreme exaggeration. For example, a man who is tired might say that he could "sleep for a year." Of course, he does not have a real desire to sleep so long. He is using exaggeration to make the point of his extreme fatigue. Many people currently use the word *fantastic* to describe almost everything, although fantastic means strange, wonderful, unreal, and illusory.

---

4. Charles E. Funk, *A Hog on Ice* (New York: Warner Publishing Company, 1948).
5. Charles E. Funk and E. J. Funk, *Horsefeathers* (New York: Warner Publishing Company, 1958).

Examination of reading selections for amelioration, generalization, pejoration, euphemism, and hyperbole can increase student sensitivity to words.

Two books by Isaac Asimov also can be used to stimulate an interest in words. These books are *Words of Science* and *Words on the Map*.[6] Students find these books enjoyable because they tell stories related to words that are used in science and on maps. Students often like to look up the meanings of the names of their favorite places, places they have visited, or the home towns of friends or relatives.

Explorations of vocabulary can also focus on the following:

1. *Acronyms*—Words composed of the first letters or syllables of longer terms, such as *SNAFU*, which means "situation normal all fouled up." This is a Navy term coined during World War II.

2. *Oxymorons*—Two incongruous words used together, such as *cruel kindness* or *broadly ignorant*.

3. *Homonyms*—also known as *homophones*—These are words that sound alike but are not spelled alike, such as *to, too, two; pare, pair; sum, some*.

4. *Heteronyms*—Words that have different pronunciations and meanings although they are spelled exactly the same, such as:

   Don't *subject* me to that experience.
   What is the *subject* of your book?

5. *Analogy*—An analogy shows a relationship or similarity between two things or ideas. Work with analogies can improve both vocabulary and reading comprehension because analogies improve thinking skills. The relationships usually expressed by analogies are:

   a. Opposites
   b. Origin
   c. Synonyms
   d. Plural
   e. Part-to-whole
   f. Function
   g. Homonyms
   h. Number
   i. Classification
   j. Process
   k. Degree
   l. Characteristic

An example of each follows:

   a. happy: sad:: up (a) over (b) down (c) high
   b. A cow is to leather as a tree is to: (a) paper (b) butter (c) farm

---

6. Isaac Asimov, *Words of Science* (Boston: Houghton Mifflin Co., 1959), *Words on the Map* (Boston: Houghton Mifflin Co., 1961).

c.   beautiful: lovely:: sad: (a) happy (b) unhappy (c) cry
d.   cow: cows:: foot: _____
e.   nose is to face as finger is to _____
f.   key: lock:: doorknob: (a) steps (b) door (c) key
g.   read: red:: fare:
h.   one: five:: nine: _____
i.   eagle is to bird as trout is to _____
j.   knife: cut:: pencil: (a) write (b) tear (c) mistake
k.   good: better:: bad: (a) worse (b) best (c) worst
l.   feathers: bird:: fur: _____

Each subject area content can lend itself to relationship exercises involving analogies. Example 5.2 is one prepared from the field of science:

Example 5.2. _____

Science analogies

a.   water/dehydration: vitamins/ (mumps, deficiency, diseases, jaundice, appendicitis)
b.   taste buds/tongue: villi/ (mouth, stomach, small intestine, colon)
c.   pepsin/protein: ptyalin/ (oils, fats, starch, sucrose)
d.   liver/small intestine: salivary glands/ (mouth, stomach, small intestine, colon)
e.   mouth/large intestine: duodenum/ (esophagus, jejunum, ileum, caecum)
f.   protein/organic nutrients: magnesium/ (peptides, feces, vitamins, minerals, salts)
g.   pancreas/pancreatic fluid: stomach/ (water, saliva, gastric juices, intestinal fluid)
h.   saliva/ptyalin: pancreatic fluid/ (trypsin, amylase, lipase, peptones)

6.   *Synonyms*—Words that have similar meanings, such as *red* and *crimson* or *walk* and *stroll*.
7.   *Antonyms*—Words that have opposite meanings, such as *walk* and *run* or *up* and *down*.

Television game shows such as "Password" and "The Wheel of Fortune" can be adapted both to motivate vocabulary interest and to teach vocabulary. Commerical games like "Scrabble" are useful in building vocabulary. Crossword puzzles and hidden word puzzles that contain commmon words and specialized vocabulary from the content areas can be constructed by both teachers and students. Figures 5.1 and 5.2 are examples of a crossword puzzle containing mathematics words and a hidden word puzzle containing science words.

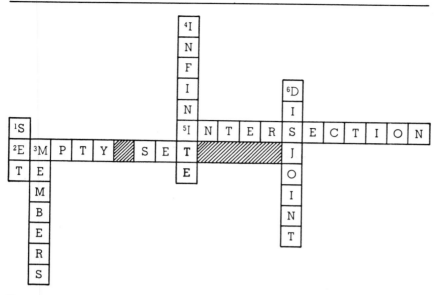

Crossword Puzzle

Across: 2. A set that has no members
         5. Sets whose members are the same

Down: 1. A collection of objects or things
         3. Things that belong to a set
         4. A set whose members cannot be counted
         6. Sets that have no members that are the same

Again, it should be emphasized that vocabulary develops out of experiences, both real and vicarious. While exercises and games are motivational and provide some experience with words, field trips to exhibits, museums, concerts, farms, and stores are even more valuable opportunities for developing concepts and vocabulary. For example, a field trip to a local dairy develops a deeper understanding of pasteurization than can reading about the process.

Television, films, flat pictures, radio, maps, charts, models, and dramatizations are forms of vicarious experience that are very valuable in the classroom for introducing and expanding vocabulary. When unfamiliar words are encountered in reading, teachers must frequently resort to one of the above mentioned media as a means of helping students understand the concepts represented by the words.

There are basic concepts about words in the English language that will help students understand vocabulary. These concepts include the following:

Word attributes

Figure 5.2 *Science hidden word puzzle*

A	L	G	A	E	C	E	L	L
M	A	S	T	A	X	O	T	I
O	P	R	O	T	I	S	T	S
E	U	G	L	E	N	A	O	S
B	O	G	I	N	E	T	A	C
A	M	O	E	B	A	S	N	G
N	B	O	T	A	N	I	S	T
R	O	T	I	F	E	R	S	X

Hidden word answers:
Across: algae, cell
      mastax
      euglena
      protists
      amoebas
      botanist
      rotifers

Down: amoeba

1. *Words name people, places, and things.* Of course, students recognize that each person has a name, and they may want to know what their names mean. For example, the name *Barbara* means stranger. The city name for Akron, Ohio, is based on the Greek word *akron* meaning "a point." Akron was so named

because it is located on the highest point of the route between Lake Erie and the Ohio River.

2. *Words can describe action.* Students can explore various action words, synonyms for action words, and the shades of meaning that are attached to these various synonyms. The class could start with the word *walk* and select synonyms such as *saunter, stroll, meander, pace,* and *tramp.* After selecting synonyms, students can discuss how the meaning varies as each synonym is used.

3. *Words can describe.* Describing words are adjectives. Students may work with various adjectives to describe a pretty girl or other topics suggested by the instructor. A pretty girl may be described as a good looking girl, a lovely lass, or a charming miss.

4. *One word may have many meanings.* Words in English may have multiple meanings; for example, the three letter word *run* has thirty-four meanings in the *American Heritage Dictionary.*[7] Following are seven examples of these multiple meanings:

    a.   I will *run* the entire distance.
    b.   He *runs* his cows in the pasture.
    c.   Jane will *run* the errand.
    d.   They will *run* John out of town.
    e.   The smugglers were *running* guns.
    f.   I have a *run* in my stocking.
    g.   *Run* this advertisement next week.

    Because words have multiple meanings, the reader must understand that a word is dependent upon context for precise meaning. The reader must use context clues to determine which of the meanings of a word is appropriate. The syntax (word order) and semantics (meanings of other words) in a sentence can help the reader select appropriate word meanings. The reader may also compare the context in which a word occurs with dictionary definitions to select the correct meaning among multiple meanings.

5. *Many words in English mean almost the same thing.* For example, think of the many words that mean *red: scarlet, magenta, ruby, flame, crimson,* and *vermillion.* Context and precision of expression determine the correct word to use among the words that have similar meanings.

---

7. William Morris, ed., *The American Heritage Dictionary of the English Language* (Boston: Houghton Mifflin Company, 1969), p. 1135.

6. *Words have denotative meanings and connotative meanings.* Denotation refers to the strict definition of a word as defined by the dictionary. Connotation refers to all of the ideas that are suggested by a term, such as the emotional reactions one has to words. For instance, the word *home* denotes the place where one lives, while it connotes warmth, love, and family. It is important to vocabulary study and reading comprehension that readers recognize the ideas connoted by the words authors use. By definition *cunning* and *astute* are very similar, but if the word *cunning* is used to describe a person it usually implies an insult, while describing a person as *astute* is a compliment.

Following is an exercise to help students understand the connotative meanings of words.

Directions: Select the word in each pair that you would prefer to use in describing yourself. Tell why you chose the word.

a. creative or screwball
b. stolid or easy going
c. thrifty or tight
d. enthusiastic or excitable
e. fat or heavy-set
f. conceited or proud

Preteach and guide Vocabulary that is sufficiently difficult or unfamiliar to impede comprehension should be introduced prior to having students read an assignment. This is particularly true for assignment materials that include technical vocabulary.

A structured overview (also called an advance organizer) may be used to introduce words and concepts to students. An advance organizer shows important relationships of concepts and the words that are labels for the concepts. The teacher who wishes to develop a structured overview should follow these steps.

1. Select the vocabulary and concepts that are essential for student understanding.
2. Organize the vocabulary in a structure that shows the relationship among the concepts.

Figure 5.3 is a structured overview developed to accompany a chapter in a secondary science textbook.

Some teachers prepare vocabulary study guides. Example 5.3 is an example from the content of business law:

Structured overview   Figure 5.3

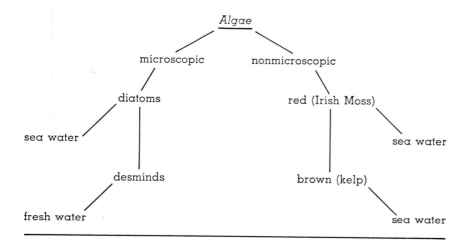

Business law vocabulary sheet   Example 5.3

Vocabulary Study Sheet for a Business Law Unit on Making Contracts

I. Match each word in the column on the left with the correct definition from the column on the right. Place the letter of the correct definition beside the number of each word.

1. contract
2. statute law
3. competent party
4. tender
5. damages

   a. a person that the law recognizes as being capable of entering into contractual relationships

   b. a legal obligation which is enforceable by law

   c. an offer to carry out an obligation

   d. a law passed by a legislative body

   e. the amount of money the law allows as compensation for a loss caused by another person

   f. person who swears that the information he has provided is true

Answer the questions below.

1. What does *breach of contract* mean? How is this meaning of *breach* related to its meaning in the sentence: "The breach in the dike was a cause for concern."?

2. What is a minor? The word *minor* comes from a Latin word. Check the dictionary to see what the Latin word meant. How is the meaning of this Latin word related to the meaning of the term *minor* in your Business Law book?

Example 5.3 (cont.)

3. What does *undue influence* mean? Use your understanding of the meaning of the prefix *un* and the meaning of the root word *due* to help you determine the meaning of *undue*.
4. In the sentence below, what is the meaning of the word *fraud*? A person who cannot read may become the victim of fraud.
5. What is a *promisor*? What is a *promisee*? Use your understanding of the meanings of the word endings to help you define these terms.

Students should be taught to scan reading materials for words that are used frequently, as these are usually key words that the reader must understand in order to comprehend content. If the student notices the words *archeologist* and *anthropology* occurring several times in a social studies textbook, he or she should consider those words as key words to learn. Focusing on key words helps make the reader more independent in expanding his vocabulary and in comprehending.

Connectives

Certain words express the great thoughts of mankind; these words are nouns, adjectives, and verbs. These are the substantive words of language. However, the full meaning of these substantive words depends upon another class of words, the thought connectors that indicate relation. These thought connectors are prepositions, conjunctions, relative pronouns, and some adverbs. Connectives are structure words that derive their meanings from their functions in sentences. For example, the connectives have been eliminated from the "Pledge of Allegiance to the Flag of the United States of America," in the following passage.

I pledge allegiance _____ the flag _____ the United States _____ America, _____ _____ the Republic _____ _____ it stands, one nation _____ God, indivisible, _____ liberty _____ justice _____ all.

Denis Rodgers researched the connectives commonly used in twelfth-grade science and social studies textbooks. Table 5.1 ranks by frequency the most common connectives in six subject areas.

Connectives signal the following relationships: positional and time relationships, equivalence, sequence, an important idea follows, contrast, qualification, and cause and effect.

Connectives that signal positional and time relationships include:

about	between	through
across	down	to
after	from	until
against	in	up
along	inside	upon

Ranking (by frequency) of the twenty most common connectives in each subject area   Table 5.1

	Overall Frequency 35 texts	Grade 6 soc. studies & science	Grade 12 geography	Grade 12 history	Grade 12 chemistry	Grade 12 biology	Grade 12 physics
but	1	1	1	1	1	1	2
if	2	2	9	5	2	2	1
when	3	3	2	12	6	9	4
because	4	4	5	9	11	8	3
however	5	10	3	8	5	3	8
as	6	5	8	6	10	7	6
although	7	11	4	3	12	11	11
thus	8	12	7	4	7	4	14
then	9	6	13	13	—	13	7
while	10	—	11	2	14	10	13
for example	11	13	12	—	4	5	9
since	12	14	15	10	3	6	12
also	13	8	10	—	9	16	10
therefore	14	—	14	16	13	14	5
so	15	—	6	—	15	20	15
even	16	7	—	7	—	12	—
perhaps	17	9	19	19	16	18	—
yet	18	15	16	14	17	17	—
such as	19	17	—	—	20	15	—
in fact	20	—	20	15	—	—	—
Connectives not in top twenty overall	so that (16) too (18) until (19) whether (20)	where (17) that is (18)	until (11) meanwhile (17) whether (18) despite (20)	if so (8) that is (18) until (19)	that is (19)	in other words (16) so that (17) on the other hand (18) consequently (19) furthermore (20)	
No. of texts examined	35	9	12	5	2	5	2

Source: Denis Rodgers, "Which Connectives? Signals to Enhance Comprehension," *Journal of Reading* 17 (March 1974):462-64.

among	like	with
around	near	without
at	of	by
before	outside	beyond
beneath		

Coordinating connectives indicate that an equivalent idea will follow. For instance, "I like cats *and* dogs." Coordinating connectives include the following: *and, likewise, also.* Some connectives signal a sequence of ideas. For example, "We went to Jane's house first, and then we went to school." Connectives that signal sequence include the following: *first, second, third,* (etc.,) *next, finally, furthermore, in addition,* and *then.* Certain connectives signal that an important idea will follow. For example, "*In summary,* the primary world problems are: overpopulation, too little food, and the lack of inexpensive sources of energy." The connectives that signal important ideas are:

thus	in brief
therefore	as a result
consequently	without question
finally	significantly
hence	unquestionably
in conclusion	absolutely
in summation (in summary)	

Contrasting ideas are signaled by some connectives. For instance, "Jane is a humanist, *but* she will not contribute to charity." The connectives that signal contrast are:

but	on the other hand
yet	otherwise
nevertheless	although
meanwhile	despite
however	

Some connectives signal qualification. For example, "I will go *if* I finish my homework." The connectives that signal qualification include:

because	since	when
if	though	while
now	where	unless

Cause and effect are signaled by certain connectives. For example, "I like May *because* she is so kind." These connectives are: *because, since, so,* and *that.*

A variety of activities can be used to help students understand and use connectives. Following are a few suggestions:

Activities

1. Read a passage orally, omitting the connectives and allow the students to supply appropriate connectives.
2. Create sentences like the following: *After the game, we went home.* Tell the students to circle the word or phrase in each sentence that answers the question you ask about connectives. For instance: Which word or phrase tells when we went home?

3. Omit connectives from written exercises, and ask the students to write the correct connectives in the blanks.

4. In written exercises, direct students to draw a line from the connective to the words it connects.

5. Use multiple-choice exercises like the following one: Directions: Read each sentence. Draw a line under the answer that tells the right meaning of the word.

   The flower is red *and* yellow.
   a. in addition to
   b. because
   c. when
   d. before

6. Ask more advanced students to circle the structure words in paragraphs and define the circled words according to their functions in the sentences in which they occur.

Focus upon essential words

Teachers cannot teach all of the unknown words in a selection. In some selections teachers may find 25 to 30 words with which students are not familiar. If the teachers were to spend only one minute per word, they would consume 25 to 30 minutes just for vocabulary development. Time and energy constraints make this kind of time utilization impossible. The logical approach to this problem is to focus on teaching only those words that are essential to comprehending the major points in the selection being read. For example, in the sentence, "The gold and magenta circus wagon pulled into town," the reader can determine that magenta is a color. The specific color is irrelevant to understanding the selection in which the sentence occurred, so time should not be spent on teaching this word.

Discussion sessions

Discussion sessions provide an informal semi-structured setting for interacting with words and using vocabulary. Discussion sessions should be planned around the vocabulary in the textbooks used by the students. Judith Crist[8] developed a model for vocabulary discussion sessions. During the first part of the general vocabulary discussion sessions the teacher introduces words in discussion; as each word is used, the word is identified and written on a chalkboard. Each participant keeps a notebook of words acquired in discussion. During the second part of the discussion period, the class is divided into pairs and discussion is renewed on a one-to-one basis with emphasis on using the new words, so students hear and speak each new word at

---

8. Judith Crist, "One Capsule a Week—A Painless Remedy for Vocabulary Ills," *Journal of Reading* 18 (November 1975): 147–49.

least once. The final part of the discussion session is writing about new words. The writings are read to the group at the beginning of the next session as a reinforcement of the lesson. Crist reports that this method has been successful and motivating for students.

Systematize strategies

A good vocabulary program helps students become independent in vocabulary growth. Students need to know methods for self-direction in vocabulary development so they may become independent. Two techniques will help students achieve vocabulary independence. The first one is establishing a word file for new words, and the second is showing students a system for learning new words.

The vocabulary file is often overlooked as a technique for developing vocabulary because it doesn't seem very exciting. However, with motivation provided by the teacher, the vocabulary file is a very effective device. Each student maintains an individual file of the new words that are encountered in his or her reading and listening. The file may be as varied as the teachers and students using it. The word cards may take the following form or any form that appeals to the teacher.

```
Word _____

Sentence in which found _____

_____

_____

Student definition _____

_____
```

For the word file to be effective the teacher must plan for evaluation of the content at regular intervals. Since the files are individual, evaluation must be planned carefully. Students may test each other in pairs, or they may construct crossword puzzles from their words for a friend to complete. The teacher may evaluate by asking students to build sentences from their words or by asking students to place their words in categories determined by the teacher. Words included in the files may be used as the content for vocabulary games. The creative mind can contribute many additional ideas for evaluation of vocabulary files.

The second aspect of developing independence in vocabulary development is to provide a specific system the student can utilize for learning new words. Have the student learn the following steps.

1. Look at the word.
2. Say the word.
3. Write the word with a synonym or brief definition.
4. Use the word in conversation.

Saying the word and writing the meaning of the word may require assistance from the teacher or a classmate, but the student should learn to rely on context clues as the first source of meaning. If context clues do not provide a meaning, then the student may discuss the word with another student or the teacher. A dictionary or thesaurus may be used for assistance if other help is not available. Once a student adapts this system or develops a system of his or her own for facilitating vocabulary acquisition, he or she can be a more independent reader.

While wide reading in and of itself may not improve vocabulary, it has the potential of so doing since the reader not only meets many new words in different fields but also becomes familiar with their different meanings in a variety of contexts. Therefore, an important goal for all content teachers is to motivate recreational and supplementary reading. The following suggestions are offered as ways of stimulating wide reading:

Wide reading

1. Consider the interests of the student. Observe him or her carefully, noting what topics he or she talks or writes about when given freedom of choice. If possible, make use of interest inventories (see Chapter 10).
2. Try to locate the "right" books to match these interests. A part of the teacher's job is to know sources of information to use to match book and student. (See "Media Selection Sources" in Chapter 3 and library (or trade) books cited for the various subject areas in Chapters 9A and 9B).
3. Make books available. Develop an attractive classroom library with books that are conducive to wide reading.
4. As a content area teacher, suggest books to students. Secondary students are accustomed to the English teacher recommending books—they are perhaps even more impressed with the suggestions made by a mathematics teacher, science teacher, social studies teacher, or others.

The relationships among ideas in English are expressed through semantics, syntax, and inflected endings. The English language relies heavily on word order to convey meaning. English sentence structure expresses meaning so well that the reader can derive quite a lot of

Language features related to sentence meaning

Syntax   information from a nonsense sentence such as: "*The nerd dracked montly.* In analyzing this sentence, *the* is a function word marking the noun *nerd.* Words like *the* indicate information about other words in the same context. *Nerd* is the subject of the sentence and a noun. *Dracked* is a verb and the *ed* ending tells the reader that the action occurred in the past. The word, *montly* probably tells how the subject *dracked.* The *ly* signals an adverb. Thus the reader arrives at sentence understanding through implicit knowledge of the grammar (syntax) of English. This understanding enables the reader to interpret and to produce grammatical sentences.

Language competence is a basic aspect of reading comprehension. The reader must learn to grasp the way meaning is expressed in English. A variety of experiences with oral and written language is useful for developing linguistic competence. Students should have opportunities to represent their own thoughts in oral and written form because these experiences will prepare them to interpret what others write and say. The more students write, the better they will understand what they are reading. Reading and writing are reciprocal processes of meaning construction that reinforce and benefit each other.

Teachers can use the four basic sentence patterns listed by Carl Lefevre[9] as a starting point for teaching syntax. Examples of the basic patterns are given in Table 5.2.

Table 5.2   *Basic sentence patterns*

Pattern	Example
1. Noun-verb	Boys run.
a. Noun-verb-adjective	Roses smell sweet.
b. Noun-verb-adverb	Boys run fast.
2. Noun-verb-noun	Boys run races.
3. Noun-verb-noun-noun	The boy gave the trophy to Susan.
4. Noun-linking verb-noun	This boy is a runner.
a. Noun-linking verb-adjective	This runner is handsome.
b. Noun-linking verb-adverb	This runner is fast.

Students may use these basic sentence patterns for writing and they may locate examples of the patterns in their reading content.

9. Carl Lefevre. *Linguistics and the Teaching of Reading* (New York: McGraw Hill, 1964) pp. 79–91.

Experience with sentences, such as making transformations from a kernel sentence, will increase reading comprehension. For example, the sentence "Susan ate a piece of cake" may be transformed as follows:

Is Susan eating a piece of cake?
Susan is not eating a piece of cake.
What is Susan eating?

A kernel sentence may be elaborated as in the following example:

Linda is eating a piece of cake.
Linda is eating a big piece of cake.
Linda is eating a big piece of chocolate cake.
Linda is slowly eating a big piece of chocolate cake.

Several techniques can be used both to assess and to increase language comprehension. The cloze procedure, which is explained in Chapter 10, is one such technique. Another is to have the student identify in a set of sentences the two sentences that have the same meaning. For example:

Doug painted the gray house.
Doug painted the house gray.
Doug painted the house that was gray.

Students can unscramble the word order of a group of words so that the words create a sentence. For example, "horse Mary have does gray a" could be unscrambled to read, "Mary does have a gray horse."

Paraphrasing is good practice for developing understanding of syntax. A sentence such as "It was John who repaired the faucet," could be paraphrased, "John fixed the faucet." Students may be asked to complete the blanks in a sentence so that the incomplete sentence has the same meaning as the complete sentence. For example:

Mary asked her mother when to leave.
Mary asked her mother when _____ should leave.

Punctuation

Punctuation is another tool authors use to signal meaning to the reader. For instance, compare the following sentences:

John ran away.
John ran away?
John ran away!

The writer has used precisely the same words in each sentence, but has varied the meaning by the punctuation. Students can be made aware of the use of punctuation through discussion. Students should be alerted to the functions of the following: *comma, question mark, exclamation point, dash, colon,* and *semi-colon.*

Figurative expressions

Figurative language is an additional aspect of language that is related to comprehension. Figurative language is a picturesque, expressive, and connotative use of language. Figurative language is based upon the use of language to create visual and emotional images in the reader's mind and to increase understanding by comparing one idea or thing with another. Language is used figuratively for several purposes. It is used to sway the reader's opinion, as in propaganda, to express difficult ideas in concrete terms, and to develop more interesting styles so readers will be motivated to read content. The most used kinds of figurative language are metaphor, simile, personification, allusion, hyperbole, and euphemism. Definitions and examples follow:

1. *Metaphor* is the comparison of things or ideas that are unlike. The word *like* or *as* is not used in making the comparison. Example: That car is a lemon.
2. *Simile* is the comparison of two things or ideas that are dissimilar, but the analogy shows how they are alike. The word *like* or *as* is used in simile. Example: That dog runs like a rabbit.
3. *Personification* is a writing technique that endows an animal or an inanimate object with human characteristics. Example: The branches of the tree reached out to hug the sky.
4. *Allusion* is indirect reference to a person, place, or a thing. Readers may encounter many allusions each day without realizing what they are. For example, the word *cereal* refers to Ceres of Greek mythology. Jim is the "last of the Mohicans."
5. *Hyperbole* and *euphemism* have been described earlier in this chapter.

Teachers may use the following activities in teaching about figurative expressions.

Activities

1. Students may create their own figurative expressions. They should be encouraged to avoid overused expressions. Example: As sweet as _____ The student should think of a word different from *honey* to use here.
2. Provide expressions and ask students to write down their interpretation of each given expression. Example: Keep your chin up. _____

3. Provide an expression with multiple-choice explanations and ask the student to select the correct explanation. Example: *He got an earful* means: (1) his ears are dirty; (b) he has water in his ears; (c) he heard some important information; (d) he heard a large amount of noise.

4. Ask students to draw figurative expressions. For example: students could illustrate an expression such as "It's raining cats and dogs."

5. Use matching activities in which the student matches the meaning of an expression with the expression. Example:

The check list of skills in Example 5.4 could be used by teachers for evaluating and monitoring the word and sentence development of their students.

Concluding comments

Example 5.4.

A check list of word and sentence skills

Experience and Concept Development
1. Has a variety of real experiences
2. Has a variety of experiences from:
   a. reading
   b. movies
   c. television
3. Labels experiences
4. Identifies likenesses and differences among things, ideas, etc.
5. Categorizes things, ideas, people, experiences
6. Uses basic concepts of time, space, size, shape, number, etc.
7. Relates experiences to reading

Language—Semantics
1. Uses correct words to label things, ideas, people, experiences
2. Formulates operational definitions
3. Uses context clues
4. Selects the proper meaning for a word with multiple meanings
5. Selects the correct word among words with similar meanings
6. Recognizes synonyms and antonyms
7. Understands denotative meanings
8. Understands connotative meanings

Language—Syntax
1. Uses complete sentences in oral language
2. Uses a variety of sentence types in oral language
3. Uses complete sentences in written language

Example 5.4 (cont.)   4. Uses a variety of sentence types in written language
5. Can transform sentences
6. Can expand kernel sentences
7. Uses syntactic clues to aid understanding
8. Groups words together in phrases
9. Uses punctuation clues to aid understanding

Self-test

1. Why is experience an important factor in reading comprehension? (a) Experience helps the reader identify main ideas. (b) Experience provides a purpose for reading. (c) Related experience enables the reader to relate to the content. (d) Experience broadens the mind.

2. How is the relationship between concept development and semantic (vocabulary) development best described? (a) No relationship (b) A labeling relationship (c) Finding likenesses and differences (d) None of these.

3. Which of these activities will enhance concept development? (a) Categorizing (b) Finding connections (c) Finding common properties (d) All of these.

4. What is word power? (a) A method of developing vocabulary. (b) The ability to solve unfamiliar words and make them a part of one's vocabulary. (c) An undesirable means of increasing vocabulary. (d) A vocabulary program published by a commercial publisher.

5. A check(✔) in the code as used in this chapter means what? (a) I know the word well and use it. (b) I know it somewhat. (c) I've seen it or heard of it. (d) I've never heard of it.

6. What does connotative meaning of words refer to? (a) The dictionary definition of a word. (b) The contextual meaning of the word. (c) The emotional reaction to a word. (d) The teacher's definition of a word.

7. What is NATO an example of? (a) Oxymoron (b) Acronym (c) Analogy (d) Homophone

8. Why is a word in isolation meaningless? (a) Words in English derive meaning from interaction with other words. (b) Words are hard to define. (c) A dictionary is necessary to determine the meaning of a word. (d) The teacher must check the meaning a student gives to a word.

9. Why are connectives important words in achieving reading comprehension? (a) They are hard to understand. (b) They are short words. (c) They have multiple meanings. (d) They signal relationships.

10. Which of the following is a kernel sentence? (a) Joe runs. (b) Linda is eating a big piece of cake. (c) Mary is going home for Christmas. (d) John and Mary are good friends.

11. Why is figurative language used by authors? (a) To create visual and emotional images (b) To vary writing style (c) To make reading more difficult (d) Both a and b.

1. Prepare a categorizing worksheet, as illustrated in this chapter, for a chapter from a content area textbook of your choice.

2. Prepare an assessment using words from a chapter in a content area book; use one or more of the four methods of testing vocabulary described in this chapter.

3. Find a trade (library) book that focuses upon words of a particular content area, such as Asimov's *Words of Science*. Share with the class how you might use it to stimulate interest in words from that subject.

4. Prepare a crossword puzzle or hidden word puzzle for a set of important terms associated with a unit of work in your content area.

5. Prepare a variety of activities that could be used to help students understand and use the connectives commonly used in your subject area.

6. Select a chapter in a content area book and select the vocabulary that you think you would teach to a class. Plan ways to teach the chosen terms.

7. Keep a vocabulary file as described in this chapter for yourself for the next eight weeks.

8. Use the checklist provided earlier to observe the word and sentence skills of two students. After completing the observation, write a brief comparison and contrast of the students' skills.

9. Below are some vocabulary terms from various content areas. Prepare a vocabulary study guide sheet for one set of them.
   Auto Mechanics: thermostat, radiator, carburetor, ammeter, armature, commutator, generator, oscilloscope, polarize, camshaft, valve-tappet.
   Music: choreographer, prologue, prompter, score, overture, prelude, libretto, aria.
   Health: bacteria, virus, protozoa, metazoa, fungi, carbuncle, psoriasis, shingles, scabies, eczema.
   Foreign language: masculine, feminine, gender, predicate, cognates, singular, consonant.
   Art: introspective, murals, appreciation, technique, expression, properties, exhibitions, contemporary, interpret.
   Driver Education: awareness, controlled emotions, maturity, irresponsible, behavioral patterns, compensate, fatigue, carbon monoxide, medication, alcohol, depressants, visual, auditory.
   Psychology: learning curve, plateau, hierarchies, massed practice, feedback, frame, negative transfer, retention, overlearning.
   Government: delinquent, incorrigibility, omnibus, exigency, indeterminate, adjudicated, arbitrariness, interrogation, formulation, juvenile.

Enrichment activities

10. Make a structured overview for a selection in a content area textbook.
11. Locate examples in content area textbooks of the types of figurative language discussed in this chapter.
12. Prepare an analogy exercise sheet (similar to the one in this chapter) for a chapter or unit in a context area textbook.

Selected references

Burmeister, Lou E. *Reading Strategies for Secondary School Teachers.* New York: Addison-Wesley, 1974. Chapter 6.

Coley, Joan D. and Linda A. Gambrell. *Programmed Reading Vocabulary for Teachers.* Columbus, Ohio: Charles E. Merrill, 1977.

Dale, Edgar, Joseph O'Rourke, and Henry A. Bamman. *Techniques of Teaching Vocabulary.* Palo Alto, Calif.: Field Educational Publications, 1971.

Dale, Edgar. *Vocabulary Development.* New York: Phi Delta Kappa, 1973.

Dechant, Emerald. *Reading Improvement in the Secondary School.* Englewood Cliffs, N.J.: Prentice Hall, 1973. Chapter 7.

Deighton, Lee C. *Vocabulary Development in the Classroom.* New York: Teachers College, 1946.

Dillner, Martha H. and Joanne P. Olson. *Personalizing Reading Instruction in Middle, Junior, and Senior High Schools.* New York: Macmillan Co., 1977. Chapter 10.

Gerhard, Christian. *Making Sense: Reading Comprehension Improved Through Categorizing.* Newark, Del.: International Reading Association, 1974.

Hafner, Lawrence. *Improving Reading in Middle and Secondary Schools.* 2nd ed. New York: Macmillan Co., 1974. Section 5.

_____. *Developmental Reading in Middle and Secondary Schools.* New York: Macmillan Co., 1977. Chapter 5.

Henry, George H. *Teaching Reading as Concept Development: Emphasis on Affective Thinking.* Newark, Del.: International Reading Association, 1974.

Karlin, Robert. *Teaching Reading in High School.* 2nd ed. Bobbs-Merrill, 1972. Chapter 6.

Miller, Wilma H. *Teaching Reading in the Secondary School,* Springfield, Ill.: Charles C. Thomas, 1974, Chapter 4.

Robinson, H. Alan. *Teaching Reading and Study Strategies.* Boston: Allyn and Bacon, 1975. Chapter 4.

Shepherd, David. *Comprehensive High School Reading Methods.* Columbus, Ohio: Charles E. Merrill, 1973. Chapter 3.

Comprehension

This chapter focuses on reading comprehension. The main topic is examined from two perspectives: (1) the major aspects of reading comprehension and (2) the techniques of instruction for developing reading comprehension.

As you read this chapter, try to answer these questions:
1. What processes occur when the reader comprehends?
2. What skills must the reader possess in order to comprehend?
3. What strategies can the teacher utilize to encourage comprehension?

Purpose-setting questions

As you read this chapter, check your understanding of these terms:

Key vocabulary

comprehension	levels of thinking	creative
preview guide	literal	Reciprocal
thinking skills	interpretive	Questioning
main ideas	(inferential)	(ReQuest)
key words	evaluative (critical)	visualizing
details	propaganda	flexibility
paragraph structure	techniques	

What is comprehension?

The greatest challenge of teaching reading to secondary students is that of building reading comprehension. Comprehension is the essence of the reading act. Although there is controversy in the field of reading regarding many aspects of the reading process, there is widespread agreement about the importance of comprehension. The reader cannot learn unless he can comprehend what the authors of his books have written, and he cannot remember what he has read unless he has understood it. The objective of all reading is to understand or comprehend what the author has written.

Reading comprehension is an abstract process that occurs in the brain; it is difficult to observe, to measure, and to teach directly. Students can discuss reading content, answer questions, and verbalize how they arrived at answers, but the actual mental process cannot be observed. A good way to explore the process of reading comprehension is to discuss reading with a reader who shares his or her thoughts as he or she reads. Example 6.1 shows an exploration of a reading incident in the life of an adult reader who read the *Akron Beacon Journal* of Sunday, December 2, 1976.

Example 6-1

As the reader sat down with a cup of coffee and the newspaper, her eyes fell on the front page headline that read: "Brrr bowl . . . Zip win warms fans." The reader knew from this headline that she was reading sports news because her background experience provided the information that the word Zip referred to the University of Akron football team, which is called the Zips or Zeppelins. They are so named because zeppelins are made of rubber and Akron is the "rubber capital of the world." Knowing that she was reading sports news carried a mental set in this reader for reading quickly and superficially because she was not a sports fan. However, this article was about an important local game and would provide some information about the game to discuss with friends and relatives. Obtaining such information provided one of her purposes for reading about the topic. The headline stated that the Zip win warms fans, indicating that the University of Akron team won the game. This was about all of the information that the reader wanted about the game. However, she remembered a conversation that she had heard in the drug store regarding the team being involved in some kind of championship competition, so she established another purpose for reading. The new purpose was to determine the title for which the Zips were competing. She skimmed the first two paragraphs of the story and learned that the game was the National Semifinals for the NCAA Division II teams. She decided at this point that she would like to find out how close the score of the game was, so she scanned the next paragraph for numerals indicative of a game score. The third paragraph provided the information that the score was 29 to 26 in an overtime game. The reader had satisfied her purposes for reading and decided that she was disappointed that she missed such an exciting game. She also felt proud that the team representing her school had *made such a good* showing in the sports world.

Although this is just one reading experience with one type of content read for rather specific purposes, examination of the reading experience in Example 6.1 provides considerable insight into reading comprehension. Notice that the reader did not read the first word in the headline first. Her eyes moved to a meaningful word, a noun, which enabled her to predict the type of content being read. The fact that this was sports news indicated a mental set for the type of reading in which the reader should engage. Reading this one word also enabled the reader to predict the topic of the article. Reading a few more words enabled the reader to use her store of information, based upon experience, to predict accurately a large portion of the article, which covered one-third of the front page of the newspaper. Detailed reading confirmed the predictions made by the reader on the basis of her sampling of the reading content. The reader had three purposes for reading that were accomplished by more careful reading of the details that supported the main idea of the article. The reader also used logic to arrive at the conclusion that the quickest way to determine the score of the game was to scan the article for numbers.

The reader whose activities were analyzed used information drawn from experience, as well as from knowledge regarding semantics, syntax, and logic, in order to comprehend. The reader used strategies for understanding that included establishing purposes for reading, reading for main ideas, and reading for details. The reader responded to the content of the article emotionally because she felt both disappointment and pride. This brief analysis reveals some of the complexities of comprehension.

Reading comprehension is processing written language to get ideas, relating ideas to experience, organizing ideas, evaluating ideas, and utilizing ideas. The reader must have some basic intellectual equipment in order to comprehend. He must have intelligence, language, and experience. Only a small portion of the information needed to comprehend comes from the printed page, while the larger portion of the information is stored in the brain. Other factors related to reading comprehension are affective dimensions, visualizing, and flexibility. The various factors will each be discussed in turn.

Experience

Readers comprehend by using their experience. The more experience a student has that relates to a topic, the better that student will be able to understand the reading content. Teachers should help students utilize their experience by developing a point of contact between the reader and the content.

One technique that helps students use their past experience to aid comprehension is the use of a preview guide. A preview guide directs the student in thinking about content of a selection prior to reading the selection. The preview guide helps the reader predict what the author will write on the basis of the reader's past experience with the subject.

A preview guide may take several forms. One very simple approach is to ask the student to write down what he knows about a topic. For example, the social science teacher who is introducing the topic of communism might ask the students to write down what they know about communism. After reading a selection on the subject, the students should look at the ideas they wrote down earlier to determine which of their ideas were accurate.

A more formal preview guide is composed of statements or questions related to the major concepts that the teacher wishes the students to understand and remember after reading the selection. A student checks the accuracy of his or her responses to the preview guide after he or she completes reading the selection. Example 6.2 is a preview guide based upon a chapter in a social studies textbook that discusses the topic of cities and suburbs.

Example 6.2   *Preview guide*

Yes	No	
_____	_____	Between 1940 and 1960, millions of Americans moved to the suburbs.
_____	_____	Transportation is not an important factor for suburbanites.
_____	_____	The influx of people has changed the nature of the suburbs.
_____	_____	Moving to the suburbs makes people very happy.
_____	_____	Commuting is one of the problems of the suburban dweller.
_____	_____	Loneliness is not a problem in suburbia.
_____	_____	A revolution in building made the suburbs possible.

Another means of developing readiness for reading comprehension and helping students utilize their experience is suggested by Richard Vacca[1]. This technique is the structured overview discussed on page 59–61 in Chapter 3 and on page 128 in Chapter 5. The structured overview enables the reader to fit his past experience into a conceptual framework so that a point of contact is developed between the reader and the content. (For a further discussion of experience as it relates to reading, refer to pages 115–18 in Chapter 5.)

---

1. Richard T. Vacca, "Readiness to Read Content Areas Assignments," *Journal of Reading* 20 (February 1977) 387 92.

The reader must use thinking skills in order to comprehend. These skills include understanding the author's organization and utilizing different levels of thinking.

Thinking skills

Comprehension of reading content requires that the reader be able to follow the author's organization of main ideas, details, paragraph structures, and whole selections.

Organization

Main ideas The use of main ideas and supporting details is one way that writers organize their ideas. Both teachers and students find that identifying the main idea is an important part of comprehension. It is impossible to analyze, synthesize, interpret or evaluate until one can identify the main idea. In order to identify a main idea, the reader must understand the selection he is reading. Readers should ask themselves who, when, where, and why questions to arrive at an understanding of the content that will enable them to locate the main idea. The main idea of a passage is the idea that the author has developed and supported by details throughout the paragraph or the selection. The main idea could be called the "big" idea the author is developing. A teacher who asks students to locate the main idea in a paragraph should be certain that there is a main idea in the paragraph. Some paragraphs present interesting information, but do not have a main idea.

Students can understand main ideas better if the teacher begins by introducing key words in sentences. Students can be directed to compose telegrams[2] to send to another person, giving such crucial information as: "Mother has had a heart attack and is very ill. Please hurry home." Through telegram exercises, students will learn to focus on key words, which are generally nouns and verbs, although other parts of speech can be important in specific messages. In the above example, students would probably select the following words, "Mother ill. Hurry home."

Activities in locating key words in sentences can be expanded to finding the key words in a paragraph. Once the key words in the sentences of a paragraph have been identified, the student can relate them to determine what big idea the key words point to. Students can sum up the relationships among the key words[3] and select the sentence that best seems to state the main idea. Following is a paragraph with the key words underlined.

A <u>dog</u> is a <u>useful</u> animal. It <u>guards</u> our <u>homes</u> from burglars and <u>alerts</u> us when <u>guests</u> are coming. The <u>dog</u> will <u>warn</u>

---

2. H. Alan Robinson, *Teaching Reading and Study Strategies* (Boston: Allyn and Bacon 1975), p. 111
3. H. Alan Robinson, *Teaching Reading and Study Strategies* (Boston: Allyn and Bacon, 1975), p. 112.

members of the <u>household</u> if <u>fire</u> breaks out in the home. Some dogs serve as <u>seeing-eye</u> dogs for <u>blind</u> people. Perhaps most important of all, dogs are loyal, loving <u>companions</u> who provide many hours of <u>pleasure</u> for their masters.

The main idea of this paragraph is the first sentence, "A dog is a useful animal." The key words of each sentence clearly point to this idea.

Following are additional strategies that teachers and students may use to increase understanding and location of main ideas.

Activities

1. Ask questions such as the following: What is this sentence, paragraph, or selection about? What do most of the key words seem to point to? What words occur most frequently? What do these frequently occurring words relate to? What idea do most of the supporting details relate to? What sentence would best summarize the frequently occurring ideas?
2. Ask: Is the main idea stated or implied?
3. Ask: Where is the main idea located in the paragraph? At the beginning, in the middle, or at the end?
4. Ask: How is the main idea developed? By example, sequence, or comparison and contrast?
5. The student can be asked to read a paragraph and select the best statement of the main idea from multiple-choice items. An example follows.

   A mutation is a change in a gene, which is the part of the cell that determines the inherited characteristics of the offspring. The changed gene is then passed on to succeeding generations. Some mutations produce only a slight change in the offspring, while others produce more drastic changes.

   Underline the answer that tells the main idea of this paragraph. (a) How scientific discoveries are made (b) What a mutation is (c) What a gene is (d) How to produce drastic changes

6. Look for words and phrases such as *first, last, the most important factor, the significant fact.* Words and phrases like these often indicate the main idea.
7. The student can be asked to read a paragraph and to select from a list of questions the question that the paragraph answers. A list of questions that could be used with the paragraph in activity number 5 above follows.
   a. How can we cause mutations?
   b. What kinds of changes do mutations cause in offspring?
   c. What is a mutation?
   d. How often do mutations occur?

8. The teacher can provide blank diagrams in which the student can place main ideas and supporting details. Following are two examples: the first example is a blank diagram, while the second is a diagram as it would be developed for the paragraph in activity number 5.

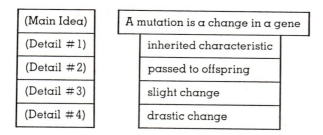

(Main Idea)	A mutation is a change in a gene
(Detail #1)	inherited characteristic
(Detail #2)	passed to offspring
(Detail #3)	slight change
(Detail #4)	drastic change

9. Students may create their own diagrams for main ideas and supporting details.

Teachers who are planning instruction on main ideas should use nonfiction for this purpose because nonfictional paragraphs are written to impart information. The student who is reading fiction for the purpose of locating main ideas may be confused by the style, plot, or moral of the story.

Details   Locating significant details enables the reader to identify main ideas. Recognizing details is an important part of the skill of identifying main ideas. Significant details are those that develop the main idea and contribute information regarding the main idea. Sometimes details are included that are interesting but do not develop the main idea. Following are some suggestions for teaching students to identify significant details.

Activities

1. Students may write down the details located in a paragraph and then categorize them as necessary and unnecessary. Following is a diagram which could be used in this exercise.

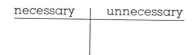

necessary | unnecessary

2. Present students with a paragraph with a detail included that does not belong in the paragraph. The students are to locate the misplaced detail. An example follows.
    Directions: Underline the sentence that is not related to the main idea.

An automobile is a useful vehicle. The owner of an automobile can travel to any place he wants at any time he wants. He or she can paint a house. He or she can go shopping in the automobile. The automobile is often used for business purposes, so it enables some people to earn a living. Automobiles come in many sizes and shapes. (The misplaced sentence is: "He or she can paint a house.")

3. Present students with a paragraph similar to the one above and a list of details. The students select the details that support the main idea. An example follows which is based on the paragraph in activity number 2.
Directions: Place an X beside each detail that supports the main idea in the paragraph.

    _____Owner can travel.
    _____Owner can go shopping.
    _____Owner can use automobile for business.
    _____Automobiles come in many sizes.
    _____They come in many shapes.

Paragraph structure The reader who successfully comprehends must adjust his or her thinking to the content of the selection being read. One of the factors to which a reader must adjust is the organization of paragraphs. Following are the most common types of paragraphs found in nonfiction writing.

1. *Introductory paragraphs*—These paragraphs are usually found at the beginning of selections and are useful for introducing a topic and giving a reader a focus for comprehending at a higher level. Introductory paragraphs give a preview of the ideas that will be presented, and they may indicate the way in which the author has organized the selection. In analyzing these paragraphs, the reader would ask him or herself questions like the following: "What do I expect this chapter will cover? How has the author probably organized the content of this chapter?" Following is an example of an introductory paragraph:

    What is reading comprehension? This is a very broad question that cannot be answered quickly or simply. This section will highlight certain salient features of the comprehension process, so that the student may better understand the process. However, any answer to such a broad question will necessarily be incomplete until better research tools become available to search out the secrets of the thinking process.

2. *Summary paragraph*—The summary paragraph is a paragraph that summarizes the ideas presented in a selection. This type of paragraph frequently occurs at the end of a chapter or at the end of a section of a long chapter. A summary paragraph may be used any place where it is useful to list information. Summary paragraphs by their nature present a concentrated collection of information; therefore, they should be read slowly and with concentration so the reader can remember the information for future reference. Following is an example of a summary paragraph:

To read means to understand. In order to read, the student must have intellectual skills that include thinking skills, language skills, and knowledge of concepts. The reader should also have certain affective skills or attitudes, values, and beliefs. These skills can either enhance or inhibit the reader's understanding. Understanding in reading is based on recognition of the author's use of style in writing, his or her way of organizing ideas, and his or her use of words, phrases, sentences, paragraphs, and selections.

3. *Main idea supported by details*—The first or last sentence in a paragraph is frequently the main idea while the other sentences in the paragraph present details that support the main idea. An example of this type of paragraph follows:

Reading enables the learner to acquire new knowledge independent of a teacher. Skill in reading enables the individual to keep up with world and local news. This skill also provides a source of entertainment for the individual. Reading is a practical skill that enables the reader to follow directions to bake a cake or to replace an electrical switch. Reading is one of the most important skills that an individual can acquire.

4. *Paragraphs of definition*—These paragraphs are developed to explain a concept or to define a term. They are usually important to the reader because they are the basis of future understanding. The reader should be alert for paragraphs of definition and note them for future reference since they are basic to understanding in many of the content areas, especially mathematics and science. An example follows:

A flexible skill group in a reading class is a temporary group of students gathered together for the purpose of learning and practicing a single reading skill. A word recognition skill or a comprehension skill might be the focus of such a group. The flexible skill group usually meets for fifteen or twenty minutes a day for two or three weeks. After the skill is learned the group is disbanded.

5. *Main idea developed by example*—In some paragraphs, the main idea is developed by example. The reader should be aware of this type of paragraph so that he or she may avoid the error that many readers make—confusing the examples with the author's main idea. The examples are used to clarify the main idea and to help prove the author's point. While reading these paragraphs one should ask oneself, "What is the big idea? What examples are used to verify the author's point?" The following is an example of a main idea paragraph developed by examples:

In the early days of the United States, reading was taught for the purpose of developing religious citizens. The Bible and the catechism were widely used for reading instruction. Other popular reading materials, such as *The New England Primer,* were composed of religious sayings such as "In Adam's fall we sinned all." The teachers in those days believed that reading religious content would develop religious citizens.

6. *Paragraphs of chronological order*—Paragraphs often present information in order of occurrence because this order clarifies the ideas presented. The reader should use the time relationship to organize the information presented for recall. The following is an example of a paragraph based upon chronological order.

The history of teaching reading in the United States is a rather long one, but it forms a circular pattern when one examines the methods used for reading instruction. The earliest method of teaching reading was the alphabetic method in which the student spelled a word and then said it. Phonics later became the accepted method through the McGuffey Readers and the Blue Back Spellers. Phonics held sway until the 1880's when the sight method was imported from Germany. The sight, or look-say, method gradually became accepted and was used almost exclusively in the United States until the early 1950's when parent and educator concern for reform of reading instruction caused publishers to move back to phonics as a basis for beginning reading instruction. This movement has gradually increased until phonics has become widely used in beginning reading instruction in the 1970's.

7. *Paragraphs of comparison and contrast*—Comparisons and contrasts can be used to clarify points that the author wishes to make. The reader should read with the following questions in mind: What is the author's main idea? What likenesses and differences does he use to illustrate his point? Students can make tables to list the likenesses and differences. Following is an example of a paragraph of comparison and contrast.

One of the main differences between beginning reading instruction with phonics and beginning reading instruction with sight words is that phonics proponents begin with the unit of sound while sight word proponents begin with the word as a unit. The phonics student memorizes sounds that serve as a basis for future learning. Sight word students quickly move into reading sentences and stories. Phonics students move more slowly at the outset, but after they learn the basic sound system of English, they move more quickly.

8. *Problem solving paragraphs*—In some paragraphs, the author states a problem for the reader and then suggests solutions for the problem. The reader of this type of paragraph should identify the problem the author has stated and the author's suggested solutions. The reader should keep in mind that the solutions are probably the author's opinions. The following questions should guide the reader: What problem is stated? Does the author present evidence that this problem exists? What solutions does the author present? Is there evidence to support the author's solutions? Following is an example of a problem solving paragraph:

Reading has become a major problem in the United States. Research indicates that young people cannot read well enough to obtain employment. Some adults cannot complete the forms necessary to obtain a driver's license, to obtain social security benefits, etc. The reading difficulties of this country could be solved if teachers were better prepared by the colleges and universities to solve the reading problems of students as they occur. If the reading difficulties were solved before they became too complex, many of the more severe reading difficulties could be prevented.

9. *Transitional paragraph*—The transitional paragraph often has one sentence that is inserted to draw the reader's attention to shifts in subject, point of view, or time. An example of a transitional paragraph follows:

Reading is a wonderful habit and can bring the habitual reader many benefits. One of the benefits of wide reading is a broad store of information. Another benefit is the opportunity to communicate with the best minds of all times.

Nevertheless, the inveterate reader has problems. One problem is that he or she may be more interested in reading than in talking with friends. Such a person may be unable to do other work because a book is calling to him or her.

Whole selections The paragraphs presented previously can be organized into selections that serve the same functions as the paragraphs. Well-written nonfiction starts with an introductory paragraph that begins with a broad general idea of the topic and narrows down to a specific point. The second section of a selection is usually the body, which develops the ideas introduced in section one. Each paragraph will usually have one main idea developed with supporting details. The paragraphs in the body may be developed by example, definition, chronological order, problem solving, or comparison and contrast. The selection is usually concluded by a summary paragraph that pulls together the ideas presented in the body of the selection. The diagram of a selection based upon this model is shown in Figure 6.1:

Figure 6.1   *Diagram of a selection*

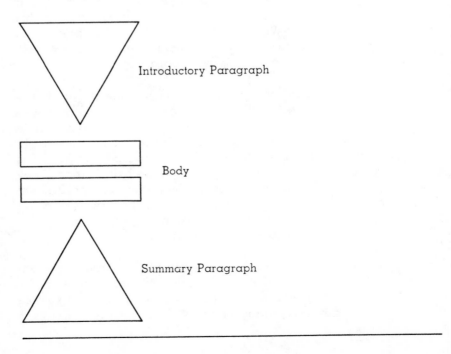

Introductory Paragraph

Body

Summary Paragraph

Activities for developing understanding of the organization of selections may include those given below:

1. Ask the students to find where the introduction of a selection is located, where the body is located, and where the summary is located.
2. Provide students with a reading selection that has been scrambled and ask them to put it into proper order.
3. Provide students with a selection that is missing an introduction or a summary and ask the students to write an appropriate introduction or summary.

A large part of reading comprehension is thinking about what one has read. Therefore, the teacher must stimulate student thinking in order to develop comprehension. Questions are one of the primary tools that teachers can use to encourage the development of thinking skills. Several factors contribute to the development of thinking skills.

Levels of thinking and questioning techniques

Readers must be able to concentrate completely on the content they are reading. If the reader's mind wanders while he or she is reading, he or she will be unable to understand the content.

The reader needs to understand what it means to demand meaning from reading. Some students are accustomed to reading words and do not realize that they must think about the ideas in the content. Teachers can help students concentrate on meaning as they read by asking them, "What is the author telling you?" Also teachers may ask students to verbalize aloud what they are thinking as they read. The outcome of this activity is similar to the analysis of reading in Example 6.1. This activity can indicate to the teacher weaknesses in each student's application of thinking skills to reading.

Another factor that influences comprehension is the availability of interesting, stimulating reading materials that reflect more than one point of view. Dull reading content does not stimulate thinking; in fact, it discourages thinking. Reading materials that provide only one point of view do not encourage students to examine and to think about ideas.

An important factor in developing thinking skills is providing an environment in which thinking can flourish. An environment that encourages thinking is created by a teacher who accepts student answers that differ from his or hers. Different points of view are tolerated in this environment. The teacher encourages students by accepting and clarifying student answers and by avoiding rejection of student answers. Often a teacher can help students think by asking "Why do you think that?" This kind of question stimulates a student to support and expand his or her answers. The thoughtful teacher also provides adequate time to think about answers to questions. When students are expected to answer questions too quickly, the quality of their answers may be lowered.

All questioning should be carefully planned so that teachers ask questions related to important ideas and concepts in the reading selection. Poorly chosen questions and questions that emphasize insignificant details are detrimental to the growth of thinking skills. For example, a question such as "What color was Mary's dress?" is an unimportant question that may prevent the reader from identifying the significant information in the selection. Teachers who are preparing to develop questions related to a reading selection should ask themselves the following questions:

1. What are the important ideas in this selection?
2. What ideas do I want the students to remember from this selection?
3. What thinking skills have the students in this group already developed?
4. What thinking skills do the students in this group need to develop?

Novice teachers or experienced teachers who are unsure of their questioning skills may wish to tape some of their lessons and classroom discussions in order to critique their questioning skills.

The teacher or student should develop purpose questions prior to reading a selection. After reading the selection, the answers to the purpose questions should be discussed. Purposes help focus students' thinking so that they understand and recall more information from reading. Reading that lacks purpose tends to be random and less meaningful. Purposes help the reader actively seek understanding. They can help students sort out important from unimportant information and to organize information.

Follow-up discussions improve understanding and encourage thinking because they allow students to see how others think about the selection. Rarely do two readers understand and react to a selection in exactly the same way. The sharing that occurs in a discussion of the selection increases student thinking.

A framework is presented below for developing thinking at four levels. The four levels of thinking are literal, interpretive, evaluative (critical), and creative.

Literal thinking This level is concerned with ideas that are directly stated in the selection. The reader should be concerned with the question "What did the author say?" or with what is stated in the lines of print. Literal comprehension includes indentification of and recall of main ideas and details. A thorough understanding of word meaning, sentence meaning, and paragraph meaning are necessary to thinking at the literal level. Questions at this level can be answered by quoting the content. The literal level of comprehension is the basic level and the level on which the other levels of comprehension depend.

Researchers have found that the literal level of understanding is surprisingly difficult for readers. William Perry[4] asked the freshmen at Harvard University to write a brief statement about what they had read in a chapter and found that only one student in 100 could achieve this literal level of reading. Amelia Melnik[5] studied ways to improve the reading of social studies material by junior high school students, and found that students believed that the question "What did the author say?" helped them the most in understanding what they read.

The main types of literal level thinking are: recognizing and recalling main ideas, recognizing and recalling details, recognizing and recalling sequence, following directions, and recognizing cause and effect. Literal level questions can be as varied as the content on which they are based.

Below, questions are suggested related to each level of thinking. They are based on a story entitled, "A New England Nun."[6] This is the story of a young woman who was engaged for fourteen years to the same man. After waiting all those years for her fiancé, she decided to break the engagement just before the wedding.

> *Literal level questions:*
> What activities gave Louisa pleasure?
> How would you describe Joe in a short paragraph?
> Who was the "New England Nun"?
> What events led to the broken engagement?

Activities such as the following can be used to increase literal understandings.

Activities

Main idea:
1. Have students read a paragraph and select the best statement of the main idea from multiple choice items.
2. Provide students with short newspaper articles in which they are to locate the main ideas.

Details:
3. Provide a paragraph that includes a number of details and ask students to list the details found in the paragraph.

---

4. William G. Perry, "Students Use and Misuse of Reading Skills: A Report of the Faculty," in Amelia Melnik and John Merritt, eds. *Reading Today and Tomorrow* (London: University of London Press, 1972), pp. 374, 372.
5. Amelia Melnik, "The Improvement of Reading Through Self-Appraisal." (New York: Columbia University, Teachers College, Unpublished doctoral dissertation, 1960), pp. 40–46.
6. Mary Wilkins Freeman, "A New England Nun," in *Where We Live* (New York: Scholastic Book Services, 1976), pp. 111–20.

Sequence:

4. Provide the students with comic strips that have been cut apart and ask them to put the comic strip in sequential order.

5. Give the students a baking mix and ask them to number, in order, the steps required to make the product. This activity can be done with directions for models of airplanes and other construction projects.

6. Provide the students with a paragraph that includes a number of activities and ask the students to put the activities in the order of occurrence. An example follows.

John had an accident as he was coming home from school. Prior to the accident he had stopped at the Red Barn for a hamburger. He had driven to school that day because he had to take his sister to the doctor's office on the way to school.

List the events in this paragraph in the order of occurrence.
   a. John took his sister to the doctor.
   b. John went to school.
   c. After school John stopped at the Red Barn for a hamburger.
   d. John had an accident.

Directions:

7. Orally direct students to draw a figure. They may check their skill at following directions by looking at the figure. For example:

Draw a vertical line ½ inch long in the middle of a piece of paper. Draw a horizontal line ½ inch wide through the middle of the vertical line.

8. For a physical education class, write a set of directions for doing a particular exercise. Give the written directions to the students to read, and then have them perform the exercise. An example follows:

Place your hands on your hips. Bend forward from the waist as far as possible. Make your torso bounce three times, pivoting at the waist. Return to an upright position. (Note the need for understanding of vocabulary terms such as *torso* and *upright*.)

Cause and Effect

9. Have students read a paragraph that contains a cause and effect relationship. State the cause of the action and have them identify the effect. Example:

    John eluded the defensive back and turned to catch the ball. The field between him and the goal was clear. "Touchdown coming up!" he thought. As the ball reached him, he took his eye off it to plan his touchdown scamper. During that instant the ball struck his chest and bounced away. "I blew it because I took my eye off the ball," John groaned.
    Question: What was the effect of John's taking his eye off of the ball?

10. Use the paragraph in activity 9 above, but state the effect and have the students identify the cause. Ask the question, "What caused John to drop the ball?"

Interpretive thinking This level is also called inferential thinking and is concerned with deeper meanings. The reader should seek to understand what the author means by the words he or she has written. This requires reading between the lines. Readers must arrive at understandings that are not stated in the text. They should synthesize information from their experience with information from reading content. The main types of inferential thinking are: recognizing the author's purpose, drawing conclusions, making generalizations, predicting outcomes, and understanding figurative language. (See Chapter 5, pages 138–39). Inferential questions do not always have right and wrong answers. The teacher should be more concerned with the logical thinking processes used by the student to arrive at a synthesis of ideas. The student should be able to support and explain his answers.

Interpretive questions based on "A New England Nun" follow:

Why do you think this story is called "A New England Nun" when it is about an engaged woman?
What caused the broken engagement?
What was the result of the broken engagement for Joe, for Lilly, and for Louisa?
Why did the author tell the reader about Caesar in such detail?

Activities such as the following may be used to develop interpretive thinking.

Activities *Author's purpose:* Writers always have some purpose for writing. They may intend to inform, to entertain, to persuade, or to fulfill some other function.

1. Have students read materials such as the following and decide what purpose the author had for writing *Kon-Tiki* by Thor Heyerdahl, *Cheaper by the Dozen* by Frank Bunker Gilbreth, or "Vote for John Smith—the People's Choice."

Drawing Conclusions: A reader must take in data and put together various clues in order to draw conclusions.

2. Give students pieces of paper describing a situation that they are to pantomime for the class to guess. For example, act out "I lost my library book." The class members must draw a conclusion about what is happening.

Making Generalizations: A generalization is a statement of a relationship between two concepts; this relationship is a broad one.[8] For example, "*all living things need food to survive*" is a generalization.

3. Ask the following two generalization questions from the area of social studies:
    a. Why do cities develop near large bodies of water?
    b. Why are new energy sources necessary for the future of the world?

Making Predictions: To make predictions, students must put together the pieces of information available and note trends. They must then project these trends into the future, deciding what events might logically follow the known ones.

4. Ask students to read the introduction to a story or selection and to anticipate what will occur in the selection.
5. Use preview guides as described on pages 145–46 of this chapter.

Evaluative thinking or **critical thinking** This is the third level of thinking. Critical reading requires that the reader make judgments about the quality, value, and validity of the content he is reading. It depends upon the ability to read well at the literal and interpretive levels. The critical reader must be able to recognize the author's purpose and the author's point of view. He must be able to distinguish fact from opinion. The reader should test the author's assertions against his own observations, information, and logic. In order to read critically, the reader must begin with an understanding of what the author is saying. He cannot read critically if he cannot grasp the author's ideas.

The critical reader should be logical and objective in evaluating content, suspending judgment while gathering the necessary data on

---

8. Arnold A. Griese, *Do You Read Me? Practical Approaches to Teaching Reading Comprehension* (Santa Monica, Calif.: Goodyear Publishing Co., 1977), p. 170.

which to base an evaluation. Suspending judgment requires that the reader avoid jumping to conclusions. The critical reader must have background experience that provides a basis for making judgments. The critical reading task should be approached with an open-minded problem-solving attitude. The critical reader should constantly ask questions about the material he is reading.

Critical reading questions based on "A New England Nun" follow:

1. Does this story portray an accurate picture of life in the late 1800's?
2. What was the real reason Louisa broke the engagement?
3. What would you have done if you were Louisa?
4. How would you have felt about the broken engagement if you were Joe?

Willavene Wolf et al.[9] have grouped critical reading skills required by nonfiction materials into three general categories: semantics, logic, and authenticity. Semantics skills include understanding the denotative and connotative uses of words, the use of vague and precise words, and the use of words in a persuasive manner. Logic skills include understanding the reliability of the author's argument, understanding the reliability of the author's statements, recognizing the use of propaganda, discriminating fact from opinion, and recognizing the various forms of persuasive writing. Authenticity skills include determining if adequate information is included, comparing this information to other relevant information, examining the author's qualifications, and using authoritative sources. Teaching suggestions for these areas are given below.

Semantics:

1. Refer to Chapter 5 for a discussion of connotative and denotative uses of words.
2. Students should be made aware that authors use "loaded" words to influence their readers. For example, many readers have unpleasant reactions to the words *un-American*, *communist*, and *radical* while reacting favorably to words like *freedom*, *peace*, and *human rights*. Ask students to find examples of the use of "loaded" words in newspapers, magazines, and textbooks.
3. Some words are used in very vague, general ways and the critical reader should be alert for these so as not to be influenced by them. (For example, the expressions "everyone is doing it" and "they say.") Examples of vague uses of words should be located by students.

---

9. Willavene Wolf, Charlotte S. Huck, and Martha L. King, *The Critical Reading Ability of Elementary School Children* (Columbus, Ohio: Ohio State University Research Foundation, 1967), pp. 20–21. (Project No. 5-1040 supported by the U.S. Office of Education.)

Logic:

1. Have students create syllogisms that state an author's premises and conclusions. The following example is based on a chapter from a social studies textbook.
    Premises:
    People with undesirable characteristics are rejected. Some "new" immigrants had undesirable characteristics.
    Conclusion:
    The "new" immigrants were rejected.
2. Have students verify the facts found in local newspaper stories.
3. Although authors may not state whether they are giving facts or opinions, sometimes there are indicators of opinions, such as the following qualifying words: *think, probably, maybe, appear, seem, believe, could,* and *should.* Have students examine sentences with the purpose of locating "opinion words." The following sentences might be used.
    a. I believe this is the best cake I have ever eaten.
    b. This symptom could mean that you are getting the flu.
    c. Jane will probably come home for vacation.
4. Drawing a diagram of the facts and opinions presented by an author will help the reader examine ideas critically. The following diagram is based upon information taken from a social studies textbook.

Facts	*Opinions*
"old" immigrants from British Isles, Germany, Scandinavia	"old" immigrants acceptable
"new" immigrants from Slavic Countries, Italy, Greece	"new" immigrants unacceptable, ignorant, greedy, diseased, criminals, insane, long-haired, wild-eyed, bad smelling

5. Recognizing propaganda is one of the logical skills required by critical readers. The following is a discussion of propaganda techniques and techniques for analyzing propaganda.
    a. *Bad names*—Disagreeable words are used to arouse distaste for a person or a thing. An example of bad names propaganda is an advertisement for weight reduction headlined with "Why be fat?"
    b. *Glad names*—This device is the opposite of bad names. Pleasant words are used to create good feelings about a

person or a thing. For example, a face cream advertisement claims that it will make your skin as "smooth as velvet."

c. *Plain Folks*—This kind of propaganda makes an effort to avoid artificiality and sophistication. Political candidates use this technique when they shake hands, kiss babies, and play with dogs. They are trying to appear like the "man next door."

d. *Transfer*—This type of propaganda attempts to transfer the reader's respect for the flag, the cross, or some other universal symbol to a person or thing. The flag is sometimes pictured in the background of an advertisement to achieve this type of effect.

e. *Testimonial*—This technique is like transfer except that a famous person gives a testimonial for a product or a person. Positive feelings for the person are supposed to be transferred to the product. For example, a famous actor may appear on television on behalf of a political candidate. Another example of a testimonial is in the advertising that features a famous athlete who claims to shave with a certain brand of razor blade.

f. *Bandwagon*—This type of propaganda is an attempt to convince the reader that he or she should accept an idea or purchase an item because "everyone is doing it." It is the kind of thinking behind a slogan such as "twenty million people can't be wrong."

g. *Card stacking*—This technique utilizes accurate information, but generally there is information omitted so that only one side of a story is told. For example, a cigarette may be advertised as smooth tasting and long lasting, but the bad effects of smoking are not mentioned.[10]

These propaganda techniques rarely occur in isolation. Many advertisements include a combination of two or more types of propaganda.

After learning to identify propaganda techniques the reader should analyze the propaganda with the following questions:

1. What technique is used?
2. Who composed the propaganda?
3. Why was the propaganda written?
4. To what reader interests, emotions, and prejudices does the propaganda appeal?
5. Will I allow myself to be influenced by this propaganda?

---

10. Nila B. Smith, *Reading Instruction for Today's Children* (Englewood Cliffs, N.J.: Prentice Hall, 1963), p 274

Authenticity

1. The writer's conclusions should be based upon adequate information. At times, the reader must seek additional data before he can evaluate the validity of an author's writing. Students can be given an article and told to check other sources of information on the topic to evaluate the validity of the information given.
2. The students can also be asked to evaluate the author's qualifications for writing on the topic at hand. Possible question items include:
    a. Would a lawyer be a qualified author for a book on writing contracts?
    b. Would a football player be a qualified author for a book on foreign policy?
    c. Would a chef be a qualified author for a book on menu-planning?
    d. Would a physician be a qualified author for a book on music theory?

Creative thinking. This is similar to critical thinking because it is thinking beyond the lines of print. However, creative reading serves a different function than critical reading. Creative reading is a deliberate effort to go beyond the information read to find new ways of viewing ideas, incidents, or characters that may stimulate novel thinking and production. Creative thinking occurs after the reader has read and understood a selection. The resulting productivity may take the form of a new idea, a new story, a design, a painting, an improved product or method, or an invention.

A creative thinker may be able to come up with several ways of solving a math problem or several approaches to an experiment in science class. A creative thinker may be able to turn a situation from a literature selection into a puppet show, a skit, a painting, or a piece of sculpture. He or she may be able to make a table in wood shop that has special useful features that no one else has considered or develop a recipe in home economics that surpasses those suggested in the book. To do these things, a creative thinker must put together things already known in new forms. Creativity is stifled if all school activities must be carried out according to the precise specifications of the teacher and if deviations from prescribed forms are invariably punished, rather than rewarded for inventiveness.

Creative thinking can be encouraged through using stimulating content and questions. Creative activities related to "A New England Nun" could take the following forms:

1. Write a new ending in which Louisa does not break the engagement.

2. Paint, draw, sketch, or model the way you visualize Louise's home.
3. Rewrite this story setting it in modern times.
4. Reread the introduction to the story. Analyze how history would have changed if more early pioneers had been timid.

Helping students question The Reciprocal Questioning (ReQuest) procedure, developed by Anthony V. Manzo, seems a promising way of improving reading comprehension as well as of helping students develop questioning techniques. ReQuest is a one-to-one teaching technique that helps students think critically and formulate questions. A condensed outline of the procedure is given below:

1. Both student and teacher have copies of a selection to be read.
2. Both silently read the first sentence of the selection. The student then asks the teacher as many questions as he or she wishes about that sentence. The student is told to try to ask the kind of questions that the teacher might ask, in the way the teacher might ask them.
3. The teacher answers the questions, requiring the student to rephrase those questions that cannot be answered because of poor syntax or incorrect logic.
4. After all the student's questions have been answered, the second sentence is read, and the teacher asks as many questions as he or she feels will profitably add to the student's understanding of the content.
5. The teacher periodically requires that the student verify his or her responses.
6. After reading the second sentence, the teacher requires integration of the ideas from both sentences.[11]

All through the interaction, the student is constantly encouraged to imitate the teacher's questioning behavior. The teacher reinforces such behavior by saying, "That's a good question," or by giving the fullest possible reply. This procedure continues until the student can read all the words in the first paragraph, can demonstrate literal understanding of what has been read, and can formulate a reasonable purpose for completing the remainder of the selection.

Affective or emotional factors are important to reading comprehension. Ruth Strang[12] studied adult readers and found that "in the majority of **Affective dimension**

---

11. Anthony V. Manzo, The ReQuest Procedure", *Journal of Reading* 13 (November 1969): 123 26.
12. Ruth Strang, *Explorations in Reading Patterns* (Chicago: University of Chicago Press, 1942), p. 6.

cases the freely written responses to reading selections were colored by the reader's prejudices and personal experiences." The reader's understanding of a passage depends to a large extent on the feelings he or she brings to the passage. A reader's emotional responses to reading content are related to his or her interests, attitudes, values, and feelings. Readers tend to read and understand best that content which reflects values and beliefs that are congruent with their own, while they have difficulty grasping views that contradict their own.

The affective dimension of comprehension is developed through a variety of materials. Students should read content that develops different points of view regarding current events, famous people, and ideas so that students are led to recognize that a variety of attitudes and values exist. Readers should examine the various points of view carefully in order to fully understand what they are reading.

Discussion is a good vehicle for developing and stimulating affective reactions of students. Questions such as the following might be used: How would you feel if you were in Mary's place? Why? Would you like to have Mary as your best friend? Why? or Why not? Questions can help the students clarify their values and attitudes. The teacher can ask students to validate and support their answers. This causes them to critically examine their attitudes.

Paying attention is an aspect of the affective area of comprehension. It is a prerequisite to comprehending and reacting to a message; to be precise, comprehension is impossible without attention. Selective attention is a directing process that focuses the individual toward the materials to be comprehended. Although attention is necessary, it is not sufficient for comprehension because the reader must have enough interest to sustain attention. Selective attention enables the reader to screen out irrelevant information and to concentrate on understanding. Selective attention causes the reader to process dates as important information when reading historical material and to process experiments as important information when reading physics.

Motivation is another factor related to the affective area of comprehension. Motivation causes the reader to focus attention and to seek understanding from reading. The reader may be motivated to read for scholastic success, for self-actualization, for curiosity, to solve problems, or for a variety of reasons. Motivation helps sustain the reader who has to read materials that are not interesting to him or her. For example, the student may read *The Decline and Fall of the Roman Empire* in order to achieve a good grade in history, but might not select this book to read without the motivation of grades.

Visualization

Visualization refers to forming mental images of the content one is reading. The reader should be able to translate words into mental images so he or she can comprehend. For example, the reader should be able to form mental images of story settings, characters, story action, geographic areas in social studies, famous historical figures, scientific experiments, and steps in mathematical problems. Visual images help the reader understand and remember what has been read.

Discussion of the language the author uses to create images and the images evoked by those words helps students concentrate on creating images. Activities that require students to picture specific scenes or persons will help them learn to visualize. For example, students can be asked to visualize their favorite places or their favorite persons. All of the activities suggested for creative comprehension help increase visualizing skill.

Flexibility in reading is necessary for good comprehension. Flexible readers adjust their rate, thinking, and approaches according to the material they are reading. Good readers are so accustomed to reading flexibly that they are not aware of the many adjustments they make as they read. They simply adjust their reading processes automatically as they move through reading material. A single page may require several adjustments on the part of the reader.   **Flexibility**

One aspect of flexibility is selecting the important ideas from among the unimportant ideas. The flexible reader reads important ideas carefully and tries to retain these ideas. This reader seeks the essence of meaning contained in material. He or she does not give each word and each phrase or even each paragraph equal attention, but selects those words, phrases, and paragraphs significant to understanding the selection. He or she reads for main ideas.

Flexibility is especially required by materials that contain a high density of facts. The reader's approach to materials containing concentrated quantities of information must be different from his or her approach to materials containing very few facts. The reader must be flexible, reading and rereading content until the desired understanding is acquired.

The competent reader reads with a flexible rate. Reading rate is governed by several factors: familiarity with the topic, the type of content, and the purpose for reading the material.

The reader's personal familiarity with the topic determines whether he or she will read rapidly, slowly, or somewhere between the two. Familiarity with a topic allows the reader to anticipate ideas, vocabulary, and phrasing used by the author so he or she can move rapidly through the material. Lack of familiarity forces the reader to read more slowly in order to understand.

The types of content read also govern rate of reading. The vocabulary burden, the number of abstract ideas, and the author's style are important factors in content that relate to how rapidly the reader can read content. Newspapers and magazines can be read more rapidly than a textbook. A novel will generally be read more rapidly than an informational book. Theoretical scientific content or statistics must be read more slowly than social studies content. Generally, mathematics is read most slowly, science is read a little more rapidly than mathematics, social science is read more rapidly than science, literature more rapidly than social science, and newspapers are read most rapidly of all.

A third factor governing rate is the reader's purpose for reading. The reader who is skimming a chapter to get a general idea of the topic will read more rapidly than the student who is studying for a final examination. The type of questions for which the student is studying should regulate the rate of reading also. Preparation for detailed factual questions requires slower reading than studying for broader, more general questions.

The flexible reader is one who is aware of those characteristics of content and of the personal characteristics that influence reading efficiency. Flexibility of reading includes a cluster of skills that are very important for good comprehension.

Concluding comments

Teachers can help students comprehend by planning specific steps designed to increase comprehension. Following are some steps which aid student comprehension:

1. Relate a topic to student experience. If the student does not have related experience, build experience through films, pictures, etc. Use experience to build interest and motivation.
2. Anticipate and preteach difficult vocabulary.
3. Anticipate and preteach concepts that students will need.
4. Help students develop purposes for reading. Use questions that focus on important information and thinking skills. Guide students to adjust rate to their purposes.
5. Have follow-up discussions based upon questions that increase student thinking and concepts. The teacher should clarify questions and concepts as needed.
6. Plan for specific comprehension skill instruction.
7. Use open-book discussions frequently. Have students refer to the book to support answers.
8. Have students reread if necessary.
9. Frequently have students paraphrase what they have read.

The check list of comprehension skills in Example 6.3 could be used by teachers for evaluating and monitoring the comprehension development of their students.

Example 6.3

A checklist of basic comprehension skills

Experience
1. Has a variety of real experience
2. Has a variety of experience from:
    a. reading
    b. movies
    c. television
3. Labels experience
4. Relates experience to reading

Thinking Skills
5. Understands author's organization of main ideas and details
6. Understands organization of paragraphs
7. Understands literal level
    a. Identifies main ideas
    b. Identifies supporting details
    c. Recalls sequence
    d. Follows directions
    e. Recognizes cause and effect
8. Understands interpretive level
    a. Predicts outcomes
    b. Draws conclusions
    c. Makes generalizations
    d. Recognizes author's purpose
    e. Understands figurative language
    f. Supports and explains answers
9. Understands evaluative level
    a. Alert to author's choice and use of words
    b. Suspends judgment
    c. Recognizes fact and opinion
    d. Follows author's logic
    e. Recognizes propaganda techniques
    f. Evaluates propaganda
    g. Evaluates author qualifications
    h. Evaluates validity of content
    i. Uses knowledge and experience to think critically
    j. Evaluates author's support for generalizations and conclusions
10. Understands creative level
    a. Responds to reading content in novel ways
    b. Develops creative productions related to reading
    c. Reads to solve problems

Affective Dimensions
11. Expects content to make sense
12. Reads with an open mind

Example 6.3 (cont.)

13. Is not excessively influenced by prejudices
14. Can understand the values of others without changing his or her own
15. Has wide interests
16. Is usually motivated to read
17. Recognizes the effect of emotions and prejudices on understanding

Visualization
18. Translates content into visual images

Flexibility of Reading
19. Selects important ideas from among the unimportant ideas
20. Rereads when density of facts presented dictates the need
21. Adjusts rate according to purpose
22. Adjusts rate according to type of material
23. Adjusts rate according to familiarity with topic

Self-test

1. Why is teaching reading comprehension a challenge? (a) Students do not like to comprehend. (b) The actual process cannot be observed. (c) Most authorities think comprehension is unimportant. (d) Teachers think it is a challenge.
2. How can a preview guide help the reader? (a) It helps one relate one's experience to the reading content. (b) It makes the pictures easier to understand. (c) It makes reading some parts of the material unnecessary. (d) It tells him what pages to read.
3. What is the purpose of the structured overview in developing readiness for reading? (a) It helps the reader understand syntax. (b) It helps the reader fit his experience into a conceptual framework. (c) It structures the entire book for the student. (d) It helps the student recognize likenesses and differences.
4. What type of meaning is understood at the interpretive level? (a) The meaning stated in the content. (b) Evaluation of ideas read (c) Meanings that are not stated in the text. (d) Applying ideas in new situations.
5. What level of thinking is recognizing main ideas? (a) Literal (b) Interpretive (c) Evaluative (d) Creative.
6. What level of thinking is making generalizations? (a) Literal (b) Interpretive (c) Evaluative (d) Creative.
7. What is one of the aspects of organization to which the reader must adjust? (a) Semantics (b) Concepts (c) Paragraph structure (d) Phonics.
8. Why do purposes for reading improve comprehension? (a) They are interesting. (b) They speed up reading. (c) They cause students to share ideas. (d) They focus the reader's thinking.

9. What levels of thinking were presented in this chapter? (a) Literal, chaining, critical (b) Literal, translation evaluation, creative (c) Literal, interpretive, evaluative, creative (d) Literal, analytic, interpretive, creative.

10. "What did the author say?" is a good question at what level of thinking? (a) Literal level (b) Inferential level (c) Critical level (d) Creative level.

11. At what level of thinking is propaganda important? (a) Literal (b) Interpretive (c) Critical (d) Creative.

12. Why should teachers allow students time to think? (a) It makes the student think. (b) It enables students to answer questions better. (c) It is the polite thing to do. (d) It provides students with a break from the work routine.

13. Which of the following does the flexible reader use to govern his rate? (a) Familiarity with the subject (b) Purpose for reading (c) The type of content (d) All of the above.

14. What kind of ideas should flexible readers look for? (a) Insignificant ideas (b) All ideas (c) Important ideas (d) None of these.

1. Read an article in the local newspaper and write down all of the thinking processes that you use to understand what you are reading.

2. Read a chapter in a book of your choice and write a question at each level of thinking related to the chapter. Share your questions with your classmates.

3. Read a current best seller and write a brief paragraph that paraphrases the book. Have a classmate who has read the same book analyze your comprehension of it.

* 4. Use the comprehension plan on page 168 and plan a comprehension lesson for a textbook selection. Use the lesson in a secondary classroom.

* 5. Use the checklist in Example 6.3 to observe the reading comprehension of two pupils. After completing the observations write a brief comparison and contrast of the students' skills.

6. Examine a selection in a content textbook and make a list of comprehension skills that could best be taught with this selection.

* 7. Visit a secondary classroom for the purpose of watching questioning procedures. What level of questions was most used? How much time were the students allowed for formulating answers?

8. Find examples of paragraphs in content area textbooks that follow organizational patterns illustrated in this chapter. Bring them to class to share and discuss with peers.

Enrichment activities

---

* These activities are designed for inservice teachers, student teachers, or practicum students.

9. Demonstrate with a peer the procedures of the Manzo ReQuest method described in this chapter.
10. Discuss this statement: Flexibility in reading is more than rate adjustment.
11. Use the "key word" idea to analyze several paragraphs in a content area textbook.

Selected references

Altick, Richard. *Preface to Critical Reading.* New York: Holt, Rinehart and Winston, 1960.

Boercker, Marguerite. *What Every Single Teacher Should Know About Language.* Clarksville, Tenn.: Queen City Publishers, 1975. Chapters 3 and 5.

Chapman, Carita. "Teaching Comprehension to the Disabled." *Journal of Reading* 20 (October 1976):37–42.

Davis, Frederick B. "Psychometric Research on Comprehension in Reading." *Reading Research Quarterly* 7 (Summer 1972):628–78.

Dawson, Mildred A., ed. *Developing Comprehension, Including Critical Reading.* Newark, Del.: International Reading Association, 1967.

Dillner, Martha A. and Joanne P. Olson. *Personalizing Reading Instruction in Middle, Junior, and Senior High Schools: Utilizing a Competency Based Instructional System.* New York: Macmillan Co., 1977. Chapters 3 and 10.

Goodman, Kenneth. "Reading: A Psycholinguistic Guessing Game." *Journal of the Reading Specialist* (May 1967):171–258.

Goodman, Kenneth S., ed. *Miscue Analysis: Applications to Reading Instruction.* Urbana, Ill.: National Council of Teachers of English, 1976.

Gray, William S. and Bernice Rogers. *Maturity in Reading: Its Nature and Appraisal.* Chicago: University of Chicago Press, 1956.

Griese, Arnold A. *Do You Read Me? Practical Approaches to Teaching Reading Comprehension.* Santa Monica, Calif.: Goodyear Publishing Company, 1977.

Hafner, Lawrence E. *Developmental Reading in Middle and Secondary Schools.* New York: Macmillan Co., 1977. Chapter 6.

Harker, W. John. *Classroom Strategies for Secondary Reading.* Newark, Del.: International Reading Association, 1977.

Herber, Harold L. and Joan B. Nelson. "Questioning Is Not the Answer." *Journal of Reading* 18 (April 1975):512–17.

Ives, Sumner. "Some Notes on Syntax and Meaning." *The Reading Teacher* (December, 1964):179–83.

King, Martha L., Bernice D. Ellinger, and Willavene Wolf, eds. *Critical Reading.* Philadelphia: J. B. Lippincott, 1967.

Lefevre, Carl A. *Linguistics and the Teaching of Reading.* New York: McGraw Hill, 1964.

Rankin, Earl F. *The Measurement of Reading Flexibility.* Newark, Del.: International Reading Association, 1974.

Robinson, H. Alan. *Teaching Reading and Study Strategies.* Boston: Allyn and Bacon, 1975. Chapter 3.

Robinson, Helen M., ed. *Sequential Development of Reading Abilities.* Chicago: University of Chicago Press, 1960.

Sanders, Norris. *Classroom Questions. What Kinds?* New York: Harper & Row, 1966.

Singer, Harry and Robert Ruddell. *Theoretical Models and Processes of Reading.* 2nd ed. Newark, Del.: International Reading Association, 1976.

Smith, Frank. *Comprehension and Learning.* New York: Holt, Rinehart and Winston, 1975.

Thomas, Ellen Lamar and H. Alan Robinson. *Improving Reading in Every Class.* 2nd ed. Boston: Allyn and Bacon, 1977.

Thorndike, Robert L. *Reading Comprehension Education in Fifteen Countries.* International Studies in Evaluation III. New York: John Wiley, 1973.

7  Reading-study skills

In this chapter consideration is given to development of more skills that enhance comprehension and retention of information contained in printed material. These skills are important in helping a student manage reading assignments in content area classes.

Study methods, such as SQ3R, EVOKER, SQRQCQ, and REAP, are described, and their usefulness in different subject areas is discussed. Attention is given to the organizational skills of outlining and summarizing and to location skills related to use of the library and use of books.

Techniques of developing report-writing skills are considered, and ways of helping students learn to read to follow directions are suggested. Consideration is given to helping students learn from the graphic aids (maps, graphs, tables, diagrams, and pictures) in their content area reading materials, as well as to helping students learn to adjust reading rate to fit their purpose and the material to be read. Two final topics of discussion are retention and test-taking.

Purpose-setting questions

As you read this chapter, try to answer these questions:

1. What are some study methods designed for use with content area reading selections?
2. What organizational skills are helpful to students who are reading material to be used later in some manner?
3. What location skills do secondary school students need in order to use the library? To use books?
4. How can a teacher prepare students for writing reports in content area classes?
5. How can you teach students to read to follow directions accurately?
6. What are the types of graphic aids found in textbooks?
7. What are some factors to consider in instruction related to reading rate?

8.   What are some suggestions that can help students retain what they read?

9.   How can teachers help students read tests with understanding?

As you read this chapter, check your understanding of these terms: **Key vocabulary**

PQRST	longitude
SQ3R	map projections
EVOKER	picture graphs (pictographs)
SQRQCQ	circle or pie graphs
REAP	bar graphs
PANORAMA	line graphs
guide words	controlled reading projectors
cross references	tachistoscopes
map legend	pacers
map scale	skimmers
graphic aids	skimming
latitude	scanning

Study methods

Many methods of approaching study-reading have been developed. The one that is probably best known and most widely used, especially for social studies and science selections, is the SQ3R method,[1] developed by Francis Robinson. The steps in the SQ3R Method are Survey, Question, Read, Recite, Review. Many of the other methods, such as PQRST,[2] are very similar to SQ3R. The steps in the PQRST method are Preview, Question, Read, Summarize, Test. Spache suggests using the PQRST procedure when reading science material, but the steps in PQRST so closely approximate the steps in SQ3R that it seems much less complicated to use SQ3R for both social studies and science materials. A study method that has been especially developed by Walter Pauk for use with prose, poetry, and drama is the EVOKER procedure.[3] EVOKER stands for Explore, Vocabulary, Oral reading, Key ideas, Evaluation, and Recapitulation. Since mathematics materials present special problems to readers, a special technique for studying mathematics has also been developed. This technique is called SQRQCQ.[4] The steps in SQRQCQ are Survey, Question, Read,

---

1. Francis P. Robinson, *Effective Study*, rev. ed. (New York: Harper & Row, 1961), chapter 2.
2. George Spache, *Toward Better Reading* (Champaign, Ill.: Garrard 1963), p. 94.
3. Walter Pauk, "On Scholarship: Advice to High School Students," *The Reading Teacher* 17 (November 1963:73 78.
4. Leo Fay, "Reading Study Skills: Math and Science," in *Reading and Inquiry*, J. Allen Figurel, ed., (Newark, Del.: International Reading Association, 1965), pp. 93–94.

Question, Compute, Question. Each of these methods will be considered in turn, as will two other general study methods, REAP[5] and PANORAMA.[6] The steps in the REAP strategy are Read, Encode, Annotate, and Ponder, whereas the steps in the PANORAMA technique are Purpose, Adapting rate to material, Need to pose questions, Overview, Read and relate, Annotate, Memorize, Assess.

SQ3R   When SQ3R is applied to a content area reading selection, a variety of reading activities must be employed. These activities are discussed below.

Survey   During the survey step, the reader reads the chapter title, the introductory paragraph(s), the bold-face and/or italicized headings, and the summary paragraph(s). The reader should at this time also inspect any graphic aids, such as maps, graphs, tables, diagrams, and pictures. This survey provides the reader with an overview of the material contained in the reading assignment and a framework into which the facts contained in the selection can be organized as the student progresses through the reading.

Question   During this step the reader is expected to formulate questions that he or she expects to find answered in the selection to be studied. The author may have provided purpose questions at the beginning of the chapter or follow-up questions at the end of the chapter. If so, the student may utilize these questions as purpose questions for the reading If not, the reader can turn the section headings into questions and read to answer self-constructed questions.

Read   This is the step in which the student reads to answer the questions formulated in the previous step. The reading will be purposeful because the student has purpose questions in mind. Notes may be taken during this careful reading.

Recite   In this step the student tries to answer the purpose questions formulated during the second step without referring to the book or any notes that were made.

Review   At this point the student reviews the material by rereading portions of the book or notes taken during the careful reading in order to verify the answers given during the previous step.

---

5 Marilyn G. Eanet and Anthony V. Manzo, "REAP—A Strategy for Improving Reading Writing/Study Skills," *Journal of Reading* 19 (May 1976) 647–52.

6. Peter Edwards, "Panorama: A Study Technique," *Journal of Reading* 17 (November 1973):132–35.

This procedure should be applied when reading prose, poetry, and drama. It is a method for "close reading." The steps are as follows: **EVOKER**

Explore Read the entire selection silently to gain a feeling for the overall message.

Vocabulary Note key words. Look up those words with which you are not familiar. Also look up unfamiliar places, events, and people mentioned in the selection.

Oral Reading Read the selection orally with good expression.

Key ideas Locate key ideas in order to help you understand the author's organization. Be sure to determine the main idea or theme of the selection.

Evaluation Evaluate the key words and sentences in respect to their contributions to developing key ideas and the main idea.

Recapitulation Reread the selection.

This study method is suggested for use with statement problems in mathematics. The steps are briefly discussed below.   **SQRQCQ**

Survey The student reads the problem rapidly in order to obtain an idea of its general nature.

Question In this step, the student determines the specific nature of the problem. Ask: What is being asked in the problem?

Read. The student reads the problem carefully, paying attention to specific details and relationships.

Question At this point, the student must make a decision about the mathematical operations to be carried out and, in some cases, the order in which these operations are to be performed. The student asks what operations must be performed and in what order.

Compute The student does the computation or computations decided upon in the previous step.

Question The student checks the entire process and decides whether or not the answer seems to be correct. He or she asks if the answer is reasonable and if the computations have been accurately performed.

REAP   This study technique encourages students to demand meaning from the reading because it requires an overt response. Not only reading skills but also thinking and writing skills, are sharpened by the use of this approach. The four steps of the technique are described below:

Read   The student reads to find out what the writer is saying.

Encode   The writer's message is translated by the student into his or her own language.

Annotate   During this step, the student writes the message. Any one of several forms of annotations may be used: heuristic, summary, thesis, question, critical, intention, and motivation annotations are all useful. Heuristic annotations consist of quotations from the selections that suggest the essence of the selections and stimulate responses. Summary annotations are brief restatements of the author's main ideas and relationships between them. A thesis annotation states the author's main premise or theme. A question annotation is a formulation of the question or questions that the annotator feels the author is answering in the selection. A critical annotation includes a statement of the author's thesis, a statement of the reader's reaction to this thesis, and a defense of the reader's stated reaction. An intention annotation states the author's purpose as it is understood by the reader. In a motivation annotation, the annotator speculates about the probable motives of the writer.[7]

Ponder   The student thinks about the author's message. Discussion with others may be a part of this step.

PANORAMA   This technique consists of eight steps that are divided into three stages. The third stage may be omitted in some cases. The stages and their component steps are described briefly below.

1. Preparatory Stage
    Purpose. The reader decides why he or she is reading the material.
    Adapting Rate to Material. The reader decides how fast the selection should be read, holding in mind the need for flexi-

---

7 Eanet and Manzo, "Reap," pp. 648 49.

bility of rate within the selection, depending upon the purpose of the reading.

Need to Pose Questions. This step is similar to the "Question" step in SQ3R. Headings of various types are converted into questions to be answered as the material is read.

2. Intermediate Stage

Overview. This step is similar to the "Survey" step in SQ3R. The main parts of the book or article are surveyed to help the student develop an idea of the author's organization.

Read and Relate. The reader uses the type of reading techniques necessary to meet his or her purposes. The reader's background of knowledge is related to the material being read. Answers to the questions posed earlier are sought.

Annotate. Annotations may be made directly in the book if this is permitted. If not, annotations can be made on separate paper. They may be made in outline form. Other ideas for annotation are mentioned in the discussion of the REAP technique.

3. Concluding Stage

Memorize. The student utilizes outlines and summaries as aids to memorization. Acronyms are used to help in remembering main points.

Assess. The student evaluates his or her efforts in relation to achievement of purposes previously stated and retention of the important parts of the material.

Organizational skills

When participating in such activities as writing reports, secondary school students need to organize the ideas they encounter in their reading. Three helpful organizational skills are outlining, summarizing, and notetaking.

Outlining

Teachers should help their students to understand that outlining is recording information from reading material in a way that makes clear the relationships between the main ideas and the supporting details. Before it is possible for the students to learn to construct an outline properly, they must have learned to identify main ideas and supporting details in reading selections. Information on how to help students locate main ideas and recognize related details is found in Chapter 6.

Two types of outlines that students may find useful are the sentence outline and the topic outline. Each point in a sentence outline is stated in the form of a complete sentence. The points in a topic outline are written in the form of key words and phrases. The sentence outline is generally easier to master since the topic outline involves an extra task—condensing main ideas, already expressed in sentence form, into key words and phrases.

The first step in making an outline is extracting the main ideas from the material and listing these main ideas beside Roman numerals in the order in which they occur. The next step is locating the details that support each of the main ideas and listing them beside capital letters below the main idea that they support. These details are indented to indicate subordination to the main idea. Details that are subordinate to these details are indented still further and preceded by Arabic numerals. The next level of subordination is indicated by lower case letters. Although other levels of subordination are possible, secondary school students will rarely have need of such fine divisions.

Some ideas about outlining that a teacher may wish to stress:

1. The degree of importance of ideas in an outline is shown by the numbers and letters used, as well as by indentation. Points that are equally important are designated by the same number or letter style and the same indentation.
2. A topic should not be subdivided unless two points of equal value can be noted under the topic. (They should not use a *I* without a *II* or an *A* without a *B*, for example.)
3. An outline should not incorporate unimportant or unrelated details.

A blank outline form may be helpful in demonstrating to students the proper form for an outline. Example 7.1 shows such a form.

Example 7.1   *Outline form*

TITLE

I. Main idea
   A. Detail supporting I
   B. Detail supporting I
      1. Detail supporting B
      2. Detail supporting B
         a. Detail supporting 2
         b. Detail supporting 2
   C. Detail supporting I
II. Main Idea
   A. Detail supporting II
   B. Detail supporting II
   C. Detail supporting II
      1. Detail supporting C
      2. Detail supporting C

Teachers can help students to see how a textbook chapter would be outlined by showing them how the headings within the chapter indicate different levels of subordination. For example, in some textbooks the title for the outline would be the title of the the chapter, Roman numeral headings would be center headings in the chapter, capital letter headings would be side headings in the chapter, and Arabic numeral headings would be italic or paragraph headings in the chapter.

One approach to helping students learn to outline their reading assignments is for the teacher to supply the students with partially completed outlines of the material and then ask the students to complete the outlines. The teacher can vary the difficulty of the activity by gradually leaving out more and more details until the students do the entire outline alone. In Example 7.2 a progression of assignments in outlining is suggested.

Progression of outlining assignments   **Example 7.2**

---

1. First Assignment
            Title (Given by teacher)
I.   (Given by teacher)
      A.   (Given by teacher)
            1.   (To be filled in by student)
            2.   (To be filled in by student)
      B.   (Given by teacher)
            1.   (To be filled in by student)
            2.   (Given by teacher)
                  a.   (To be filled in by student)
                  b.   (To be filled in by student)
II.   (Given by teacher)
      A.   (Given by teacher)
      B.   (To be filled in by student)

2. Second assignment
            Title (Given by teacher)
I.   (Given by teacher)
      A.   (To be filled in by student)
      B.   (To be filled in by student)
            1.   (To be filled in by student)
            2.   (To be filled in by student)
II.   (Given by teacher)
      A.   (To be filled in by student)
      B.   (To be filled in by student)

---

3.   Third assignment—Only skeleton outline is given by teacher. Student fills in all parts.

Title _____

I.
   A.
   B.
   C.
      1.
      2.
II.
   A.
      1.
         a.
         b.
      2.
   B.

Outlining practice should probably be offered in every subject area because of the differences in organization of material among the disciplines. A standard form, used throughout the school, will decrease confusion among the students.

Summarizing   Summaries of reading assignments can be extremely valuable to secondary school students when they are studying for tests. The summaries have to be good ones to be helpful, however. In order to write a good summary, a student must restate what the author has said in a more concise form. The main ideas and essential supporting details of a selection should be preserved in a summary, but illustrative material and statements that merely elaborate upon the main ideas should not be included. The ability to locate main ideas is therefore a prerequisite skill for learning how to write good summaries. (Development of this skill is discussed in Chapter 6.)

A student must understand the material in order to write a good summary of it. He or she must comprehend the relationships between the main ideas appearing in the material and must record the material in such a way that these relationships are apparent.

The topic sentence of a paragraph is a good summary of the paragraph, if it is well-written. Practice in finding topic sentences of paragraphs, therefore, is also practice in the skill of summarizing paragraphs.

Summaries of longer selections may be constructed by locating the main ideas of the component paragraphs and combining these ideas into a summary statement. Certain types of paragraphs can generally be disregarded when writing summaries of lengthy selections. Introductory and illustrative paragraphs are ones that add no new ideas and, therefore, are not helpful in constructing a concise overview of the material. Students who write summaries of their reading assignments may wish to compare their summaries with concluding or summary paragraphs written by the author to make sure that they have not omitted essential details.

When writing summaries, the students should not only try to limit the number of sentences used, but should also try to limit the number of words used within sentences. Words unnecessary for conveying the meaning of the sentences can be omitted. For example,

> *Original sentence:* A match, carelessly discarded by an unsuspecting tourist, can cause the destruction by fire of many acres of trees that it will take years of work to replace. *Changed sentence:* Carelessly discarded matches can result in extensive destruction of forested areas by fire.

Students can be given short passages with which to practice summarizing skills. The sample paragraph below could be used.

> Voters in Hawk County defeated a proposed half-cent increase in sales tax on Tuesday. Their sales tax rate will continue to be 6 percent. The additional revenue from the tax would have been applied to educational needs in the county, if the measure had passed. Of 2,031 voters who cast ballots Tuesday, however, only 500 voted in favor of the increase.

Practice in summarizing is most effective if the material being summarized is taken from textbooks the students are currently studying or other material that they are expected to read in connection with classwork. The teacher may give the students a section of the textbook to read and three or four summaries of the material. The students can be asked to choose the best summary from those presented and asked to tell why the other summaries were not as good. This is good preparation for the independent writing of summaries by the students.

Notetaking

Taking notes on readings done for classes can be helpful as an aid to memory. Well-constructed notes can make rereading of the material at a later time unnecessary and can thus save students time and effort. In order to take good notes the students are forced to think about the material being read, and, because of this, they will be more likely to remember it when they need to use it. It is also true that the simple act of writing the ideas will help to fix them in the students' memories.

Students should be encouraged to use a form of notetaking that helps them most. Some may utilize outline form when taking notes on an assignment in a textbook. Others will wish to write a summary of the

textbook materials. They need opportunities to practice both procedures. Ideas for practice are suggested in the two preceding sections
of this text.

Notes for a research paper can be especially effective when made
on index cards that can be later sorted into topics to be covered in the
paper. If note cards are used, each one should include the source of
the information so that the paper can be well-documented. Examples
of note cards are shown below:

1st reference from source

> Buttinger, Joseph. "Indochina." *Encyclopedia
>   Americana*, 1968, XV, 68d.
>
>
> Chinese are the largest minority group in the countries
> of Cambodia, Thailand, Malaya, and Vietnam.

Source previously used

> Buttinger, p. 68d.
>
>
> The Chinese tend to be city-dwellers.

Incomplete sentences

> Buttinger, p. 68d.
>
>
> First inhabitants of Indochina—probably Negritos.
> Next—Malayo-Indonesians.

Some guidelines for notetaking that may be helpful to students
include:

1. Key words and phrases should be used in notes.
2. Enough of the context must be included to make the notes
    understandable after a period of time has elapsed.

3. The bibliographical reference should be included with each note card or page.
4. Direct quotations should be copied exactly and should be used sparingly.
5. Notes should clearly differentiate between direct quotations and reworded material.
6. Notes should be as brief as possible.
7. Use of abbreviations can make notetaking less time consuming. Examples: ∴ for therefore; w/ for with; = for equals.

Teachers may be able to help their students learn to take good notes by "thinking through" a textbook assignment with them in class, emphasizing the points that should be included in a good set of notes. Students then can be encouraged to take notes on another assignment and compare them with a set of notes the teacher has constructed over the same material.

Location skills

In order to take part in many study activities, students need to be able to find the necessary reading material. The teacher can help students with these tasks by showing them location aids that exist in libraries and books.

Libraries

Teachers may neglect to teach students location skills connected with the library because they feel that the librarian should perform this task. The librarian, however, may feel that he or she is not supposed to function as an instructor. Because of these conflicting viewpoints, students may receive no instruction in the use of the library, even though they are encouraged to use it for both reference work and recreational reading. This problem can be solved if teachers and librarians work cooperatively to develop the skills needed for effective library use.

The librarian can help by showing the students the location of books, periodicals, card catalogs, and reference materials (dictionaries, encyclopedias, atlases, *Reader's Guide to Periodical Literature*, and others) in the library; by explaining the procedures for checking books out and returning them; and by clarifying the rules relating to behavior in the library. The librarian can also demonstrate the use of the card catalog and the *Reader's Guide* and explain the arrangement of books in the library. (The Dewey Decimal System is the arrangement most commonly used in school libraries in the United States for classifying nonfiction books.) Posters may be constructed and displayed in the library to remind the students of check-out procedures, library rules, and arrangement of books. One possible poster might list the major divisions of the Dewey Decimal System. These divisions are indicated below.

000–099: Generalities
100–199: Philosophy and Psychology
200–299: Religion
300–399: The Social Sciences
400–499: Language
500–599: Pure Sciences
600–699: Technology (Applied Sciences)
700–799: The Arts
800–899: Literature
900–999: General History and Geography[8]

Other posters which might be profitably displayed in the library could include samples of the different types of cards that are found in the card catalog. Examples are shown below and on page 187.

Subject Card

```
Historical Fiction


U    Uris, Leon
       Armageddon
     Doubleday & Company, Inc., © 1964.
```

Author Card

```
U    Uris, Leon


       Armageddon
     Doubleday & Company, Inc. © 1964.
```

The librarian can be extremely helpful to the teacher. He or she may

1. help the teacher locate both printed and nonprinted materials related to current units of study.

---

8. Melvil Dewey, *Dewey Decimal Classification and Relative Index* (Lake Placid Club, N.Y.: Forest Press, 1971).

2. help the teacher plan a unit on use of reference materials in the library.

3. help the teacher discover reading interests of individuals and specific groups of students.

4. alert the teacher to professional reading materials in his or her content area.

Content area teachers will often want students to make use of the library. Simply telling them to do so is insufficient preparation. Students need guidance for each library assignment. If students are expected to use the card catalog to locate reference books or recreational reading selections, they should be reminded that the cards in the card catalog are filed alphabetically and that there are subject, author, and title cards for each book. A brief review of the Dewey Decimal System of classification may be advisable if nonfiction books are to be located.

If material in popular magazines is to be sought by the students, the teacher might review or initially teach the use of the *Readers' Guide to Periodical Literature* in which articles from approximately 160 popular magazines are indexed. Each article is indexed under the subject and the author's name. Sometimes an article is included under the title also. A pamphlet entitled *How to Use the Readers' Guide to Periodical Literature*[9] is a useful source for the teacher.

Title Card

> *Armageddon*
>
> U Uris, Leon
>   *Armageddon*
> Doubleday & Company, Inc. © 1964.

Cross Reference Card

> Zeus
>
> see
>
> Greek Mythology

---

9. *How to Use the Readers' Guide to Periodical Literature*, rev. ed. (New York: H. W. Wilson, 1970).

Social studies teachers may wish to teach students to use *The New York Times Index,* which is a subject index of articles from the *New York Times.* Since dates of the articles' publication are included, students may use this index as an aid to locating articles in local papers on the same subjects.

The location of material within informational books and special reference books (encyclopedias, dictionaries, almanacs, atlases) found in the library is also a concern of the content area teacher. Finding a book on a subject is useless if the student cannot then find within the book the information that is needed. Skills needed for this task are discussed below.

Books   Most informational books offer students several special features that help them locate needed material. Content area teachers will find that explaining the functions of prefaces, tables of contents, indexes, appendixes, glossaries, footnotes, and bibliographies will be well worth the effort because of the increased efficiency with which the students will be able to use books.

Prefaces and/or introductions When a content area teacher presents a new textbook to secondary school students, he or she should ask them to read the preface and/or introduction to the book to obtain an idea about why the book was written and the manner in which the material is to be presented. The teacher can then explain the function and importance of these book parts in books used for outside research reading.

Table of contents The table of contents of a new textbook should also be examined on the day the textbook is distributed. The students can be reminded that the table of contents tells what topics the book includes and the pages on which these topics begin. They should be led to understand that the table of contents makes it unnecessary to look through the entire book to find the section of interest at the moment. A brief drill with the textbook can help to emphasize these points. Questions such as these can be asked:

1. What topics are covered in this book?
2. What is the first topic that is discussed?
3. On what page does the discussion about _____ begin? (This question can be repeated several times with different topics inserted in the blank.)

Indexes The students need to understand that an index is an alphabetical list of items and/or names mentioned in a book and the pages upon which these items or names appear. Many books contain one general index, but some contain subject and author indexes as well as other specialized indexes (for example, a first line index in a poetry or music book). Most indexes contain both main headings and subheadings. Students generally need practice in using index headings to locate information within their books. After a preliminary lesson on what an index is and how it is useful in locating information, the teacher might present a lesson on the use of an index similar to the one in Example 7.3.

Lesson idea on index practice   **Example 7.3**
_____

The teacher should use the student's own textbooks whenever possible in the teaching of index use. This lesson idea can be modified for use with an actual index in a content area textbook. The sample index given here is not from an actual textbook.

> *Sample Index*
> Absolute value 145, 174–175
> Addition
>   of decimals, 101
>   of fractions, 80–83
>   of natural numbers, 15–16, 46–48
>   of rational numbers, 146–48
>   of real numbers, 170
> Angles, 203
>   measurement of, 206–207
>   right, 204
> Axiom, 241
> Base
>   meaning of, 5
>   change of, 6–7

The teacher can ask the students to use the index to answer the following questions:

1. On what page would you look to find out how to add decimals? Under what main topic and subheading did you have to look to discover this page number?
2. On what page will you find *base* mentioned?
3. What pages contain information about absolute value?
4. On what pages would you look to find out about measurement of angles? What main heading did you look under to discover this? What subheading did you look under?

Example 7.3 (cont.)

5. Where would you look to find information about adding real numbers? Would you expect to find any information about real numbers on page 146? Why, or why not?
6. Is there information about addition of natural numbers on pages 46–48? Is information on this topic found on any other pages?

The following questions can be incorporated into the lesson if an actual index is being used.

7. Find the meaning for *base* and read it to me. Did you look in the index to find the page number? Could you have found it more quickly by looking in the index?

Appendixes   Students can be shown that the appendixes in their textbooks and in other books contain information that may be helpful to them. Bibliographies or tabular material may appear in appendixes. At times students may need to use this material, but they will not use it if they do not know where to find it.

Glossaries   Glossaries are often found in content area textbooks. Students can be taught that glossaries are similar to dictionaries, but include only words presented in the books in which they are found. Glossaries of technical terms can be of much help to students in understanding a book's content. The skills needed for proper use of a glossary are the same as those needed for using a dictionary. (See Chapter 4 for a detailed discussion of use of the dictionary.)

Footnotes   Footnotes inform students of the source or sources of information included in the text. If further clarification of the material is needed, a student may use the footnote to guide him or her to the original source.

Bibliographies   Bibliographies may refer students to other sources of information about the subjects discussed in a book. Students can be encouraged to turn to these sources for clarification of ideas and/or for additional information on a topic. The bibliography at the end of a chapter in a textbook is generally a list of references that the author(s) consulted when preparing the book or references that contain additional information about the subject. Some books contain bibliographies that list books by a particular author or that suggest lists of appropriate selections for particular groups. Bibliographies are extremely valuable aids for students doing assigned research activities.

Special reference books   Secondary school students are often called upon to find information in such reference books as encyclopedias, dictionaries, almanacs, and atlases. Unfortunately, many students have reached junior high or high school unable to use such books effectively.

Important items related to effective use of reference books include:

1. Knowledge of alphabetical order. (Most secondary school students will have mastered alphabetical order, but a few will need help.)
2. Knowledge that encyclopedias, dictionaries, and some atlases are arranged in alphabetical order.
3. Ability to use guide words. (Knowledge of location of guide words on a page and understanding that they represent the first and last entry words on a dictionary or encyclopedia page.)
4. Ability to use cross references. (Related primarily to use of encyclopedias.)
5. Ability to use pronunciation keys. (Related primarily to use of dictionaries.)
6. Ability to choose from several possible word meanings the one that most closely fits the context in which the word was found. (Related to use of dictionaries.)
7. Ability to interpret the legend of a map. (Related to use of atlases.)
8. Ability to interpret the scale of a map. (Related to use of atlases.)
9. Ability to locate directions on maps. (Related to use of atlases.)
10. Ability to determine which volume of a set will contain the information being sought. (Related primarily to use of encyclopedias.)
11. Ability to determine key words under which related information can be found.

Because encyclopedias, almanacs, and atlases are often written on extremely high readability levels, teachers should use caution in assigning work in these reference books. Students are not likely to profit from trying to do research in books written on their frustration levels. When students are asked to look up material in books that are too difficult for them to read with understanding, they tend to copy the material word-for-word instead of trying to extract the important ideas.

Various aspects of dictionary use are discussed in Chapter 4. Many skills related to the use of an atlas are included in the section of this chapter that is concerned with reading maps. Some learning activities that may be useful in the teaching the use of the encyclopedia are discussed below. Worksheets such as the one in Examples 7.4 and 7.5 can be used.

Example 7.4

Worksheet on using the encyclopedia

Pretend you have an encyclopedia whose volumes are arranged so that there is one volume for each letter of the alphabet. Look at the following names and decide which volume of the encyclopedia you would have to use to find each one. Write the letter of the volume in the space provided beside the name. When you finish, use the answer key to check your work. If you don't understand why you made your mistakes, ask the teacher for an explanation.

_____ Richard Nixon
_____ Marie Curie
_____ Clara Barton
_____ Martin Van Buren
_____ Martin Luther King
_____ Robert Louis Stevenson
_____ John Paul Jones
Answer key: N, C, B, V, K, S, J

Example 7.5

Worksheet on using the encyclopedia

Look up each of the following topics in the encyclopedia. On the line beside each topic, write the letter of the volume in which you found the topic and the page number on which the topic is discussed.

1. Tennis   _____
2. Solar system   _____
3. U.S. Constitution   _____
4. Lobster   _____
5. Oleander   _____
6. Sampan   _____
7. Education in Sweden   _____
8. Computer use in library systems   _____

Because different encyclopedias vary in content and arrangement, students should be taught to use several different sets. They should be asked to compare the entries in several different sets on a specified list of topics. They may also be asked to compare different sets of encyclopedias on an overall basis, noting such features as types of index used, number of volumes, ease of reading, and recentness of publication.

Report writing   Content area teachers often assign reports to be written on topics related to the content area. Sometimes the students are allowed to choose their own topics for reporting. In other instances, the teacher may ask each student to write on a predetermined topic. The process below can be followed in helping students prepare good reports. The first step mentioned will not be applicable if the teacher chooses the topic.

Step 1. Select a topic. The topic selected must be pertinent to the content area material being studied. It should be chosen because of its interest value for the reporter and for the rest of the class if the reports are to be shared. Ordinarily, students choose topics that are much too broad for adequate coverage. The teacher needs to help the students narrow their topics so that the task of preparing the report is more manageable.

Step 2. Collect information on the topic. Students use the location skills discussed in the previous section of this chapter in order to collect information from a variety of sources. The organizational skill of notetaking covered earlier will also be essential for use at this point.

Step 3. Organize the material. Outlining the information collected is the main activity in this step. Material from the different sources used must be fused together at this time. Sequence and relationship of main ideas and details are important considerations in forming the outline.

Step 4. Write a first draft. Utilizing the outline just formulated and the notes compiled, the students write an initial draft of the report.

Step 5. Proofread the first draft. The students now read the first draft of the report to check for sentence and paragraph sense, cohesiveness of the information, appropriate usage, correct spelling, and proper punctuation. They check to make sure that all material is properly documented.

Step 6. Revise the report. The students make needed changes in the initial draft and rewrite the report in a form acceptable for submission to the teacher.

In order to help students perform effectively on an assigned written report, the teacher can do much to prepare them for the experience. A procedure that a teacher might follow is described below.

1. Name a broad topic related to the course of study. Ask the students for suggestions as to how the topic could be narrowed to make it more manageable. Consider a number of acceptable topics that might be derived from the original topic.

2. Choose one of the acceptable narrowed topics. Take the students to the library and have them locate sources of information on the topic. Ask each of them to take notes from at least one source, being sure to record bibliographic information.

3. Return to the classroom. As a class, synthesize the notes into a single outline. (Use the chalkboard or overhead projector.)

4.   Write the report from the outline as a whole-class or small-group activity, utilizing the teacher or student leaders as scribes.

Following the above procedure will help students know what to expect when they are asked to work on individual reports. Help with skills of notetaking, outlining, summarization of information, and location of information should be a prerequisite for assignment of a written report.

Reading to follow directions

Secondary school students are constantly expected to follow written directions both in the classroom and in common everyday experiences. Teachers write assignments on the chalkboard or distribute duplicated materials that have directions written on them. Textbooks and workbooks in different content areas contain printed directions that students are expected to follow. This is particularly true of science, mathematics, and vocational education books, but it holds to some degree in all subject areas. In Chapters 8–10, examples of reading tasks in different subject areas that require students to follow directions are given. This section will consider the general problem of following directions, especially in everyday activities.

Young people and adults alike find themselves surrounded with situations in which they need to be able to follow directions to carry on their daily activities. Many of these people fail to succeed at tasks they attempt either because they do not know how to read to follow directions or because they ignore the directions and try to perform the task without understanding the sequential steps which compose it. Almost everyone is familiar with the saying, "When all else fails, read the directions." This tendency to take printed directions lightly may have been fostered in the classroom. Teachers hand out printed directions and proceed to explain them orally. Teachers also often tell students each step to perform as they progress through the task, rather than asking the students to read the directions and point out which parts need clarification for them. These actions promote a general disregard for reading directions.

Experiences in following directions that are a part of general life activities include traffic signs, recipes, assembly and installment instructions, forms to be completed, voting instructions, registration procedures, and many others. Traffic signs give a single direction on each sign. These directions are vital ones if a person wishes to avoid bodily injury, misdirection, fines, or other penalties. The other activities mentioned above involve multiple steps to be performed. Failure to complete the steps properly may result in penalties: inedible food, nonworking appliances, receipt of incorrect merchandise, and a variety of other possibilities.

Teachers are in an excellent position to show students the importance of being able to follow written directions. They are also in a position to show students techniques for reading directions with understanding.

Following directions requires two basic comprehension skills—the ability to locate details and the ability to detect sequence. Each step in a set of directions must be followed exactly and in the appropriate sequence. Because of this, reading to follow directions is a slow and deliberate task. Rereading is often necessary. A procedure such as the following may prove helpful.

1. Read the directions from beginning to end to get an overview of the task performed.
2. Study any accompanying pictorial aids which may help in understanding one or more of the steps or in picturing the desired end result.
3. Read the directions, visualizing each step to be performed. Read with an open mind, disregarding your own preconceived ideas about the procedure involved.
4. Take note of such key words as *first, second, next, last,* and *finally.* Let these words help you picture the order of the activities to be performed.
5. Read each step again, just before you actually do it.
6. Carry out the steps in the proper order.

Students will learn to follow directions more easily if the presentation of activities is scaled in difficulty from easy to hard. Teachers can start with one-step directions and then progress to two-step, three-step, and even longer sets of directions as the proficiency of the students increases.

Some activities for developing skill in following directions are suggested below.

Activities

1. Give students a paragraph containing key direction words (*first, next, then, last, finally,* etc.) and ask them to underline the words that help to show the order of events.
2. Prepare ditto masters containing directions for Japanese paper folding activites. Provide the students with paper, and ask them to follow the directions.
3. Use worksheets similar to the one in Examples 7.6 and 7.7 to make a point about the importance of following directions.

Example 7.6

Worksheet on following directions

Questionnaire

Read all of this questionnaire before you begin to fill in the answers. Work as quickly as you can. You have five minutes to finish this activity.

Name _____

Address _____

_____

Phone Number _____

Age _____

What is your father's name? _____

What is your mother's name? _____

What is your mother's occupation? _____

Do you have any brothers? _____ If so, how many? _____

Do you have any sisters? _____ If so how many? _____

Do you plan to go to college? _____ If so, where? _____

What career are you most interested in? _____

How many years of preparation past high school will be necessary if you pursue this career? _____

Who is the person that you admire most? _____

What is this person's occupation? _____

After you have completed reading this questionnaire, turn the paper over and write your name on the back. Then give the paper to your teacher. You should have written nothing on this side of the page.

Example 7.7

Worksheet on following directions

Carefully follow the directions given in the sentences below:

1. Circle the numeral that stands for the larger number: 11, 52, 4, 16, 21, 32, 35, 15.
2. Underline the first and last numeral in this list: 2, 7, 1, 4, 3, 8.
3. Draw a line through the third word in this sentence.
4. Circle each word in this sentence that begins with the letters *th.*
5. Add 44 and 76. Take the result and subtract 10. Divide that result by 10. Place your answer on this line. _____
6. Circle every noun in this sentence.

4. Make it a practice to refer students to written directions instead of telling them how to do everything orally. Ask the students to read the directions silently and then tell you in their own words what they should do.

5. Teach the meanings of words commonly encountered in written directions, such as *affix, alphabetical, array, estimate,*

example, horizontal, phrase, and *vertical.* Other words that might need attention are listed in an article by Helen Newcastle.[10]

6. Have the students follow directions in order to make something from a kit.

Any exercises for improving the ability to understand details and detect sequence will also help students in their attempts to improve skills in following directions. See Chapter 6 for ideas in these areas.

Graphic aids

Textbooks contain numerous graphic aids to readers that are often disregarded by students because they have had no training in the use of such aids. Maps, graphs, tables, charts and diagrams, and pictures can all help the students to understand the textbook material better if the students are given assistance in learning to mine the information from these graphic aids.

Maps

Maps may be found in social studies, science, mathematics, and literature textbooks, although they are most common in social studies textbooks. Since maps are generally included in textbooks to help clarify the narrative material, students need to be able to read maps in order to fully understand the material being presented.

Students may have received some background in map reading techniques in the elementary school, but many have not had any structured preparation for reading maps. Therefore, secondary school students may vary greatly in their abilities to handle assignments containing maps. A survey of map-reading skills should be administered early in the school year by a teacher who expects map reading to be an assigned activity at frequent intervals throughout the year. Below are some useful questions for surveying map-reading skills. They are related to the map on page 198.

1. What kind of information does this map supply?
2. What symbol indicates a metropolitan area with a population from 500,000 to 1,000,000?
3. What is the distance from Birmingham to Atlanta?
4. What lakes are shown on the northern boundary of this map?
5. What are possible reasons for the areas of severe air pollution shown on the map? The polluted rivers and lakes?

---

10. Helen Newcastle, "Children's Problems with Written Directions," *The Reading Teacher* 28 (December 1974):294.

Figure 7.1   *Air and water pollution in the United States*

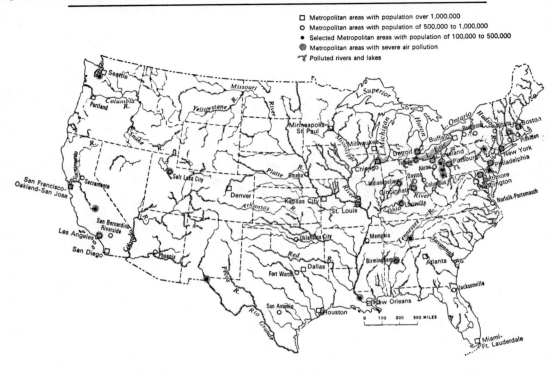

Source: Henry F. Graff, *The Free and the Brave*, p. 695. Copyright 1972 by Rand McNally & Company. Reprinted by permission.

After a survey of map-reading skills has been administered, the teacher should systematically teach any of the following skills that the students have not yet mastered:

1. Locating and comprehending the map title
2. Determining directions
3. Interpreting a map's legend
4. Applying a map's scale
5. Understanding latitude and longitude
6. Understanding common map terms
7. Making inferences concerning the material represented on a map
8. Understanding projections

The first step in map reading should be examining the title of the map to determine what area is being represented and what type of information is being given about the area. Map titles are not always located at the tops of the maps, as students often expect them to be. Therefore, the titles may be overlooked unless students are alerted to the fact that they may need to scan the map to locate the title.

Next the students should locate the directional indicator on the map and orient themselves to the map's layout. They should be aware that north is not always at the top of a map, although many maps are constructed in this manner.

Interpretation of the legend or key of the map is the next step in reading the map. The legend contains an explanation of each of the symbols used on a map. Without understanding of these symbols, the map is incomprehensible.

In order to determine distances on a map, the map's scale must be applied. Because it would be highly impractical to draw a map the actual size of the area represented (for instance, the United States), maps show areas greatly reduced in size. The relationship of a given distance on a map to the same distance on the earth is shown by the map's scale.

An understanding of latitude and longitude may be helpful in reading some maps. A system of parallels and meridians can enable a reader to locate places on a map using coordinates of degrees of latitude and longitude. Parallels of latitude are lines on a globe which are parallel to the equator. Meridians of longitude are lines which encircle the globe in a north-south direction, meeting at the poles.

There are many common map terms that students need to understand in order to comprehend maps that they are expected to read. Among these terms are *latitude* and *longitude*, of course, as well as *Tropic of Cancer*, *Tropic of Capricorn*, *north pole*, *south pole*, *equator*, *hemisphere*, *peninsula*, *continent*, *isthmus*, *gulf*, *bay*, and many others.

Teachers should encourage more than simple location activities with maps. They should ask students to make inferences concerning the material represented on maps. For example, for a map showing the physical features of an area (mountains, rivers, lakes, deserts, swamps, etc.), the students might be asked to decide what types of transportation would be most appropriate. This type of activity is extremely important at the secondary level.

Students may have a need to understand different types of projections. Flat maps and globes can be compared to illustrate distortion. Inexpensive globes can be taken apart and flattened out to show one common type of projection.

It may be helpful to students to relate a map of an area they are studying to a map of a larger area that contains the original area. For example, a map of Tennessee can be related to a map of the United States. In this way, the position of Tennessee within the United States becomes apparent.

Many types of maps may be found in content area textbooks. Among these types are road maps, relief maps, physical maps, vegetation maps, political maps, product maps, population maps, and weather maps. All of these types of maps require students to apply some or all of the map skills discussed above. Each type of map may require special explanation, because each type may present unique problems to the reader.

Further suggestions for working with map reading skills are given below.

Activities

1. Ask students to construct a map of an area of interest to the particular class (for example, a map of recreation facilities in the town in a health or physical education class). Help them to draw the map to scale. (The aid of a mathematics teacher may be desirable.) Make sure they include a title, a directional indicator, and a legend.

2. When a map is encountered in a content area textbook, guide them through use of the legend by asking questions such as the following:
   Where is there a railroad on this map?
   Where is the state capitol located?
   Where do you find a symbol for a college?
   Are there any national monuments in this area? If so, where are they?

3. Work with map terminology by having students point out on a wall map such features as *gulf* and *peninsula*.

Graphs   Graphs often appear in social studies, science, and mathematics books, and sometimes appear in books for other content areas. Graphs are used to make comparisons among quantitative data. There are four basic types of graphs:

1. Picture graphs, which compare quantities using pictures.
2. Circle or pie graphs, which show relationships of individual parts to the whole.
3. Bar graphs, which use vertical or horizontal bars to compare quantities.
4. Line graphs, which show changes in amounts.

Picture graphs (or pictographs)   Picture graphs are easier to read than the other types. Visualization of data is aided by use of this type of graph. The reader must remember, however, that only approximate amounts can be indicated by pictographs, making it necessary to estimate amounts when interpreting these graphs. An example of a pictograph is shown in Figure 7.2.

Sample picture graph   Figure 7.2

Population of Kingsley (1974–1978)

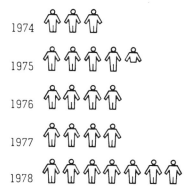

1974

1975

1976

1977

1978

= 1000 people

Circle or pie graphs   Proportional parts of a whole can be shown most easily through use of circle or pie graphs. These graphs show the percentage of the whole that each individual part represents. An example of a circle graph is shown in Figure 7.3.

Bar graphs   Bar graphs are useful for comparing the sizes of several items or the size of a particular item at different times. These graphs may be either horizontal or vertical. Examples are shown in Figure 7.4.

Line graphs   Line graphs can depict changes in amounts over a period of time. Line graphs have vertical and horizontal scales. Each point that is plotted on a line graph has a value on both scales. An example of a line graph is shown in Figure 7.5.

Reading graphs   Students can be taught to discover from the title what comparison is being made or information is being given, to interpret the legend of a picture graph, and to accurately derive needed information from a graph.

Figure 7.3   *Sample circle graph*

Monthly Budget

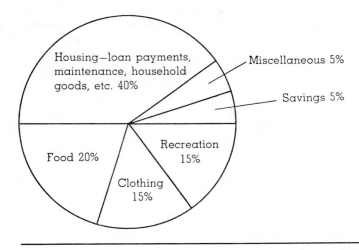

One of the best ways to help students learn to read graphs is to have them construct graphs themselves. Below is a list of examples of types of graphs students might construct.

1. A picture graph showing the number of tickets to the senior prom purchased by each homeroom.
2. A circle graph showing the percentage of each day that the student spends in various activities (sleeping, eating, studying, etc.).
3. A bar graph showing the number of outside readings completed for English class during each grading period.
4. A line graph showing weekly quiz scores of one student during one six week period.

The teacher can also construct graphs such as the ones in Figures 7.2, 7.3, 7.4, and 7.5 and ask the students to answer questions about them. Some sample questions follow:

Figure 7.2: Sample Picture Graph
1. What does each symbol on this graph represent?
2. What time period does this graph cover?
3. During what year did Kingsley have the largest population?
4. Approximately how many people lived in Kingsley in 1976?

Sample bar graphs Figure 7.4

Percent of Voters for John Drew

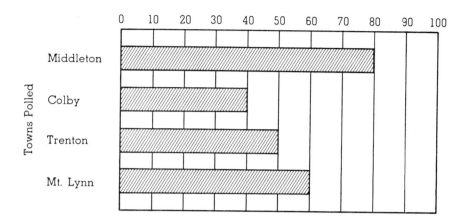

Immigration to the United States 1830–1970

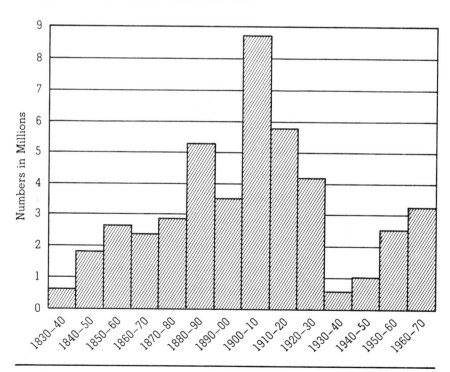

Source: Graff, Henry F. *The Free and the Brave* (Chicago: Rand McNally & Company, 1972) 520.

Figure 7.5   *Sample line graph*

Describe the increase in cotton production that took place after the cotton gin came into use.

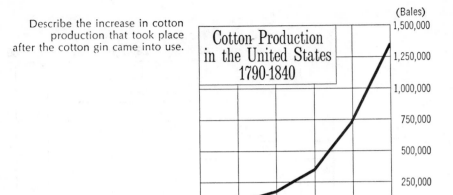

Source: Henry F. Graff, *The Free and the Brave* p 353. Copyright 1972 by Rand McNally & Company. Reprinted by permission.

Figure 7.3: Sample Circle Graph
5. What kind of information does this graph contain?
6. What budget item consumes the most money?
7. What percentage of the budget is allocated for food?
8. What does the "Miscellaneous" category mean?

Figure 7.4: Sample Bar Graphs
9. What is the topic of the second sample bar graph?
10. How many people immigrated during the years 1910–20?
11. During what ten year span did the largest number of people immigrate?
12. During what ten year span did the smallest number of people immigrate?
13. What percent of the voters from Middleton were for John Drew?
14. In which of the four towns was John Drew least popular?
15. In which of the four towns did John Drew have the most support?
16. In which town were 40 percent of the voters for John Drew?

Figure 7.5: Sample Line Graph
17. What time period is depicted on this graph?
18. What does the vertical axis represent?
19. What does the horizontal axis represent?
20. What was the trend in cotton production over the years represented?

21. Did the invention of the cotton gin in 1793 have an effect on cotton production? Describe the effect.

Tables

Tables may be found in reading materials of all subject areas. Tables contain information arranged in vertical columns and horizontal rows. One problem that students have with reading tables is extracting the particular facts needed from a large mass of available information. The large amount of information provided in the small amount of space on tables can confuse students unless the teacher provides a procedure for reading tables.

Just as the titles of maps and graphs contain information about their content, so do the titles of tables. In addition, as tables are arranged in columns and rows, the headings for these columns and rows can also provide information. Specific information is obtained by locating the intersection of an appropriate column with an appropriate row. An example of a table is Table 7.1.

Average temperatures in Darby and Deal for June–December 1977 (in degrees)   **Table 7.1**

		Months						
		June	July	August	September	October	November	December
Towns	Darby	70°	72°	75°	74°	65°	65°	60°
	Deal	68°	69°	71°	70°	65°	64°	58°

Questions such as the following could offer the students practice in reading tables.

1. What type of information is located in Table 7.1?
2. What are the column and row headings? What are the subheadings?
3. What time period is covered by the table?
4. Which of the two towns has the lowest average temperatures over the time period represented?
5. What was the average temperature for Darby in October 1977?
6. In what month did Darby and Deal have the same average temperature?
7. What is the unit of measurement used in this table?

Charts and diagrams

Charts and diagrams appear in textbooks for many different content areas. They are designed to help students picture the events, processes, structures, relationships, or sequences described by the text. At times they may be used as summaries of the text material.

Students must be made aware of the abstract nature of charts and the fact that they often distort information or over-simplify it. Interpretation of the symbols found in charts and understanding of the perspective used in diagrams are not automatic. Teachers must provide practice in such activities.

The examples in Figures 7.6, 7.7, and 7.8 show how visual aids can be used in textbooks.

Figure 7.6   *The circumpolar constellations*

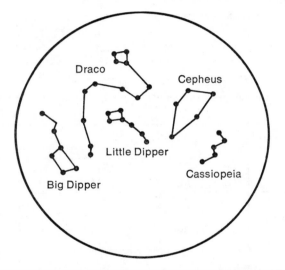

Source: Abraham, Norman, *et al.*, *Interaction of Earth & Time* (Chicago: Rand McNally & Company, 1972): 48.

Another example of a diagram is a floor plan. See Chapter 9B, page 289.

Numerous types of charts and diagrams are used in the various content areas: "tree" diagrams (English); "flow" charts (mathematics); process charts (science); and so on. Careful instruction in how to read such charts and diagrams must be provided if interpretation of content material is to be achieved.

Pictures

Today it is a rare content area textbook that contains no pictures. The pictures are designed to illuminate the material described in the textbook, as well as to interest the students. They may be photographs that offer a highly realistic representation of the concepts, people, or places discussed or line drawings that are somewhat more abstract in

Movement in an ice sheet   **Figure 7.7**

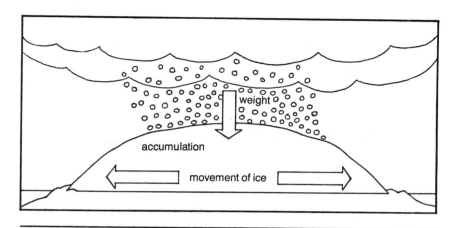

weight

accumulation

movement of ice

Source: Abraham Norman et al., *Interaction of Earth & Time*, (Chicago: Rand McNally & Company, 1972):292.

Units of measure derived from the human body   **Figure 7.8**

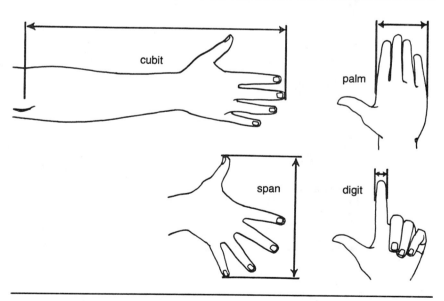

cubit

palm

span

digit

Source: Abraham, Norman, et al., *Interaction of Matter & Energy* (Chicago: Rand McNally & Company, 1973): 148.

nature. Cartoons are special types of pictures which contain special symbols that the students need to understand. Cartoons often distort the things they represent in order to make a point. Students must be made aware of this fact and encouraged to read cartoons critically.

Pictures are frequently seen by students as mere space fillers, reducing the amount of reading they will have to do on a page. Therefore, the students may pay little attention to the pictures, although the pictures are often excellent sources of information.

Since pictures are representations of experiences, they may be utilized as vicarious means of adding to a student's store of knowledge. Teachers should help students mine information from pictures in their textbooks by encouraging them to study the pictures before and after

Figure 7.9   *A picture from a current science textbook*

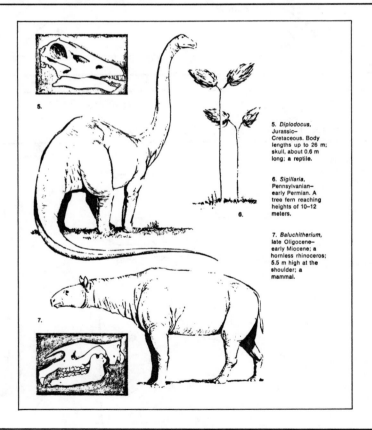

5. *Diplodocus,* Jurassic– Cretaceous. Body lengths up to 26 m; skull, about 0.6 m long; a reptile.

6. *Sigillaria,* Pennsylvanian– early Permian. A tree fern reaching heights of 10–12 meters.

7. *Baluchitherium,* late Oligocene– early Miocene; a hornless rhinoceros; 5.5 m high at the shoulder; a mammal.

Source: Abraham Norman, et al., *Interaction of Earth & Time,* p. 203. Copyright 1972 by Rand McNally & Company. Reprinted by permission.

reading the text, looking for the purpose of the picture and specific details presented. This picture study may aid in retention of the material involved.

Study time will be more efficiently used if students are taught to vary their reading rates to fit their purposes and materials than if such instruction is neglected. Making such adjustments is known as flexibility of rate. Light fiction being read strictly for enjoyment should be read much faster than a science experiment that the student must perform. When reading to find isolated facts, such as names and dates, rapidly scanning a page for key words is more reasonable than reading every word of the material. When reading to determine main ideas or organization of a selection, skimming is more reasonable than reading each word of the selection. Tests of a student's ability to vary reading rate are useful.[11]

Adjusting Rate to fit Purpose and Materials

Students frequently have the idea that everything should be read at the same rate. Thus, some of them read novels as slowly and deliberately as they read their mathematics problems. These students will probably never enjoy reading for recreation because they work so hard at reading and it seems to take so long. Other students move rapidly through everything that they read. In doing so, they generally fail to grasp essential details in content area assignments, although they "finish" reading all of the assigned material. Rate of reading should never be considered apart from comprehension. Therefore, the optimum rate for reading any material would be the fastest rate at which an acceptable level of comprehension can be obtained. Teachers who wish to concentrate upon improving their students' reading rates should include comprehension checks with all rate exercises.

Naturally it is desirable for a person to read each type of material at the fastest possible speed that will meet his or her purposes. This speed will vary from an extremely slow rate for savoring the beauty of phrasing in a poem to a very rapid rate for getting a general overview of the news stories appearing on the front page of the paper.

Work on increasing reading rate should not receive emphasis until basic word recognition and comprehension skills are thoroughly under control. Improvement in these skills often results in increased rate without any special attention to rate.

---

11. Educational Developmental Laboratories in Huntington, N. Y., publishes a group of Reading Versatility Tests which require students to use different reading approaches.

Factors affecting rate   There are many factors that influence the rate at which a person can read a particular selection. Some of these factors include the following:

1. Factors related to the material
   a. Size and style of type
   b. Format of the pages
   c. Use of illustrations
   d. Organization
   e. Writing style of the author
   f. Abstractness or complexity of ideas
2. Factors related to the reader
   a. Background of experiences
   b. Reading ability
   c. Attitudes and interests
   d. Reason for reading

Obviously, these factors will differ with each selection that is read. Realizing this, the idea that all materials can be read equally effectively at the same rate is exposed as unreasonable.

Poor reading habits may greatly decrease reading rate. Among such habits are excessive vocalization (forming each word as it is read); sounding out all words, familiar and unfamiliar; excessive regressions (going back and rereading previously read material); and pointing at each word with the index finger. Concentrated attention to these problems can yield good results. Often a secondary school student simply needs to be made aware of the habit that is slowing him or her down and given some suggestions for practice in overcoming it. Use of the machines cited in the next section of this chapter has often helped in overcoming some of these problems.

Techniques of increasing rate and encouraging flexibility   Many methods have been devised for helping students increase or adjust their rates of reading. These approaches include use of special machines, timed exercises, skimming and scanning exercises, and flexibility exercises.

Machines   The machines commonly used for increasing rate are controlled reading filmstrip projectors, controlled reading motion picture projectors, tachistoscopes, pacers, and skimmers. Use of machines often motivates students to improve rate skills.

Controlled reading filmstrip projectors use sets of specially developed filmstrips. The stories printed on the filmstrips are exposed to the students a line at a time or a segment of a line at a time as a scanner moves across the line of print in a left-to-right sequence. The rate of presentation can be adjusted to fit the student or students using the material. Some of these films are accompanied by excellent books that emphasize comprehension through encouraging a preview of the material before the machine is used, programmed study of vocabulary, and checks for comprehension.

Films to increase rate are available for use with ordinary 16-millimeter motion picture projectors. The films let the reader view parts of a line in a left-to-right progression. The material before and after the highlighted portion is obscured. The speed of the film can be varied in some cases by changing projector settings. The wide speed variations possible with the filmstrip projectors mentioned above are not possible with these films. Comprehension questions are included.

Tachistoscopes are devices that present printed materials for brief periods of time (for example, $\frac{1}{100}$ of a second, one second, etc.). Tachistoscopic attachments are available for use with filmstrip or slide projectors or overhead projectors. Some are independent devices. Some of them have electronically controlled exposures, some mechanically controlled exposures, and some manually controlled exposures. Hand tachistoscopes (see Chapter 5) can be constructed for individual use and operated manually. These devices are designed to encourage students to take in more print in a single fixation and to shorten fixation time.

Pacers have arms, beams of light, or shades that move down the page of printed material from top to bottom at regulated speeds. The student tries to read below the moving bar or within the beam of light.

A skimmer has a bead of light that moves down the center fold of the book at a rapid rate to encourage the reader to keep up an appropriate rate when skimming. Only one company offers a machine of this type.

Some commonly used rate machines include the following:

1. All-Purpose Electric Tachistoscope, Lafayette Instrument Company
2. AVR Flash-Tachment, Audio Visual Research
3. AVR Reading Rateometer, Audio Visual Research
4. EDL Controlled Reader and EDL Controlled Reader Jr., Educational Developmental Laboratories
5. EDL Skimmer, Educational Developmental Laboratories
6. EDL Tach-X Tachistoscope, Educational Developmental Laboratories
7. Flashmeter, Keystone View Company
8. Keystone Reading Pacer, Keystone View Company
9. PDL Perceptoscope, Perceptual Development Laboratories
10. Phrase Flasher, Reading Laboratory Incorporated
11. Readermate, Singer-Graphlex
12. Shadowscope Reading Pacer, Psychotechnics, Inc.
13. SRA Reading Accelerator, Science Research Associates

14. Tachisto-Flasher, Learning Through Seeing, Inc.
15. Tachisto-Viewer, Learning Through Seeing, Inc.

Timed readings Timed readings are often extremely effective in helping students increase their reading rates. Two types of timed readings are common: (1) reading for a fixed period of time and then counting the number of words read and computing the words read per minute, and (2) reading a fixed number of words, computing the time elapsed while reading, and deriving a rate score in words per minute.

Timed readings should always be accompanied by comprehension checks. An extremely high rate score is of no use if the student fails to comprehend the material. Teachers should encourage rate increases only if comprehension does not suffer. Some students need help in basic reading skills before they will be able to participate profitably in these rate-building activities.

Graphs can be kept of timed rate exercises over a period of weeks or months. Seeing visible progress can motivate students to work on improving rate. Comprehension charts should also be kept in order to view rate increase in the proper perspective.

Timed readings are more satisfactory rate-building exercises than are machine oriented exercises. The main reason for this is that machines will not always be available to push students to read rapidly, and eventually they must learn to operate without a machine for a crutch.

Skimming and scanning techniques Skimming and scanning are special types of rapid reading. Skimming refers to reading to get a general idea or overview of the material, and scanning means reading to find a specific bit of information. Skimming is faster than rapid reading of most of the words in the material because, when a person skims material, he or she reads selectively. Scanning is faster than skimming because only one bit of information is being sought. When scanning, a person runs his or her eyes rapidly down the page concentrating on the particular information being sought.

Skimming techniques are used in the survey step of the SQ3R method discussed earlier in this chapter. Teachers can help develop skimming skills as they work to teach this study method.

Other skimming activities include:

1. Give the students a short period of time to skim an assigned chapter and write down the main ideas covered.
2. Ask students to skim newspaper articles and match them to headlines written on the board. Have a competition to see who can finish first with no errors.

3. Give the students the title of a research topic and have them skim an article to decide whether it is pertinent.

Scanning activities are easy to design. Some examples are:

1. Have the students scan a telephone book page to find a specific person's number.
2. Have the students scan a chapter in history to find the date of a particular happening.
3. Have the students scan a textbook to find information on a particular person.

Students need to scan for key words related to the specific facts that they seek. An exercise in generating key words related to a specific topic may be beneficial.

Flexibility exercises Since not all materials should be read at the same rate, students need assistance in determining appropriate rates for different materials. One type of flexibility exercise would be a group of questions such as the ones below, followed by a discussion of the students' reasons for their answers:

1. What rate would be best for reading a statement problem in your mathematics textbook?
2. Could you read a television schedule, a newspaper article, or a science textbook fastest and still achieve your purpose?
3. Is skimming an appropriate way to read a science experiment?
4. What technique of reading would you use to look up a word in the dictionary?

Retention

Secondary school students are expected to retain much of the material that they are assigned to read in their content area classes. Retention is demonstrated in different ways. When a student recognizes a word or a sound-symbol association learned previously, he or she exhibits retention of this information. If the student fails to recognize the previously learned information, retention is faulty for some reason. If a person who has learned a rule for decoding printed words is asked to state the rule and is able to do so, he or she can be said to have recalled it. Failure to recall the rule is evidence of lack of retention.

Two ways of enhancing retention have already been discussed extensively in this chapter. They are use of study methods and use of study guides. Teachers can help students apply these techniques and others that will facilitate retention of material. Some suggestions that the teacher may offer include:

1. Always read study material with a purpose. If the teacher does not supply you with a purpose, set purposes of your own. Having a purpose for reading will help you extract meaning from a passage, and material that is meaningful to you will be retained longer.

2. Try to grasp the author's organization. This will help you to categorize concepts to be learned under main headings, which are easier to retain than small details and which facilitate the recall of these related details. In order to accomplish this task, outline the material.

3. Try to picture the ideas the author is attempting to describe. Visualization of the information being presented will help you remember it longer.

4. As you read, take notes on important points in the material. Writing information can help you to fix it in your memory.

5. After you have read the material, summarize it in your own words. If you can do this, you will have recalled the main points, and the rewording of the material demonstrates your understanding.

6. When you have read the material, discuss the assignment with a classmate or a group of classmates. Talking about the material facilitates remembering it.

7. Apply the concepts that you read about if it is possible. Physical or mental interaction with the material will make retention more likely.

8. Read assignments critically. If you question the material as you read, you will be more likely to remember it.

9. If you wish to retain the material over a long period of time, use spaced practice (a number of short practice sessions extended over a period of time) rather than massed practice (one long practice session). Massed practice facilitates immediate recall, but for long-term retention distributed practice produces the best results.

10. If you plan to recite the material to yourself or another student in order to increase your retention, do so as soon as possible after reading the material for the greatest benefits. Always check on your accuracy and correct any error immediately so that you will not retain inaccurate material.

11. Overlearning facilitates long-term retention. To overlearn something you must continue to practice it for a period of time after you have initially mastered it.

12. Mnemonic devices can help you retain certain types of information. (For example, remember that there is "a rat" in the middle of "separate.")

Teachers can also facilitate retention of material by their students by offering them ample opportunities for review of information and practice of skills learned and by offering positive reinforcement for correct responses given during these practice and review periods. Class discussion of material to be learned will help to aid retention of the material. Emphasis on classifying the ideas found in the reading material under appropriate categories can also help.

Sometimes secondary school students fail to do well on tests, not because they do not know the material, but because they have difficulty reading and comprehending the test. Teachers can help by giving students suggestions about ways of reading different types of tests.   **Test-taking**

Essay tests often contain the terms *compare, contrast, trace the development, describe, discuss,* and many others. Teachers can explain what is expected in an answer to a question containing each of these terms and any other terms that they may plan to use. This will help prevent students from losing points because they "described" instead of "contrasted." For instance, if students are asked to compare two things or ideas, the teacher generally expects both likenesses and differences to be mentioned. If they are asked to contrast two things or ideas, differences are the important factors. If the students are asked to describe something, they are expected to paint a word picture of it. Sample answers to a variety of different test questions utilizing the special vocabulary may be useful in helping students understand what the teacher expects.

> Example: Contrast extemporaneous speeches and pre-pared speeches. Answer: Extemporaneous speeches are given with little advance thought. Prepared speeches are usually preceded by much thought and research. Prepared speeches often contain quotations and paraphrases of the thoughts of many other people about the subject. Extemporaneous speeches can contain such material only if the speaker has previously become very well informed in the particular area involved. Assuming little background in the area by the speaker, an extemporaneous speech would be likely to have less depth than would a prepared speech since it would involve only the immediate impressions of the speaker. Prepared speeches tend to be better organized than extemporaneous speeches because the speaker has more time to marshall his thoughts and arrange them in the best possible sequence.

Objective tests must be read carefully. Generally, every word in an item must be considered. Teachers should emphasize the importance of considering the effect of words such as *always*, *never*, and *not*, as well as others of this general nature. Students need to realize that all parts of a true-false question must be true, if the answer is to be *true*. They also need to realize that all possible responses for a multiple-choice question need to be read before an answer is chosen.

Teachers can also help students do better on tests if they offer suggestions on how to study for different types of tests. Some useful hints would include the following.

1. When studying for essay tests:
   a. Remember that your answers should include main ideas, accompanied by supporting details.
   b. Expect questions that cover the most important topics covered in the course, since only a few questions can be asked, due to limited time.
   c. Expect questions that are broad in scope.
   d. Consider the important topics covered, and try to guess some of the questions that the teacher may ask. Prepare good answers for these questions and try to learn them thoroughly. You will probably be able to use the points you learn in answers for the test, even if the questions you formulated were not exactly the same as the ones asked by the teacher.
2. When studying for objective tests:
   a. Become familiar with important details.
   b. Consider the types of questions that have been asked on previous tests, and study for those types. If dates have been asked for in the past, learn the dates in the material.
   c. If listing questions are likely, especially sequential listings, try preparing mnemonic devices to aid you in recalling the lists.
3. Learning important definitions can be helpful for any kind of test, and they can be useful in answering many essay questions.
4. Apply the suggestions listed in the section on "Retention."

When teachers construct tests, they need to take care to avoid making the test harder to read than the original material was. If this situation exists, a student may know the material required, but the readability level of the test may be so high that he or she is unable to comprehend the questions. The student may then make a low score on a test because of the teacher's poor test preparation, rather than the student's poor knowledge of the concepts involved.

1. What does SQ3R stand for? (a) Survey, Question, Read, Recite, Review (b) Seek, Question, Read, Review, Report (c) Sequential Questioning, Read, React, Report (d) None of the above.

2. For what content area is SQRQCQ designed? (a) English (b) History (c) Science (d) None of the above.

3. Which statement below is true of outlining? (a) A main topic may have a single subdivision. (b) Indention helps to show the degree of importance of ideas in an outline. (c) Roman numeral headings are subordinate to capital letter headings. (d) None of the above.

4. Which is/are example(s) of organizational skills? (a) Outlining (b) Summarizing (c) Notetaking (d) All of the above.

5. Which of the following are contained in the card catalog? (a) Subject cards (b) Author cards (c) Title cards (d) All of the above.

6. Which of the following statements is *not* true? (a) Glossaries are found in many content area texts. (b) Skills needed to use glossaries are the same as those needed for use of the dictionary. (c) Glossaries include mainly general vocabulary words. (d) None of the above.

7. What should students know about guide words? (a) They represent the first and last entry words on a page. (b) They represent the first two entry words on a page. (c) They are found in the preface of the book. (d) None of the above.

8. What should be avoided when written reports are assigned to students? (a) Organizational skills should be stressed before starting the process. (b) The teacher should guide the students through a report-writing experience before they are asked to write independently. (c) Use of a single source of information should be encouraged. (d) None of the above.

9. Which skill(s) are involved in reading to follow directions? (a) The ability to locate details. (b) The ability to detect sequence. (c) Both of the above (d) Neither of the above.

10. Which statement describes the legend of a map? (a) It is the history of the area represented in the map. (b) It contains an explanation of each of the symbols used on the map. (c) It is located in the top, left-hand corner of the map. (d) None of the above.

11. What type of graph is easiest to read? (a) Pictograph (b) Circle graph (c) Line graph (d) Bar graph

12. What is a problem in reading charts? (a) They are generally filled with too much unimportant information. (b) They often over-simplify information. (c) Both of the above. (d) Neither of the above.

13. What is meant by flexibility of rate? (a) Reading all material as rapidly as possible. (b) Varying reading rate to fit purposes and materials. (c) Rapid reading without regard for comprehension. (d) None of the above.

14. Which factor(s) affect rate? (a) Size and style of type. (b) Author's writing style. (c) Reader's background of experiences. (d) All of the above.

15. What kind of rate machine has an arm that moves down a page of printed material from top to bottom at regulated speeds? (a) Tachistoscope (b) Controlled reading filmstrip projector (c) Pacer (d) None of the above.

16. Which of the following represents the fastest reading rate? (a) Skimming (b) Study reading (c) Scanning (d) None of the above.

Self-test

17. Which of the following can improve retention? (a) Discussing the assignment with a classmate. (b) Applying the concepts presented in the assignment. (c) Reading the assignments critically. (d) All of the above.

Enrichment activities

* 1. Teach one of the study methods described in this chapter to a class of secondary school students. Work through it with them step-by-step.

2. Make a bulletin board that would be helpful to use when teaching either outlining or notetaking. Display it either in your college classroom or in a secondary school classroom.

3. Make a set of sample card catalog cards for ten or more books. Plan a lesson on use of the card catalog. Teach this lesson to a group of your classmates. *Teach the lesson in a secondary school classroom, if possible.

4. Plan a lesson on use of the index for a secondary level textbook of your choice. Teach the lesson to a group of your classmates. *Teach the lesson in a secondary school classroom, if possible.

5. Collect materials that secondary level students often need to read to follow directions. Discuss with your classmates how you could help the students learn to read these materials more effectively.

* 6. Guide a group of secondary school students through the process of writing a group report.

7. Take a content area textbook at the secondary level and plan procedures to familiarize students with the parts of the book and the reading aids the book offers.

8. Visit a secondary school library and listen to the librarian explain the reference materials and library procedures to the students. Evaluate the presentation, and decide how you might change it if you were responsible for it.

9. Collect a variety of types of maps. Decide which features of each map will need most explanation for students.

10. Collect a variety of types of graphs. Make them into a display that could be used in a unit on reading graphs.

11. Develop a procedure to help secondary school students learn to be flexible in their rates of reading. Use materials of widely varying types.

*12. Examine several of your old tests. Decide what reading difficulties they may present to your students. Isolate special words for which meanings may have to be taught.

---

*   These activities are designed for inservice teachers, student teachers, or practicum students.

Aukerman, Robert. *Reading in the Secondary School Classroom.* New York: McGraw-Hill, 1972. Chapters 4 and 5.

Baker, William D. *Reading Skills.* Englewood Cliffs, N.J.: Prentice-Hall, 1974. Chapters 5, 6, 9, 13, 14, 15.

Berger, Allen. "Increasing Reading Rate With Paperbacks." *Reading Improvement* 9 (Winter 1972): 78–84.

Burmeister, Lou E. *Reading Strategies for Secondary School Teachers.* New York: Addison-Wesley, 1974. Chapters 5 and 11.

Burron, Arnold and Amos L. Claybaugh. *Using Reading to Teach Subject Matter.* Columbus, Ohio: Charles E. Merrill, 1974. Chapters 2 and 4.

Dechant, Emerald. *Reading Improvement in the Secondary School.* Englewood Cliffs, N.J.: Prentice-Hall, 1973, Chapter 8.

Dembo, Myron H. and Donald A. Wilson. "A Performance Contract in Speed Reading." *Journal of Reading* 16 (May 1973): 627–33.

Dewey, Melvil. *Dewey Decimal Classification and Relative Index.* Lake Placid Club, N.Y.: Forest Press, 1971.

Dillner, Martha H. and Joanne P. Olson. *Personalizing Reading Instruction in Middle, Junior, and Senior High Schools: Utilizing a Competency-Based Instructional System.* New York: Macmillan Co., 1977. Chapters 4 and 10.

Eanet, Marilyn G. and Anthony V. Manzo. "REAP—A Strategy for Improving Reading/Writing/Study Skills." *Journal of Reading* 19 (May 1976): 647–52.

Edwards, Peter. "Panorama: A Study Technique." *Journal of Reading* 17 (November 1973): 132–35.

Fiddler, Jerry B. "Contemplative Reading: A Neglected Dimension of Flexibility." *Journal of Reading* 16 (May 1973): 622–26.

Figurel, J. Allen, ed. *Reading and Inquiry.* Newark, Del.: International Reading Association, 1965.

Hafner, Lawrence, E. *Developmental Reading in Middle and Secondary Schools.* New York: Macmillan Co., 1977. Chapter 7.

Hafner, Lawrence E. *Improving Reading in Secondary Schools: Selected Readings.* New York: The Macmillan Co., 1967. Sections 6 and 9.

Herber, Harold E., ed. *Developing Study Skills in Secondary Schools.* Newark, Del.: International Reading Association, 1965. Chapters 1, 3, 4, 5, 6, 7, 8.

How to Use the Readers' Guide to Periodical Literature. New York: H. W. Wilson, 1970.

International Reading Association. *Reading Instruction in Secondary Schools.* Newark, Del.: IRA, 1964. Chapter 4.

Karlin, Robert. *Teaching Reading in High School.* Indianapolis: Bobbs-Merrill, 1972. Chapters 7 and 9.

———. *Teaching Reading in High School: Selected Articles,* Indianapolis: Bobbs-Merrill, 1969. Chapters 7 and 9.

McIntyre, Virgie. *Reading Strategies and Enrichment Activities for Grades 4–9.* Columbus, Ohio: Charles E. Merrill, 1977. Chapter 9 and Appendix.

Newcastle, Helen. "Children's Problems with Written Directions." *The Reading Teacher* 28 (December 1974): 292–94.

Pauk, Walter. "The Art of Skimming." *Reading Improvement* 2 (Winter 1965): 29–31.

———. "On Scholarship: Advice to High School Students." *The Reading Teacher* 17 (November 1963): 73–78.

**Selected
references**

————. "Study Skills! That's the Answer!" *Reading Improvement* 10 (Winter 1973): 2–6.

Putnam, Lillian R. "Don't Tell Them to Do It . . . Show Them How." *Journal of Reading* 18 (October 1974): 41–43.

Robinson, Francis P. *Effective Reading.* rev. ed. New York: Harper & Row, 1961 Chapter 2.

Schale, Florence. "Three Approaches to Faster Reading." *Reading Improvement* 2 (Spring 1965): 69–71.

Schubert, Delwyn G., ed., and Theodore L. Torgerson, consultant. *Readings in Reading: Practice-Theory-Research.* New York: Thomas Y. Crowell, 1968. Chapters 29, 32, 78, 79, 80.

Shepherd, David L. *Comprehensive High School Reading Methods.* Columbus, Ohio: Charles E. Merrill, 1973. Chapter 5.

Spache, George. *Toward Better Reading.* Champaign, Ill.: Garrard, 1963.

Thomas, Ellen Lamar and H. Alan Robinson. *Improving Reading in Every Class: A Sourcebook for Teachers.* Boston: Allyn and Bacon, 1972. Chapter 4.

Vacca, Richard. "Readiness to Read Content Area Assignments." *Journal of Reading* 20 (February 1977): 387–92.

The demands and common elements of content reading

8

This chapter explores the demands made on the reader by content reading materials. The common elements within content textbooks are examined.

As you read this chapter, try to answer these questions:

1. What are the basic differences between narrative writing and expository writing?
2. What characteristics of content materials may create problems for the reader?
3. How would you respond to this comment: There is a unique list of reading skills needed for each content area.

Purpose-setting questions

As you read this chapter, check your understanding of these terms:

content area
  reading
narrative
  materials
abstract concepts

technical
  (specialized)
  vocabulary
compact style
organization style

readability
flexible rate
graphic aids
writing patterns

Key vocabulary

There are fundamental differences in the written material of different specialized subject areas. Content reading materials are written in a different style and at a higher level of readability than the narrative materials often used for developmental reading instruction. Each discipline has its own body of concepts and vocabulary, its own style of writing, and its own style of organizing and presenting information. Furthermore, students read content materials for different purposes

The need for reading instruction with specialized subject matter

than those for which they read a novel or a short story. They use reading as a tool for learning. For many years, teachers assumed that students who could successfully read basal readers could read subjects such as science, social studies, and mathematics with equal success. Research and classroom experience have led educators to realize that reading in the content areas makes greater demands on the reader than reading narrative materials. If the student does not receive direct instruction in how to read various types of content material, he or she may tend to read all content materials in the same way as narrative material. This can defeat the learning process.

The problems involved in reading content area material are increased by the current "knowledge explosion." Knowledge is multiplying at such a rapid rate that schools can not teach all the knowledge worth having. Furthermore, many facts that are learned quickly become obsolete. Alvin Toffler writes in *Future Shock* that[1]

> at the rate at which knowledge is growing, by the time the child born today graduates from college, the amount of knowledge in the world will be four times as great. By the time that same child is 50 years old, it will be 32 times as great, and 97 percent of everything known in the world will have been learned since the time he was born.

To cope with this situation, the student must become an independent, self-directed learner and relearner, which requires the student to use reading as a means of acquiring knowledge.

Students in today's schools are expected to read large amounts of material. Textbooks are frequently supplemented by outside reading from reference materials of many kinds. Students must be able to adjust to many types of content materials. They must learn to compare and contrast the ideas of several authors and to reach conclusions on the basis of their reading. Also, inductive teaching methods require greater independence on the part of the student when reading in the various curricular areas. Since the advent of inductive teaching, students have been inundated with books, newspapers, and magazines where once they had to read only one textbook. Students must read widely and organize and structure their reading so they can participate in class discussions and write reports.

The demands of content reading   One of the best ways to become acquainted with the demands of content reading is to examine both content materials and narrative materials. Compare the excerpts from secondary textbooks given in

---

1. Alvin Toffler, *Future Shock* (New York: Bantam Books, 1970), p. 157–158.

Examples 8.1 and 8.2. Example 8.1 is from a secondary literature book and Example 8.2 is from a secondary science book. What similarities can you find?

Passage from a literature book   **Example 8.1**

You must hear, besides the first spring notes of the bluebird and the robin, four bird songs this spring. First (1) the song of the wood thrush or the hermit thrush, whichever one lives in your neighborhood. No words can describe the purity, the peacefulness, the spiritual quality of the wood thrush's simple "Come to me." It is the voice of the tender twilight, the voice of the tranquil forest, speaking to you. After the thrush (2) the brown thrasher, our finest, most gifted songster, as great a singer, I think (and I have often heard them both), as the southern mockingbird. Then (3) the operatic catbird. She sits lower down among the bushes than the brown thrasher, as if she knew that, compared with him, she must take a back seat; but for variety of notes and length of song, she has few rivals. I say *she,* when really I ought to say *he,* for it is the males of most birds that sing, but the catbird seems so long and slender, so dainty and feminine, that I think of this singer as of some exquisite operatic singer in a woman's rôle. Then (4) the bobolink; for his song is just like Bryant's bubbling poem, only better! Go to the meadows in June and listen as he comes lilting and singing over your head.

There are some birds that cannot sing: the belted kingfisher, for instance; he can only rattle. You must hear him rattle. You can do as well yourself if you will shake a "pair of bones" or heave an anchor and let the chain run fast through the hawsehole. You then must hear the downy woodpecker doing his rattling *rat-ta-tat-tat-tat-tat* (across the page and back again), as fast as *rat-ta-tat* can *tat.* How he makes the old dead limb or fence-post rattle as he drums upon it with his chisel bill! He can be heard half a mile around.

Then high-hole, the flicker (or golden-winged woodpecker), you must hear him yell, *Up-up-up-up-up-up-up-up-up-up-up-up*—a ringing, rolling, rapid kind of yodel that echoes over the spring fields.

Source: Dallas Sharp, *The Year-Out-of Doors.* Copyright 1917 by the Houghton Mifflin Co., Boston, Mass. Reprinted with permission.

Passage from a science book   **Example 8.2**

Learning in Birds. Some of the songs that birds sing are short and simple, whereas others are quite complicated. Is a bird's song an example of an inborn behavior? Or must a bird learn the songs that its parents sing? The following experiments were conducted at Rockefeller University to study these questions.

A group of white-crowned sparrows was studied. As the adults reproduced, the individual offspring were placed inside sound-proof boxes so that they were isolated from each other as well as from their parents. The boxes were equipped with microphones and speakers. The microphones picked up

**Example 8.2
(cont.)**

the sounds made by each sparrow, and a recording was made. The speakers allowed the experimenters to play selected sounds to each sparrow.

The design of the experiments called for isolating the birds at various ages. Some birds were isolated as soon as they hatched, others when they were five days old, still others when they were ten days old, and some after they were ten days old. All the sparrows were kept in isolation until they were more than one hundred days old.

The sounds made by the birds were analyzed on an electronic machine called a *sound spectrograph*, which produced a chart called a *sound spectrogram*. Using the sound spectrograms, the experimenters could make accurate comparisons of sounds. The results of the experiments are below.

1.   Sparrows that were isolated before they were ten days old did not produce songs that matched those of normal, adult sparrows.

2.   Sparrows isolated after 50–100 days did produce songs similar to those of normal, adult sparrows.

3.   Sparrows that were isolated before ten days of age that heard the tape-recorded songs of normal, adult birds sometime after they were ten days old, and before they were 50 days old, did reproduce normal adult songs.

4.   Sparrows which did not hear normal, adult songs until after they were 50 days old failed to reproduce them, and their songs differed little or not at all from birds that heard no song after 10 days of age.

What conclusions can you draw from these experiments? Is the normal, adult song of the white-crowned sparrow an inborn or a learned behavior? What happens to young sparrows that are not raised with adults? How is age associated with learning?

From *Exploring Life Science* by Walter A. Thurber, Robert E. Kilburn, and Peter S. Howell. © Copyright 1975 by Allyn and Bacon, Inc. Reprinted by permission of Allyn and Bacon, Inc.

Each of the passages explores the same topic, the songs of birds. The passage from the literature book describes the songs of birds in an easy to read manner that relates to the reader's own experience. The author uses vivid descriptive terms such as *purity, peacefulness, tender twilight, tranquil forest, gifted songster, dainty and feminine.* The reader is carried along by the description of each of the various birds' songs. The birds are characterized with descriptive terms; the catbird is described as the "operatic catbird," and the thrush is described as "the brown thrasher, our finest, most gifted songster."

The author of this passage is sharing his pleasure in the song of birds with the reader. He is also creating the mood of a June morning, which will encourage the reader to go out in search of the birds' songs. The reader is reading for the purpose of enjoying the mood created by the author's description. The mood and meaning of the selection are apparent to the reader. The reader does not have to analyze, synthesize, or reach a conclusion in order to understand.

The reader of the passage from the science textbook must read a very compact style that includes very few descriptive words. The reader must understand technical terms such as:

inborn behavior
experiment design
electronic machine
sound spectrograph
sound spectrogram
white-crowned sparrow

The reader must be able to read about the design of the experiments and then must synthesize the findings of the four studies to reach a conclusion regarding the singing of the sparrows. The reader's purpose is to reach an understanding of how birds learn to sing as a part of understanding a broader concept of inborn behavior. The reader must study this content carefully to remember the information for future reference.

Examination of the preceding passages shows some of the demands that are placed on the reader by content reading. The following discussion examines each of these demands in detail.

Basic concepts

Content textbooks are designed to teach the basic concepts of the disciplines to students. The concepts of content area materials range from concrete to abstract. The difficulty in understanding concepts increases in direct proportion to the abstractness of the concept because the more abstract a concept is, the more difficult it is to learn. Content area writing abounds in abstract concepts, such as *freedom*. A simple definition of a concept like *freedom* does not teach the reader the concept; it is only after much experience with various types of freedom that the reader will begin to comprehend the concept. Content materials tend to include a larger number of unfamiliar, abstract concepts than do narrative materials. Content area concepts may be unrelated to the experience of the reader, while the concepts found in narrative reading are more often familiar.

Concepts found in curricular material are often developed in a pyramid fashion. Students are expected to understand and remember key concepts that will serve as a basis for later learning, although the author may not make an association between earlier and later concepts. For example, in Example 8.2, taken from a science book, the reader is expected to understand the concept of how birds learn to sing; this understanding will help the reader understand inborn behavior and evaluate examples of inborn behavior. In this instance, the burden of learning is on the reader. The student who misses one concept cannot easily acquire later concepts. The student may be expected to develop an understanding of basic concepts almost entirely from reading.

Vocabulary   Concept development is linked to vocabulary development because one's vocabulary provides labels for the concepts one has acquired. Words are also an author's vehicle for expressing ideas; therefore, they are important to the reader. The vocabulary of the reading materials used in elementary schools is carefully controlled. Such material does not prepare the reader for the large number of important, unfamiliar words that will be encountered in secondary textbooks. Content materials may introduce ten or more new words per page. These words are often not repeated; thus the reader is not given an opportunity to reinforce knowledge of the new words.

The vocabulary of content materials presents other problems for the reader; for instance, one of the difficult problems encountered in content materials is the extensive specialized vocabulary of the content fields. The technical vocabulary of a field may be entirely new to the reader, and the concepts on which the vocabulary is based may be unfamiliar and abstract. In science, a reader meets words like *solar*, *planet*, and *minerals*; in social studies, words such as *culture*, *longitude*, and *adaptation*. The abstractness of such words causes difficulty because the student remembers best words that are meaningful to him or her.

A further aspect of the vocabulary problem in content materials is the use of common words in new and technical contexts. Words such as *matter*, *composition*, *series*, and *mouth* have both general and specialized meanings, which may be confusing to the reader. For example, *mouth* may refer to an oral cavity in the face; it may refer to the natural opening of a river, harbor, or a cave; or it may refer to the mouthpiece of a musical instrument. Words may shift meanings in a single selection, and the reader must be alert for these changes. Both technical and general vocabulary present a major hurdle for the reader of content materials.

Writing style   The style of writing used in content textbooks is very demanding because it is highly compact. Each word is so important that the reader cannot skip words and maintain an understanding of the content read. The compactness of expository writing is the result of compressing a large number of ideas into a few lines of print. One paragraph in a social studies textbook may cover 100 years of time, or a social studies textbook may devote only a paragraph to the Presidency of Franklin Delano Roosevelt, while other books are entirely devoted to this subject. A paragraph cannot reveal character and provide insights for the reader in the same manner as a book. A paragraph in a science book may discuss a major discovery that is based on a number of concepts, and each sentence may include several important details. The author cannot explore each scientific principle in great detail due to the limitations of space.

Writers in each of the content areas have special styles of organizing and expressing information. Knowledge in any discipline is more than a mere collection of facts. Knowledge is better described as an understanding of an interrelationship of ideas. For example, cause and effect and temporal order of events are two types of organization that are characteristic of social science writing. In reading science, knowledge is often organized around experiments. The reader must learn to identify the types of organization used in each content area and approach the material accordingly.

Organizational style

The compactness of ideas, the terseness of writing, the presentation of concepts, the patterns of writing used to structure knowledge, and the technical vocabulary create a high level of readability in content textbooks. A number of research studies have explored the difficulties students encounter when reading content textbooks. Charles Peters,[2] who studied the presentation of concepts in social studies books, found that presenting concepts in a different style than usually used in textbook writing enhanced reading comprehension. John Lee and Lee Anderson[3] researched eleventh-grade students' understanding of vocabulary in American history. They found that concepts were presented in a superficial manner which prevented students from developing understanding. Robert Ratcliffe[4] analyzed the representation of ideas in American history textbooks at fifth-grade, eighth-grade, and eleventh-grade levels. He found that the major causes of misunderstanding were insufficient definitions, details, and examples.

Readability

Classroom teachers frequently observe that the readability of content textbooks may run one or two grade levels above their grade placement. Ronald Hash[5] applied two readability formulae to three randomly selected social studies textbooks and found a range of levels as great as six years within some materials. These research studies indicate that reading content materials places great demands on the reader.

Reading in content area materials is a demanding task for the student. The reader's objectives include expanding knowledge and solving

Understanding level

2. Charles W. Peters, "The Effect of Systematic Restructuring of Material upon the Comprehension Process," *Reading Research Quarterly* 11 (1975–76): 87–111.

3. John R. Lee and Lee F. Anderson, "New Approaches to the Material for a Sequential Curriculum on American Society for Grades Five to Twelve." Vols. 1–2 (Evanston, Ill.: Social Studies Curriculum, Northwestern University, 1970).

4. Robert H. Ratcliffe, "A Critical Analysis of the Treatment Given Representative Social Science Ideas in Leading Eleventh-Grade American Textbooks" (Evanston, Ill.: Unpublished Doctoral dissertation, Northwestern University, 1966).

5. Ronald J. Hash, "The Effects of a Strategy of Structured Overviews, Level Guides and Vocabulary Exercises on Student Achievement, Reading Comprehension, Critical Thinking and Attitudes of Junior High School Classes in Social Studies," (Buffalo, N.Y.: Unpublished Doctoral dissertation, State University of New York at Buffalo, 1974), pp. 20–25.

problems. Reading for these purposes requires high levels of understanding on the part of the reader. Readers must locate information, evaluate information, relate information to other sources, and organize information so they can understand it.

Flexible rate Reading content materials requires adjusting one's rate of reading to the purpose for which one is reading; for example, the reader who is studying for an examination will read more slowly than one who is skimming an assignment for class discussion. The nature and difficulty of the materials being read further influences reading rate. A theoretical psychiatric presentation, such as *Man's Search for Meaning* by Victor Frankl, requires slower reading than the evening newspaper.

Rate is also influenced by the reader's familiarity with the content and his or her background experience. The rates a reader may adopt range from fast skimming, to cursory reading, to study reading, to the slow critical reading. (A further discussion of adjusting rate to fit purpose and material is found in Chapter 7.)

Graphic aids Graphic aids are widely used in content reading materials; therefore the reader must be able to use these aids to achieve comprehension. Content books contain pictures, graphs, charts, tables, and maps. The purpose of these aids is to express relationships in a condensed sort of language. The reader must be able to interpret graphic aids and to integrate the ideas with the content. Students are often unaware of the value of graphic aids, so they disregard these parts of the textbook without attempting to interpret them. (See Chapter 7.)

Interest An interest in the content being read is essential to reading comprehension. Content that holds no interest for the reader is difficult to understand. The content fields are concerned with areas of interest that the average reader may not have developed. The reader is usually uninterested in content that is removed from his or her experience. Since the student who is reading content textbooks may be essentially unmotivated, teachers must build motivation into their lessons to help students build broader interests and increase their comprehension.

Summary statement This section of Chapter 8 has pointed out some major differences between narrative and content area reading through emphasizing characteristics of content materials. Table 8.1 summarizes these ideas.

Characteristics of narrative and content material   Table 8.1

Narrative	Content
1. Tells story (characters, plot, theme, setting)	1. Provides information
2. General descriptive vocabulary frequently repeated	2. Specialized and technical vocabulary infrequently repeated
3. Calls for character identification	3. Calls for interaction with subject matter
4. Attention held by plot or description	4. Attention supported by form of presentation and organization
5. Use of single story or book	5. Use of supplementary materials, reference sources
6. Concepts often based on reader's experiences	6. Unfamiliar abstract concepts, concisely presented, and developed in pyramid fashion
7. Elaborate writing style	7. Terseness of writing style
8. Read for entertainment	8. Read to expand knowledge and solve problems
9. Read fairly rapidly	9. Requires slower, more flexible rate
10. Words convey meaning	10. Graphic aids (pictures, graphs, charts, tables, maps, etc.) are widely used
11. Varying readability level	11. High readability level
12. Mostly literal/interpretive levels of comprehension	12. Critical/creative levels of comprehension, as well as literal/interpretive levels

Within the content areas, there are general abilities and skills needed in most subjects. Some are cited below:

Common elements within the content areas

Abilities and skills

1. Recognizing words and developing vocabulary.
2. Understanding special concepts and technical vocabulary.
3. Discovering main ideas and supporting details.
4. Locating facts or specific details.
5. Organizing complex material by determining sequence, drawing conclusions, and finding cause and effect relationships.
6. Locating information and using reference materials.
7. Learning graphic aids and symbols common to each area.
8. Adjusting rate to purpose, difficulty, and type of material.
9. Studying and evaluating the material intelligently.
10. Developing the habit of extensive reading.

In other words, Chapter 4's Word Recognition Skills, Chapter 5's Vocabulary Development, Chapter 6's Comprehension, and Chapter 7's Reading/Study Skills are processing elements common to all subject matter material. In another way of stating this idea, *common reading skills* include (1) word recognition, (2) understanding at literal, interpretive, critical, and creative levels, and (3) making use of different speeds according to intent of reading and the nature of the subject matter. Additionally, some *study skills* common to reading any content area include (1) location of information, (2) organization, and (3) evaluation.

There are few special skills that can be associated exclusively with a specific content area. A few skills have close associations with particular areas: reading maps and time lines is largely considered in the field of social studies; formulas are associated with the field of science; mathematical symbols permeate mathematics; and understanding characters or enjoying sensory impressions are highlights of reading literature. But most reading skills are equally applicable to all content areas. It is true that certain skills may be utilized more frequently in one subject area than another. For example, the ability to note causes and effects is probably needed more frequently in social studies and science than in any other areas. But seeing cause and effect is a creative level skill used with content material other than social studies and science. Categorizing skills are needed in the reading of science material, especially biology, but they are also essential in reading social science and mathematics. Drawing conclusions cannot be thought of as belonging exclusively to any one area of the curriculum. In the course of a day, a student may be asked to draw conclusions about the main reasons for the conflict of World War II (social studies), about which geometry theories correctly apply to a problem situation (mathematics), and about the classification of a rock according to the minerals it contains (science). The ability to cope with precise, compact writing is needed with mathematics materials, but it cannot be disassociated from the reading of certain forms of literature, such as poetry. In brief, content material calls for an extensive development of essential reading skills, not a totally different configuration of skills for each content area.

Vocabulary   But what about the specialized vocabulary of each subject area? For example, vocabulary is a strong contributing factor in the difficulty of reading in chemistry. Not only is there a voluminous number of new technical words in chemistry, but many of these words are confusingly close to one another in meaning. There is no question that a number of words and concepts closely associated with each content area should be taught. An important shortcoming of past teaching has been a failure to recognize this need—and an even greater need to focus upon the student's deficiencies in overall language and concept development. For example, in a business education text, the word *commission* may be defined as "the allowance made to an agent for transacting business for another." It should be apparent that a reader needs an extensive command of language (*allowance, agent, transacting*) in order to interpret this definition. In addition, the reader must store other meanings for the term *commission* in order to understand it in other contexts, including: a warrant granting certain powers and imposing certain duties, authority to act as agent for another, a body of persons charged with performing a duty, the doing of some act, and a certificate conferring military rank and authority. Other examples of special vocabulary can easily be culled from various areas, as suggested below:

Industrial arts—polarize, bore, plane
Music—prologue, score
Government—omnibus
Algebra—variable, cancellation, premise, inverse
Psychology—plateau
Physical education—mount, routine, pike

Very few words have only one fixed meaning. The meaning of a word met in one content textbook may be inappropriate to the use of the word in another setting. Teaching special meanings for the technical vocabulary in a content area will not alone solve the problem of reading in the content areas. The technical words in a content textbook are only a small part of the words that the student must deal with in reading that text. The language facility that students need in mining the content areas goes beyond a list of technical words—they need to develop and expand concepts through their acquaintance with the homonyms, homographs (words that look alike and are often confused in meaning), high frequency root words, and the like that appear in their content reading materials.

This chapter concludes with a preview of the treatment of the various content areas presented in Chapters 9A and 9B. For the sake of explication, the patterns of writing most used in different subject areas are suggested below:

Writing patterns

Social Studies
1. Cause-and-effect pattern (ascertaining causes and effects).
2. Main ideas and supporting details pattern.
3. Chronological or sequential events pattern (events in specific time sequence).
4. Comparison and/or contrast pattern (comparing likenesses and/or differences).
5. Question and answer pattern.
6. Combination of patterns.

Reading maps, graphs, charts and pictures is prominently associated with social studies. Two additional major emphases of this content area are the reading of propaganda and the reading of newspapers and magazines.

Science
1.   Classification pattern (systems and subsystems).
2.   Instructions for an experiment (following directions).
3.   Explanation of a technical process (often accompanied by diagrams).
4.   Detailed statement-of-facts pattern (detailed facts).
5.   Cause-and-effect pattern.

Also, the use of abbreviations and equations is prominently associated with the reading of science materials.

Mathematics
1.   Problem pattern (word or verbal problem).
2.   Explanatory pattern (expounding a mathematical process).
3.   Graph and chart pattern.

Another common aspect of mathematics content books is the use of special symbols, signs, and formulae.

Literature
1.   Fictional patterns (novels, novellas, short stories).
2.   Nonfiction patterns (essays, criticism, true stories).
3.   Poetry (narrative, descriptive, lyric).
4.   Drama (tragedies, comedies, serious plays).

How-to-do-it directions are prominent in vocational-technical materials, as are diagrams, drawings, graphs, charts, and tables. These are also prevalent in the content areas of physical education, driver education, art, and music.

It has been pointed out that a pattern is not restricted to one subject area alone. Some patterns are used in several subjects. For example, in an essay or biography, the detailed statement-of-facts pattern sometimes appears, although more infrequently than it appears in science. Also cause-and-effect relationships appear within literature, but not as prominently as in the subject areas of social studies and science. (See the "Cause-and-Effect" examples from social studies and science materials in Chapter 9A.) Abbreviations and equations appear in science textbooks, but also in mathematics textbooks. For example, reading the temperatures of $0°$ C or $32°$ F in science material is similar to symbol reading in mathematics. (See the symbol reading example in Chapter 10.) Mathematical problems are presented not only in mathematics textbooks, but also in science textbooks, especially chemistry and physics. The explanatory pattern is used frequently in both mathematics and science textbooks. The explanation of a technical process (for example, "How a Television Works") is quite similar to an explanatory pattern in mathematics (such as "How Multiplying Negatives Result in a Positive"). Of course, graphs and charts appear as visual aids in mathematics, science, social studies, and other subjects. A single chapter in any content area textbook may contain several of these patterns.[6]

It is hoped that the information about writing patterns and high frequency skills suggested in the following Chapters 9A and 9B will help teachers help their students to read in the respective subject areas with greater understanding.

Concluding comments

This chapter has served as an introduction to the following chapters of 9A and 9B. It seems desirable to alert the reader to the fact that only special features of each subject area are discussed in Chapters 9A and 9B—such as technical vocabulary, writing patterns, prominent skills associated with the subject, common aspects of certain subject materials, the scope of materials for reading, and suggestions for helping with some of the reading tasks posed.

While considering the individual content areas in Chapters 9A and 9B, the reader should keep in mind the broader recommendations, appropriate for all subjects, that are made in this book for the integration of reading into the content areas. Eight principles of basic instruction form the framework for overall planning. They are:

1. Gain a reasonable estimate of each student's reading ability. (See Chapter 10.)
2. Further diagnose the ability to read material in the specific content area. Such diagnosis includes use of the cloze procedure and informal skills inventories as described in Chapter 10.
3. On the basis of findings, provide material at the student's instructional level. (See Chapters 3 and 10.)
4. Prepare the student for the reading assignments. This includes use of structured overviews and directed reading

---

6. All writers do not use exactly the same terms or categories for the major writing patterns in subject matter content. For example, H. Alan Robinson (*Teaching Reading and Study Strategies: The Content Areas*, Boston: Allyn and Bacon, 1975) uses the following format for explaining forms, presenting examples, and providing strategies for helping readers unlock ideas within each pattern of writing:

Social Studies: Topic Development, Enumeration, Generalization, Sequence, Comparison or Contrast, Effect-Cause, and Question-Answer.

Science: Enumeration, Classification, Generalization, Problem Solution, Comparison or Contrast, Sequence.

Mathematics: Concept Development, Principle Development, Problem Solving.

English: Short Stories, Novels, Drama, Poetry, Essays, Autobiographies, and Biographies.

The reader is encouraged to explore the Robinson book and others in conjuction with reading of Chapters 9A and 9B.

lessons as explained in Chapter 3, as well as the teaching of technical vocabulary as discussed in Chapters 4 and 5.

5. Help guide the student's reading. This may be done through the use of study guides (see Chapter 3), interpretation at various thinking levels (see Chapter 6), and becoming aware of patterns of writing and high frequency skills associated with the content area. (See Chapters 9A and 9B.)

6. Reinforce through practice the vocabulary (see Chapters 4 and 5) and reading-study skills (see Chapter 7) pertinent to the content area.

7. Assist student retention. Provide test-taking helps. (See Chapter 7.)

8. Extend interests of students. Stimulating recreational and supplementary reading in the content area is the key device.

Such teaching procedures integrate reading with the teaching of the content areas. The content area teacher is the best qualified person for implementing these proposals since he or she is most knowledgeable in (1) identifying content material demands, (2) setting purposes and teaching technical vocabulary, (3) identifying important concepts to be arrived at, (4) knowing how to best read and study the text, and (5) using resource materials to develop and broaden experiences and to motivate student interest.

Self-test

1. Which of the following styles of writing is used in most content textbooks? (a) Expository (b) Narrative (c) Fictional (d) None of these.

2. Which of the following factors represents fundamental difficulties a student encounters when reading content materials? (a) Vocabulary (b) Language patterns (c) Printing (d) Both a and b.

3. Which of the following phrases explains the pyramid development of concepts in content textbooks? (a) The content is written in the form of a pyramid. (b) The content teaches students how to understand pyramids. (c) Each concept developed depends upon previously developed concepts. (d) Concept development helps students measure pyramids.

4. Which type of vocabulary creates a comprehension problem for many students? (a) Technical vocabulary (b) Sight words (c) Spelling vocabulary (d) None of these.

5. What does the term *compact style* mean as it relates to content materials? (a) Many ideas per sentence and paragraph (b) Smaller print used (c) Fewer pictures used (d) Lack of explanations

6. What is the main objective of content reading? (a) Entertainment (b) Expanding knowledge (c) Fulfilling teacher assignments (d) Completing the curriculum.

7. Which of the following are graphic aids used in textbooks? (a) Maps (b) Graphs (c) Pictures (d) All of these.

8. What word best describes the concepts usually presented in content textbooks? (a) Long (b) Abstract (c) Familiar (d) Funny
9. Why are concepts presented in content materials difficult for students? (a) Students do not want to learn them. (b) They are not colorful. (c) They are abstract. (d) None of these
10. Why do writers of content textbooks use different styles for organizing information? (a) To make the books interesting (b) Because they like to write in different ways (c) To explain the knowledge of the discipline (d) To make reading easier
11. What does the term *flexible rate* mean? (a) Reading very rapidly (b) Adjusting rate to the type of content being read (c) Using a tachistoscope for reading (d) Reading very slowly
12. How many special reading skills are unique to one specific content area? (a) Few (b) Many (c) Depends upon content area (d) None
13. Which is an example of a reading study skill common to any content area? (a) Rate adjustment (b) Location of information (c) Determining organization (d) All of these
14. In which subject area are cause-and-effect patterns probably most frequent? (a) Literature (b) Health (c) Social studies (d) Mathematics

---

Enrichment activities

1. Select a content textbook and a literature book at the same grade level and compare them on the following points: (a) number of adjectives and adverbs. (b) abstract concepts. (c) types of organization of content.
* 2. Visit a classroom at a secondary level and interview students regarding their reading interests. Compare their stated reading interests with the topics in their content textbooks.
* 3. Interview a good secondary school reader regarding the reading problems he or she encounters. Interview a student who is not a good reader regarding his or her reading problems. Compare the responses of the two students.
4. Use a readability formula to evaluate the readability level of a content textbook. (See Chapter 3.)
5. Select a content textbook and locate in the textbook an example of each reading demand cited in this chapter.
6. Select a paragraph from a content textbook and rewrite it in an easier-to-read fashion.
7. Discuss the following statements: "The major problem in teaching any content area is the specialized vocabulary of that subject," and "There has been an overemphasis upon specialized vocabulary in the content areas."
8. Make a list of several of the words and definitions provided in the glossary of a content book. What information is needed to

---

* These activities are designed for inservice teachers, student teachers, and practicum students.

interpret the definitions? What other meanings must the reader know to understand the words in other contexts?

9. Begin to collect patterns of writing as classified in this chapter (and in Chapters 9A and 9B) from content area textbooks. Try to find examples where the same pattern is used in several subject areas. Also try to find an example where the pattern occurs mostly in a single content area.

10. Find a representative passage from a content area textbook. Bring a copy of it to class for discussion purposes. List as many of the reading demands cited in this chapter as you can find in the selection. Cite the exact words, phrases, or sentences that illustrate each reading demand.

Selected references

Aukerman, Robert. *Reading in the Secondary School Classroom.* New York: McGraw-Hill, 1972. Chapters 7–12.

Burmeister, Lou E. *Reading Strategies for Secondary School Teachers.* New York: Addison-Wesley, 1974. Chapters 6–9.

Dechant. Emerald. *Reading Improvement in the Secondary School.* Englewood Cliffs, N.J.: Prentice Hall, 1973. Chapter 9.

Dillner, Martha and Joanne Olson. *Personalizing Reading Instruction in Middle, Junior, and Senior High Schools.* New York: Macmillan Co., 1977. Chapter 6.

Earle, Richard A. *Teaching Reading and Mathematics.* Newark, Del.: International Reading Association, 1976.

Hafner, Lawrence. *Improved Reading in Middle and Secondary Schools.* 2nd ed. New York: Macmillan Co., 1974. Section 10.

———— *Developmental Reading in Middle and Secondary Schools.* New York: Macmillan Co., 1977. Chapters 8–19.

Herber, Harold. *Teaching Reading in Content Areas.* Englewood Cliffs, N.J.: Prentice Hall, 1970.

Karlin, Robert. *Teaching Reading in High School.* 2nd ed. Indianapolis, Ind.: Bobbs-Merrill, 1972. Chapters 8, 12.

———— *Teaching Reading in High Schools: Selected Articles.* Indianapolis, Ind.: Bobbs-Merrill, 1969. Chapter 12.

Marksheffel, Ned. *Better Reading in Secondary Schools.* New York: Ronald Press, 1962. Chapter 8.

Miller, Wilma H. *Teaching Reading in the Secondary School.* Springfield, Ill.: Charles C. Thomas, 1974. Chapters 11–18.

Robinson, H. Alan. *Teaching Reading and Study Strategies.* (Boston: Allyn and Bacon, 1975). Chapters 6–10.

Robinson, H. Alan and Ellen Lamar Thomas, ed. *Fusing Reading Skills and Content.* Newark, Del.: International Reading Association, 1969.

Shepherd, David. *Comprehensive High School Reading Methods.* Columbus, Ohio: Charles E. Merrill, 1973. 8–12.

Thelen, Judith. *Improving Reading in Science.* Newark, Del.: International Reading Association, 1976.

Reading in the content areas: part 1

This chapter explores the specific reading skills required by the following content subjects: the social sciences, the sciences, mathematics, English (language arts), and foreign languages.

As you read this chapter, try to answer these questions:

1. What are the reading skills you think are required in such fields as social studies, science, mathematics, language arts, and foreign languages? Make a list of skills for each subject. As you read this chapter, check to see if your predictions are accurate.
2. What common writing patterns appear in these content areas?

Purpose-setting questions

As you read this chapter, check your understanding of these terms:

Key vocabulary

expository writing
writing patterns
cause and effect
   patterns
main idea and
   supporting details
chronological and
   sequential
comparison and
   contrast

classification
experimental
explanation of a
   process
detailed
   statement-of-fact
problem-solving
word (verbal)
   problem

graphs and charts
poetry
drama
fiction
nonfiction
individualized
   reading

The social sciences include economics, sociology, political science, history, geography, civics, and anthropology. One of the goals of schools in the United States is to perpetuate the principles of democratic government; therefore, social studies are the core of the overall curriculum. Being able to read social studies content material helps

The social sciences

237

students become effective citizens of a democracy. To achieve this goal students must develop reading skills that will enable them to:

1. understand the ideas and viewpoints of others.
2. acquire and retain a body of relevant concepts and information.
3. think critically and creatively, thus developing attitudes and values and learning to make decisions.

Vocabulary, style, and organization

Technical vocabulary contributes to the difficulty some students experience when reading social studies. Students must learn the meanings of such words as *barriers, dominion, democracy, domestic, tyranny,* and *expansion* in order to understand social studies material. A student must comprehend 75 percent of the ideas and 90 percent of the vocabulary of a social studies selection to read it at an instructional level, thus to learn something from it and to avoid frustration.[1] Even higher levels of understanding and vocabulary knowledge are required to achieve independent reading levels. (Refer to Chapter 5, pages 118 to 135, for vocabulary teaching techniques.)

Social science materials are written in an expository style, which is a precise, factual way of writing. Example 9A.1 serves as an example of this style of writing. As you read this example, note the lack of description. Also note the use of technical language that must be defined so the reader can understand the content. Several technical terms are introduced in the short section of material. The reader must both understand the technical terms and remember them in future reading of economics. The reader must also read the graph and relate it to the content of the selection.

Authors use a variety of organizational patterns for developing topics in social science textbooks. The most common organizational patterns are:

1. Regional—Topics are developed according to regions such as the Middle-East, North America, etc.
2. Chronological—Topics are developed according to periods of time, usually beginning in the past and moving toward the present.
3. Movements—A book is organized around major movements in history such as the Industrial Movement.

---

1. Wayne L. Herman, Jr., "Reading and Other Language Arts in Social Studies Instruction: Persistent Problems," in *A New Look at Reading in the Social Studies,* Ralph Preston, ed. (Newark, Del.: International Reading Association, 1969), p.5.

4.   Concepts—Concepts such as culture, transportation, or economics often serve as an organizing focus.

The reader can usually determine the organization of a book by
reading the preface and the table of contents. Recognition of the
organizational pattern should provide a mental set that will aid the
reader in understanding what he or she is reading.

Students should understand that authors cannot include all of the
available information on a topic in a single social science textbook;
each writer selects information to include according to his or her point
of view and purpose. This necessary brevity makes critical reading

Sample Social Science Material   **Example 9A.1**

Gross National Product

The figures relating to the size, growth, and distribution of a
country's population interest economists because they are associated
with the total performance of that country's economy—the production
of goods and services. Economists measure total performance by
computing Gross National Product (GNP), *the total market value of all
goods and services produced in a given year*. Diagram E shows the
components of GNP and their relative size in a recent year.

DIAGRAM E: ITEMS IN GROSS NATIONAL PRODUCT

GOVERNMENT
Highways
Defense
Education

NONDURABLE GOODS
Food
Clothing
Medicine

SERVICES
Transportation
Utilities
Entertainment

DURABLE GOODS
Automobiles
Appliances

CAPITAL EQUIPMENT AND CONSTRUCTION
Factories
Machinery
Houses

Goods can also be classified in other
ways. Some goods are primarily for the
use of consumers; others are used primarily by those people who manufacture or
produce other goods. The former category, "consumer goods," would include
such items as clothing, television sets,
refrigerators, shoes, and food. The latter
category, "producer or *capital* goods,"
would include machines, tools, factory
buildings, and any other items used to
produce still *other* goods.

The category of "services" includes
what we pay for automobile and television repairmen, the fees of doctors and
lawyers, the salaries and incomes of
musicians, actors, and writers, and pay-
ments for other kinds of services
provided by American private enterprise.

Comparisons of GNP figures for various years can give you an idea of the
changes in the total economy of a country. It is also helpful to know what
changes in GNP mean in terms of the population. Therefore,
economists measure GNP *per capita* (per person) by dividing the GNP
by the total population. You should realize that GNP *per capita* is
purely a statistical device and does not measure or describe how the
GNP is *actually* distributed among the individual members of the
total population.

Graph F contains the figures for both GNP and GNP *per capita*
during selected historical periods. Did the GNP grow at a faster or
slower rate than the population as a whole? How do you account for
this? Why does the increase in GNP *per capita* apparently increase less
than the total GNP?

GNP reflects the total amount of goods and services produced in
an economy, but we are also interested in the changing composition

Source: from *Land of Progress*, page 168, by Irwin Unger and H. Mark Johnson © Copyright 1975 by Ginn
and Company (Xerox Corporation). Used with permission.

important in the social sciences. The reader must read more than a single textbook in order to achieve a full understanding of a topic. Critical reading is especially important when an author does not write just about *what* has happened, but about *why* events have occurred. Biases are likely to appear when an author explains causes of events. An author's point of view is affected by the following factors.[2]

1. author's age.
2. author's nationality.
3. author's religion.
4. author's political views.
5. author's race.
6. author's family history.
7. author's sex.
8. audience for whom author is writing.

Writing patterns   As well as organizing and introducing topics according to one of the four common patterns cited earlier, an author can structure ideas and concepts in a variety of ways. These include structuring according to:

1. cause and effect.
2. main idea and supporting details.
3. chronological or sequential events.
4. comparison and/or contrast
5. questions and answers.
6. a combination of ways. (The first five ways of organizing information rarely exist in isolation, but are often used in combination.)[3]

Cause and effect is a frequently used writing pattern in social science materials. Each of the social sciences is concerned with chains of causes and effects where one cause results in certain effects that become the causes of other effects. Example 9A.2 shows cause and effect writing.

Example 9A.2   *Sample cause and effect writing*

Where formerly the British had been willing to relax the mercantile system to let the colonists trade with countries outside the Empire, they now tightened up on the laws. In addition, the British taxed the colonists to obtain revenue, giving as the reason the high cost of victory over the French and the need for maintaining

---

2. Irwin Unger and H. Mark Johnson, *Land of Progress* (Lexington, Massachusetts: Ginn and Company (Xerox Corporation): 1975, p. 29.

3. Nila Banton Smith. "Patterns of Writing in Different Subject Areas," *Journal of Reading* 8 (November 1964): 100–1.

troops in the colonies to forestall future wars and keep the Indians in check. The colonists objected to taxation on the ground that they had no representation in Parliament to defend their interests.

Taxation, the quartering of troops in the colonies, the closing of the western frontier: these and other measures led to violence on the part of both British and Americans. The Boston Massacre of 1770 was caused by the unwelcome presence of British redcoats, who fired on a jeering, rock-throwing Boston mob that had gotten out of control. The Boston Tea Party of 1773, where British tea was thrown into the harbor, was a violent protest against a very moderate tax placed on that product. Such incidents widened the rift, causing the Americans to convene Continental Congresses to promote united action against the homeland.

Even after the violence flamed into open warfare at Lexington Green and Concord, Massachusetts, the Americans still hoped to reconcile with the British. When they refused, Thomas Paine and other advocates of independence led the Americans to accept their destiny and to sever ties with the motherland.

From *Land of Progress* by Irwin Unger and H. Mark Johnson, © Copyright 1975 by Ginn and Company (Xerox Corporation). Used with permission.

The following techniques are useful in helping students develop the skills required to understand cause and effect patterns.

Activities
1. State some effects and ask students to identify the causes. Ask them to answer the question, "Why did this happen?" after reading the material in Example 9A.2.
   a. The colonists objection to taxation was caused by _____
   _____.
   b. The taxes levied on the colonists by the British were caused by _____.
2. State some causes and ask students to identify the effects. Have them answer the question, "What did this fact cause?"
   a. The cost of the French war and the cost of maintaining troops in the colonies caused _____.
   b. The British levied taxes on the colonists which caused
   _____.
3. Develop a chart like the following to relate causes and effects.

Cause	Effect
French war and maintaining colonial troops	Taxes levied on colonists
Taxes levied by British	Boston Tea Party
Taxation, quartering of troops in colonies, closing western frontier	Violence such as Boston Massacre and Boston Tea Party

4. Develop a matching exercise to match causes and effects.

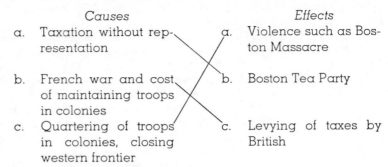

Causes	*Effects*
a. Taxation without representation	a. Violence such as Boston Massacre
b. French war and cost of maintaining troops in colonies	b. Boston Tea Party
c. Quartering of troops in colonies, closing western frontier	c. Levying of taxes by British

The *main idea and supporting details* pattern of organizing knowledge is also used frequently in social science materials. The main idea is the "big idea" or the broad general idea that is supported by details in a selection.

Example 9A.3 provides an example of the main idea and supporting details pattern.

Example 9A.3   *Sample pattern of main idea and supporting details*

Colonial Government

Each of the thirteen mainland colonies had its own local government. These dealt with the wide range of day-to-day problems of crime, business contracts, health, safety, and family concerns that occur in every community. The local laws to handle these problems were passed by the colonial legislatures. These lawmaking bodies normally consisted of two houses, a lower house elected by the voters, and an upper chamber usually called the Council chosen by the Governor. The appointed Council was obviously not as democratic as the lower house. But even in the house, voting was restricted to white males who owned a certain amount of property or paid a certain amount of taxes.

The governors were powerful men. They could propose new laws and veto those passed by the legislatures. They could also suspend the colonial legislatures when they disliked what they were doing. The governors were appointed by the king of England and his advisers.

Besides controlling the colonies through the governors, Great Britain also exercised control through various other bodies in England. For example, Parliament could make laws for the entire Empire, including the colonies.

From *Land of Progress* by Irwin Unger and H. Mark Johnson, © Copyright 1975 by Ginn and Company (Xerox Corporation). Used with permission.

The techniques discussed in Chapter 6 for understanding main ideas may be used to teach this pattern. Outlining, which is discussed in Chapter 7, is useful for helping students comprehend this pattern. Following is an outline based on the above selection.

    I.   Each colony had local government
        A.   Day to day problems handled
            1.   crime
            2.   business
            3.   health
            4.   safety
        B.   Colonial legislature (lawmaking body) composed of two houses
            1.   upper house—appointed by governor
            2.   lower house—elected by voters
        C.   Voters (white male property owners and/or taxpayers)

In the *chronological or sequential events* pattern of writing, events are arranged in order of occurrence; thus, a chronological pattern presents a sequence based on time and space. Students should be helped to develop a concept of time by considering its relationship to their own lives. Understanding time is necessary to reading social science material with understanding. However, memorization of dates his little value as compared to thinking about and understanding what one has read. Since indefinite time references such as "in early days" or "in ancient times" may confuse the reader, teachers should prepare students for these references and discuss their meanings.

An example of the chronological pattern of writing is in Example 9A.4.

Sample of chronological pattern of writing　　　　　　　　　**Example 9A.4**

Civil War
The war began in April, 1861, at Fort Sumter, South Carolina, where Federal troops were stationed on an island in Charleston harbor. Confederate forces opened fire after the Union garrison refused to surrender. Southern artillery soon pounded Fort Sumter into submission.

Four years later—after Bull Run, Shiloh, Gettysburg, and Appomattox—it was all over. Northern industrial might and doggedness overpowered Southern chivalry and heroism. In the modern world, then emerging, slavery had to be abolished once and for all, and Americans on both sides of the Mason-Dixon line today do not regret it. As of April, 1865, a reunited nation, forged in the fires of civil war, started patching its wounds and looking towards the future.

Understanding chronological patterns may be developed by the use of the following techniques.

Activities

1. Guide students to understand blocks of time. Seeking relationships among events helps students comprehend time. Given the material in Example 9A.4, the student should understand that the twenty years prior to the Civil War was the period when the immediate causes of the war became apparent and that a great many factors which led to the war developed during that period. The war itself lasted from 1861 until 1865. It was followed by the Reconstruction period. Each of these three blocks of time are interrelated. A time line can help students understand blocks of time in a concrete way.

Civil War

April, 1861	*April, 1865*
War began	War ended
nation divided	nation reunited
some states left	beginning of
union	Reconstruction
	period

2. Relate a time sequence to a student's own experience with time and help the student develop a concept of the past, present, and future. The student can relate historic occurrences to his or her lifetime and the lifetimes of his or her parents and ancestors. For example, the Civil War probably occurred in the lifetime of the great, great grandparents of present-day students.

Past	*Ancestors*
Civil War	great, great grandparents
World War I	great grandparents
World War II	grandparents
Korean Conflict	parents
Present	student
Future	descendants

Comparison and/or contrast patterns are used to explain social science ideas. Basically this pattern uses likeness and differences as a means of developing understanding. Example 9A.5 shows this writing pattern.

Example 9A.5   *Sample of comparison/contrast writing pattern*

Though he was an aristocrat, Jefferson held remarkably democratic political views. He had strong faith in the people and hoped the United States would become a nation of sturdy, independent farmers living under a government that emphasized local self-rule. Jefferson favored the Constitution, but he did not wish to see too much power slip into the hands of the Federal government. Where the constitution was unclear, he preferred to see the power remain in the hands of the states.

Hamilton had little patience with Jefferson's states' rights views. He wanted a strong and active national government that would attract the support of merchants and businessmen and help make the country powerful and rich.

Unlike Jefferson, Hamilton favored stretching the meaning of the Constitution, if necessary, so that Congress could pass laws that would strengthen the Federal government. For example, Hamilton wanted a national bank, run in the interests of the government and private business. Nowhere did the Constitution say that such a bank could be chartered, and Thomas Jefferson argued that, *strictly* speaking, there could be no bank, if it was not mentioned. But Alexander Hamilton noted that, according to the Constitution, Congress may "borrow money on the credit of the United States." These words, *loosely* speaking, authorized the establishment of a national bank, Hamilton insisted — and he had his way! The Bank of the United States was started in 1791.

Hamilton and his followers were known as "loose constructionists" in interpreting the Constitution. They formed the conservative Federalist party to which our first two Presidents, George Washington and John Adams, belonged. Supreme Court Chief Justice John Marshall used a loose construction approach in a series of momentous decisions that established the authority of the Federal government over the state governments.

Jefferson and his states' rights supporters were "strict constructionists." Their views were upheld by the liberal Antifederalist, or Democratic-Republican, party. Jefferson's belief in a relatively weak national government won strong support in the Southern states.

From *Land of Progress* by Irwin Unger and H. Mark Johnson, © Copyright 1975 by Ginn and Company (Xerox Corporation). Used with permission.

Understanding of the comparison and/or contrast pattern can be developed through use of the following techniques.

Activities

1. A chart can be developed that shows comparisons and contrasts. The following chart is based on the Example 9A.5 selection and shows the contrasts between Jefferson and Hamilton.

Jefferson	Hamilton
Self-rule	Strong national government
States rights	Opposed states rights
Constitution to protect states from interference of federal government.	Constitution to expand power of Federal government
Opposed national bank	Wanted national bank
"Strict Constructionist"	"Loose Constructionist"

2. The teacher may provide contrasts and ask the students to locate comparisons or, from the example selection provided, the teacher may provide Jefferson's points of view and ask the students to locate the contrasting views of Hamilton.

Jefferson	*Hamilton*
Believed in states rights	
Opposed national bank	

A *question and answer* pattern is sometimes used to organize social science materials. In this pattern, the author asks a question that he answers for the reader. The reader should be able to recall the questions the author poses and identify the answers provided. Example 9A.6 suggests this style of writing.

Example 9A.6   *Sample question/answer writing pattern*

Now, how accurate are these descriptions that we read? Did the people who wrote them tell the absolute truth? This is a difficult question to answer! Though everyone tries to be honest and accurate in describing what he sees, his feelings color his reporting. For example, a reporter who is sympathetic with workers conducting a strike will probably write an account of the strike which favors those workers. Another reporter who opposes the strike can be expected to offer a somewhat different version of the same event. By the same token, the activities of the President of the United States (whoever he may be) are generally presented with a note of approval by those writers who support him, and with a note of disapproval by his opponents. These slanted feelings or prejudices are called *bias*, a concept which will be dealt with throughout this unit.

Sources. Historians usually classify records as one of two types: primary or secondary sources. Eyewitness accounts of historical events are called primary sources. These sources consist of contemporary newspaper accounts, chronicles, letters, diaries, and speeches. Secondary sources, such as textbooks, are written by authors who study the primary sources and try to interpret and explain their true meaning. The texts' authors then present us with their version of history, in their own words. Both primary and secondary sources have built-in advantages and limitations for the student of history.

Which source—primary or secondary—would probably contain more historical data and information? Which source would probably be more free from bias or personal feeling? Is history what *actually* happened, or what people *think* happened? Is there any way to discover what *actually* happened? These are hard questions that historians must face.

Trying to find the truth of history by sifting through primary and secondary sources is no easy task. As you can imagine, you will encounter many different interpretations of historical figures, trends, and events, depending on the bias and viewpoint of the people reporting them.

From *Land of Progress* by Irwin Unger and H. Mark Johnson, © Copyright 1975 by Ginn and Company (Xerox Corporation). Used with permission.

In a *combination pattern* of writing the student should identify the kinds of writing patterns used and the teacher should use the techniques suggested for these individual patterns to help the student understand the selection.

In addition to learning to recognize the organizational patterns used for writing social science materials, the reader should develop skills for reading propaganda, maps, graphs, charts, and pictures.

Additional skills

Nila Smith has defined propaganda as a "deliberate attempt to persuade a person to accept a point of view or take a certain line of action."[4] Although textbooks are often thought of as being free of propaganda, if Smith's definition is applied, it becomes apparent that readers encounter propaganda in textbooks as well as in newspapers and magazines. Students should learn to identify and analyze the propaganda devices used in books, magazines and newspapers. Techniques for identifying and analyzing propaganda are discussed in detail in Chapter 6.

Readers of social studies materials are frequently asked to refer to maps. They should develop a sense of direction and an understanding of distance as they learn to read maps. Students need to have experience in reading a variety of maps, such as physical, political, population, and economics maps. They also should practice relating maps to written content. Refer to Chapter 7 for a discussion of map reading skills.

Graphs and charts are vehicles for presenting information in a concise manner. Frequently students skip graphs and charts because they do not recognize the value of the information contained in them. However, students can and should learn to use the information from these sources effectively.

Students should use the following steps when reading a graph or chart:

1. Read the title to determine exactly what information is being given.
2. Read the figures or labels and be sure that you grasp what they stand for.

---

4. Nila B. Smith, *Reading Instruction for Today's Children* (Englewood Cliffs, N.J.: Prentice Hall, 1963), p. 273.

3. Study the graph or chart and make comparisons among the different items illustrated.
4. Interpret the significance of the chart or graph as a whole.[4]

Pictures in social studies textbooks also convey information to the reader who considers them carefully. The reader should examine pictures and read captions and relate the information to the textual content in order to achieve a full understanding.

Using newspapers and magazines   Newspapers and magazines are excellent media for reading instruction because they are readily available and they treat a wide variety of subject matter. Newspapers and magazines are highly motivating for secondary students because they focus on the present. They are interesting to students who have been turned off by formal reading materials. Newspapers have the added advantage of providing a fresh set of materials each day. Magazines enable students to pursue special interests in depth.

Readability   The interest level, the style of writing, and the vocabulary of newspapers and magazines make them very readable for secondary students. The daily newspaper in many cities is easier to read than the textbooks students are using in school. A recent analysis of the readability of the front page of a daily newspaper in a large North Carolina city revealed that the front page ranged from seventh grade to tenth grade in readability. A similar analysis of the front page of a weekly newspaper from a small Ohio town revealed a readability of fourth-grade level. The readability of different sections of newspapers varies; however, newspapers generally are easier to read than textbooks. An analysis of the readability of an article in a current women's magazine revealed a readability of fourth-grade level; however, the readability of magazines varies from article to article. The readability of different magazines also varies considerably.

Reading skills that can be taught with newspapers and magazines   Newspapers and magazines can be used to develop reading skills that range from decoding to critical and creative reading. Following is a list of skills that can be taught through these media:

1. Word identification and recognition
2. Vocabulary
3. Literal reading
4. Interpretive reading

---

5. Nila Banton Smith, "Patterns of Writing in Different Subject Areas," *Journal of Reading* 8 (November 1964): 101

5. Critical reading
6. Creative reading
7. Flexible rate
8. Reading pictures, charts, graphs, and maps

Techniques for developing reading skills with newspapers and magazines Ideas for the eight skills cited above are presented in turn.

Activities

1. Word identification and recognition
   a. Practice decoding unknown words through use of context
   b. Practice identifying common words as sight words.
2. Vocabulary
   a. Learn the meanings of the special terms of journalism, such as *beat, deadline, linotype,* and *byline.*
   b. Work crossword puzzles found in newspapers and magazines.
   c. Study abbreviations and acronyms found in newspapers and magazines, such as *FBI, CIA,* and *WIN.*
   d. Locate examples of vivid language used to describe sports events.
   e. Find examples in which the same word is used with different meanings. For example, in one selection the word *run* may mean a run in a baseball game, while in another selection it may mean a run in a stocking.
   f. Suggest synonyms and antonyms for words used in newspapers and magazines.
3. Literal reading
   a. Locate the main points in an article and the writer's support for his main points.
   b. Read the classified advertisements to find a job students would like to fill and write a letter of application responding to the qualifications listed in the advertisement.
   c. Ask specific literal questions related to news stories or advertisements, such as: Who won the baseball game? Which grocery has the cheapest coffee?
   d. Locate *who, where, when, why,* and *how* in a newspaper story.
   e. List in sequence the steps of a how-to-do-it article.
   f. Follow directions for making an item found in a newspaper or magazine.
   g. Examine a newspaper to determine the percentage of space used for advertising.

4. Interpretive reading
    a. Identify the point of view of an editorial.
    b. Compare two editorials for likeness, difference, and point of view.
    c. Compare the treatment of a news event in a news story and in an editorial.
    d. Find examples of an author's interpretation in a news story.
    e. Ask questions such as the following:
        1) How does one reporter's writing differ from another reporter's writing?
        2) What can you learn about the author from the way he writes news stories?
    f. Ask students to state the effects they anticipate as the result of a news event. This exercise may be developed in the form of a chart such as the following:

News Event	*Effects*

5. Critical reading
    a. Analyze articles, editorials, and advertisements for examples of fact and opinion.
    b. Analyze the connotative use of words in newspapers to influence the reader.
    c. Analyze news stories related to controversial topics for bias.
    d. Evaluate the effectiveness of editorials in achieving their purposes.
    e. Determine whether the writer of a news story was well informed.
    f. Ask questions such as the following:
        1. Did the writer omit important information?
        2. Does the story fit with what the reader knows from past experience?
    g. Analyze advertisements to find examples of various types of propaganda.
    h. Analyze advertising to determine if it appeals to emotions or logic.
6. Creative reading
    a. Write an advertisement for an item or service that is advertised in a newspaper or magazine.

    b.   Rewrite a news story to improve it.

    c.   Write a letter to the editor on a topic of concern.

    d.   Create a cartoon relating to a controversial issue or personality.

    e.   Write a review of a movie or a television show.

    f.   Dramatize a news story.

7. Flexible rate

    a.   Ask students to suggest the rates at which various sections of the newspapers or magazines should be read.

    b.   Ask students to make a list of the purposes they have for reading newspapers and magazines.

    c.   Skim news stories and advertisements for main ideas.

    d.   Scan the entertainment section to locate the time of the late showing of a movie.

8. Reading pictures, charts, graphs, and maps

    a.   Learn to identify the different types of pictures used in newspapers, such as file photographs, on the spot photographs, and drawings.

    b.   Analyze the information provided in graphs, maps, and charts.

    c.   Discuss the value of pictures, graphs, maps, and charts for illustrating the news.

Sample lesson plan for developing reading skills with the newspaper   **Example 9A.7**

Objectives:
To identify fact and opinion in a news story
To identify bias in a news story
To suggest effects of a news event

Material:
Articles from several newspapers relating to the Supreme Court ruling that allows lawyers to advertise routine legal services.

Introduction:
Ask the students if they have heard any discussion or read anything about the Supreme Court ruling. Ask the students what they think about advertising by lawyers. Have them supply reasons.

Purposes for silent reading:
Do the authors of these articles agree with your opinion?
Do the writers present any advantages or disadvantages of this advertising?
Do you think the writers are biased in their presentations of the story?

Example 9A.7 (cont.)   *Silent reading:*
Allow sufficient time for silent reading of the selections.

Follow-up discussion:
Discuss the questions posed as silent reading purposes as well as the following questions.
Did the writers of these articles all have the same attitude regarding the topic?
Were they expressing fact or opinion? How do you know they were stating facts or opinions?
Why do you think the writers were biased if they were?

Extension activities:
The class members may conduct a poll to determine how many people are opposed to this ruling and how many in favor of the ruling. The class may analyze the reasons for voting yes or no.
The students may locate further information on the topic by reading additional newspapers and magazines.
The class may develop a chart of the effects of this ruling based upon their reading, discussion, and poll.

Sources of newspaper teaching materials   The following materials are available from the sources cited.

American Newspaper Publishers Association Foundation, 750 Third Avenue, New York, N.Y. 10017.
  Daily Newspaper in the School Curriculum
  The Teacher and the Newspaper
  Units on the Study of the Newspaper for English Classes, Grades 7–12
  How to Get More Out of Your Newspaper
  Remedial Reading and the Newspaper

Chicago Tribune Educational Services, 654 Tribune Tower, 435 North Michigan Ave., Chicago, Ill. 60611.
  Catalysts for Change: Secondary Level Social Sciences
  Innovate! A Generative Guide to Inquiry Teaching of Communication Skills.

Miami Herald, 1 Herald Plaza, Miami, Fla. 33101.
  Conner, B. G. and R. E. Bullington, *The Living Textbook: A Teacher's Manual for the Use of the Newspaper in the Classroom.*

Educational Services Program, Detroit Free Press, 321 West Lafayette, Detroit, Mich. 48231.
  Detroit Free Press: The Story of a Newspaper
  Using the Newspaper's Weather Column: A Teacher's Guide

Using the Newspaper in the Classroom: Junior High School Teacher's Manual

National Council for the Social Studies, Department of the National Education Association, Washington, D.C. 22325
How to Use Daily Newspapers.

The New York Times Curriculum Aids, College and School Service, 229 West 43 St., New York, N.Y. 10036
Get More out of Your Newspaper
Introduction to a Good Reading Habit
The New York Times in the Economics Classroom
The New York Times in English Classes
The New York Times Enriching the Curriculum
The New York Times in Problems of Democracy Courses
The New York Times in the "New" Social Studies

The goal of scientific study is to help people understand their world. In many respects, science is an expression of man's curiosity about the world and efforts to explain the objects and events of the world.   **Science and health**

The objectives of science education for secondary students are twofold. The first objective is to develop scientific literacy, "the ability of an intelligent layman to read scientific literature and to understand its implications for the culture."[5] Scientific literacy enables the consumer to recognize that science can solve many of man's universal problems, but in doing so it creates new problems. For example, the present environmental crisis was partially created by the same technology that gave the world a cleaner, whiter laundry.

A second goal of science education is to introduce science to young people who may pursue scientific careers. Adolescence is a period of exploration during which students study many areas to find special interests that they may pursue in the future.

Science education requires students to competently read scientific material so they can develop the basic concepts of science. Successful reading of scientific content requires that the reader think like a scientist. Scientific content is written in a very terse style, and the factual content is very dense. The reader must read very slowly and pay careful attention to the concepts, details, and generalizations presented. He or she must read for exact meaning. The reader cannot   **Style and vocabulary**

---

5. George G. Mallinson, "Reading in the Sciences: A Review of the Research," in *Reading in the Content Areas* (Newark, Del.: International Reading Association, 1972), p. 145.

skip any portion of the content, because it has no meaning out of context. In order to read in this manner, the student must understand the many technical words that are used in scientific materials and be able to follow the patterns of writing used to structure scientific writing.

Many specialized, technical terms are used in writing science materials. Scientific vocabulary rapidly becomes obsolete because constant new discoveries cause some terms to become useless while adding new technical terms. An activity to use to help students learn scientific vocabulary is presented below. (Refer to Chapter 5 for techniques for teaching vocabulary and to Chapter 4 for word recognition techniques.)

Activity

Have students make an illustrated dictionary of scientific terms. An example of an entry in such a dictionary follows.

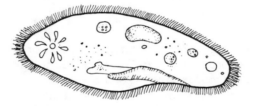

A paramecium is a one-celled animal that is found in the scum on pond water.

paramecium

Writing patterns   The patterns of writing used in scientific materials include classification, experiment, explanation of a technical process, detailed statement of facts, cause and effect, and the problem pattern.[7]

The *classification* pattern consists of information ordered under common headings and subheadings. The information sorted in this way may consist of living things, objects, or ideas. The classification pattern is a type of outlining that shows the relationships among concepts and the distinguishing characteristics. This pattern is comparable to the pattern of main ideas and supporting details. Example 9A.8 shows this pattern.

Example 9A.8   *Example of classification writing pattern*

Nonmicroscopic Algae. Probably the best place to observe large algae is along a rocky seacoast when the tide is low. Nearly all plants which grow attached to rocks lying between high and low tide are algae. Many plants

---

7. Nila B. Smith, "Patterns of Writing in Different Subject Areas. *Journal of Reading* 8 (October 1964): 34.

which do not appear to be green have their chlorophyll masked by other red or brown colored chemicals.

Classifying Algae. Plant scientists called botanists have the task of deciding whether a particular plant is an alga. They do not use the size of a plant as the deciding factor. Thus, not all algae are small. Instead, in order for a plant to be an alga, it must contain chlorophyll and have no roots, leaves, or special tissues for transporting food, water, and minerals through the plant. By this definition, algae can be small or large.

To simplify the task of learning about the thousands of different algae, botanists have grouped algae by color into small subgroups. These subgroups are called the green, blue-green, red, brown, and golden algae (or diatoms). The pictures on these pages show examples of each subgroup. Which types did you find in your culture? Look for examples of other types on your next visit to the seashore.

Uses of Algae. Diatoms, the important food source for water animals, are also useful to us in other ways. Rich deposits of diatoms decompose to form diatomaceous earth, whose properties make it useful as a filter, an insulator, an absorber, and as a fine polish in grinding lenses.

Source: Walter A. Thurber, Robert E. Kilburn, and Peter S. Howell, *Exploring Life Science*, page 6. Copyright 1975 by Allyn and Bacon, Inc. Reprinted with permission of Allyn and Bacon, Inc.

The techniques for teaching main ideas found in Chapter 6 and the techniques for teaching outlining found in Chapter 7 may be used to teach this pattern of writing to students. Following is a classification outline based on Example 9A.8.

I. Classification–Algae
    A. Distinguishing characteristics
        1. Contain chlorophyll
        2. Have no roots
        3. Have no leaves
        4. Have no tissues for transporting food, water or minerals
    B. Classified by color
        1. Green
        2. Blue-green
        3. Red
        4. Brown
        5. Golden

The *experimental* pattern of writing is frequently used in scientific materials because experiments are the basis of scientific knowledge and advancement. The reader must be able to read experiment directions and translate these into action. The reader must carry out the directions precisely and carefully observe the outcomes. The purpose of an experiment is comparable to that of a main idea, and experimental directions are comparable to details. Example 9A.9 presents this pattern of writing.

Example 9A.9   *Sample experimental pattern of writing*
_____ _____

Making a Model Cell. Obtain a glass or plastic tube about the size of a test tube with the end broken. If necessary, smooth the sharp glass edges by holding them in a hot flame.

Cover the smoother end of the tube with a piece of cellophane tubing, held in place by a rubber band as shown above. Hold the covered end of the test tube under water to make certain that water won't leak under the rubber band into the tube. Use this apparatus as a model cell in the following experiments.

Diffusion through a Membrane. Half fill a model cell with 0.1 percent starch mixture. Place the model cell in a beaker of water so that the level of liquid outside the tube is the same as the level inside. Add about 10 drops of iodine to the water in the beaker.

After several hours, note which region has changed color. Explain the color change. What substance passed through the membrane?

_____

Source: Walter A. Thurber, Robert E. Kilburn, and Peter S. Howell, *Exploring Life Science*, page 28. Copyright 1975 by Allyn and Bacon, Inc. Reprinted by permission of Allyn and Bacon, Inc

Following are the steps a reader should use when reading an experiment.

1.   Ask the following questions:
   a.   What am I to find out?
   b.   What materials are needed?
   c.   What processes are used?
   d.   What is the order of the steps in the experiment?
   e.   What do I expect to happen?
2.   Perform the experiment.
3.   Observe the experiment.
4.   Compare the outcomes to predicted outcomes. (Success or failure of an experiment is determined by the learning that takes place.)

Explanation of a process is another pattern of writing used in science materials. Its name explains the objective of this style of writing; it explains a process. The process explained may be a biological process, like the digestive process, or it may be a technical process, such as how an engine operates. Diagrams usually accompany this kind of pattern, so the reader must fuse content information with the diagram information in order to understand the process. Example 9A.10 illustrates an explanation of a process pattern.

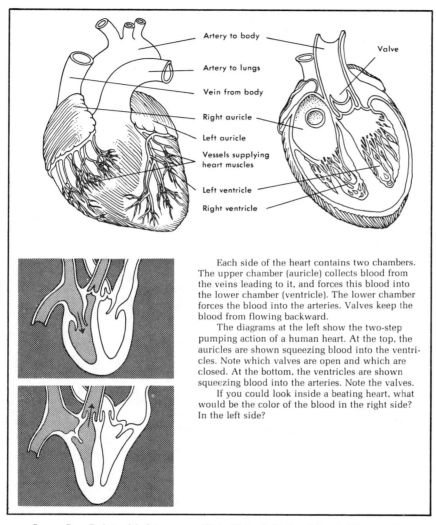

Each side of the heart contains two chambers. The upper chamber (auricle) collects blood from the veins leading to it, and forces this blood into the lower chamber (ventricle). The lower chamber forces the blood into the arteries. Valves keep the blood from flowing backward.

The diagrams at the left show the two-step pumping action of a human heart. At the top, the auricles are shown squeezing blood into the ventricles. Note which valves are open and which are closed. At the bottom, the ventricles are shown squeezing blood into the arteries. Note the valves.

If you could look inside a beating heart, what would be the color of the blood in the right side? In the left side?

Labels on diagram:
- Artery to body
- Valve
- Artery to lungs
- Vein from body
- Right auricle
- Left auricle
- Vessels supplying heart muscles
- Left ventricle
- Right ventricle

Source: From *Exploring Life Science* page 129, by Walter A. Thurber, Robert E. Kilburn, and Peter S. Howell. © Copyright 1975 by Allyn and Bacon, Inc. Reprinted by permission of Allyn and Bacon, Inc.

Techniques that will help students comprehend the explanation of a process are as follows:

1. Have them attempt to restate the explanation in their own words.
2. Have them reread the explanation of a process to check their comprehension.

3. Have them study the sequence of steps in this pattern and attempt to recall the process by recalling the steps in sequence. An example of this technique based on an example of the process style of writing follows:
   a. veins bring blood to
   b. upper chamber (auricle) forces blood into
   c. lower chamber (ventricle) forces blood into
   d. arteries
   e. valves prevent blood from going backward
4. Give the reader an unlabeled diagram to use to illustrate a process such as the following:

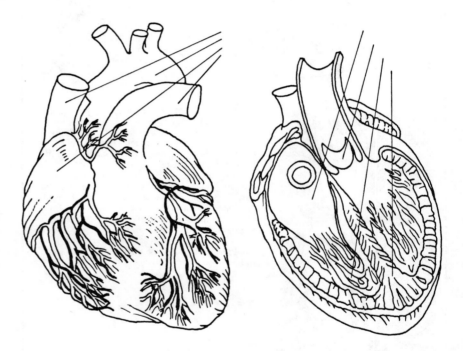

The *detailed statement of fact* pattern usually provides a definition or a statement of a scientific principle. Information is usually very dense in this pattern. Understanding the information in this style of writing is usually necessary for development of basic scientific understandings. The reader may be unable to build later concepts if he or she does not understand the information presented in a detailed statement of fact. The information, principles, or definitions in such a pattern should be understood before preceeding to future assignments. This style of writing requires a very slow rate of reading. A diagram or a picture may be included with the detailed statement of fact. If one is included, the reader should relate the content to the diagram or picture. Example 9A.11 shows this style of writing.

Sample of detailed statement of fact writing pattern   Example 9A.11

Instinct. A caterpillar makes a cocoon. After a time it comes out of the cocoon as a butterfly. The butterfly unfolds its newly formed wings, lets them dry, and flies away. The caterpillar never learned how or when to build a cocoon. The butterfly did not need practice to fly away. One other curious thing: all caterpillars of the same kind build exactly the same kind of cocoon.

A spider egg raised away from any other spider develops into a young spider. When the young spider has developed to the point where it can spin a thread, it begins to build a web. The pattern of the web is the same as those spun by other spiders of the same kind.

These are examples of complicated behavior that is practiced by all the animals of the same kind. These behaviors are inborn. Apparently these behaviors are inherited just as you inherit the color of your eyes, hair, skin, and other features from your parents. Ethologists call these behaviors *instincts.* Instincts are inborn and practiced by all animals of the same kind.

Source: Walter A. Thurber, Robert E. Kilburn, and Peter S. Howell, *Exploring Life Science*, page 237. Copyright 1975 by Allyn and Bacon, Inc. Reprinted by permission of Allyn and Bacon, Inc.

The teacher may use the following techniques to help students understand this pattern of writing.

Activities
1. This pattern can be read like one with main ideas and supporting details. In Example 9A.11, instincts is the main idea and the supporting details are behaviors such as flying, making a cocoon, and spinning a web.
2. The student should reread this pattern as many times as are necessary for him to understand the information, principle, or definition being explained.
3. Ask the student to suggest additional applications or examples to illustrate his understanding. For Example 9A.11, the student could list additional behaviors that are instincts.

The *cause and effect* pattern is concerned with scientific causes and effects. Example 9A.12 illustrates the cause and effect style of writing in scientific materials.

Sample cause and effect pattern   Example 9A.12

Beef and pork are popular foods. Over 50 percent of the fat in these foods is saturated. Fish and chicken fat contain only about 25–30 percent saturated fats.

Example 9A.12 (cont.)   Doctors have recently discovered that people who develop heart disease usually have been living on diets which contain too much fat, and too much of their fat intake has been saturated fat. Why are increasing numbers of doctors recommending that we eat less fat, less beef and pork, more chicken and fish, fewer fried foods, and that fried foods be fried in vegetable oil? Study the table on the next page. Suggest foods that you should eat less of in your diet. Suggest other foods which might be substituted in your diet.

Source: Walter A. Thurber, Robert E. Kilburn, and Peter S. Howell, *Exploring Life Science*, page 50. Copyright 1975 by Allyn and Bacon, Inc. Reprinted by permission of Allyn and Bacon, Inc.

Table 9A.1 shows a cause and effect guide for the preceding science selection in Example 9A.12.

Table 9A.1

Cause	Effect
eating saturated fat	heart disease
beef and pork 50% saturated fat	heart disease
fish and chicken 25–30% saturated fat	less heart disease

A variation of this idea is illustrated in Example 9A.13, a cause and effect study guide.

Example 9A.13

Cause and effect study guide
Directions: Read the selection to identify cause and effect relationships. Place effects in one list and causes in another. With a partner, read aloud to relate each cause and effect. Then place letters in the correct blanks below.

Effects
a.   Firmness of plants
b.   Seeds develop
c.   Growing of embryo
d.   Pollinated by bees
e.   Plant dies

Causes
___ 1.   Pistils receive pollen grains
___ 2.   Supply of food in endosperm or cotyledons
___ 3.   Cellulose
___ 4.   Vascular system does not receive nutrients
___ 5.   Brightly colored sepals

For additional teaching suggestions to use with this style of writing, see the cause and effect pattern in social studies.

The *problem solving* style of writing is used in scientific materials where the author describes a real or hypothetical problem and its actual or suggested solution. For example, a writer might use this style of writing to explain how a vaccine was developed for polio. Example 9A.14 contains this style of writing.

Sample problem solving style of writing   **Example 9A.14**

Penicillium Mold. The mold named *Penicillium* is generally more common than bread mold. Each circular growth in the dish below is a colony of *Penicillium* mold. Two days ago, three small mold samples were placed on this *culture* dish. A thin layer of thousands of bacteria were also added to the culture dish. The food in the culture dish provided food for each bacterium, so each one grew and divided in half. In a half hour or so, each new cell grew and divided again. After two days, a thin white layer of bacteria almost completely covered the surface.

Note the large growths of *Penicillium.* The bacteria do not grow and divide in the region surrounding the mold. Can you propose a hypothesis to explain why the bacteria don't grow near the mold?

For many years, cultures of bacteria and molds just like the one here were observed by microbiologists. They had seen this type of growth hundreds of times before, but no one ever stopped to wonder why. But an English microbiologist, Dr. Alexander Fleming, did. His hypothesis was that the mold might be giving off a chemical which diffuses outward. This chemical killed bacteria, and so the bacteria could not grow close to the mold.

The unknown chemical was isolated and tested against other bacteria. Then it was tested on animals with this bacterial disease, and finally on diseased human volunteers.

All test results were favorable and the new wonder drug, penicillin, resulted from these research studies. Chemicals, such as penicillin, which act this way on bacteria are called *antibiotics* (*anti*–against; *biotic*–life).

Source: Walter A. Thurber, Robert E. Kilburn, and Peter S. Howell, *Exploring Life Science*, pages 16–17. Copyright 1975 by Allyn and Bacon, Inc. Reprinted by permission of Allyn and Bacon, Inc.

To teach students to read and understand this style of writing, the teacher may use the following techniques.

Activities
1. Ask the student to identify the problem and state it in his or her own words.
2. Ask the student to locate the solution or solutions suggested by the author.
3. Ask the student to prepare a problem and solution statement similar to the following:

Problem: Why don't bacteria grow and divide in the region surrounding bread mold?

Solution: Fleming found that mold gave off a chemical that killed the bacteria. He isolated the chemical and tested it against bacteria. He tested the chemical on animals with bacterial disease. He tested the chemical on diseased human volunteers.

Additional skills   In addition to understanding technical terminology and styles of organizing science materials, the reader of science must have mathematics skills and must memorize abbreviations and equations used in scientific content. Example 9A.15 contains scientific writing that requires the use of these skills.

Example 9A.15   *Sample of additional skills for reading science materials*

Measuring Food Energy. Food energy is measured in *calories*. These should be called *large calories* because each one is 1000 times larger than the small calories used by chemists and physicists. Food tables give energy values in large calories.

Calorie measurements are made in the metric system. A large calorie can raise the temperature of 1000 grams (about one quart) of water 1° Celsius (about 2° Fahrenheit). The same amount of energy can lift 45 kilograms (100 pounds) about 9 meters (30 feet).

Suppose that 1000 grams of water is warmed 5° C by the heat from a burning marshmallow. How much energy did the marshmallow add to the water?

Energy of a Nut Meat. Pour 250 grams (a cupful) of water into a thin metal dish and record the water temperature with a Celsius thermometer. Burn a nut meat under the pan and take the temperature of the water again. Calculate the heat gained by the water (250 grams of water heated 4° C represent one calorie).

What are some sources of error in this experiment? Why must you expect your results to be smaller than those given in food tables?

CALORIE CALCULATIONS

Large Calories

$$= \frac{Temp\ change \times wt\ of\ H_2O}{1000}$$

$$= \frac{7° \times 250\ grams}{1000}$$

$$= 1.75\ calories$$

Source: Walter A. Thurber, Robert E. Kilburn, and Peter S. Howell *Exploring Life Science*, page 50. Copyright 1975 by Allyn and Bacon, Inc. Reprinted by permission of Allyn and Bacon, Inc.

Understanding abbreviations and equations must be practiced until the student has memorized those that are necessary for understanding.

Personal health is a scientific subject taught in many schools in conjunction with physical education. Textbooks are generally used in teaching this subject, even if no textbook is used for the activity portions of the course.

The vocabulary of health may include medical terminology and scientific terminology that are difficult for many students to understand. Teachers of health should use the suggestions related to science materials since similar styles of writing are used in science and health.

Resource books and magazines

1. Booklists

   H. J. Deason, *The AAAS Science Book List*, 3rd ed., Washington, D.C.: American Association for the Advancement of Science.

   M. E. Gott and J. R. Wiles, *High Interest—Low Vocabulary Science Books*, Boulder, Colo.: School of Education, University of Colorado.

   Robert Leibert, *A Place to Start*, Kansas City, Mo.: Reading Center, University of Missouri.

   H. Logasa and N. J. Brooklawn, *Science for Youth, An Annotated Bibliography for Children and Young Adults*, Ocean City, N.J.: McKinley Publishing Co., 1963.

2. Book Clubs

   Falcon Book Club, Young Reader's Press, 1 W. 39th Street, New York, N.Y. 10018

   Popular Science Book Club, 44 Hillside Ave., Manhasset, N.Y. 11030

3. Magazines

   American Forest, American Forestry Association, 919 17th St. NW, Washington, D.C. 20016.

   Animal Kingdom, New York Zoological Society, 185th St. and Southern Blvd. New York, N.Y. 10033

   Audubon Magazine, National Audubon Society, 1130 Fifth Ave., New York, N.Y. 10028

   Chemistry, American Chemical Society, 1155 16th Street NW, Washington, D.C. 20036

   Current Science and Aviation, American Education Publications, 1250 Fairwood Ave., Columbus, Ohio 43216

   Junior Natural History, American Museum of Natural History, Central Park West at 79th St., New York, N.Y. 10024.

   Popular Mechanics, Popular Mechanics Co., 575 Lexington Ave., New York, N.Y. 10022

Popular Science Monthly, Popular Science Publishing Co., 535 Lexington Ave., New York, N.Y. 10017

Science Digest, The Hearst Corporation, 959 Eighth Ave., New York, N.Y.

Science Reading Adventures, American Education Publications, Columbus, Ohio 43216

Science World, Scholastic Magazines, Inc., 50 W. 44th St., New York, N.Y. 10036

Today's Health, American Medical Association, 535 N. Dearborn Street, Chicago, Ill. 60610

Mathematics

Mathematics is a very important discipline because mathematics is used in many areas of work and study. For example, mathematics is used in science, industrial arts, economics, engineering, home economics, business, architecture, and many other areas. Mathematics also is used in everyday life in many ways, such as telling time, making change, playing games, and participating in hobbies. Mathematics is concerned with the study of qualities, of quantities, and of relationships through the use of numbers, symbols, and words. The mathematics student must have reading skills in order to acquire the concepts of mathematics. Language is used to explain the concepts of mathematics; therefore, there is a high correlation between reading ability and mathematics achievement.

Words and symbols

Mathematics requires highly abstract thinking because it is concerned with ideas and symbols rather than things. Mathematics is a highly compressed system of language wherein one symbol may represent several words; for example, the symbol $>$ represents the words *greater than*. Written mathematics is different from the writing in other subjects because mathematics writing is more dense and contains more ideas in each line and on each page than is generally true of other disciplines. In mathematics, words and symbols are mixed; so comprehension depends not only on words and word relationships, but the relationships between words and symbols. The reader of mathematics must be able to read symbols, signs, abbreviations, exponents, subscripts, formulae, equations, geometric figures, graphs, and tables as well as words.

Vocabulary study is an essential aspect of a program to teach students to read mathematics. The student must read mathematics with great precision; he or she cannot skip words or fill in from context. It is important that the reader understand the precise meaning of each word because the meaning of a single word may alter the meaning of an entire passage. The reader also must integrate the words into thought units and understand relationships among words.

Following are some activities to help the reader of mathematics better understand the terminology of the discipline of mathematics. The first activity was suggested by Richard Earle in his book, *Teaching Reading and Mathematics.*[8] Earle suggested four means of definition to be used with all students in mathematics. The four types of definition are formal definition, listing of characteristics, simulated examples, and real life examples. Following are examples of each type of definition.

1. Formal definition: A square is a parallelogram that has four right angles and four sides of equal length.
2. Listing of characteristics: Several things are true about any square. It has only two dimensions, length and height. It has exactly four sides, each one a straight line of equal length. It has four interior angles, which total exactly 360 degrees. Each angle is a 90 degree angle.
3. Simulated example: Squares drawn on a chalkboard, cut from paper or other material, or pointed out in drawings or pictures.
4. Real life example: Natural occurrences that exemplify square formation. Manmade objects that utilize squares as industrial, architectural, or decorative features. Natural occurrences used might be the shape of a yard or a field, while manmade occurrences might be a window pane, a room, a piece of furniture.

Earle suggests other activities which are useful for developing understanding of mathematical terms. They are shown in the following example.

Activities
1. The student is asked to check the characteristics that describe the term.
   A set
   _____ is a collection of objects
   _____ has members
   _____ has common properties
   _____ includes dissimilar objects
   _____ can be an empty set
   _____ has fractional numbers[9]

8. Richard Earle, *Teaching Reading and Mathematics* (Newark, Del.:International Reading Association, 1976), p. 18.
9. Richard Earle, *Teaching Reading and Mathematics* (Newark, Del.: International Reading Association, 1976), p. 20.

The exercise can be reversed because a single definition may describe several terms used in mathematics.

2. Have the student identify multiple terms that describe the term.

Can be an *average*.

_____ mode   _____ median

_____ mean   _____ numeral

_____ addend   _____ circle[10]

In addition to needing preciseness of vocabulary knowledge, the reader of mathematics needs to read slowly and analytically, because reading mathematics requires concentration. The reader should read actively, with a pencil in hand to take notes and to practice working examples of the processes that are introduced.

Writing patterns A mathematics textbook is different from textbooks in the other content areas. A logical sequence of mathematics skills, concepts, and principles is presented in a style that requires that the reader become skillful in understanding the following patterns of writing: the problem pattern, the explanatory pattern, graphs and charts.

The greatest difficulty that readers of mathematics usually encounter is reading and understanding *word problems* (verbal problems). These are mathematics situations stated in words and symbols. Following is an example of the writing used in verbal problems.

> The Boodle Noodle Company is running a contest in which they will send the winner some money every day for one month. The amounts are $100 the first day, $200 the second day, $300 the third day, and so on. If the month has 30 days and you win the contest, how much money will the Boodle Noodle Company send you altogether?[11]

I. E. Aaron suggests nine steps to guide the reading of word problems. The steps are as follows:

1. Read the problem quickly to get an overview.
2. Reread the problem, this time at a slower rate, to determine what facts are given.
3. Think of the specific question to be answered.
4. Think of the order in which the facts are to be used in answering the question raised in the problem.
5. Think of the operations required for solving the problem.

---

10. *Ibid.*, p. 21.
11. Source: Harold R. Jacobs, *Mathematics A Human Endeavor*, page 47. Copyright 1970 by W. H. Freeman and Company.

6. Estimate an answer that seems reasonable.
7. Work the problem by performing the appropriate operation.
8. Compare the answer with the estimated answer.
9. Go back to the first step if the answer seems unreasonable.[12]

The *explanatory pattern* is generally used to explain a process to the student. This pattern is usually accompanied by an example to which the reader must relate the content. Example 9A.16 contains this pattern of writing.

Sample explanatory writing pattern   **Example 9A.16**

HAVE you ever gotten a chain letter? In 1935 a chain letter craze started in Denver and swept across the country. It worked like this. You receive a letter with a list of five names. You send a dime to the person named at the top, cross the name out, and add your own name at the bottom. Then you send out five copies of the letter to your friends with instructions to do the same. When your five friends send out five letters each, there will be 25 in all. If none of the 25 persons getting these letters breaks the chain, 125 more letters will be sent, and so on.

Let's list these numbers in order, starting with the one letter you receive.

$$1 \quad 5 \quad 25 \quad 125 \ldots$$

This is a number sequence because each number follows the last according to a uniform rule. The rule however is to *multiply* by 5 (*not* add 5), so this is not an arithmetic sequence. It is called a geometric sequence and the diagram at the top of this page shows that the numbers are growing faster and faster.

A number sequence that is built by always *multiplying by the same number* is called a **geometric sequence.**

If we represent any term in the "chain letter" sequence by n, the next term is $5n$.

From *Mathematics A Human Endeavor*, by Harold R. Jacobs. W. H. Freeman and Company. Copyright © 1970.

Techniques a teacher may use to help students comprehend this style of writing are as follows:

Activities

1. The student should work through the example to determine whether he or she understands the process.
2. The reader should restate the process in his or her own words.
3. The student should apply the new process by locating additional situations in which the process can be used.

---

12. I. E. Aaron, "Reading in Mathematics," *Journal of Reading* 8 (May 1965): 391–95, 401.

Graphs and charts are often used to represent mathematical concepts in mathematics materials, as well as in other content textbooks and other materials such as newspapers and magazines. The graph in Example 9A.17 appears in a mathematics textbook.

Figure 9A.17 *Sample graph in mathematics reading material*

The bar graph shows stopping distance in feet for certain speeds under average road conditions. The shaded part of each bar shows the distance traveled before the driver can react (reaction time) by touching his brake. The entire bar shows stopping distance. Use the graph in Exercises 3 and 4.

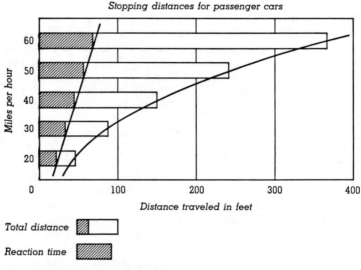

3. Suppose you connect the midpoints of the tops of the bars on reaction time. What kind of relation would describe the figure?
4. Would a linear function be a model of the total stopping distance? Explain.

Source: From *Harbrace Mathematics Introduction to Secondary Mathematics 2* page 234, by Joseph N. Payne, David W Wells, and George A Sponner. Copyright © 1972, 1967 by Harcourt Brace Jovanovich, Inc , and reprinted with their permission

The teacher should use graphs and charts that represent data with which students are familiar, such as basketball or football scores. The teacher may ask students questions that require them to refer to a graph or chart for answers. Following are examples of questions:

1. What is the title of this graph or chart?
2. What type of graph is this? (bar graph, etc.)
3. Who would find the information in this graph useful?

The reader of mathematics must learn to read the special symbols, signs, and formulae which are used in mathematics textbooks. Reading and understanding these is similar to learning to read a foreign language. Example 9A.18 is a selection from a mathematics textbook that contains this type of writing.   **Additional skills**

Additional reading skills in mathematics textbooks   **Example 9A.18**

Every mathematical curve can be associated with an equation. For example, curve C, which you drew in Set I, has the equation

$$x^2 + y^2 = 256,$$

and curve A has the equation

$$64x^2 + 100y^2 = 6,400.$$

To get a better idea of the relationship between curves and equations, we will draw graphs for a couple of equations and see what they look like.

What curve has the equation

$$x^2 + y^2 = 25?$$

To answer this, we will plot some points whose x and y coordinates "fit" the equation. For example, (5, 0) is one of these points, because

$$5^2 + 0^2 = 25,$$

and $(-3, -4)$ is another of these points, because

$$(-3)^2 + (-4)^2 = 25.$$

To save you the trouble of doing a lot of arithmetic, some more points have been worked out for you.

From *Mathematics A Human Endeavor*, by Harold R. Jacobs. W. H. Freeman and Company. Copyright © 1970.

Teachers should help the students relate meaning to the specialized features used. Students should practice reading this type of content until they have a thorough knowledge of the meaning. Students should memorize the meaning of basic mathematics symbols, signs, and formulae.

Aftermath, Palo Alto, Calif.: Creative Publications, 1971.   **Some high interest**
Isaac Asimov, *Of Time and Space and Other Things*, New York: **materials for**
  Doubleday, 1965.   **mathematics**
E. T. Bell, *Men of Mathematics*, New York: Simon and Schuster,   **classrooms**
  1937.

W. A. Ewbank, *A Downpour of Math Lab Experiments*, Birmingham, Mich.: Midwest Publications, 1970.

Clifton Fadiman, *Mathematical Magpie*, New York: Simon and Schuster, 1962.

Oswald Jocoby, *Mathematics for Pleasure*, New York: McGraw-Hill, 1962.

Modern Math Games, Activities, and Puzzles, Belmont, Calif.: Fearon, 1970.

NCTM, *Experiences in Mathematical Ideas*, Volumes I and II, Washington, D.C.: National Council of Teachers of Mathematics, 1970.

Mary O'Neill, *Take a Number*, Garden City, N.Y.: Doubleday, 1968.

Think Lab, Chicago: Science Research Associates, 1974.

English (language arts)   The language arts include reading, writing, speaking, and listening. Language arts materials includes all types of literature including fiction, nonfiction, drama, and poetry. The language arts are concerned with communication between the sender of a message and the receiver of a message. Both the sender and the receiver must have command of the English language in order to communicate effectively; therefore, study of the language arts is largely concerned with effective use and appreciation of the English language. Literature is a part of language arts study because it is the content of the language arts.

Effective reading of language arts content requires that the reader understand specialized vocabulary such as *adjective*, *drama*, *precis*, and *haiku*. (For suggestions regarding vocabulary development refer to Chapter 5.)

General reading skills are required to read each type of literature. The reader should be sensitive to the author's use of language. He or she should be alert to the words and phrases that are repeated. Authors also emphasize words and phrases through typographical aids and punctuation. They frequently define words that are important to the reader's understanding.

The reader should seek to understand the form or design that the author has used to structure his or her ideas. Authors of each type of literature organize their ideas into patterns that are important to understanding. For example, nonfiction may be organized into introduction, body, and summary while fiction is organized around a plot.

Readers should be encouraged to read actively. They should become so involved with the selection they are reading that they feel as if they were living the story or poem.

Reading straight through a fiction selection helps students understand the entire plot, the character development, and setting. In nonfiction, the reader should read through the entire selection in order to grasp the concepts being developed and in order to evaluate the importance of ideas. If reading of a selection is broken down into chapters, stanzas, or smaller parts, the reader will probably not have an opportunity to grasp the whole selection.

A directed reading lesson is one way teachers can help students read and understand the various forms of literature. Following are the steps of a directed reading lesson.

1. Build the background necessary for understanding the selection. The teacher may use pictures, film, television, or objects as necessary to build background understandings. Sensitize students to the author's use of language. It may be useful to read aloud sentences, phrases, and paragraphs that characterize the author's style.
2. Establish purposes for silent reading. Refer to Chapter 3 for additional discussion of this topic.
3. Read the selection silently.
4. Discuss the selection. Emphasize important ideas such as character development and growth. Encourage students to interpret and respond to selections in relation to their own experience.
5. Plan for extension of ideas and/or learnings derived from reading the selection. Extension may take the form of reading related selections for the purposes of comparison or contrast. Reading of drama may be extended by acting out the play.

The following techniques are useful for increasing understanding of various types of literature.

Types of literature

Activities

1. Ask students to read and react to the selection. Reactions should be on the basis of background experience.
2. Students should ask themselves questions such as the following:
   a. What is the selection about? The student should paraphrase what the author is saying.
   b. Is the story true or make-believe?
   c. What is the significance of this selection?
3. Ask students to give examples of points the author made.
4. Ask students to list key words and phrases used by the author.

5. Students should classify a selection as poetry, drama, fiction, or nonfiction before reading in order to understand the characteristics of the type of literature they are reading.

The *fictional* form of writing is an imaginative expression of the author's ideas. The author shares an experience with the reader through relating the incidents of a story. Readers usually seek intrinsic probability in a story; they like to feel that the story could have happened.

Fictional stories are told through use of the plot, which is the plan of the story, includes episodes to develop the story, and moves to a climax, which is the high point of the action. Frequently the author seeks to build suspense regarding the outcome of the story in order to hold the reader's interest.

Characters often tell the story. The personalities of characters are revealed through their actions and thoughts, through the thoughts and actions of other characters regarding the character, through conversation, and through the statements of a narrator. The reader usually prefers three-dimensional characters who reveal both good and bad qualities. Characters who are too good or too evil are not believable.

The setting of a story is the time and place of the story. The significance of time and place differ from story to story. Setting is probably most significant in historical fiction. Generally time and place influence the food, clothing, speech, actions, and thoughts of the characters.

The mood of a story is developed through the author's style of writing. The author expresses mood through word choice and sentence structure. He or she creates imagery through symbolic techniques such as simile and metaphor. The author may also develop mood through the symbolism used.

The theme of a story is the purpose for which the author wrote the story: What is the writer trying to say to his audience? Themes are often very old ideas told in different ways through different plots, characters, settings, and moods. For example, the struggle of a teenager to grow up is a common theme in adolescent literature.

Teachers may use techniques such as the following to help students understand fiction.

Activities

1. Ask students to locate the author's stylistic techniques that create mood.
2. Ask the students to draw a line that illustrates the plot. An example of this technique follows on page 273.
3. Ask students to select characters who are well developed, three-dimensional characters and compare them with characters who are not well developed.

Climax

Incidents

Falling action

4. Discuss with students the ways in which the story would change if the setting were changed.

Example 9A.19 is an illustrative reading lesson based on the "Legend of Sleepy Hollow."

Illustrative literature lesson   **Example 9A.19**

Introduction
Do you know any good ghost stories? Have you ever sat around with a group of friends telling ghost stories? How did you feel later, particularly if you had to go some place alone? You probably felt the way Ichabod Crane felt in this story after he listened to some ghost stories and rode home alone over country roads. The story you are going to read is a ghost story. The characters in this story include: a worthy pedagogue; a rantipole hero; a ripe, melting and rosy-cheeked maiden; and a contented farmer. After you read the story, try to name each of the characters listed. As you read this story think about these questions: What factors created an atmosphere for the ghost to appear? What happened to Ichabod?

Vocabulary
Match each of the words with a definition

words	definitions
continual reverie	German soldier
Hessian trooper	Bible study
spectre	constant daydream
psalmody	ghost

Discussion Questions
1. How would you characterize the residents of Sleepy Hollow?
2. Is the setting important in this story? Why?
3. Do you think Katrina was really interested in Ichabod? Why?
4. How are Brom Bones and Ichabod Crane alike? How are they different?
5. What was the point of view of this story?
6. Do you agree with the old man about the purpose of this story? What do you think the purpose was?

Activities
1. Write a paragraph telling what you would have done if you were Ichabod.

Example 9A.19 (cont.)

2. Read another story written by Washington Irving and compare it to the "Legend of Sleepy Hollow."
3. Draw a picture of the way you visualize Ichabod.

(Note: Study guides as explained in Chapter 3 may be used in conjunction with such directed reading lessons.)

Nonfiction writing is precise, factual writing. Nonfiction writing is frequently used to develop concepts. Nonfiction is an objective way of writing, and emotions play little or no role. Nonfiction is usually organized around an introduction, a body, and a summary. Main ideas and supporting details patterns are used in writing nonfictional materials. Since nonfiction is usually written to develop concepts, technical vocabulary is generally used. (Refer to Chapter 8 for additional information about nonfiction.)

Poetry is a condensed form of writing. The author states ideas in a succinct fashion. Poetry is usually written to express the thoughts and emotions of the author. Frequently poets cause the reader to appreciate familiar things and ideas in a new way. Poetry may also tell a story. Well-written poetry stimulates the imagination of the reader. Poets use rhythm and rhyme to express their ideas and to stimulate the reader. Poets also frequently use imagery to help a reader see or feel a particular place or thing.

Teachers may use the following techniques with poetry:

1. Poems should be read aloud.
2. Poems should be read in their entirety for appreciation.
3. Poems usually should be read twice in order to achieve full appreciation.
4. The reader may compare prose and poetry on the same topic in order to understand the succinctness of poetry.

Drama is literature written to be acted. The writer intends for characters to speak the lines and for the audience to see the action. Drama includes stage directions that the reader must read in order to understand the story. The reader should pay attention to all information in parentheses and italics. The name of the speaker is printed before his or her lines, so the reader must be alert to the names of the speakers in order to follow the speeches and the action. In drama the characters are responsible for telling the story.

The following teaching procedures may be used for drama.

1. Ask the students to visualize the action.
2. Have the students read the speeches aloud to aid comprehension.
3. Have the students act out the described actions in order to arrive at a better understanding of the action.

For additional details on and illustrations of applying reading strategies to literature, see:

Backner, Saul, "Teaching Reading and Literature to the Disadvantaged Part 1—A Definition," *Journal of Reading* 17 (April 1974): 512–16. (This is a series of seven articles. Parts II-VII appear in *Journal of Reading* (Oct. 1974–Mar. 1975).

Chester, S. Alan, "Integrating the Teaching of Reading and Literature," *Journal of Reading* 19 (February, 1976): 360–66.

Donlan, Dan, "Developing a Reading Participation Guide for a Novel," *Journal of Reading* 17 (March 1974): 439–43.

Finder, Morris, "Teaching to Comprehend Literary Texts—Poetry," *Journal of Reading* 14 (March 1971): 353–58, 413–19.

Finder, Morris, "Teaching to Comprehend Literary Texts—Drama and Fiction," *Journal of Reading* 17 (January 1974): 272–78.

Frain, Emma Carville, "Book Reports—Tools for Thinking," *Journal of Reading* 17 (November 1973): 122–24.

Gebhard, Ann O., "Poetry—And Test of Comprehension," *Journal of Reading* 17 (November 1973): 125–28.

Larson, Martha L., "Reader's Theatre: New Vitality for Oral Reading," *The Reading Teacher* 19 (January 1976): 359–66.

McKenna, Michael, "Shakespeare in Grade 8," *Journal of Reading* 19 (December 1975): 205–7.

Muller, Al, "New Reading Material: The Junior Novel," *Journal of Reading* 18 (April 1975): 531–34.

Ritt, Sharon Isaacson, "Journeys: Another Look at the Junior Novel," *Journal of Reading* 19 (May 1976): 627–34.

Thompson, Richard F., "Teaching Literary Devices and the Reading of Literature," *Journal of Reading* 17 (November, 1973): 113–18.

Twining, James E., "Reading and Literature: The Heterogeneous Class," *Journal of Reading* 18 (March 1975): 475–80.

Composition and grammar

These books, whether studied in a page-by-page manner or utilized as reference tools, can present difficulties unless some reading guidance is provided in the form of previewing, discussion, and conducting of a few directed lessons.

Frequently, these textbooks follow an expository pattern of explaining a concept or idea, illustrating it, developing a definition or generalization, and then providing application exercises. A large number of paragraphs are definitional, as explained in Chapter 6. Many details are packed into each page, making rather uninteresting reading though often clearly presented. Frequently, the material is almost in outline form, requiring the ability to note topics and subtopics. Once the student learns to recognize the consistent pattern in a given text, he or she often can use the book independently.

Individualized reading

Individual differences increase as students go through school, and this results in a wide variation in the reading abilities of secondary students. Students in a secondary class can vary in reading level from low elementary to college. This creates a great problem for the secondary teacher. Individualized reading provides an opportunity for the teacher to meet the individual needs of students in reading.

An individualized reading program is one in which the students select the materials they wish to read, based upon their needs and interests. They read these books at their own rate. After the books are completed, the teacher and each student usually have an individual conference to discuss the books.

A wide selection of books related to different interests and written at varying reading levels should be available for an individualized reading program. Multiple copies of popular books should be available. Some teachers allow students complete freedom in choosing the books they read; however, some students require guidance in selecting interesting reading materials that they are able to read.

The individual conference between teacher and student enables the teacher to evaluate the student's reading skills, comprehension, and interests. The conference provides a time for the teacher and the student to interact so the student may ask questions and read aloud without embarrassment. During the conference the teacher frequently asks vocabulary and comprehension questions. During the conference, the teacher should ask the student to read a brief section of the book aloud in order to evaluate his or her skills.

Some teachers require students to complete culminating activities related to their books. These activities enable students to share ideas they have read with their classmates. These activities are at the creative reading level; see Chapter 6 for suggestions.

Individualized reading does not just include individual activities. Group activities have an important role in this program. The teacher may discover that the majority of the class has the same reading problem and may choose to work with the group on this skill. For example, a number of students may encounter difficulties with figurative language. Because of this problem the teacher may do some exercises related to this skill with the group. Another opportunity for group activities arises when a number of students have read the same book and these people gather for a group discussion of the book.

Individualized reading offers opportunities for students to read materials that interest them at their own levels and rates. It provides opportunities for the teacher to work with individual problems.

Three references that reveal some of the beneficial effects of individualized reading are:

Faber, Daniel, *Hooked on Books* (New York: Putnam, 1968).
Faber, Daniel, *The New Hooked on Books* (New York: Putnam, 1976).

Wigginton, E., *The Foxfire Book* (Long Island, New York: Doubleday, 1972).

Some special courses within the language arts include the following. **Other language arts**

Journalism (See the Newspapers and Magazines section earlier in
this chapter.)
Speech (See Chapter 6, Levels of Thinking.)
Theatre (See Drama earlier in this chapter.)

The study of foreign language is valuable in today's world due to **Foreign language**
increased travel and communication among the people of the world.
The study of foreign language has an additional value in that it helps
students understand the culture of another country. Foreign language
instruction should have a meaningful approach that results in the
ability to use a language functionally.

Readiness is an important factor in reading a foreign language.
The teacher must build a point of contact between the reader and the
content he or she is reading. Students should be exposed to oral
language to develop listening comprehension of the language they
are learning. Listening comprehension precedes reading comprehension. Recordings and foreign language broadcasts on radio and
television provide opportunities for students to develop listening
comprehension.

Students should be taught the concepts and the vocabulary used
in the selections they are preparing to read. Discussion and practice of
common phrases and expressions is useful in developing readiness to
read. The use of context as an aid to understanding vocabulary should
be stressed in reading a foreign language. In addition, the teacher
should provide purposes to guide the students' silent reading.

Reading content written in a foreign language presents problems
parallel to those of reading English. The reader must learn the
semantics and syntax of the language being studied. The student
should have opportunities to listen to the language, speak the
language, read the language, and write the language. Teachers can
use the same methods in teaching students to read a foreign language
as are used in teaching them to read English.

Following are some specific techniques useful in helping students
develop comprehension of a foreign language.

Activities
1. Teach students to use a foreign language dictionary.
2. Encourage the student to write his or her own ideas in the
    language being studied.

3. List words in English that are derived from the language studied.
4. Ask students to describe a basketball or football game in the language.
5. Provide students with direction cards written in English. The student must then state the directions in the foreign language. Example: You go into a department store and find the children's department.
6. The above activity can be reversed with the directions printed in a foreign language and the student stating them in English.
7. Have students write in a foreign language an advertisement to sell an automobile.
8. Provide students with grocery advertisements and ask them to write the word from a foreign language for each item in the advertisement.
9. Provide students with objects to categorize by form, function, color, or texture in the foreign language.

Concluding comments   A checklist of content reading skills is presented in Example 9A.20 as a summary of the major points developed in this chapter. Such a checklist may be used for evaluating students, groups, or classes. The teacher attempts to determine the students' performance for each skill and checks under *yes* or *no*. This information is valuable when providing strategies and materials for instruction.

Example 9A.20   *Checklist of content reading skills*

NAME _____ SCHOOL _____
GRADE _____
The reader of content materials is able to read with understanding the following:

                              Yes   No

Social Studies
    Technical vocabulary
    Cause and effect
    Chronology
    Comparison/contrast
    Question and answer
    Main idea and supporting details
    Critical reading
    Graphs and charts
    Pictures
    Newspapers and Magazines

Science   Yes   No
    Technical vocabulary
    Experiment
    Classification
    Explanation of a technical process
    Detailed statement of fact
    Cause and effect
    Problem
    Mathematics applications

Mathematics
    Technical vocabulary
    Symbols
    Problem
    Explanatory
    Graphs and charts
    Formulae

Language Arts
    Vocabulary
    Structure
    Unity of selection
    Appreciation

    Fiction
        Plot
        Characterization
        Setting
        Mood
        Theme

    Nonfiction
        (Refer to Chapter 8 for points about expository writing)

    Poetry
        Rhyme
        Rhythm
        Imagery
        Condensed form

    Drama
        Stage directions
        Plot of play
        Theme of play

Foreign Language
    Vocabulary
    Foreign language dictionary
    Context

Self-test

1. What level of vocabulary understanding should a student achieve in order to read social studies at an instructional level? (a) 50% (b) 25% (c) 75% (d) 90%

2. What style of writing is used in social studies content? (a) Fictional (b) Expository (c) Narrative (d) Stream of consciousness

3. Which patterns of writing are most used in writing social studies content? (a) Comparison/contrast (b) Chronological (c) Cause and effect (d) All of these

4. Why is critical reading of social studies content necessary? (a) Students enjoy being critical. (b) Critical reading is necessary to literal comprehension. (c) Authors may have bias. (d) It is included in the curriculum.

5. Why are graphs and charts used in textbooks? (a) To make the text more interesting (b) To brighten the book (c) To make the text more difficult (d) To present information in a concise manner

6. Which of the following is the best example of a scientifically literate person? (a) One who enjoys reading science (b) One who reads a large amount of science (c) An intelligent, understanding reader of science (d) A professional scientist

7. Why should scientific content be read slowly? (a) The vocabulary is difficult. (b) Content can't be skipped because the material has no meaning out of context. (c) The teacher prefers it. (d) Both a and b.

8. Which of the following styles of writing science materials are most used in science textbooks? (a) Experiment (b) Explanation of a technical process (c) Classification (d) All of these

9. Which of the following definitions explains the detailed statement of fact as found in science materials? (a) Provides a label for the diagram (b) Provides a definition or statement of a principle (c) Is necessary for conducting an experiment (d) Describes a process

10. Why is mathematics considered abstract? (a) It is difficult. (b) The symbols represent ideas. (c) It is compactly written. (d) All of these.

11. Which of the following factors contribute to the problems of reading mathematics? (a) One symbol may represent several words. (b) Mathematics is a difficult subject for many students. (c) Too many problems are introduced on a single page. (d) Too many examples are given.

12. Which of the following areas are included in the language arts? (a) All foreign languages (b) Reading, writing, listening, speaking (c) The use of language in art (d) Social studies, mathematics, science

13. What is the basic goal of reading language arts materials? (a) Understanding between sender of a message and receiver of a message (b) Speaking clearly (c) Learning specialized vocabulary (d) Diagraming sentences

14. What are the basic types of literature? (a) Comics, drama, and fiction (b) Fiction, nonfiction, poetry, and drama (c) Drama and poetry (d) None of these

15. What is the plot of a story? (a) The time and place (b) The way the author uses language (c) The plan of the story (d) The message of the story

1. Compare the discussion of a famous person as presented in a social studies textbook and in a trade book.
2. Compare the presentation of a topic in a science book with the presentation of the same topic in a trade book.
3. Develop a bibliography of trade books that could be used by students who are unable to read the textbook.
*4. Use the checklist in Example 9A.20 to analyze the content reading skills of a student.
5. Describe how individualized reading might be utilized or adapted for use in your content area.
6. Demonstrate how magazines and newspapers may be used in your content area.
7. Prepare a cause-and-effect chart for some topic in a content area.
9. Report to the class on one of the literature articles cited on page 275.
10. Check professional journals (such as *Social Education, Science Teacher, Mathematics Teacher, English Journal*) for articles dealing with reading of content material. Share your findings with the class.
11. Check the readability level of a textbook and/or supplementary material used for one of the subjects treated in this chapter (See Chapter 3)
12. Prepare a directed reading lesson for one of the subjects treated in this chapter. (See Chapter 3)
13. Prepare a three-level study guide for a selection from one of the subjects treated in this chapter. (See Chapter 3)
14. Prepare a structured overview for a mathematics or science unit of work. (See Chapter 3)
15. Prepare a vocabulary exercise (anagram, maze, puzzle, scramble, or other challenging variation) for one of the subjects treated in this chapter. (See Chapter 5)
16. Select a study skill appropriate to one of the subjects treated in this chapter. Describe how you would teach it. (See Chapter 7)

Enrichment activities

Artley, A. Sterl. "Critical Reading in the Content Area." *Elementary English* 36 (February 1959): 122–30.

Aukerman, Robert C. *Reading in the Secondary Classroom.* New York: McGraw Hill, 1972. Chapters 7–10.

Braam, Leonard S. and Marilyn A. Roehm. "Subject Area Teachers Familiarity with Reading Skills." *Journal of Developmental Reading* (Spring 1964): 188–96.

Selected references

---

* These activities are designed for inservice teachers, student teachers, or practicum students.

Burmeister. Lou E. *Reading Strategies for Secondary School Teachers.* Reading, Mass.: Addison Wesley, 1974. Chapters 8 and 9.

Burron, Arnold and Amos L. Claybaugh. *Using Reading to Teach Subject Matter.* Columbus, Ohio: Charles E. Merrill, 1974.

Donlan, Dan. "Multiple Text Programs in Literature." *Journal of Reading* 19 (January 1976): 312–319.

Earle, Richard. *Teaching Reading and Mathematics.* Newark, Del.: International Reading Association, 1976.

Forgan, Harry W. and Charles T. Mangrum. *Teaching Content Area Skills* Columbus, Ohio: Charles E. Merrill, 1976.

Hafner, L. E. *Improving Reading in Middle and Secondary Schools.* 2nd ed. New York: Macmillan Co., 1974.

———*Developmental Reading in Middle and Secondary Schools.* New York: Macmillan Co., 1977. Chapters 8–15.

Herber, Harold. *Teaching Reading in Content Areas.* Englewood Cliffs, N.J.: Prentice Hall, 1970.

Howes, Virgil. *Individualizing Instruction in Reading and Social Studies.* New York: Macmillan Co., 1972.

Johnson, Roger and Ellen B. Vardian. "Reading, Readability and the Social Studies." *The Reading Teacher* 26 (February 1973): 483–88.

Karlin, Robert. *Teaching Reading in High School.* 2nd ed. Indianapolis: Bobbs Merrill, 1972. Chapters 12 and 13.

———"What Does Educational Research Reveal about Reading and the High School Student?" *The English Journal.* 58 (March 1969): 386–95.

Laffey, James L. *Reading in the Content Areas.* Newark, Del.: International Reading Association, 1972.

Lowell, Stephen S. *The Newspaper Comes to the Classroom.* Portland, Maine: J. Weston Walch, 1973.

Lunstrum, John P. "Reading in the Social Studies: A Preliminary Analysis of Recent Research." *Social Education* (January 1976): 10–18.

Maney, Ethel S. "Literal and Critical Reading in Science." *Journal of Experimental Education* 27 (September 1958): 57–64.

Marksheffel, N. D. *Better Reading in the Secondary School.* New York: Ronald Press, 1966.

Piercey, Dorothy. *Reading Activities in Content Areas.* Boston: Allyn and Bacon, 1976. Chapters 5, 7, 11, 13, 14.

Preston, Ralph. *A New Look at Reading in the Social Studies.* Newark, Del.: International Reading Association, 1975.

Robinson, H. Alan. *Teaching Reading and Study Strategies.* Boston: Allyn and Bacon, 1975. Chapters 6–9.

Robinson, H. Alan. "Reading Skills Employed in Solving Social Studies Problems." *The Reading Teacher* 18 (January 1965): 263–69.

Robinson, H. Alan and Ellen Lamar Thomas. *Fusing Reading Skills and Content.* Newark, Del.: International Reading Association, 1972.

Robinson, Helen M. "Developing Critical Readers." in Russell Stauffer ed. *Dimensions of Critical Reading*, XI. Newark, Del.: University of Delaware, 1964. Pp. 1–12.

Sargent, Eileen E., Helen Huus, and Oliver Andersen. *How To Read a Book.* Newark, Del.: International Reading Association, 1970.

Schulwitz, Bonnie Smith. *Teachers, Tangibles, Techniques: Comprehension of Content in Reading*. Newark, Del.: International Reading Association, 1976.

Shepherd, David L. *Comprehensive High School Reading Methods*. Columbus, Ohio: Charles E. Merrill, 1973.

————"Teaching Science and Mathematics to the Seriously Retarded Reader in the High School." *Reading Teacher* 17 (September 1963): 25–30.

Strang, Ruth, Constance M. McCullough, and Arthur E. Traxler. *The Improvement of Reading*. 4th ed. New York: McGraw Hill, 1967. Chapters 8–10.

Thelen, Judy. *Improving Reading in Science*. Newark, Del.: International Reading Association, 1976.

Thomas, Ellen Lamar and H. Alan Robinson. 2nd ed. *Improving Reading in Every Class*. Boston: Allyn and Bacon, 1977. Chapters 6 and 7.

West, Gail B. *Teaching Reading in Content Areas: a Practical Guide to the Construction of Student Exercises*. Orlando, Florida: Sandpiper Press, 1974.

9B  Reading in the content areas: part 2

This chapter explores the reading skills required by the content of school subjects not treated in Chapter 9A. The general reading skills required by vocationally-oriented subjects and the specific reading skills required by industrial arts, business education, home economics, physical education, driver education, art, and music are considered.

Purpose-setting questions

As you read this chapter try to answer these questions:
1. Why do subjects such as industrial arts, business education, home economics, physical education, driver education, and fine arts require reading competence?
2. What general reading skills are required by industrial arts, business education, and home economics?
3. What specific reading skills are required by physical education and driver education?
4. What specific reading skills are required by fine arts subjects?

Key vocabulary

As you read this chapter, try to understand the meaning of these terms:

vocational subjects	graphics	business education
expository style	industrial arts	home economics
visualizing		

Industrial arts, business education, and home economics

The subjects considered in this section are those that prepare students for specific trades or occupations. Reading competence is closely related to student success or failure in these subjects. The educational objective of these areas is to educate a worker who is careful, organized, effective, and efficient and who has mastered occupational skills. Teachers also hope to foster healthy attitudes toward work. In order to achieve these goals, students must become widely acquainted with the reading materials that relate to their areas. Therefore, the students must have adequate reading skills. They should receive direct reading instruction to help them read specialized materials with success.

The subjects considered in this section are often motivating to students, since they tend to select them to fulfill direct interests and future goals. Students who have had little motivation for reading in the past may be stimulated to read by their desire for success in these areas. Therefore, reading instruction in these specialized fields can be beneficial.

The range in reading achievement among students who elect occupationally-oriented studies tends to be broader than among students who choose academic areas, because college bound students generally elect academic subjects, while vocational subjects are selected both by very bright students and by students who are unable to succeed in academic subjects. Some students who are not competent readers choose to study vocational subjects because they believe that they can avoid reading by following a vocational course of study. These students are shocked to discover the volume and difficulty of reading required in vocational studies. Unfortunately for the poor reader, there is no subject in the secondary curriculum that does not require reading skill.

Features of the reading material Since the volume of print used in vocational subjects appears small, students and teachers may misjudge the level of reading required. Even the rather brief sets of directions frequently found in these materials require precise, careful reading. Vocational subjects are written in an expository style that is very concise. This style requires that the reader read with precision, follow directions, and put ideas and words into action through application.

These subjects require visualization of drawings, labels, and directions. The reader must be able to visualize how a dress will look when it has been constructed, or anticipate how a recipe will taste when cooked.

Generally vocational materials include three kinds of writing: a presentation of factual information, how-to-do-it directions, and suggestions for problem solving. Example 9B.1 shows these types of writing in vocational content materials. The first part of the selection, taken from an industrial arts textbook, provides information regarding painting. The authors provide problem-solving information when they explain that filler or putty will not cover up poor workmanship. This selection also provides how-to-do-it material in the form of directions for mixing paint.

Common aspects of vocational materials

Example 9B.1 *Sample type of writing in vocational materials*

Painting

Paint is the most widely used finishing material, and it can be applied with reasonable success by the household mechanic. It is an *opaque finish* because it completely covers the surface without allowing the color or grain to show through.

In general paint is made of pigments, such as white lead and zinc white, and vehicles, such as lineseed oil, turpentine, and in some cases, color pigment and drier.

Paint may be purchased in a wide range of prices. The price, however, is not a guarantee of quality. You will be wise to buy standard brands with a known reputation. Cheap paint is apt to be more expensive in the long run because it may not give long service and much time and labor may be wasted on it.

1. Sealers and Fillers. Before a surface is painted, a thin paint or specially prepared undercoating should be applied. After this filler has dried, the job should be sanded down.

Sizing is a special type of filler used on newly plastered walls before they are painted. Glue, with a consistency of paint or very thin varnish, is often used as sizing.

Wood with major defects can often be made usable with plastic wood or crack filler which is available in sealed cans and can be used like putty. These fillers can be sanded to a smooth surface.

The true craftsman does not use filler or putty to cover up poor workmanship. Fillers will not correct poor planing and sanding; putty will not hide hammer dents; and plastic wood cannot repair broken edges.

2. Mixing Paint. Although many people buy ready-mixed paint, the home craftsman should be able to mix his own. Use the following procedure when mixing paint.

1. Shake the can vigorously. (The dealer will sometimes do this with a special machine.)
2. Open the can with a cover remover.
3. Pour one-third of the paint into an extra can. This will be mainly oil.
4. Mix the remaining paint thoroughly with a paint paddle.
5. Pour the paint from the extra can back into the paint can and mix it thoroughly.
6. Pour the paint back and forth in the two cans until it is well mixed.
7. Old paint which contains lumps should be strained through cheesecloth or a silk stocking.

When you are ready to paint, pour about half the paint into an empty can so that all the paint will not be lost in case of an accident. Stir the paint from time to time to keep the pigment and vehicle from separating.

Source: Estell Curry, Rolland Pardonnet, Russell Symes, *General Industrial Arts*, pp. 59–60. Copyright 1967 by Van Nostrand Company, Princeton, N.J.

Technical vocabulary Each vocational subject has extensive technical vocabulary, as well as common vocabulary words that have specific meanings in each subject area. *Credit* is an example of a common word that has a specific meaning when used in bookkeeping. A general meaning of the word *credit* is acknowledgment of the source of an idea. For example, "Bill gave John *credit* for the new product." In bookkeeping the word *credit* refers to a bookkeeping entry that shows money paid on an account. For example, "You may place this entry on the *credit* side of the ledger." The technical vocabulary of a subject usually represents concepts that are essential to reading that subject with understanding. Teachers of vocational subjects often have an advantage because the vocabulary usually represents concrete concepts, which are easier to teach than more abstract ideas. For example, *sauté* is a word used in home economics to represent a way of cooking food which can be demonstrated to students; *debit* represents a specific bookkeeping concept that can be concretely illustrated for the student.

Teachers should take advantage of the concrete nature of vocabulary and concepts and teach them by relating the printed words to student experience. Teachers may use concrete objects, illustrations, and examples to develop understanding of concepts. Direct instruction for technical vocabulary should be planned so that students acquire the necessary language for reading vocational materials. (Refer to Chapter 5 for vocabulary teaching techniques.)

Following directions Each subject requires that the student read directions and translate them into action. The reader of industrial arts must read directions for operating and repairing various pieces of equipment. The reader of home economics must be able to follow the directions for cooking a recipe or constructing a garment. The student of business education reads directions for operating business machines and for setting up bookkeeping systems.

Reading directions requires that the student read slowly and precisely. The student should be prepared to reread in order to achieve complete understanding. The reader of directions should be guided by the following questions.

1. What am I trying to do? (What is the task?)
2. What materials are required?
3. Do I understand all of the terms (words) used in these directions?
4. What is the sequence of steps?
5. Have I omitted anything?
6. Am I ready to perform the task?
7. Was I successful in accomplishing the task?

Directions in vocational materials provide immediate feedback as to how well a student has read them because following them usually results in a concrete, observable outcome. For example, if a machine in the industrial arts shop does not work due to the student's failure to follow directions, this result is obvious. Failure to follow directions in baking a cake will be apparent when the student observes or eats the cake.

Example 9B.2 is a set of directions from a home economics book.

Example 9B.2   *Directions from a home economics book*

A Gravy for Beef Pot Roast

1 small marrow bone, 2½ to 3 in.	Simmer bone in water for 1 hour; remove bone.
1½ c. cold water	Add flour to ½ c. cold water and shake.
4 T. flour	Add enough water to stock to make 2 cups.
½ t. salt	Pour stock into cooking pan and add
gravy coloring	thickening; stir until thick and smooth.
	Add a few drops of gravy coloring if gravy is light.
	Serve in a gravy container at the table.

Source: Irene McDermott, Jeanne L. Norris, and Florence Nicholas, *Homemaking for Teen-Agers*, Book 2, 3rd ed., p. 550. Copyright 1972 by Chas. A Bennett, Co., Inc., Peoria, Ill.

The reader could apply the following suggested questions and activities to the example.

1. What am I trying to do? (To make gravy for beef pot roast.)
2. What materials are required? (2½ to 3 inch marrow bone, 1½ cup cold water, 4 tablespoons flour, ¼ teaspoon salt, gravy coloring)
3. Do I understand the terms? (marrow, simmer, stock, thickening)
4. What is the sequence of steps? (a) simmer bone, b) remove bone from stock, c) add water, d) pour stock into pan, e) add thickening, f) stir, g) add coloring, h) serve)
5. Have I omitted anything? (No.)
6. Complete the steps.
7. Was I successful in accomplishing the task? (If the gravy is smooth and tasty, the student has succeeded.)

Interpreting graphics   Students in these areas must be able to read a variety of graphic materials, such as blueprints, drawings, cutaways, patterns, pictures, and sketches. Readers must be able to visualize these graphic materials and must understand the three-dimensional aspects of the graphics they are studying. They must also interpret the scales and legends that accompany graphics so as to interpret the materials being read. Examples 9B.3 and 9B.4 show two types of

Floor plan from an industrial arts textbook   Example 9B.3

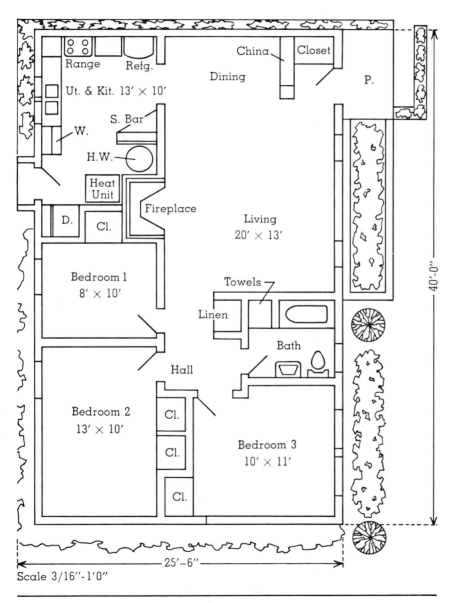

Source: Donald Lux and Willis Ray. *The World of Construction.* Bloomington, Illinois: McKnight and McKnight Publishing Co., 1970, p. 9.

graphics that students commonly encounter. Example 9B.3 is from industrial arts materials, and Example 9B.4 is from home economics content. (Also see Chapter 7.)

Example 9B.4   *Sample home economics reading content*

Homemaking For Teen-agers — Book II

GENERAL ALTERATIONS
To Lengthen

• Cut the pattern apart on the alteration line.
• Pin or tape one section to tissue paper.
• Measure the desired amount to be added and draw a line on the tissue paper.
• Pin or tape the other section of the pattern to this line. Keep grain line markings straight.
• Connect cutting lines, fold lines, and darts.

To Shorten

• Measure from the alteration line the amount that needs to be shortened and draw a second line across the pattern.
• Fold the pattern on the alteration line

and bring the folded edge to the second line.

• Pin or tape in place. Keep grain line markings straight.
• Straighten the cutting line.

Where to Lengthen or Shorten

If you examine a pattern, you will notice that the instructions "lengthen or shorten here" are placed where the alteration will not interfere with the lines of the garment. In the case of a flared skirt, any change in length can usually be made at the hemline. For straight skirts, the alteration is made between the hipline and hemline; in the bodice, between the bustline and waistline.

For sleeves, there are two alteration lines—one above the elbow and one below. To determine where to alter, compare your arm

---

Source: Irene McDermott, Jeanne Norris, and Florence Nicholas. *Homemaking for Teen-Agers*. Book II, 3rd ed., p. 264. Copyright 1972 by Chas. A. Bennett Co., Inc., Peoria, Ill.

In reading the blueprint in Example 9B.3, several abilities are needed. The ability to interpret the scale of the drawing is important. The teacher could use such activities as the following to encourage the students to apply the scale:

1.   Have students study the scale of the blueprint, apply it, and describe the actual dimensions of Bedroom 1.
2.   Have students draw a 4′ by 4′ area to the scale given on this blueprint.

There is also a need to interpret special symbols, such as the symbol ' for *feet*, the symbol " for *inches*, and the symbol $\times$ for *by*. Abbreviations for several words must be interpreted.

In reading the pattern in Example 9B.4, the student must coordinate the text with the illustrations. Directions must be followed carefully and in sequence.

Reading and study of printed materials The reader of these materials must adjust his or her rate as needed. Where the content requires it, the student must read slowly and with precision while less difficult material may be read more rapidly. Rate should be adjusted to the purposes for reading, the type of content, and the student's familiarity with the subject.

Students should also be taught to reread content until they achieve comprehension. Many students expect to achieve full understanding from one reading of a selection. This is often impossible. Written directions are rarely understood with only one reading. It is important that teachers help students realize that rereading is both a normal procedure and, at times, a necessary one.

Industrial arts, business education, and home economics are usually very motivating areas of study for students; therefore, the students' interests will help sustain them while reading content materials. Students will frequently be able to read materials well beyond their usual reading levels due to their interest in the topic. Thus it is very important that each classroom have a classroom library of reading materials related to its subject matter. Teachers should use these materials to develop the reading interests of their students, as well as to increase their understanding of the content area. (A list of suggested materials for a classroom library is included for the subjects treated in this chapter.)

A problem-centered approach to reading is useful in the classroom. In industrial arts class, a student may need to know how to finish a piece of wood, and the proper reference can be offered to help solve the problem while encouraging the student to read.

Teachers should make a particular effort to introduce the textbook to their students. Students in vocationally-oriented classrooms tend to ignore the textbook because they think it is unnecessary. After students learn the variety of information available in the textbook, they will use the textbook more frequently. Instruction that familiarizes the students with the textbook will help them use it more effectively to acquire background information and to solve problems. Following are some questions that could be used on a worksheet to introduce students to their textbooks. These questions are based on an industrial arts textbook, but they can be adapted to any subject area.

1. How many chapters are in this book?
2. Which chapter discusses floor plans?

3. On what page can scale drawings be found?
4. What is the copyright date of this book?
5. Is this a current book?
6. Who wrote this book?
7. Is the author qualified in this field?
8. Turn to page 205 of the glossary. What are oleum spirits?
9. How does the drawing on page 9 help you?

The teacher of these subjects should use directed reading lessons to help the students understand textbook materials. Since some poor readers elect to study vocational subjects, they may require specific reading instruction. Example 9B.5 is a description of a directed reading lesson based on home economics.

Example 9B.5   *Directed reading lesson*

1. *Introduction* (readiness). What kind of fabric is used in the clothing you are wearing today? What is your favorite kind of fabric? Here is a box of various types of fabric. Look at each piece and try to determine the contents of each piece of fabric.
2. *Vocabulary and concepts.* Discuss and pronounce each vocabulary word. Be certain students have a concept for each type of fabric by giving them labeled samples of each to examine.

wool	brocade
synthetic fabric	lamé
satin	velvet
cotton	

3. Provide students with *silent reading purposes* such as the following: How do you choose a suitable fabric to make a dress? How are synthetic fabrics different from natural fabrics?
4. Have the students *read the lesson silently.*
5. *Discuss* the silent reading purposes and ask discussion questions such as the following: Do you prefer natural or synthetic fabrics? Why? What are the advantages of natural fabrics? What kind of dress pattern would you choose for a brocade fabric?
6. Have students reread as necessary to solve the problem of selecting an appropriate fabric for their next garment.

Some students will be unable to handle reading material that is contained in the textbook. Supplementary materials written on a lower difficulty level are needed. Available materials include the following:

1. From Frank E. Richards Publishing Co., Inc., 330 First Street, Box 370, Liverpool, N.Y. 13088:
   a. *You*, by Clare Tremble—a hardbound social adjustment textbook.

b. *The Bank Book*, by John D. Wool—a worktext on understanding banking.
c. *Application Forms*, by Benjamin Piltch—a step-by-step approach.
d. *Shop Made Easy*, by Frank Cattaneo—on use of hand tools for wood, metal, mechanical drawing, and plastics.
e. *Working With Wood*, by Herbert Horwitz—basic worktext with photographs.
f. *What is Electricity?*, by Dr. Eileen L. Corcoran and John R. Pavka—a paperback text.

2. From Fearon Publishers, Inc., 6 Davis Drive, Belmont, CA 94002:
    a. *Going Places With Your Personality: A Guide To Successful Living*, by Charles H. Kahn, Robert Tong, and Wing Jew—designed for grades 7–12; reading level is grade 2.7.
    b. *Planning Meals and Shopping*, by Ann A. Weaver—reading level is grade 2.5.
    c. *Getting Ready to Cook*, by Ann A. Weaver—reading level is grade 2.8.
    d. *The Young Homemaker's Cookbook*, by Ann A. Weaver—reading level is grade 2.9.
    e. *Planning for your Own Apartment*, by Virginia S. Belina—reading level is grade 3.0.

This section deals with specific applications of skills to particular subject areas. Examples for each different area are included.

Application to specific subjects

Industrial arts Industrial arts include instruction related to machine operation, wood-working, auto-shop, drafting, and radio and television repair. Obviously, these areas encompass a large technical vocabulary that must be understood. Following are examples of important technical words: *carburetor, muffler, jack plane, bar clasp,* and *wood rasp*. The reader must learn the technical name and function of tools and parts that are used in the various machines. Example 9B.6 shows writing from an industrial arts textbook. Notice which technical terms are essential to understanding the selection.

Writing example from an industrial arts textbook

Example 9B.6

4. *Paint Thinners.* Most paint is of the right consistency for a final coat when the can is first opened. The thinner, however, evaporates rapidly when exposed to the air, and must be replaced from time to time. For this reason you should be

Example 9B.6 (cont.)   familiar with the various types of thinners. Remember that the quality of a paint can be spoiled by using a poor thinner or the wrong quantity of a good thinner.

Paint must be thinned with turpentine; lacquer with lacquer thinner; and shellac with alcohol. *Never use gasoline for thinning paint or cleaning brushes. It is very dangerous.*

Linseed oil is really a vehicle for the lead and color in paint. However, it is used to thin exterior paint for the priming coat. It is made from flax seed and comes in two forms, raw and boiled. Boiled linseed oil is generally used with exterior paint because it dries faster than raw linseed oil.

Turpentine is a thinner for both inside and outside paints. It has a tendency to cause paint to dry faster and to have a dull finish. Turpentine is made of the distilled sap of pine trees.

Turps, synthetic turpentine, or *oleum spirits* are all names for a mineral-oil substitute for turpentine. It is cheaper than turpentine and is quite widely used. It is also satisfactory for cleaning brushes.

Source: Estell Curry, Rolland Pardonnet, and Russell Symes, *General Industrial Arts* (Princeton, N.J.: Van Nostrand Co., 1967), p. 61.

The reader of the selection in Example 9B.6 must understand the following essential words in order to understand the selection:

paint thinners	shellac
consistency	linseed oil
evaporates	vehicle
exposed	lead
thinned	dull finish
turpentine	turps
lacquer	synthetic turpentine
lacquer thinner	oleum spirits

Many of the technical terms that are needed in industrial arts classes are related to tools and equipment. Labeling such tools and equipment clearly in the classroom can help students learn to recognize these words when they appear in textbooks.

Demonstrations of processes can clarify the printed explanations that students must understand. For example, the teacher might illustrate the process of replacing the jets on a carburetor.

As stated earlier, the reader of industrial arts material must learn to follow step-by-step directions for operating equipment, constructing tables, or installing a carburetor. He or she must be able to follow the directions on "job sheets," which are used in industrial arts classes for assigning daily work. Safety rules are important concepts to be understood by industrial arts students. Reading such rules is essential to the students' well-being.

Example 9B.7 is a selection from an automobile repair textbook and shows the need for coordinating text material with illustrative diagrams. The diagram is designed to help the student understand what the technical term *tram rod* represents and to help the student visualize what is meant by taking "two opposite diagonal measurements." Teachers should encourage students to study the diagrams carefully in order to increase their understanding of the textual material. In order for the illustrations to be fully comprehended, the students need to realize that one represents a cutaway section of an automobile body. They also need to realize that the lines with arrows represent measurement lines and that a special symbol (") is used to represent the word *inches*.

Selection from an automobile repair textbook   Example 9B.7

Checking the Body for Misalignment

There are two ways of aligning or squaring up an automobile body—by using a tram rod (Figure 15-37) or with a steel measuring tape. The alignment is determined by taking two opposite diagonal measurements, using either body bolts or accurately measured-off chalk marks as reference points. It is very important that all measurements be taken from bare metal areas. If the two opposite diagonal measurements are the same, that particular section or area of the body is in alignment (see Figure 15-38).

Tram Rod

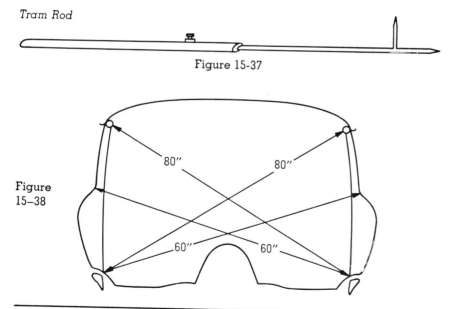

Figure 15-37

Figure 15-38

Source: A. Tait, A. G. Deroche, N. N. Hildebrands, *The Principles of Autobody Repairing and Repainting,* p. 337. Copyright 1971 by Prentice-Hall, Inc., Englewood Cliffs, N.J. Reprinted with permission.

When using the passage in Example 9B.7, the teacher can urge students to use context clues to clarify the meaning of the term *aligning.* Use of structural analysis can then help them determine the meaning of the term *alignment.*

Reference reading is also necessary for industrial arts students because they often must locate information in books such as *Machinery's Handbook*[1] or automobile repair manuals. In order to do this reading, the student must use the index and table of contents to locate the information necessary for answering specific questions or solving problems. He or she may have to refer to an appendix or glossary. After finding the general area in which the information is located, the student should skim or scan to find the specific location and then switch to careful reading for details.

Example 9B.8 *Selection from a basic electricity textbook*

Appendix D

Graphic Symbols for Electrical and Electronic Diagrams

Graphic Symbols for Electrical Diagrams

The graphic symbols used for electrical diagrams come from two general sources. One is from the field of communications, the other from the industrial field. In most instances, the same symbols are used for both types of diagrams. There are, however, some differences, as shown in the following list.

	Communication	Industrial
Amplidyne		
Capacitors		
capacitor, fixed		
capacitor, variable		
Cell		
single cell		
battery		
Fuse		
Generators		
a-c generator		
armature and slip rings (if any)		
field coil		
d-c generator		
armature, commutator, and brushes		
field coil		
Ground		

Source: A. Marcus and W. Marcus, *Basic Electricty,* Englewood Cliffs, N.J.: Prentice Hall, Inc., 1974, p. 393.

---

1. Holbrook Horton, ed., *Machinery's Handbook* (New York: The Industrial Press, 1964). ·

The portion of an appendix presented in Example 9B.8 is from a book on basic electricity. It is essentially a picture dictionary of graphic symbols representing electronic parts. The student reading a schematic diagram in the textbook or elsewhere can refer to this appendix, find the symbol that he or she does not know, and check to see what it represents. If the student is drawing a schematic, he or she can look up the representation for any part to be included in the schematic.

In addition, industrial arts students generally read trade literature such as *Popular Mechanics* and *Mechanics Illustrated*. They should read periodicals of the trade to learn about new products, materials, and techniques. Periodicals provide general information that is useful to students in the various trades.

Critical reading skill is necessary for industrial arts students. They must evaluate the information they read. For example, students must read labels of products critically to evaluate products for the task at hand. Students may have to evaluate the suitability of a blueprint. They also need to read contracts and invoices critically. (See Chapter 6.)

Some library (or trade) books available in the area of industrial arts include:

Baker, Eugene, *I Want to be a Draftsman*, Chicago: Children's Press, 1976.

Esterer, Arnulf, *Tools, Shapers of Civilization*, New York: Messner, 1966.

Greens, Carla, *I Want to be a Mechanic*, Chicago: Children's Press, 1959.

Harwood, Mark, *Fun with Wood*, New York: Grossett, 1972.

Hellman, Hall, *The Lever and the Pulley*, Philadelphia: Lippincott, 1971.

Lincoln, Martha and Katharine Lorres, *Workshop of Your Own*, Boston: Houghton Mifflin, 1959.

Meyer, Carolyn, *Saw, Hammer and Paint*, New York: Morrow, 1973.

Seidelman, James E., *Creating with Wood*, New York: Crowell, 1969.

Sootin, Harry, *Experiments with Machines and Matter*, New York: Norton, 1963.

Business education Business education includes bookkeeping, typing, shorthand, business mathematics, and business law. These subjects have a heavy load of technical vocabulary. (For example: *assets, liabilities, balance sheet, debit, credit.*) When possible, the teacher should relate technical vocabulary to the experience of the students; technical terminology should also be taught with concrete materials. Example 9B.9 is a selection from a business education textbook. Note the technical vocabulary, which includes: *property* *taxes, real estate, personal property, exempted, mortgage, general property tax, taxable value, local assessors, and estimated market value.*

Example 9B.9 *Sample technical vocabulary from a business education textbook*

Property Taxes

A *property tax* is one levied upon real estate or any personal property that has value and that can be bought and sold. This tax is based upon the assumption that the ownership of property is an indication of the owner's ability to pay tax. In some states certain property, such as real estate owned by churches, is exempted from the general property tax. In other instances a taxpayer may be exempted from paying tax on the full value of the property if there is a mortgage on it. In other cases, local governments may exempt certain individual or business property from the general property tax in order to attract new industry.

Since the property tax is based upon value, it is necessary to determine the taxable value of the property. Local assessors estimate the value of the property. The assessed value (usually a percentage of the estimated market value) of the property becomes the basis for calculating the amount of tax the owner should pay.

Source: Donald P. Kohns, *Credit and Collections* (Cincinnati, Ohio: South-Western Publishing Co., 1968), p. 129.

Example 9B.10 is a section from a business textbook. In teaching from this selection, the teacher should strongly encourage the use of context clues. The following questions would help to focus the students' attention on word meanings they could ascertain from studying the context:

1. What are *guides*? (Text has direct definition.)
2. What are *captions*? (Synonym is used.)
3. What does *alphabetic range* mean? (Example is given.)

Example 9B.10 *Sample selection from a secretarial office textbook*

Guides

Guides are heavy cardboard sheets which are the same size as the folders. Extending over the top of each guide is a tab upon which is marked or printed a notation or title called a *caption*. The caption indicates the alphabetic range of the material filed in folders behind the guide. For example, a guide may carry the caption *A* which would tell the secretary that only material starting with the letter *A* would be found between that guide and the next guide. This tab may be part of the guide itself, or it may be an attached metal or plastic tab. Sets of guides may be purchased with printed letters or combinations of letters and numbers that may be used with any standard filing system. Other guide tabs are blank, and the specific captions are made in the user's office.

Source: James R. Meehan et al., *Secretarial Office Procedures*, 8th ed. (Cincinnati, Ohio: South-Western Publishing Co., 1972), p. 409.

Business subjects require that the student read with great accuracy. Even a very small error can be disastrous for a reader in these areas. For example, an error in bookkeeping could make a company appear to be making a profit when they are actually losing money. An error in transcribing shorthand could change the entire meaning of a letter to a client or business associate and have widespread consequences for the poor secretary who made the error. Business students should have a clear understanding of how meaning is conveyed through the grammar of English, and they should concentrate on reading for meaning. The student who is reading with an effort to grasp ideas is less likely to make errors.

Fluency and accuracy in shorthand is increased when the student practices reading shorthand aloud at sight. Also students should be taught to phrase their reading of shorthand to increase fluency and accuracy.

Business education students must be able to read graphs, charts, tables, balance sheets, invoices, and tax forms. Table 9B.1 is a table from a business education book; refer to Chapter 7 for the steps to follow in reading tables.

Table from a business education textbook   Table 9B.1

Taxable* income	Amount of tax	Percent of taxable income
$ 1,000	$ 145	14.5
2,000	310	15.5
10,000	2,190	21.9
20,000	6,070	30.4
100,000	55,490	55.5

*Taxable income is income after all allowances for exemptions and personal deductions have been subtracted.

Source: Roman Warmke, Euguene Wyllie and Beulah Sellers, *Consumer Decision Making* (Cincinnati, Ohio: South-Western Publishing Co., 1972), p. 128.

The teacher might use Table 9B.1 to let students practice the skills involved in reading tables. He or she might ask the following questions:

1. What does the asterisk beside the heading *Taxable Income* tell you to do?
2. If a person's taxable income is $100,000, what would the tax be? What percent of the taxable income is that amount?
3. At what level of taxable income does a person pay 21.9% of his or her taxable income?

Business students must learn to use reference materials such as *Coffin's Interest Tables*,[2] financial handbooks, and handbooks of business mathematics. (See Chapter 7.)

Home economics Home economics is a much more complex subject than it may appear on the surface. This area of study includes child care, consumer economics, foods and nutrition, clothing and textiles, design, management, housing, home furnishings, and personal growth and development.

Home economics content includes a large quantity of difficult vocabulary. (For example, *sauté, parboil, top sirloin, top stitch,* and *French seam.*) The reader must be helped to understand the concepts represented by this vocabulary. Example 9B.11 contains a section from a home economics textbook. Notice that the reader must understand the following terms (technical vocabulary is starred; the other words are difficult general vocabulary terms): *compels, payroll deduction,* authorize, specified, pay period,* lump sum,* bonds,* deducted,* transfer, checking account,* savings account,* systematically.* (See Chapter 4 for word recognition techniques and Chapter 5 for vocabulary development strategies. For example, working with root words can help students understand the words *deduction, deducted,* and *systematically.*)

Example 9B.11   *Sample money management selection from a home economics book*

Payroll Deduction Plans
Many people feel the need of a savings method that reminds or compels them to save regularly. The payroll deduction plan is one such arrangement. You authorize your employer to take a specified amount out of your pay each pay period. In some cases, this amount is just held and given to you in one lump sum at a specified time, perhaps just before vacation. Usually though, this method operates as a "bond-a-month" plan in which your employer purchases Series E bonds for you. By having the money deducted from your pay, you take care of saving first, before you get the money.

A similar plan is one in which you authorize the bank to transfer so much each month from your checking account to a savings account. In either case, you are admitting that you don't trust yourself to save systematically.

Source: Irene McDermott, Jenne L. Norris, and Florence Nicholas, *Homemaking for Teenagers,* Book 2, 3rd ed., p. 143. Copyright 1972 by Chas. A. Bennett Co., Inc., Peoria, Ill.

---

2. John E. Coffin, *Coffin's Interest Tables* (Philadelphia: John C. Winston Co., 1953).

Students of home economics find it necessary to read diagrams, patterns, drawings, graphs and charts. This requires that the student be able to visualize the finished product of a pattern or floor plan. The reader must be able to read mathematics symbols and legends to understand the graphics. Table 9B.2 is a table taken from a home economics textbook. (Refer to Chapter 7 for the steps to use in reading tables.)

Sample table in home economics textbook   **Table 9B.2**

Homemaking For Teen-agers — Book II

NUTRITIVE VALUE OF FOODS—Continued

Food, approximate measure	Water	Food energy	Protein	Fat	Carbohydrate	Calcium	Iron	Vitamin A value	Thiamin	Riboflavin	Niacin	Ascorbic acid
	Percent	Calories	Grams	Grams	Grams	Milligrams	Milligrams	International units	Milligrams	Milligrams	Milligrams	Milligrams
Miscellaneous Items—Continued												
Soups:												
Canned, condensed, ready-to-serve:												
Prepared with an equal volume of milk:												
Cream of chicken... 1 cup.....	85	180	7	10	15	172	.5	610	.05	.27	.7	2
Cream of mushroom 1 cup.....	83	215	7	14	16	191	.5	250	.05	.34	.7	1
Tomato........... 1 cup.....	84	175	7	7	23	168	.8	1,200	.10	.25	1.3	15
Prepared with an equal volume of water:												
Bean with pork.... 1 cup.....	84	170	8	6	22	63	2.3	650	.13	.08	1.0	3
Beef broth, bouillon consomme... 1 cup.....	96	30	5	0	3	Trace	.5	Trace	Trace	.02	1.2	......
Beef noodle....... 1 cup.....	93	70	4	3	7	7	1.0	50	.05	.07	1.0	Trace
Clam chowder, Manhattan type (with tomatoes, without milk)..... 1 cup.....	92	80	2	3	12	34	1.0	880	.02	.02	1.0	......
Cream of chicken... 1 cup.....	92	95	3	6	8	24	.5	410	.02	.05	.5	Trace
Cream of mushroom. 1 cup.....	90	135	2	10	10	41	.5	70	.02	.12	.7	Trace
Minestrone........ 1 cup.....	90	105	5	3	14	37	1.0	2,350	.07	.05	1.0	......
Split pea......... 1 cup.....	85	145	9	3	21	29	1.5	440	.25	.15	1.5	1
Tomato........... 1 cup.....	90	90	2	3	16	15	.7	1,000	.05	.05	1.2	12
Vegetable beef.... 1 cup.....	92	80	5	2	10	12	.7	2,700	.05	.05	1.0	......
Vegetarian........ 1 cup.....	92	80	2	2	13	20	1.0	2,940	.05	.05	1.0	......
Dehydrated, dry form:												
Chicken noodle (2-oz. package) ... 1 pkg......	6	220	8	6	33	34	1.4	190	.30	.15	2.4	3
Onion mix (1½-oz. package)......... 1 pkg......	3	150	6	5	23	42	.6	30	.05	.03	.3	6
Tomato vegetable with noodles (2½-oz.pkg.) 1 pkg......	4	245	6	6	45	33	1.4	1,700	.21	.13	1.8	18
Frozen, condensed:												
Clam chowder, New England type (with milk, without tomatoes):												
Prepared with equal volume of milk... 1 cup.....	83	210	9	12	16	240	1.0	250	.07	.29	.5	Trace
Prepared with equal volume of water.. 1 cup....	89	130	4	8	11	91	1.0	50	.05	.10	.5	......
Cream of potato:												
Prepared with equal volume of milk... 1 cup.....	83	185	8	10	18	208	1.0	590	.10	.27	.5	Trace
Prepared with equal volume of water.. 1 cup.....	90	105	3	5	12	58	1.0	410	.05	.05	.5	......
Cream of shrimp:												
Prepared with equal volume of milk... 1 cup.....	82	245	9	16	15	189	.5	290	.07	.27	.5	Trace
Prepared with equal volume of water.. 1 cup.....	88	160	5	12	8	38	.5	120	.05	.05	.5	......
Oyster stew:												
Prepared with equal volume of milk... 1 cup.....	83	200	10	12	14	305	1.4	410	.12	.41	.5	Trace
Prepared with equal volume of water... 1 cup.....	90	120	6	8	8	158	1.4	240	.07	.19	.5	......
Tapioca, dry, quick-cooking 1 cup.....	13	535	1	Trace	131	15	.6	0	0	0	0	0
Tapioca desserts:												
Apple............ 1 cup.....	70	295	1	Trace	74	8	.5	30	Trace	Trace	Trace	Trace
Cream pudding........ 1 cup.....	72	220	8	8	28	173	.7	480	.07	.30	.2	2
Tartar sauce............. 1 tbsp.....	34	75	Trace	8	1	3	.1	30	Trace	Trace	Trace	Trace
Vinegar............... 1 tbsp.....	94	Trace	Trace	0	1	1	.1	......	......	......	......	......
White sauce, medium..... 1 cup.....	73	405	10	31	22	288	.5	1,150	.10	.43	.5	2
Yeast:												
Baker's, dry, active..... 1 pkg......	5	20	3	Trace	3	3	1.1	Trace	.16	.38	2.6	Trace
Brewer's dry.......... 1 tbsp.....	5	25	3	Trace	3	17	1.4	Trace	1.25	.34	3.0	Trace
Yoghurt. See Milk, Cheese, Cream, Imitation Cream.												

Source: Irene McDermott, Jenne L. Norris, and Florence Nicholas. *Homemaking for Teenagers.* (Book II), 3rd ed., pg. 528. Copyright 1972 by Chas. A. Bennett Co., Inc., Peoria, Ill.

The teacher can use such a table to give students practice in reading tables. Questions such as the following could be posed:

1. What is the subject covered in this table?
2. How much water is found in a package of Baker's dry, active, yeast?
3. How much iron is found in one cup of frozen condensed cream of shrimp soup, prepared with an equal volume of water?

Note that the students must be able to utilize several levels of subheadings under the main headings given for foods. They must be aware of the different units of measure used for the nutrients, and they need to be able to read numbers expressed in decimals. Abbreviations for package, tablespoon, and ounce must be interpreted in order to read some of the table entries.

Students of home economics are required to scan labels for specific information. For example, they must scan labels on foods,

Example 9B.12 *Example of label information*

Source: Irene McDermott, Jenne I. Norris, and Florence Nicholas. *Homemaking for Teenagers.* (Book II), 3rd ed. Peoria, Illinois Chas. A. Bennett Company, Inc., 1972, p. 534. Reprinted by permission of National Canners Association.

fabrics, and cleaning products to determine the amounts contained in the packages. The readers must also determine whether the products are suitable for their needs. For example, when planning special diets the students must locate information regarding the amount of carbohydrates, fats, proteins, and other nutrients in a food. Example 9B.12 shows label information a reader must interpret.

The student is required to read directions in home economics which include technical vocabulary. Additionally, following the directions precisely and in the proper sequence is necessary for achieving the desired outcome. Note the sequence and the technical words in Example 9B.13, which contains directions taken from a home economics textbook.

Example of directions in a home economics textbook   **Example 9B.13**

Prepare the Pattern and Fabric For Cutting
Regardless of what you are making, you will follow the same general procedure in cutting out a garment. If you followed the plan in Book I, and made the suggested projects, you have already gone through the steps at least five or six times. By now you should be thoroughly familiar with them and be able to proceed automatically.

Check body measurements with your pattern and, if necessary, make pattern alterations.

Prepare fabric for grain perfection.

Check fabric carefully for one-way, match, diagonal, or any other feature that must be taken into consideration for correct cutting.

Pin pattern pieces to fabric according to cutting layout on the instruction sheet.

Cut out.

Transfer pattern markings to the fabric.

Source: Irene McDermott, Jenne L. Norris, and Florence Nicholas, *Homemaking for Teenagers*, Book 2, 3rd ed., p. 263. Copyright 1972, by Chas. A. Bennett Co., Inc., Peoria, Ill.

Home economics students must be able to read critically to evaluate a recipe for use. A student must compare and contrast the information provided regarding various products to determine which is most appropriate for his or her needs. The homemaker must read and evaluate information regarding sewing techniques or cooking procedures to determine which technique will make the work easier. New equipment that appears on the market must be evaluated for efficiency and to determine whether the cost of such equipment is worth the advantages it offers. One new piece of equipment that many homemakers have been evaluating is the microwave oven.

The home economics student reads newspapers, magazines, sewing books, and cookbooks. These materials frequently must be read in the same way reference books are read. The student should use the index to locate information, scan for the needed information, and read for details.

The following library, or trade books, in the area of home economics are available.

Isabella Beeton, *The Book of Household Management*, New York: Farrar, Straus and Giroux, 1969.

Psyche Cattell, *Raising Children with Love and Limits*, Camden, N.J.: Nelson, 1974.

Fitzhugh Dodson, *How to Parent*, Los Angeles: Nash, 1970.

Frank Donovan, *Block Printing in Textiles: A Complete Guide*, New York: Watson-Guystill, 1961.

Lillian Gilbreth, *Management in the Home*, New York: Dodd, 1954

Jean Gillies, *How to Run Your House: Without Letting it Run You*, New York: Doubleday, 1973.

Leland Gordon, *Economics for Consumers*, 6th ed., Princeton, N.J.: Van Nostrand, 1972.

Leonard Groupe, *Going Broke and How to Avoid it*, New York: Crowell, 1972.

Norma Hallen, *Textiles*, New York: Macmillan, 1973.

B. R. Hergehahn, *Shaping Your Child's Personality*, Englewood Cliffs, N.J.: Prentice-Hall, 1972.

Samuel Karelitz, *When Your Child is Ill*, New York: Random House, 1969.

Charles Klamkin, *How to Buy Major Appliances*, New York: Regency, 1973.

Marvin Klapper, *Fabric Almanac*, New York: Fairchild, 1966.

Mary Lynch, *Sewing Made Easy*, New York: Doubleday, 1969.

Adele Margolis, *How to Make Clothes that Fit and Flatter*, New York: Doubleday, 1969.

———— *Fashion Sewing for Everyone*, New York: Doubleday, 1974.

Nell Nichols, *Farm Journal's Country Cookbook*, New York: Doubleday, 1959.

Patricia Perry, *The Vogue Sewing Book*, New York: Doubleday, 1970.

Virginia Pomeranz, *The First Five Years: A Relaxed Approach to Child Care*, New York: Doubleday, 1973.

Martin Poriss, *How to Live Cheap but Good*, New York: American Heritage, 1971.

Carmella Riehl, *Family Nursing and Child Care*, Peoria, Ill.: C. A. Bennett, 1961.

Irma S. Rombauer and Marion Rombauer Becker, *Joy of Cooking*, Indianapolis: Bobbs-Merrill, 1971.

Reay Tannahill, *Food in History*, New York: Stein and Day, 1973.

Auren Uris, *Executive Housekeeping*, New York: Morrow, 1976.

David Van Dommellon, *Decorative Wall Hangings: Art with Fabric*, New York: Funk and Wagnalls, 1962.

Anne Willan, *Grand Diplome Cooking Course*, New York: Danbury Press, 1972.

A variety of reading skills are also required by other school subjects. Physical education, driver education, art, and music will each be discussed in turn.

Other school subjects

Physical education is a particularly valuable area of study today due to the increased amount of leisure time available to Americans. Also the great national interest in physical fitness has created a surge of interest in physical education. The content of physical education can be used to motivate reluctant readers because students who will not read other materials often willingly read physical education materials.

Physical education

Physical education is frequently taught without textbooks, but reading skills are required even when textbooks are not used. Students have to be able to read the rules and directions for playing games. They may read books that will help them improve their techniques in various sports. For example, there are many books available to help one improve one's golf swing.

Reading physical education material requires a number of reading skills. There is an extensive specialized vocabulary in this reading content. Each sport has a separate set of terms to be learned. (For example, *love, touchdown, foul,* and *guard.*) Notice that the word *love* from tennis and the terms *foul* and *guard,* which apply to several sports, are multiple meaning terms for which students have other meanings in their everyday vocabularies.

The team and individual sports taught in physical education classes utilize much special equipment. In order to learn the names and functions of the various pieces of equipment, the students could illustrate each piece of equipment, label it, and describe its function. A notebook could be maintained for this purpose, with the equipment for each sport categorized and alphabetized.

Reading physical education materials also requires that the reader follow the sequence of game directions and relate the directions to diagrams for game play. Frequently the reader must relate written content to diagrams and drawings in order to achieve understanding. Diagrams in games such as football can be quite complex. Understanding some games requires that the reader study drawings of referees' hand signals and remember the meanings of the signals in order to play the game.

Figure 9B.1 shows some referee's hand signals that students may have to interpret. The students have to translate the stick drawings into actual actions.

Figure 9B-1   *Diagram of referee's hand signals*

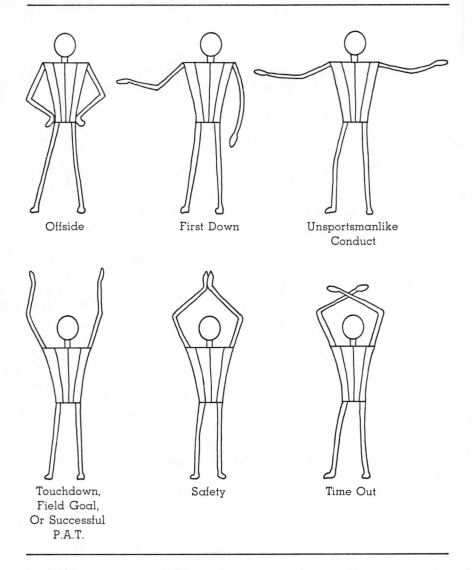

Offside

First Down

Unsportsmanlike
Conduct

Touchdown,
Field Goal,
Or Successful
P.A.T.

Safety

Time Out

The reader of physical education materials should learn to read
graphs and charts that contain data regarding games and plays. The
sports section of local newspapers is useful for developing these skills.
(See Chapter 7 for details regarding the reading of graphs, charts, and
diagrams.)

Reading can increase the enjoyment of spectator sports. As the
student learns more about the fine points of soccer, hockey, and

professional football, he or she can increasingly enjoy watching these games. Students also enjoy reading about the lives of current sports figures. Physical education teachers can encourage reading in this area by creating bulletin boards relating to books about sports and sports figures. They can refer students to books and magazines that can stimulate the student's interest in reading. Some library or trade books available in the area of physical education include:

Coombs, Charles, *Be a Winner in Track and Field*, New York: William Morrow, 1975.

Duroska, Lud, ed., *Great Pro Running Backs*, New York: Grossett and Dunlap, 1973.

Engle, Lyle Kenyon, producer, *Stock Car Racing U.S.A.*, New York: Dodd Mead, 1973.

Knosher, Harley, *Basic Basketball Strategy*, Garden City, N.Y.: Doubleday, 1972.

Kozuki, Russell, *Karate for Young People*, New York: Sterling, 1974.

Olson, James T., *Billie Jean King. The Lady of the Court*, Chicago: Creative Education, 1974.

Van Riper, Guernsey, *Behind the Plate: Three Great Catchers*, Champaign, Ill.: Garrard Press, 1973.

Driver education

Driver education classes are provided for secondary students in order to prepare them to drive safely, efficiently, and effectively. Driver education courses usually include a section of theory that is taught with a textbook; this is followed by practical application of driving skills and actual driving practice. The majority of young people look forward to acquiring a driver's license with great anticipation because a driver's license is one of the symbols of entering adulthood. For modern teenagers, learning how to drive is almost like passing the rites of adulthood of earlier societies. Since driving is a very significant skill for young people, reading driver education content and related materials is very important for secondary students. Students are highly motivated to read these materials; therefore, driver education content is useful for developing reading skills.

Readers of driver education content utilize skills similar to those needed for the other content areas. They must be able to interpret the following types of content: technical vocabulary, cause and effect relationships, directions, inferences, comparisons, pictures, diagrams, symbols, and mathematical material. In addition, readers must be able to read at the literal, interpretive, and critical levels. They must be able to visualize what they are reading so that they can translate words into action as they move from the textbook to actual driving practice.

Understanding the technical vocabulary used in driver education materials is essential to understanding the content and translating the content into action. The technical vocabulary of such materials usually represents concrete concepts relating to driving skill and automotive equipment. The student who has had little or no experience with an automobile is at a disadvantage because he or she has had no experience with the concepts represented by the words. This problem can be overcome by showing the student the object or process represented by the terms. Following are examples of the technical words found in driver education materials: *crosswalk, oversteering, intersection, collision, accelerator, right-of-way, regulatory signs, vehicle malfunction,* and *gauges.* (Refer to Chapters 4 and 5 for vocabulary teaching suggestions.)

In addition to the terms used in driver education materials, the reader must be familiar with a variety of writing patterns used to organize the content. Cause and effect writing is often used in helping the reader understand how to operate a vehicle. Example 9B.14 provides a sample of cause and effect writing from a driver education textbook.

Example 9B.14   *Writing pattern in a driver education textbook*

Identifying Traffic Events

Drivers who become skillful at identifying deal with the most important events in driving. They make their identifications based on information from all the senses. When a driver hears a small explosion and feels a shakiness in his car's movement (sensing), he concludes that he might have a flat tire (identifying). If he hears a siren and sees other drivers slowing or pulling over to the curb (sensing), he concludes that an emergency vehicle might be approaching (identifying).

As these examples show, identification, a *mental* process, relies heavily on sensing, a *physical* process. A driver must be in the best possible physical and mental condition to identify properly.

Source: Richard W. Bishop, Robert M. Calvin, Kenard McPherson. *Driving: A Task-Analysis Approach* (Chicago: Rand McNally and Company, 1975), p. 120.

The reader should analyze the content so that he or she can identify causes and effects. Following are suggestions for analyzing cause and effect writing; they are based on Example 9B.14.

Activities

1. The reader may make a diagram of causes and effects such as the following:

Causes	Effects
flat tire	shakiness
siren (emergency vehicle)	pull to the curb

2. The teacher may state the effects and ask the students to identify the causes, as in this example.
   a. Cause:_____
      Effect: Shakiness
   b. Cause:_____
      Effect: Pull to the curb

Another method of organizing content in driver education materials is through directions. The selection from a textbook in Example 9B.15 requires that the reader read a set of directions in sequence. He or she must also be able to translate these directions into action.

Directions from a driver education textbook   Example 9B.15

To back straight, use these procedures:
1. Turn your head and look backward to make sure the way is clear.
2. Keep your foot pressed on the brake until you are ready to move.
3. Shift to reverse gear.
4. Turn your body to the right, placing your left hand at the top of the steering wheel so that you have enough leverage to turn it.
5. If possible, place your right arm on the seat back to support yourself.
6. Look over your right shoulder.
7. Release pressure on the brake pedal.
8. Correct steering as necessary.
9. Glance forward briefly to see where the front of the vehicle is going. Look back over your shoulder.
10. Brake to a stop. Turn your body back to its normal sitting position. Shift to park or drive gear. If you are parking, set the park brake.

Source: Richard W. Bishop, Robert M. Calvin, Kenard McPherson, *Driving: A Task Analysis Approach* (Chicago: Rand McNally and Co., 1975), p. 85.

Following are suggestions for teaching the reading of directions in driver education materials, based on Example 9B.15.

Activities

1. The student may be presented with a set of directions from which a step has been omitted and the student is asked to state the omitted step. For example:

      a. Turn your head and look backward to make sure
the way is clear.

      b. ?

      c. Shift to reverse gear.

2. The student may be presented with a set of scrambled directions and asked to put them in the proper sequence. For example:

Directions: Number the following steps for backing in a straight line using the correct sequence.

    ( ) Look over your right shoulder.

    ( ) Turn your head and look backward to make sure
the way is clear.

    ( ) Shift to reverse gear.

    ( ) Turn your body to the right, placing your left
hand on the top of the steering wheel so that you
have enough leverage to turn it.

In addition to reading the organizational patterns cited previously, the reader of driver education materials frequently must identify main ideas and supporting details in order to understand the content. Chapter 6 presents a number of suggestions to aid the student in reading main ideas and supporting details.

The content of driver education and the actual driving process require that the reader make predictions based upon inferences and comparisons. Inferences that are the result of observation of surrounding conditions and traffic signs enable the driver to predict the road conditions to be encountered. The driver can compare present conditions with past driving experiences so as to predict how to react to traffic situations. The reader must be able to make inferences and comparisons based on written information. The selection from a driver education textbook in Example 9B.16 explains the role of prediction in driving.

Example 9B.16 *Prediction in driver education material*

When you make driving comparisons, ask yourself these questions: Is this situation like others I have been in? What happened in the other situation(s)? Could the same thing happen again in this situation? These questions, your assessments, and your assumptions will help you predict what could happen in a traffic situation.

Prediction as a Process
Prediction involves making *assessments* and *interpretations.* After you have sized up a situation, recognized assumptions, and made comparisons, you must

test the results mentally before you make a final prediction. You will need to assess (determine) two things: how much information you have, and how valuable the information is to you. In other words, you must *look* at the traffic scene for information it provides and *match* the information with your knowledge and experience. You then interpret or translate the information into a picture that has meaning for you.

Assessing information is a mental process. The information you must work with includes traffic laws that apply, the different vehicles present and what these vehicles can and cannot do, the maneuvers which different drivers are performing, the way your own vehicle is working, the roadway design, and general human behavior. When you process all this information, you will be able to answer the following questions: What will it do and how much? Is it a hazard or a threat? What is the amount or degree of risk?

You must remember the traffic laws that apply to the situation. From your past driving experience, you also must determine if other drivers obey all or some of the laws that apply. This present and recalled information helps you predict what a vehicle will do.

You can better predict "how much" a vehicle will do if you determine what each of the vehicles present is capable of doing. You must predict how each vehicle, including your own, can accelerate, decelerate, and corner. You must determine if your own vehicle is working properly. Recalling how and where different maneuvers are performed and how the roadway design affects the maneuvers also helps you determine what a vehicle will do, how much it will do, and if it is a hazard or threat.

Source: Richard W. Bishop, Robert Calvin, Kenard McPherson, *Driving: A Task-Analysis Approach* (Chicago: Rand McNally and Company, 1975), p. 137.

Following are examples of questions that teachers can use for developing skill in making predictions:

Inferences: Inferences enable the driver to predict his or her actions. Read the following question and answer it.

> If you were driving an automobile that was traveling at 45 miles per hour and you encountered a sign that indicated a sharp curve and a sign below it that said 35 M.P.H., what inference would you make?

Comparison: The driver can predict how he or she should drive by comparing present conditions with previous experience. Following are questions that will help the driver make helpful comparisons. Read them and answer them.

1. Compare driving a truck with driving an automobile.
2. If you were driving through a snow storm what comparisons could you make which would help you decide how to drive?
3. If you saw a horse running toward the road, what would you do? What previous experiences helped you make your decision?

The reader of driver education materials and the driver must be able to identify traffic signs. The excerpt from a driver education textbook in Figure 9B.2 shows examples of common traffic signs.

Figure 9B.2   *Common traffic signs*

Source: Richard W. Bishop, Robert M. Calvin, Kenard McPherson. *Driving: A Task-Analysis Approach.* Chicago: Rand McNally and Co., 1975, p. 25.

The following questions can be used to ensure that the students determine the meanings of the road signs in Figure 9B.2.

1. Is a curve indicated by any of the signs shown? If so, draw a picture of the sign.
2. What is the meaning of the sign that has two people pictured on it?
3. Which sign indicates the highway that is being used?
4. Which sign tells you the maximum (top) speed allowed on the highway?

The reader of traffic signs should learn to use color, size, and shape as a means of identifying them. Flash cards that show the various traffic signs are useful in helping students memorize these signs.

Driver education textbooks also include diagrams to help students understand various driving situations and driving related information. Figure 9B.3 is an example of a diagram from a driver education textbook. (page 314)

The teacher can help students understand such diagrams by using the following steps:

1. Provide the student with a blank diagram and the written directions. The student should draw in the automobile and number the steps the driver should take in order to turn left.
2. Provide the student with the complete diagram and ask him to write the directions for turning left in the correct sequence.

The driver education student must be able to read and compute mathematical material in order to understand the content. Figure 9B.4 shows the type of mathematics skills required by driver education materials. (page 315)

The reader of Figure 9B.4 may be helped in the following ways:

1. Ask the student to explain the main idea of the chart.
2. Ask the student to explain the significance of the information.
3. Ask the student how many car lengths are required to stop when the car is traveling 50 miles per hour.
4. Ask the student to explain how he or she would apply this information when driving.

Teachers of driver education should encourage students to think at the literal, interpretive, and critical levels in order to achieve understanding of the content. (Refer to Chapter 6 for a discussion of these levels.)

There are a number of supplementary, reference, and recreational resources available for the driver education library. Several are suggested, on pages 315 and 316.

Figure 9B.3 *Diagram from driver education textbook*

Turning Right

The Approach
1. Be sure the planned turn is legal.
2. Check for traffic ahead, to the sides, and behind, using both inside and outside rearview mirrors.
3. Signal and move into the proper lane and lane position.
4. Signal to turn right.

The Condition
5. Adjust speed to about 10 mph before the turn and keep the car wheels straight.
6. Check the intersection for vehicles and pedestrians.
7. Check the inside rearview mirror for following vehicles.

The Performance
8. Begin hand-over-hand steering just as the front end of the vehicle reaches the intersection curb line.
9. As the front end of the vehicle reaches the proper lane, unwind the steering wheel while accelerating gently.
10. Straighten the car in the lane and accelerate according to road and weather conditions.

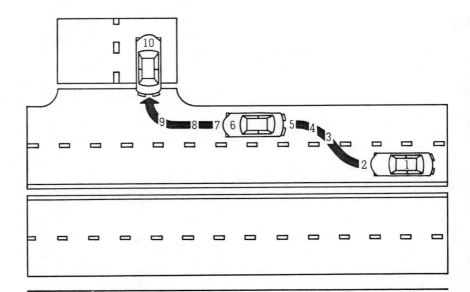

Source: From Richard W Bishop Robert M Calvin Kenard McPherson *Driving A Task-Analysis Approach*, p 80 Copyright 1975 by Rand McNally and Company Chicago

Mathematics used in driver education material   Figure 9B.4

Average Stopping Distance at Different Speeds

Stopping distances may vary because of differences in road and weather conditions. The figures here are based on tests utilizing new cars with properly adjusted brakes and on dry, level concrete surfaces. Reaction time is based on average reaction time of three-quarters of a second.

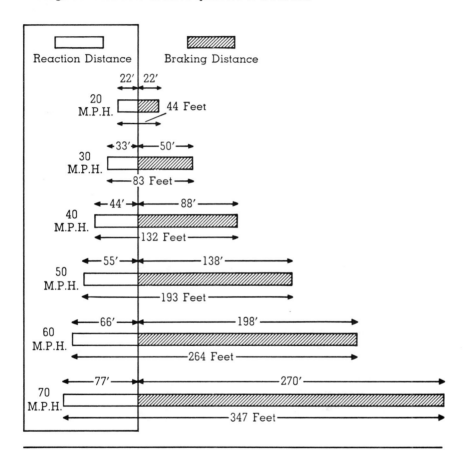

Source: From Richard W. Bishop, Robert Calvin, Kenard McPherson, *Driving: a Task-Analysis Approach*, p 41. Copyright 1975 by Rand McNally and Company, Chicago.

James E. Aaron, *Driver and Traffic Safety Education*, New York: Macmillan, 1966.

Benjamin C. Bogue, *The Driver's Handbook*, Washington, D.C.: The National Safety Foundation, 1966.

———— *Your Driver's Examination and Road Test*, Washington, D.C.: The National Safety Foundation, 1974.

Patty De Roulf, *A Woman and Her Car*, Indianapolis: Bobbs Merrill, 1974.

Merle E. Dowd, *How to Save Money When You Buy and Drive Your Car*, Englewood Cliffs, N.J.: Parker Publishing Company, 1967.

Lester B. Forrest, *Automobile Drivers*, Bronxville, N.Y.: Cambridge Publishing Company, 1955.

H. T. Glenn, *Youth at the Wheel*, Peoria, Ill.: Bennett Publishing Company, 1958.

Anthony Harding, ed., *Cars in Profile*, New York: Doubleday, 1973.

Ralph Nader, *Unsafe at any Speed; the Designed-In Dangers of the American Automobile*, New York: Grossman, 1965.

Ken W. Purdy, *Young People and Driving; The Use and Abuse of the Automobile*, New York: John Day, 1967.

John Stevenson, *Learning to Drive*, New York: Arco Publishing Company, 1974.

Art   Many students with special interests and talents choose to study art; therefore, art can be used to motivate these students to read. These students will read in order to pursue their special interests. Art students read to solve problems and to study the styles of various artists. They frequently enjoy reading about the lives of artists because they can relate to these people due to their common interests. Books enable art students to study the art of certain historical periods in depth. Students can also study the art of specific ethnic groups through books.

The art student must learn to read the technical vocabulary of artists. (For example, *impressionist, watercolors,* and *oils.*) Example 9B.17 includes material from a textbook used for teaching art. As you read this brief selection, note the many technical words and expressions used. (For example, *linear perspective, diminishing contrasts, hue, value, intensity of color, texture, achieve deep penetration, two dimensional surface, infinite concept, atmospheric perspective, pictorial composition, theme, picture plane, volume of deep space, softening edges of objects, scale,* and *middle ground.*)

Example 9B.17   *Sample passage from an art textbook*

Problem 1

In conjunction with linear perspective, artists of the past frequently used diminishing contrasts of hue, value, and intensity of color and texture to achieve deep penetration of space on a two-dimensional surface. This is known as the infinite concept of space or atmospheric perspective.

Create a pictorial composition based on the theme "Objects in Space." Conceive of the picture plane as the near side of a volume of deep space. Use the indications of space suggested in the opening paragraph, plus softening edges of objects as they are set back in depth. The human figure may be used to help suggest the scale of objects in space. Foreground, middle ground, and deep space may be indicated by the size of similar objects.

___

Source: Otto Ocvirk, Robert Bone, Robert Stinson, and Philip Wigg, *Art Fundamentals Theory and Practice* (Dubuque, Iowa: William C. Brown) 1975: 114.

An activity that can be used to develop art vocabulary is presented below:

Art Vocabulary Game.
Objective: To provide practice in associating words with colors.
Materials needed: Set of cards with hues (as listed below), set of cards with color words

vermillion	cinnamon	burgundy
cerise	ocher	sloe
puce	sepia	ecru
indigo	magenta	ivory

Directions for Activity: This game is one in which a student accumulates "books" (sets of two) of matching cards. The regular rules of a card game may be used. (This activity can be played by two or more. The one who can match the most cards correctly within a specified period of time wins.)

The art student finds it necessary to read directions for using various types of media and materials. These directions must be followed precisely to achieve the desired effect; therefore he or she must read carefully for details.

The art student must critically evaluate various types of materials and media by reading labels. It is also necessary for the student to read reference materials, art history, biographies, and critical reviews of artists' works found in newspapers. Magazines such as *Arts and Activities, School Arts, Popular Photography,* and *Craft Horizons* provide current information and ideas for the art student. Some library books available in the area of art include:

Chase, Alice Elizabeth, *Famous Paintings for Young Peole,* New York: Platt, 1951.

Chase, Alice Elizabeth, *Looking At Art,* New York: Crowell, 1966.

Glubok, Shirley, *The Art of America Since World War II,* New York: Macmillan Co., 1975.

Glubok, Shirley, *The Art of America in the Early Twentieth Century,* New York: Macmillan Co., 1974.

Glubok, Shirley, *The Art of the New American Nation,* New York: Macmillan Co., 1972.

Marshall, Anthony D., *Africa's Living Arts,* New York: Watts, 1970.

Moore, Clyde B., *Frederic Remington, Young Artist*, Indianapolis: Bobbs-Merrill, 1971.

Raboff, Ernest, *Leonardo da Vinci*, New York: Doubleday, 1971.

_____ *Marc Chagall*, New York: Doubleday, 1968.

_____ *Pablo Picasso*, New York: Doubleday, 1968.

Stone, David K., *Art in Advertising*, New York: Pitman Publishing, 1971.

There are many books on painting, drawing, stitchery, weaving, printmaking, and the like. All require reading of illustrations and diagrams. (See Chapter 7.)

Music   Music students usually have special interests and talents. Therefore, music can serve as a vehicle to interest these students in learning to read well.

Music students are expected to read and interpret a large number of musical terms such as *sonatina, spiritoso, andante,* and *allegretto.* In addition, special symbols are used in music. These symbols aid the student in interpreting the music. Students must be able to recognize symbols for such things as treble clef, bass clef, notes (whole, half, quarter, etc.), rests (varying values corresponding to note values), sharps, flats, crescendo, and diminuendo. The teacher must frequently demonstrate the musical terms and concepts for students in order for them to understand. Print alone cannot convey musical concepts. For example, the teacher might illustrate playing a song *pianissimo* and playing the same song *forte,* or he or she might illustrate a *crescendo* followed by a *diminuendo.* Example 9B.18 is a selection from a secondary school music textbook. Note that the student must read the words of the song, the notes, and specialized directions. In addition, the music student must coordinate all of the information he or she has read with his or her fingers and/or voice.

Oftentimes students have trouble reading the songs in music books, particularly when words are presented in syllabic form. Several specific procedures may be utilized to help:

1. Provide background information about the song.
2. Present the words of the song in poem form on a ditto sheet (to avoid confusion that may result from all the accompanying signs and symbols on a music sheet).
3. Discuss any words that may not be recognized or comprehended as well as the overall meaning of the lyrics.
4. Cooperatively, the teacher and students should divide the words into syllables. A ditto sheet may again be prepared with words in this form.

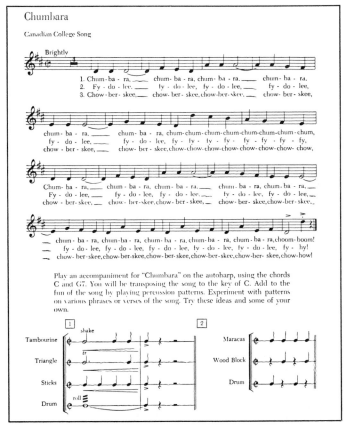

Source: Beth Landis and Lara Haggard. *Exploring Music.* New York: Holt Rinehart, 1968, p. 150.

After the musical aspects of the song are taught, the students can use the ditto sheet (with divided words) to sing from. Later, they may use the music books that contain the syllabicated words along with the notes and other symbols.

Music students use reading skills in several ways. They must learn to sight read music quickly. To achieve this, the student must practice identifying music notes rapidly; sometimes flash cards are useful for developing this skill. Learning to read musical phrases aids the student in achieving accuracy and speed. Music students read the words of songs which frequently involve rather difficult words; so a meaningful approach that utilizes context clues helps the student. They may also read forewards to collections of music which explain the background and nature of the music. This helps the music student understand and interpret the works.

The music student is often required to read a variety of materials related to music. He or she reads materials such as *Etude* magazine, biographies of musicians, music history, and critical reviews in local newspapers. Some library books available in the area of music include:

Barclay, Pamela, *Duke Ellington: Ambassador of Music*, New York: Creative Education, 1974.

Davis, Marilyn Kornreich, *Music Dictionary*, New York: Doubleday, 1956.

Dublowsky, John, *Music in America*, New York, Crowell-Collier Press, 1967.

Hosegawa, Sam, *Stevie Wonder*, New York: Creative Education, 1975.

Levine, Jack, *Understanding Musical Instruments: How to Select Your Instrument*, New York: Warne, 1971.

Montgomery, Elizabeth, *The Story Behind Pop Songs*, New York: Dodd, 1958.

Morse, Charles, *Roberta Flack*, New York: Creative Education, 1975.

Warren, Fred, *The Music of Africa*, Englewood Cliffs, N.J.: Prentice Hall, 1970.

Self-test

1. Why do vocational students need reading instruction? (a) So they can read vocational materials in class. (b) So they can read well enough to get a job. (c) Both *a* and *b* (d) Neither *a* nor *b*.

2. Why do poor readers often choose to study vocational subjects? (a) They are more interesting. (b) The students think they will be required to do less reading. (c) The students choose them for fun. (d) The students want to learn to read.

3. Vocational materials usually include three writing types. Which of the following is *not* one of the three? (a) Factual information (b) How-to-do-it material (c) Stories (d) Problem solving.

4. The technical vocabulary of industrial arts, business education, and home economics is which of the following? (a) Often concrete so it can be illustrated and demonstrated (b) Hard to pronounce (c) Difficult to teach (d) Abstract.

5. How must the reader of vocational materials read directions? (a) Quickly (b) Skip them (c) Precisely and carefully (d) Memorize them.

6. Why do readers of vocational subjects have an advantage when they read directions? (a) The directions are short. (b) They are easy. (c) The reader receives feedback regarding the success of his or her reading. (d) Following directions is fun.

7. What factors do not influence the rate used by the reader of vocational materials? (a) Purposes for reading (b) Type of content (c) Familiarity with the subject (d) None of the above.

8. Why is critical reading important to industrial arts students? (a) They must evaluate material on labels. (b) They must pronounce the words. (c) Both *a* and *b* (d) Neither *a* nor *b*.
9. Which of the following reference works would a business education student use? (a) A shorthand book (b) *Coffin's Interest Tables* (c) *Encyclopaedia Britannica* (d) Both *a* and *b*.
10. Which of the following is *not* a reason for critical reading in home economics? (a) To evaluate new equipment (b) To evaluate the contents of food products (c) To select recipes (d) To read for pleasure.

1. Select a set of directions from a subject treated in this chapter and rewrite the directions in simpler language for poor readers.

   Enrichment activities

2. Develop an annotated bibliography of materials which could constitute a classroom library in one of the subjects treated in this chapter. Indicate readability levels whenever possible.
3. Make a dictionary of terms for use in one of the areas treated in this chapter. You could use drawings and pictures from magazines, catalogues, and newspapers to illustrate the dictionary.
4. Collect pamphlets, magazines, newspapers and library books that could be used to develop understanding of vocabulary and concepts of poor readers in a subject treated in this chapter.
5. Select a section in a textbook on a subject treated in this chapter. Make a reading lesson plan for the selected section.
6. Prepare a presentation, describing how you would help teach a student to read one of the following: (a) an invoice or balance sheet; (b) a contract; (c) a tax form; (d) a physical education activity or game; (e) a critical review of art or music; (f) a specialized handbook; (g) a reference source.
7. Read several of the articles cited in Selected References on one of the subjects treated in this chapter. Report to the class on the suggestions for teaching reading in this area.
8. Examine textbook materials from industrial arts, business education, and home economics textbooks. Locate examples of the common reading problems.
9. What are some library (trade) books available for the areas of industrial arts, home economics, and business education other than these suggested in this chapter? Include some high interest, low vocabulary materials.
10. Prepare a three-level study guide for a selection from one of the subjects treated in this chapter. (See Chapter 3)
11. Prepare a vocabulary exercise (anagram, maze, puzzle, scramble, or other challenging variation) for one of the subjects treated in this chapter. (See Chapter 5)
12. Select a study skill appropriate to one of the subjects treated in this chapter. Describe how you would teach it. (See Chapter 7)

Selected references

Ahrendt, Kenneth M. and Shirley S. Haselton. "Informal Skills Assessment for Individualized Instruction" *Journal of Reading,* 17 (January 1973): 52–57.

Aukerman, Robert C. *Reading in the Secondary Classroom.* New York: McGraw-Hill Book Company, 1972. Chapters 11 and 12.

Carney, John J. and William Losinger. "Reading and Content in Technical-Vocational Education." *Journal of Reading* 19 (October 1976): 14–17.

Danneman, Jean. "Reading: The Road to Shorthand Skill." *Business Education World* 40 (January 1960): 26.

Earle, Richard and Linda S. Perney. "Reading the Words in Music Class." *Music Educator's Journal* 59 (December 1972): 55–56.

Forgan, Harry W. and Charles T. Mangrum. *Teaching Content Area Reading Skills.* Columbus, Ohio: Charles E. Merrill, 1976.

Garbutt, Douglas. "An Investigation into Students' Understanding of Some Accounting Terms." *Journal of Business Education* 40 (April 1965): 298–301.

Hafner, Lawrence E. *Improving Reading in Middle and Secondary Schools.* 2nd ed. New York: Macmillan Co., 1974.

——— *Developmental Reading in Middle and Secondary Schools.* New York: Macmillan Co., 1977. Chapters 16, 17, and 19.

Hafner, Lawrence E., Wayne Gwatney, and Richard Robinson. "Reading in Bookkeeping: Predictions and Performance." *Journal of Reading* 14 (May 1971): 16–18.

Harrison, Lincoln J. "Teaching Accounting Students to Read." *Journal of Business Education* 35 (January 1960): 167–70.

Johnson, Joyce D. "The Reading Teacher in the Vocational Classroom." *Journal of Reading* 17 (October 1974): 27–29.

Karlin, Robert. *Teaching Reading in the High School.* 2nd ed. Indianapolis: Bobbs Merrill, 1972. Chapter 12.

Levine, Isidore N. "Solving Reading Problems in Vocational Subjects." *High Points* 43 (April 1960): 10–17.

Musselman, Vernon A. "The Reading Problems in Teaching Bookkeeping." *Business Education Forum* 14 (December 1959): 5–7.

Piercey, Dorothy. *Reading Activities in Content Areas.* Boston: Allyn and Bacon, 1976. Chapters 9, 11, and 12.

Robinson, H. Alan. *Teaching Reading and Study Strategies in the Content Areas.* Boston: Allyn and Bacon, 1975. Chapter 10.

Robinson, H. Alan and Ellen L. Thomas. *Fusing Reading Skills and Content.* Newark, Del.: International Reading Association, 1969.

Robinson, Richard D. "Business Teachers are Reading Teachers." *Journal of Business Education* 44 (February 1969): 201–2.

Schulwitz, Bonnie S. *Teachers, Tangibles and Techniques.* Newark, Del.: International Reading Association, 1975.

Wulffson, Don L. "Music to Teach Reading." *Journal of Reading* 14 (December 1970): 179–82.

Young, Edith M. and Leo V. Rodenborn. "Improving Communication Skills in Vocational Courses," *Journal of Reading* 19 (February 1976): 373–77.

Assessment procedures

10

A major purpose of this chapter is to assist the content area teacher in determining whether students possess the reading and study skills necessary to successfully deal with the materials of his or her course. To so evaluate, the content teacher must be aware of the reading and study skills appropriate to his or her particular subject.

This chapter discusses six major assessment procedures: (1) standardized tests of reading achievement; (2) informal tests of reading achievement; (3) observation checklists; (4) self-assessment; (5) attitude measures; and (6) reading interest inventories. Each is an important tool and serves certain purposes.

As you read this chapter, try to answer these questions:

Purpose-setting questions

1. What are some representative standardized reading tests, and how can test results be used to help a teacher plan an instructional program?
2. What are some informal measures of reading achievement, and how can results of each be used to help a teacher plan an instructional program?
3. What types of questions and record-keeping systems may be utilized for observation checklists related to reading achievement?
4. What are some self appraisal techniques to help students evaluate reading strengths and weaknesses?
5. What measures of attitudes toward reading are helpful to the teacher in individualizing the instructional program?
6. What is a "reading interest inventory" and how may the results be used by the teacher to enhance an instructional program?

As you read this chapter, check your understanding of these terms.

Key vocabulary

standardized reading test	graded word list	informal reading inventory
	independent reading level	

survey reading test
diagnostic reading
   test
validity
grade equivalent
percentile rank
stanine
aptitude tests
reading expectancy
test norms

instructional
   reading level
frustration reading
   level
group reading
   inventory
skills inventory or
   test

capacity
   (potential)
   reading level
cloze test
   procedure
reading
   autobiography

Standardized tests of reading achievement

Standardized reading tests yield objective data about reading performance. Ideally, they are designed so that each response to a test item is subject to only one interpretation. Authors of standardized tests sample large populations of students to determine the appropriateness of test items, and they seek to verify the validity and reliability of test results so that schools can be confident that the tests measure what they are supposed to measure and do so consistently.

There are various types of standardized reading tests:

1. Survey test, which measure general achievement in a given area, such as reading.
2. Diagnostic tests, which analyze and locate specific strengths and weaknesses and may suggest causes.
3. Oral tests, which analyze and locate strengths and weaknesses of oral reading.
4. Study skills tests, which measure ability to utilize techniques essential for enhancing comprehension and retention, such as study methods, locating and organizing information, adjusting rate of reading, etc.

A bit more needs to be said about the validity and reliability of a test. A valid standardized reading test represents a balanced and adequate sampling of the instructional outcomes (knowledges, skills, etc.) that it is intended to cover. Validity is best judged by comparing the test content with the related courses of study, instructional materials, and educational goals of the class. Evidence about validity is nearly always given in the test manual of directions; such information may be checked against the impartial opinions of educational professionals and by a careful inspection to see if the test is designed to measure what one wants to measure.

The reliability of a test refers to the degree to which the test gives consistent results. One way of establishing reliability is by giving the same test twice to a large group of pupils. If each student makes practically the same score in both testing situations, the test is highly consistent and reliable. If many students make higher scores in one testing situation than in the other, the test has a low reliability. Another method of measuring reliability is to compare students' scores on the odd-numbered items with their scores on the even-numbered items; if they are in the same rank order, or if they have a high correlation, the test is reliable. A third method of measuring reliability is to compare one form of a test to an equivalent form of the test. A test used to compare the average scores of different classes does not have to be highly reliable, as low reliability is unlikely to affect the comparisons. However, when measuring the level of achievement of an individual student, only a test of high reliability should be used as it is necessary to find his or her specific, not comparative, level of achievement. While a test of low reliability cannot be very valid, high reliability does not guarantee that a test is valid.

The most common ways in which results of standardized tests are expressed are: (1) grade scores or grade equivalents, (2) percentile ranks, and (3) stanines.

Grade equivalent indicates the grade level, in years and months, for which a given score was the average score in the standardization sample. For example, if a score of 25 has the grade equivalent of 8.1, 25 was the average score of pupils in the norm group who were in the first month of the eighth grade. If a pupil (not in the norm group) who is in the first month of the eighth grade were to take the same test and score 25 correct, his or her performance would be at "grade level," or average for his or her grade placement. If that pupil, were to get 30 right, or a grade equivalent of 9.1, he or she would have done as well as the typical ninth grader in the first month. Similarly a 6.3 grade equivalent for an eighth grader would mean that he or she is performing the way the average pupil in the third month of sixth grade would perform on that test.

Percentile rank expresses a score in terms of its position within a set of 100 scores. The percentile rank indicates the precent of scores of the norm group that are equal to or lower than the given score. Thus a result ranked in the 35th percentile is regarded as equivalent to or surpassing the results of 35 percent of the persons in the norm group. A student who scores in the 83rd percentile as compared with the local school's norms may only score in the 53rd percentile if his or her score is based on national norms.

A *stanine* ranks a test score in relation to other scores on that test. (The term is derived from the words *standard* and *nine*.) A stanine is expressed as a value from one to nine on a nine point scale. Thus, the mean score of the standard population has a stanine value of 5. Verbal descriptions often assigned to stanines are as follows:

stanine 9—highest performance
stanines 7 and 8—above average
stanines 4, 5, and 6—average
stanines 2 and 3—below average
stanine 1—lowest performance

Through the use of test norms, one student's score may be compared to the scores of other students of similar age and educational experience. It can be useful to determine how a student's performance on one test compares with his or her performance on other tests in a battery and to determine how his or her performance on a test compares to his or her performance on the same test administered at another time. However, scores from two different kinds of standardized reading tests cannot be easily compared since the tests probably differ in purpose, length, and difficulty. Even the results of the same test administered on successive days may vary, depending on the reliability of the test and other factors related to the student.

Representative standardized reading tests

The four major types of standardized reading tests are discussed below.

Survey A survey test measures general achievement in a given area, such as reading. The results can show how well students are performing. By examining a student's score in relation to scores of others, the teacher obtains an impression of the student's reading achievement. Looking at a number of students' scores gives an indication of the range of reading achievement in the class.

For example, the distribution in Table 10.1 approximates the range of reading achievement scores for a tenth-grade class. A cursory examination of the distribution shows that one-third of the students are performing well below grade level, one-third within a year or two of grade level, and one-third well above grade level. A teacher who has this information at the beginning of the school year knows that it is necessary to make provisions for individual differences. A single score represents the student's overall achievement and does not reveal how the student will perform on specific reading tasks. However, some reading survey tests designed for secondary school students have separate sections on vocabulary, comprehension, and reading rate. Such tests yield separate scores for each section. A wise teacher will not merely be concerned with a student's total achievement score but will want to determine if the student is equally strong in all areas tested or if he or she is stronger in one area than another. Furthermore, a careful examination of student responses to individual test items might provide the teacher with information about more specific reading requirements. One way to learn more from testing is to go over the test items with the student to see if he or she can explain his or her responses. It is possible that correct responses were reached in inappropriate ways, or that a student guessed a number of the answers.

Range of reading scores in a tenth-grade class   Table 10.1

Grade Score	Students
15.0–15.9	1
14.0–14.9	1
13.0–13.9	4
12.0–12.9	4
11.0–11.9	2
10.0–10.9	6
9.0– 9.9	2
8.0– 8.9	3
7.0– 7.9	5
6.0– 6.9	1
5.0– 5.9	1
	N = 30

Some survey reading tests include:

1. *Burnett Reading Series: Survey Test*, New York: Scholastic Testing Services, 1970. (Includes subtests on vocabulary, comprehension, rate, and accuracy. For grades 7–13.)
2. *California Achievement Tests: Reading*, rev. ed., Monterey, Calif.: California Test Bureau—McGraw-Hill, 1970. (Includes subtests on vocabulary and reading comprehension. Level 4 for grades 6–9; Level 5 for grades 9–12.)
3. *Cooperative English Tests: Reading Section*, rev. ed., Princeton, N.J.: Educational Testing Service, 1960. (Includes subtests on vocabulary and comprehension. Level 2 for grades 9–12).
4. *Gates-MacGinitie Reading Tests*, rev. ed., New York: Teachers College Press, 1970. (Includes subtests on speed and accuracy, vocabulary, and comprehension. Survey E for grades 7–9; Survey F for grades 10–12.)
5. *Iowa Silent Reading Tests*, rev. ed., New York: Harcourt Brace Jovanovich, 1970. (Includes subtests on vocabulary, comprehension, directed reading, and reading efficiency. Level I for grades 6–9; Level II for grades 9–12.)

6. *Nelson-Denny Reading Test*, rev. ed., Boston: Houghton-Mifflin, 1973. (Includes subtests on vocabulary, comprehension, and rate. For grades 9–16.)

7. *Reading Test: McGraw-Hill Basic Skills System*, New York: McGraw-Hill, 1970. (Includes subtests on rate, flexibility, retention, skimming and scanning, and comprehension. For grades 11–14.)

8. *Sequential Tests of Educational Progress*, Series II: Reading, Princeton, N.J.: Educational Testing Service, 1969. (No subtests. Level 2 for grades 10–12; level 3 for grades 7–9.)

9. *Stanford Achievement Test: High School Reading*, rev. ed., New York: Harcourt Brace Jovanovich, 1965. (No subtests. For grades 9–12.)

10. *Traxler High School Reading Tests*, rev. ed., Indianapolis: Bobbs-Merrill, 1967. (Includes subtests for story comprehension, word meaning, and paragraph comprehension. For grades 9–12.)

Example 10.1   *Iowa silent reading tests*

Reproduced from the *Iowa Silent Reading Tests*, copyright 1973 by Harcourt Brace Jovanovich, Inc. Reproduced by special permission of the publisher.

A profile sheet from *Iowa Silent Reading Test* is presented in Example 10.1 to give an indication of the content of the test and the recording of results.

Diagnostic   A diagnostic test helps to locate specific strengths and weaknesses and possibly suggests causes for them. There are few group diagnostic reading tests at the secondary level; these include:

1. *Diagnostic Reading Tests,* Mountain, N.C.: Committee on Diagnostic Reading Tests, 1947. (Includes subtests on vocabulary in four subject areas, comprehension, rates of reading, and word attack. Upper level for grades 7–13.)
2. *Doren Diagnostic Reading Test of Word Recognition Skills,* Circle Pines, Minn.: American Guidance Service, 1973. (For grades 1–9.)
3. *Stanford Diagnostic Reading Test,* New York: Harcourt Brace Jovanovich, 1973. (Includes subtests for comprehension, vocabulary, syllabication, phonics, and rate. Brown Level, grades 5–8; Blue Level, grades 9–12.)

Stanford diagnostic reading test   **Example 10.2**

| | TEST 2 | TEST 3 | TEST 4 | TEST 1 | TEST 5 Reading Comprehension | | |
	Auditory Discrimination	Phonetic Analysis	Structural Analysis	Auditory Vocabulary	Literal Comprehension	Inferential Comprehension	Comprehension Total
Raw Score							
	9	9	9	9	9	9	9
	8	8	8	8	8	8	8
S	7	7	7	7	7	7	7
T A	6	6	6	6	6	6	6
N	5	5	5	5	5	5	5
I N	4	4	4	4	4	4	4
E	3	3	3	3	3	3	3
	2	2	2	2	2	2	2
	1	1	1	1	1	1	1

Pupil Information Box

Name

Teacher   Grade

School

City   State

Today's Date
            month   day   year

Date of Birth
            month   day   year

Reproduced from the *Stanford Diagnostic Test.* Copyright 1976 by Harcourt Brace Jovanovich, Inc. Reproduced by special permission of the publisher.

A profile sheet from the *Stanford Diagnostic ·Reading Test* is presented in Example 10.2 to give an indication of the content of the test and the recording of results.

Oral Several oral reading tests are available for students at the secondary level. The oral reading tests must be given on an individual basis and require preparation for their administration. Presumably the kinds of errors a student makes when reading orally serve as a clue to the kinds of errors made when reading silently. This may or may not be true. But oral reading tests are valuable diagnostic tools for some students who are having serious reading problems. They include:

1. *Gilmore Oral Reading Test*, new ed., New York: Harcourt Brace Jovanovich, 1965. (Includes subtests for accuracy, comprehension, and rate. For grades 1–8.)
2. *New Gray Oral Reading Test*, Indianapolis: Bobbs-Merrill, 1967. (Includes subtests for accuracy and comprehension. For grades 1–16.)
3. *Slosson Oral Reading Test*, East Aurora, N.Y.: Slosson Educational Publications, 1963. (For grades 1–12.)

A sample of the record booklet for *Gray Oral Reading Test* is presented in Example 10.3 to give an idea of the recording of results.

Study skills There are several tests that chart the ability to use references, maps, indices, dictionaries, and graphs. These include:

1. *S.R.A. Achievement Series: Work Study Skills*, Chicago: Science Research Associates, 1964. (For grades 6–9.)
2. *Work-Study Skills: Every Pupil Test of Basic Skills*, new ed., New York: Harcourt, Brace and World, 1949. (For grades 5–9.)

Other types of standardized tests There are several special types of standardized instruments which measure specific areas. Some of these include:

1. *ANPA Foundation Newspaper Test*, Princeton, N.J.: Cooperative Tests and Services, 1969. (Includes simulated newspapers to test newspaper reading ability. For grades 7–12.)
2. *California Phonics Survey*, Monterey, Calif.: California Test Bureau—McGraw-Hill, 1963. (Includes subtests on vowel and consonant confusions, reversals, configuration, endings, negatives-opposites–sight words, and rigidity. For grades 7–16.)
3. *Pupil Placement Tests*, Boston: Houghton-Mifflin, 1970. (Includes subtests on word recognition, oral sight reading, and listening. For use in determining independent, instructional,

Example 10.3

EXAMINER'S RECORD BOOKLET

for the

GRAY ORAL READING TEST

FORM C

Name *Bill R.*

School *Windhurst High*

City *Windhurst*

Examiner *R. Jones*

Grade *10*   Age *15.6*

Teacher *Smith*   Sex *M*

State

Date *October 18, 1962*

SUMMARY

Pas-sage Number	No. of Errors	Time (in Seconds)	Pas-sage Scores	Compre-hension
1.	—	—	9	—
2.	—	—	9	—
3.	—	—	9	—
4.	—	—	9	—
5.	0	16	9	4
6.	1	17	8	4
7.	2	34	3	4
8.	2	62	2	1
9.	3	74	1	1
10.	7	108	0	0
11.	7/	—	0	0
12.	/22			
13.				
Total Passage Scores			59	
Grade Equivalent			8.7	

TYPES OF ERRORS

1.	Aid	0
2.	Gross Mispronunciation	2
3.	Partial Mispronunciation	14
4.	Omission	1
5.	Insertion	1
6.	Substitution	0
7.	Repetition	4
8.	Inversion	0 /22

OBSERVATIONS
(Check statement and circle each part)

Word-by-word reading
✓ Poor phrasing
Lack of expression
Monotonous tone
Pitch too high or low; voice too loud,
    too soft, or strained
Poor enunciation
✓ Disregard of punctuation
✓ Overuse of phonics
✓ Little or no method of word analysis
✓ Unawareness of errors
Head movement
Finger pointing
Loss of place

COMMENTS: *Read passages through 7 with ease then began to sound unfamiliar words losing meaning.*

Source: From the *New Gray Oral Reading Test*. Indianapolis, Indiana: Bobbs-Merrill, 1967.

frustration and potential reading levels. For grades 1–9.)

4. *Reader's Inventory*, Huntington Park, N.Y.: Educational Developmental Laboratories, 1963. (Includes subtests on reading interests, attitudes, habits, visual conditions, background, expectations in reading. For grades 9–16.)

5. *Test of General Educational Development*, Washington, D.C.: American Council on Education, 1970. (Includes subtests on interpretation of reading materials in the natural sciences, social studies, and literature. For grades 9–16.)

Several group aptitude (general academic ability) tests used in the secondary school are listed below:

1. *California Short-Form Test of Mental Maturity*, Monterey, Calif: California Test Bureau, 1963. (For K-college level.)

2. *Kuhlmann-Anderson Intelligence Test*, 7th ed., New York: Psychological Press, 1963. (For grades 7–9 and 9–13.)

3. *Lorge-Thorndike Intelligence Tests*, multi-level ed., Boston: Houghton-Mifflin, 1966. (For grades 3–13.)

4.   *Otis-Lennon Mental Ability Test*, New York: Harcourt Brace Jovanovich, 1970. (Intermediate for grades 7–9; Advanced for grades 10–12.)

Most mental tests for secondary school level students require reading. Results often place the poor reader in the dull-normal category, possibly underestimating his or her real ability. Such students should be measured by a test that does not require reading for a more valid assessment. The test must be individually administered, and may require special training for administration.

Intelligence tests scores are useful in identifying the under-achiever. A student's score on a standardized reading test only indicates present performance and not the performance of which the student may be capable. An intelligence test score can indicate a student's capability level, which can then be compared with his or her actual performance. Whether or not the student is performing up to capacity can be determined. One commonly used formula for finding this information, suggested by Guy Bond and Miles Tinker,[1] is given below:

$$\frac{IQ}{100} \ (years \ in \ school) + 1.0 = Reading \ Expectancy$$

Thus, a mid-year eighth grader who scored 150 on an intelligence test would have a reading capacity or expectancy of twelfth-grade level:

$$\left(\frac{150}{100} \times 7.5\right) + 1.0$$
$$(1.50 \times 7.5) + 1.0$$
$$(11.25) + 1.0$$
$$12.25$$

Because of the differences in students' backgrounds of experience and because of the limitations of standardized tests, caution should always be exercised in the use of such formulas. Experience indicates that most formulas for predicting reading potential are least accurate for extremely good and extremely poor readers.

There is a second way of estimating a student's potential. The student's listening ability is a good indicator of the level on which he or she could be reading. The following tests provide a measure of the student's listening comprehension:

1.   *Brown-Carlson Listening Comprehension Test*, New York: Harcourt Brace Jovanovich, 1955. (Includes subtests on imme-

---

1.   Guy L. Bond and Miles A. Tinker, *Reading Difficulties: Their Diagnosis and Correction*, 2nd ed. (New York: Appleton-Century Crofts, 1967), p. 93.

diate recall, following directions, recognizing transitions, recognizing word meanings, and lecture comprehension. For grades 9–adult.)

2. *Durrell Listening-Reading Series,* New York: Harcourt Brace and World, 1969. (Advanced level for grades 7–9.)

3. *Sequential Tests of Educational Progress: Listening,* Princeton, N.J.: Educational Testing Service, 1957. (For grades 4–14.)

In choosing a test for use, several factors should be considered. For example, a test is inappropriate if the sample population used to standardize it is significantly different from the class or group to be tested. A description of the norm population is usually contained in the test manual. Even a test that is based on populations of children from a wide variety of rural and urban centers and of various social, racial, and ability levels and of different sexes and races is not always the most appropriate. Some publishers have begun to standardize according to a particular geographic region or a particular educational reference group. In many cases, local norms may be more appropriate to use.

Selecting and using standardized tests

In addition to measuring the reading skills it claims to measure (validity) and having subtests that are long enough to yield reasonably accurate scores, a test should not result in a chance score, with students obtaining high score by luck, guessing, or other factors (reliability). The more reliable tests have a reliability coefficient of .90 with subtests above .75.

As a summary, the following ideas on test selection and evaluation are proposed for consideration:

1. Determine the purpose for testing. Is it to compare class achievement with national or local norms or to determine the status of a class or individual to learn whether corrective steps should be taken? Is it to evaluate an on-going developmental reading program or specific reading skills? Is it to serve as a screening device in order to determine the need for further testing?

2. Locate suitable tests. Probably the most useful single source of assistance in locating suitable tests is the *Seventh Mental Measurement Yearbook,* edited by Oscar K. Buros, cited below.

3. Evaluate tests in terms of such items as the following:
   a. Age-grade level. Is it suitable for intended students?
   b. Reliability. Does it yield consistent results?
   c. Validity. Does it actually measure what it is supposed to measure?

d.   Adequacy of the manual. Is adequate information given regarding the reliability and validity of the test?

e.   Relevance of the norms provided. Are the norms based on sound sampling procedures and are aids (profiles, etc.) provided for their interpretation?

f.   Appropriateness of the content. Is it fair to minority groups and inner-city students?

g.   Ease of administration. Are directions for administering the test clear and concise?

h.   Time. Can the average student attempt at least half of the items within the time range?

i.   Economy. What is the initial cost? Are test books reusable? Is scoring easy?

j.   Availability of alternate, equivalent forms. Can the test be used for test-retest comparisons?

A good way to become familiar with a test is to take it yourself and then to administer it to a few students. Specimen sets of tests are available from publishers at a reasonable cost. Also see Suggested Enrichment Activities # 1 for an outline to use for evaluating a standardized reading test.

For readers who are interested in more detailed descriptions of particular tests, the following collections of reviews on reading tests are suggested. Also see Appendix D.

O. K. Buros, *Mental Measurement Yearbook*, 7th ed., Highland Park, N.J.: Gryphon Press, 1972.

————, *Reading Tests and Reviews*, Highland Park, N.J.: Gryphon Press, 1968.

————, *Reading Tests and Reviews*, II, Highland Park, N.J.: Gryphon Press, 1975.

William Blanton et al., eds., *Reading Tests for the Secondary Grades: A Review and Evaluation*, Newark, Del.: International Reading Association, 1972.

At this point, one of the most important precautions about the results of standardized tests must be mentioned. The results do not indicate the level of reading instruction or assignments to give to a student. Based on the result of administering questions to a particular norming group, the grade norm for a test is the average number of items that students get correct at a particular grade level. A score of 9.0 may indicate only that student who is just beginning ninth grade had 50 items correct. It does not mean that the student who had 50 items correct can necessarily read 9.0 grade level material. In fact, the grade score a student gets on a silent reading test usually tells you that material at that level is too difficult for him or her. More will be said about this and what to do about it in the following section dealing with informal tests of reading achievement.

There are several informal (nonstandardized) measures of reading achievement which can be useful to the teacher in revealing student reading achievement. Four of these kinds of measures will be discussed in this section: (a) vocabulary assessment, (2) group reading inventory, (3) skills inventories, and (4) informal reading inventories, including the cloze procedure. (Informal assessments for word analysis skills—contextual, structural, phonic, and dictionary—have been presented in Chapter 4.)

Informal tests of reading achievement

As noted earlier in the listing of standardized survey reading tests, there are several formal measures of this aspect of reading. One informal diagnostic device is discussed below.

Vocabulary

San Diego Quick Assessment   This is a graded word list that may be used to determine reading level and detect errors in word analysis. The information provided may be used to group students or to select appropriate reading materials for them. To administer this device, the teacher should follow the steps below.

1.   Type out each list of ten words on an index card.
2.   Begin with a card that is at least two years below the student's grade level.
3.   Ask the student to read the words aloud; if he or she misreads any on the initial list, drop to easier lists until he or she makes no errors.
4.   Encourage the student to attempt to read aloud the words he or she does not know so that the techniques the student uses for word identification can be determined.
5.   Have the student read from increasingly difficult lists until he or she misses at least three words on a list.

The level at which a student misses no more than one out of ten words is his or her *independent reading level* (the level of material that he or she can read successfully without teacher aid). Two errors on a list indicates the *instructional level* (this is the reading level of the material to be used under teacher guidance). Three or more errors indicate that the level is too difficult for him or her (called the *frustration level*).

Lists are available for preprimer level up to the eleventh grade; for practical purposes, only the lists for the grades 4 through 11 are presented in Table 10.2.

Table 10.2   *Graded word list for quick assessment*

Grade 4	Grade 5	Grade 6	Grade 7
decided	scanty	bridge	amber
served	business	commercial	dominion
amazed	develop	abolish	sundry
silent	considered	trucker	capillary
wrecked	discussed	apparatus	impetuous
improved	behaved	elementary	blight
certainly	splendid	comment	wrest
entered	acquainted	necessity	enumerate
realized	escaped	gallery	daunted
interrupted	grim	relativity	condescend

Grade 8	Grade 9	Grade 10	Grade 11
capacious	conscientious	zany	galore
limitation	isolation	jerkin	rotunda
pretext	molecule	nausea	capitalism
intrigue	ritual	gratuitous	prevaricate
delusion	momentous	linear	risible
immaculate	vulnerable	inept	exonerate
ascent	kinship	legality	superannuate
acrid	conservation	aspen	luxuriate
binocular	jaunty	amnesty	piebald
embarkment	inventive	barometer	crunch

Source: M. LaPray and R. Ross, "The Grade Word List: A Quick Gauge of Reading Ability," *Journal of Reading* 12 (January 1969): 305–7. Reprinted with permission of the authors and the International Reading Association.

Other vocabulary lists may be helpful for particular students. For example, there are several lists of high-frequency words that may be checked, particularly for the very disabled secondary school reader:

1. Dolch, Edward, *A Manual for Remedial Reading*, Champaign, Ill.: Garrard Publishing Co., 1945. (Page 29 gives the Dolch Word List).
2. Dolch, Edward W., "95 Nouns Common to Three Word Lists," in *Teaching Primary Reading*, Champaign, Ill.: Garrard Publishing Co., 1950, p. 269.

3. Fry, Edward, *Instant Words*, Sunland, Calif.: Learning Through Seeing. (The list appears in *Elementary English* 34 (November 1957): 456–58; and also in Edward B. Fry, *Reading Instruction for Classroom and Clinic*, New York: McGraw-Hill, 1972, pp. 58–63.)

4. Johns, Jerry, "A List of Basic Sight Words for Older Disabled Readers," *English Journal* 61 (October 1972): 1057–59.

5. Johnson, Dale D., "The Dolch List Reexamined," *The Reading Teacher* 24 (February 1971): 455–56. (Gives the 220 most frequently used words in the Kucera-Francis Corpus)

A group reading inventory of content material may be taken by having students read a passage of 1,000 to 2,000 words from their textbooks and asking certain types of questions. This procedure can give some indication of how well students read a particular textbook. Content books to be studied should be written on a student's instructional or independent level; trade and supplementary books should be on a student's independent level.

Group reading inventory (G.R.I.)

Usually the selection used in an inventory is chosen from an early part of the textbook. The teacher introduces the selection and directs the students to read it for the purpose of answering certain kinds of questions. As students read, the teacher writes the time on the chalkboard at 15 second intervals; each student writes down the last time recorded when he or she finishes reading the passage. Later, a words-per-minute score is computed by dividing the time into the total number of words in the passage. For example, if the passage is 1,000 words long and the student reads it in 4 minutes, the student would divide 4 into 1,000 to get a 250-words-per-minute score. When finished reading, the student closes the book and answers a series of questions on such things as:

1. vocabulary (word meaning, word recognition, context, synonyms, antonyms, syllabication, accent, affixes).
2. literal comprehension (main ideas, significant details, sequence, following directions, etc.).
3. interpretive comprehension (evaluative and inferential).

A sample group reading inventory from a secondary level history textbook is provided in Example 10.4. (Also see the Shepherd citation in Selected References for other examples of group reading inventories.)

Sample group reading inventory   **Example 10.4**

Name _____ Date _____

Motivation Statement: Read to find out why the Confederation

Example 10.4 (cont.)

Congress was unable to settle its foreign problems.

Selection: *Dealing with Other Countries.*

The men who represent one country as it deals with other nations are called *diplomats.* Their work is called *diplomacy,* or the *foreign relations* of their country. The foreign relations of the Confederation were not very successful. Congress did not have the power to make the states or the people follow the agreements that it made with other countries. Under these conditions other nations had little respect for the United States.

The British had promised in the Treaty of Paris to leave the territory they had agreed was now part of the United States. Instead, they remained in their forts along the Great Lakes. They also used their Indian friends to keep settlers out of the Northwest Territory. There was much fighting between the frontiersmen and England's Indian allies.

Why did the English hold these forts? They hoped to keep their fur trade and the control it gave them over some Indian tribes. They even hoped to set up an Indian nation north of the Ohio River. Suppose the American government failed to last. Some British leaders thought that they could then move back into control of their former colonies. The reason they gave for keeping their grip on the Northwest was that the United States had not kept its treaty promise to help British creditors collect their debts in America.

In 1784 Congress tried to settle some of its problems with England. It sent John Adams to London. He tried to get the British to give up the forts on American soil and to increase trade with the United States. The British refused to give up the forts until American debtors had paid the money owed to British creditors since before the Revolutionary War. They refused to make any kind of trade treaty. Adams tried for three years, but could not get the British to change their minds.

Congress also tried to settle its troubles with Spain. In the Treaty of Paris, England had given Americans the use of the Mississippi River and the right to store their goods at New Orleans. This agreement was most important to the people who had moved into Kentucky and Tennessee. They had to use the Mississippi to get their goods to market. They also needed the right to deposit, or keep, their goods in New Orleans until a ship could load them for the trip across the ocean.

Spain held the lower Mississippi and New Orleans. Its rulers would not accept the agreement made by the British and Americans. They also hoped the new nation would not succeed so they could take part of it. Spanish officials urged the settlers south of the Ohio to secede, or take their territory out of the United States. They could then join the Spanish empire. Spain would give them the use of the Mississippi and New Orleans. Spain was still a strong nation. It proved this by getting Indians to attack the pioneers who settled near Spanish territory, and by holding onto Natchez, in American territory.

But Spain was willing to discuss such problems. In 1785 Don Diego de Gardoqui became the first Spanish minister to America. He and John Jay, the American Secretary of Foreign Affairs, soon began to bargain. By this time Spain had closed the lower Mississippi to American trade. Jay was told by Congress that he must get Spain to allow such trade. Don Diego was willing, but only if Spain would control the Mississippi, most of what is now Alabama and Mississippi, and parts of Tennessee, Kentucky, and Georgia. Spain claimed this land because it had held parts of it while fighting the British as allies of the United States during the Revolutionary War. Don Diego also asked that Spain should hold all lands south of the thirty-fifth parallel.

John Jay refused to accept such claims. He insisted that the United States would accept only the terms of the Treaty of Paris, which made the thirty-first parallel the boundary between Florida and the United States. Businessmen in the North and East wanted to build up their trade with Spain. In August, 1786, Congress changed its position. It told Jay that he could give up American rights on the Mississippi River for 25 years, if Spain would in turn agree to allow more American trade in Spanish ports. This would have helped the businessmen of New England, but would have hurt the farmers and settlers in the South and West. There was a bitter debate in Congress, and the men who represented seven of the states voted for this plan. This was two states less than the nine that had to agree before Congress could make a treaty. The talks between Spain and the United States then ended. The problems between the two countries were not settled until the Pinckney Treaty of 1795.

Relations with France were also poor. Thomas Jefferson became our minister to France. He wrote that the French showed him little respect. The leaders of the French government were angry because the United States could not repay its wartime debts. However, Jefferson did get them to agree to allow more trade by American ships.

The Confederation had no army, and could not do much about Indian attacks. It could not open up the Mississippi, build up trade with Europe, or make needed agreements with foreign governments. More people began to wonder why they had to have such a weak national government.

Source: Boyd Shafer et al., *A High School History of Modern America*, 2nd ed.,pp. 104–5. Copyright 1973 by Laidlaw Bros., River Forest, Ill. Used by permission of Laidlaw Brothers, a Division of Doubleday and Co., Inc.

Questions: (Vocabulary)
1. What is meant by the term *diplomacy?*
2. Define *secede.* Define *allies.*
3. What is a synonym for the word *treaty?*
4. Divide the word *Confederation* into syllables.
5. Write the definition of the word *relations* as used in the passage.

Example 10.4 (cont.)   6. What did the author mean by "keeping their grip on the North-west"?

(Literal Comprehension)

(Detail)   1. What job did John Jay have in the Confederation government?

(Detail)   2. Why did the English remain in forts along the Great Lakes?

(Detail)   3. Why was the Treaty of Paris important to the people of Tennessee and Kentucky?

(Sequence)   4. List, in order, the sequence of steps in the discussion of problems with Spain.

(Interpretive Comprehension)

(Evaluation)   1. Do you agree with the directive of Congress to Jay in 1786? Why or why not?

(Inference)   2. What do you think the people began to want from their national government? What makes you think this?

(Conclusion)   3. Why did the U.S. under the Articles have so much difficulty in dealing with other nations?

Materials are suitable for instructional purposes if the student can comprehend 75 percent of (or answers six out of eight questions about) what he or she reads. If students can comprehend 75 percent of what they read, their comprehension will increase if teachers introduce specialized vocabulary words, help with comprehension, teach a study method, and provide specific purposes for reading. Of course students have many different reading levels, depending upon their interests and the background information that they may possess on any specific topic. Thus, there is a need to apply a group reading inventory to texts in each specific content area. Where the student comprehends 90 to 100 percent of what he or she reads (answers 9 questions out of 10 correctly), the material can be classified as being on his or her *independent* level. Where the student comprehends 50 percent or less of what he or she reads (answers 5 questions out of 10 correctly), the material is on his or her *frustration* level. Students scoring 70 percent or below on a set of materials should be given an inventory on easier material; those who score 90 percent or above should be given an inventory on more difficult material.

Finally, such an inventory may be individually administered. In such a case, the teacher receives more information by listening to the student read orally. The only variation in procedure is that, after checking comprehension, the teacher tells the student to read the selection out loud and follows along on a second copy. The teacher marks on the second copy the following types of errors:

1. Each unknown word that must be supplied by the teacher (place *p* above unknown word).
2. Each word or word part that is mispronounced (underline mispronunciation, indicating given pronunciation above word).
3. Each omitted word or word part (circle omission).
4. Insertion of words not in the text (place caret and word above where insertion was made).
5. Reversals of word order or word parts (use reversal mark—∼).
6. Repetitions (use wavy underline).

Ignoring of punctuation marks. Spontaneous corrections may be marked as well, although they should not be scored as errors. Mispronounced proper names and differences due to dialect should also not be counted as errors. Some teachers have found it effective to tape a student's oral reading, replaying the tapes to note the errors in performance. Material in which the student can recognize 95 percent of the words can be classified as suitable for instructional purposes.

Below is an illustration of a part of a marked oral reading passage.

"There is (a) time in every man's education when he arrives at the
p conviction that envy is *ignorance;* that imitation is suicide; that he
must take himself for better, for worse, as his portion . . .
Ralph Waldo Emerson, "Self-Reliance."

Skill inventories

Many content teachers want to know if the students have developed the specific reading skills that are necessary to succeed in their content areas. The following skills are common to all content areas:

1. Understanding and using parts of textbooks (table of contents, index, list of illustrations, appendices, bibliography, glossary).
2. Interpreting maps, tables, charts, graphs, diagrams, cartoons.
3. Knowing specialized vocabulary.
4. Using reference materials (encyclopedias, dictionaries, supplemental reference books).
5. Recognizing special symbols, formulas, and abbreviations.

Other necessary general skills are using study methods, outlining, taking notes, and reading at a flexible rate. Of course, general comprehension skills are involved in all content areas, as suggested in the group reading inventory. The following items may be used to prepare skill assessments:

1. Parts of textbooks—Have students make use of different aids in their textbooks, such as preface, index, vocabulary lists, appendices, and the like.
2. Maps, tables, charts, graphs, diagrams, cartoons—Use examples from the students' textbooks and ask students to answer questions you have prepared.
3. Specialized vocabulary—Use words from the glossaries of textbooks or supplemental materials that you use.
4. Reference materials—Use the reference materials that are available for your content area, and develop questions to see if students know the various reference sources and how to use them.
5. Symbols, abbreviations, and formulas—See if students can recognize the most frequently used symbols and abbreviations in your content material.

In the following Examples, some sample reading skills tests are provided. Each deals with a separate skill area, and each example comes from a different content area.

Example 10.5   *Using parts of a textbook—skill inventory*

Directions: Use your textbook to answer the following questions:
1. What is the title of your book?
2. When was it published?
3. Who wrote the book?
4. What are the titles of the first three chapters?
5. How are the chapters arranged or grouped?
6. On what page does Chapter 4 begin?
7. Find the meaning of the term _____ (such as "air mass").
8. On what page is there a chart showing _____ (such as *stars* and *constellations*)?
9. What does the map on page ____ tell you?
10. On what page does the book explain the construction of a _____ (such as *hydrometer*)?
11. What index entries are given for _____ (such as *latitude*)?

Below are two columns of words or phrases. Match the expression from the right-hand column with the one that means the same, or almost the same, thing in the left-hand column.

____Index	1. Name of book
____Table of contents	2. Part of book giving additional information, such as notes and tables
____Bibliography	

_____Appendix
_____Glossary
_____Preface
_____Title
_____Copyright Date

3. Introduction
4. List of books for further reading
5. Alphabetical list of topics with the page on which each is found
6. Year when book was published
7. List in front of book with chapter headings or topics in sequence and page on which each begins
8. List of words with their meanings

Reading tables, maps, and graphs—skill inventory   **Example 10.6**

Directions: Look at the table below and answer the following questions.

The Boron Family

Name	Symbol	Atomic Number	Atomic Weight	Number of Electrons Per Group				
Boron	B	5	10.8	2	3			
Aluminum	Al	13	27.0	2	8	3		
Gallium	Ga	31	69.7	2	8	18	3	
Indium	In	49	114.8	2	8	18	18	3
Thallium	Tl	81	204.4	2	8	18	32	18	3

Source: Norman Abraham, et al., *Interaction of Matter and Energy.* p. 90. Copyright 1973 by Rand McNally.

1. What is the symbol for aluminum?
2. What is the electron grouping for Indium?
3. Sixty-nine and seven tenths is the atomic weight for which element?
4. What is the atomic number for Boron?
5. What is the name for this set of elements?

Directions: Study the map on page 344 and answer the questions about it.

Study the map carefully. Then tell whether the statements about the map are true or false:
1. The Zimbabue Culture was located south of the equator.
2. The Sahara Desert takes up most of the southern part of Africa.
3. Cultures that traded across the Indian Ocean would most likely have been located in eastern Africa.
4. Ethiopia, Nubia, and Egypt were all located near the waters of the Nile River.
5. One could travel by water from Rhodesia to Egypt.
6. The Nok and Zimbabue Cultures were located along the coast of Africa.

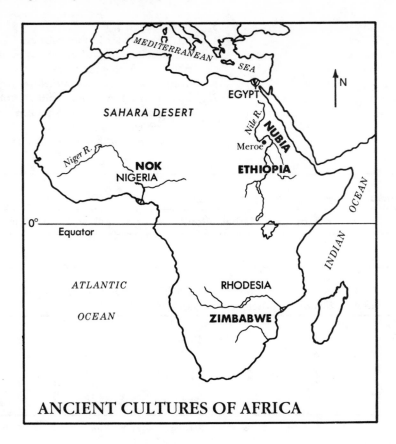

ANCIENT CULTURES OF AFRICA

Source: Sol Holt and John R. O'Connor, *Exploring World History*, p. 49. Copyright 1969 by Globe Book Co., New York.

Directions: Look at the graph below and answer the questions about it.

1. Was there a steady growth of voters from 1824 to 1860?
2. Around what year was there a sudden increase in popular votes cast in presidential elections?
3. Does the graph show the percentage of voting-age citizens participating in presidential elections?
4. For what years are complete data not provided?
5. About what percent of Americans took part in the 1824 presidential election?
6. About what percent of Americans voted in the 1972 presidential election?

Percentage of the total population voting in presidential elections

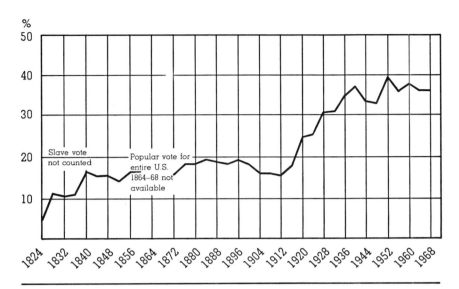

Source: Historical Statistics and Statistical Abstract

Using reference sources—skill inventory   **Example 10.7**

Directions: Answer the following questions (based on English classroom reference sources).

1. What library aid will tell you the library number of a book?
2. What is a biography?
3. What is the difference between fiction and nonfiction?
4. Explain to what each circled numeral of this entry from *Reader's Guide to Periodical Literature* refers.

    ① AIRPLANES
      ② Electra on public trial.   L. Davis   il   Flying
                                      ⑦   ⑧   ⑨

    68: 46–7⁺ F′ 61
    ③   ④   ⑤ ⑥

5. Describe the content of *Dictionary of American Biography*.
6. Describe the content of *Granger's Index to Poetry*.
7. Where could you find an alphabetical listing of words with synonyms and antonyms instead of definitions?
8. What information may be found in the *Reader's Encyclopedia*?
9. Where might you find short stories listed by title, author, subject?
10. What information may be found in *Book Review Digest*?

11. What information may be found in *Cumulative Book Index?*
12. Where might you go to find the answer to the question "Is Steinbeck's *The Grapes of Wrath* considered to be one of his better works?"

Directions: Find the following words in a dictionary and list the guide words and numbers of the pages on which they fall.

Word	Guide Words	Page number
anachronism		
aphorism		
assonance		
denouement		
epigram		
foreshadowing		
irony		
soliloquy		

Directions: Use a set of encyclopedias, such as *The World Book.* Answer the following questions.
1. What is the purpose of an encyclopedia?
2. What are the meaning and purpose of the guide letter or letters on the cover of each volume?
3. What are the meaning and purpose of *guide words?*
4. What is meant by *cross reference?*
5. What is the purpose of the bibliographies at the end of articles?
6. Where is the index located in the encyclopedia?

Example 10.8   *Vocabulary—skill inventory*

Directions: Explain the following terms concisely (Chapter 5, "Elections," in *American Government* by Allen Schech and Adrienne Pfister, Boston: Houghton-Mifflin, 1972, served as the source of vocabulary items.)

suffrage	closed primary
franchise	open primary
poll tax	plurality
suffragettes	presidential preference primary
literacy tests	favorite son
voting register	electoral votes
absentee ballot	electoral college
Australian ballot	office line ballot
party line ballot	caucus ballot
short ballot	

Directions: Look at the following words. Write the syllables of each word.

discriminations	residency
compulsory	nomination

convention   primary
candidates   delegates
expenditures   amendment
registration

Directions: Pronounce each word orally.

majority   eligibility
precinct   candidates
registrars   campaign
strategy   qualification

Directions: Define the italicized words.

The word *primary* suggests a first election—a nominating election held sometime before a regular election. A person who runs in a primary election needs only a *plurality* to win his party's nomination. A run-off by the two persons with the most votes may be required if no candidate receives a *majority*.

In the *closed* primary, the voter receives only the ballot of his own party; this is different from the *open* primary.

Special symbols and abbreviations   **Example 10.9**

Directions: Supply the missing parts.

Mathematical Symbols

Idea	Symbol	Read	Example
Operation:			
Addition	$+$	_____	_____
Subtraction	$-$	_____	_____
Multiplication	$\times$ or ( )	_____	_____
Division	$\div$	_____	_____
Relation:			
Equality	$=$	_____	_____
Inequality	$\neq$	_____	_____
Greater than	$>$	_____	_____
Greater than or equal to	$\geq$	_____	_____
Less than	$<$	_____	_____
Less than or equal to	$\leq$	_____	_____
Grouping:			
Parentheses	( )		_____
Brackets	[ ]		_____
Braces	{ }		_____
Vinculum	——		_____

Exercises

1.   Use symbols to write each expression in the shortest way you can.
     a.   five plus seven   i.   3 times y
     b.   3 plus 4   j.   9 more than 6

Example 10.9 (cont.)

c. x increased by 6

d. 6 decreased by x

e. a plus b

f. 7 minus 5

g. y is equal to 5

h. x minus y

k. 9 is greater than 6

l. m times r

m. 3 times a times b

n. x times y times z

o. the product of b and r

2. Write each expression in symbols.

a. the product of i, r, and t

b. 3 is not equal to 8

c. y is greater than 4

d. m is less than 12

e. x divided by 3

f. a equals the product of b and h

g. v divided by the product of l and w

h. x is less than y and greater than z

i. a times the sum of r and s

j. the quotient of 6 and c

k. y is greater than or equal to the sum of a and b

3. Express in symbols.

a. 25 minus the sum of 5 and 12. Multiply the result by 2.

b. m plus the difference between a and b. Multiply the result by s.

c. The product of a and b is greater than their sum.

d. The quotient of x and y is less than their difference.

e. The quotient of m and n is not equal to their product.

4. Express in words.

a. $5 + 2$

b. $5 > x$

c. $b + x$

d. $x - y$

e. $x \div y$

f. $y < 7$

g. xy

h. $\dfrac{ab}{p}$

i. prt

j. $(\frac{1}{2})h(a + b)$

k. $3b + 5xy$

l. $a(r + t)$

m. $5x - (3 + y)$

n. $\dfrac{3c - 5d}{7x}$

o. $2m \le 5r$

p. $2x \ne 5y$

5. If Walter has earned twice as many dollars as his younger brother, Harold, and Harold has earned x dollars, how many dollars has Walter earned? How many dollars have both earned together?

6. Mary has twice as many shells in her collection as Tom, but she has 4 shells less than Ann. How many shells has Mary if Ann has x shells? How many shells has Tom?

7. The sum of Jerry's and Bob's weights is less than that of their wrestling coach, Mr. Harvey. Let J, B, and H represent the weights of these persons, respectively, and express the relation between their weights.

8. Three boys compared their times in running the 100-yard dash. George was first, Bill was second, and Marvin was third. Write 6 relations to compare each boy's running time to that of the other two. Use T_1 as George's time, T_2 as Bill's time, and T_3 as Marvin's time. (T_1 is read "T sub one." This is a common way to distinguish between several quantities of the same kind.)

9. Express in symbols the fact that the average of 5 and 9 is less than the average of 4, 8, and 12.

10. Express in symbols the fact that the average of 4 and *s* is greater than the average of *a*, *b*, and *c*.
11. Express in symbols the fact that *B* is at least as great as *A*, but no greater than *C*.

Source: Glenn D. Vannatta et al, *Algebra One* (Columbus, Ohio: Charles E. Merrill Publishing Co., 1970), p. 708.

Study methods—skill inventory   Example 10.10

Directions: Answer the following questions about how you read and study your assignments.
1. Do you skim material before reading it in detail?
2. Do you summarize the selection after you read it?
3. Do you raise questions when reading and then read to find the answers?
4. Do you note key statements in your text during study?
5. Do you review the previous assignment before proceeding to read the current one?
6. When you sit down to study , do you make an effort to read as rapidly and as carefully as you can?
7. Do you immediately reread sections of your assignment that are not clear?
8. Are you careful not to skip graphs, tables, and charts when you read your assignment?
9. Do you take notes of key ideas after you have read each section?

Outlining/taking notes—skill inventory   Example 10.11

Directions: Read the selection below. Outline what you have read as you would a reading assignment in your course. (Use one main idea and four subtopics.)

India Is a Crowded Peninsula

    1. We know of the Far East as an area where hundreds of millions of people live. Red China today has more than 700 million people and India has almost 500 million people. These two nations have the largest populations in the world. Great numbers of the Chinese and Indian people live in crowded river valleys. It was in these same fertile river valleys that the ancient Indian and Chinese civilizations began about 5,000 years ago.

    2. India is part of a large peninsula shaped like a triangle, in the southern part of Asia. A peninsula is a land almost completely surrounded by water except for a small part which is attached to the mainland. This peninsula is about half the size of the United States. Today it includes two countries—India and Pakistan. The giant Himalaya Mountains, the highest in the world, separate India almost completely from the rest of Asia on the north. The Himalaya Mountains extend to the southwest, too. With water on three sides of the land and mountains on the north side, the early Indian people could live

Example 10.11 (cont.)   with little fear of invasion. There were passes in the mountains, however, and some invaders were able to get through to the river valleys. The snow and rain from the northern mountains fed the waters of the Indus and Ganges Rivers of India. (Map, page 41). Large numbers of people were able to live in the valleys of these rivers.

Source: Sol Holt and John R. O'Connor, *Exploring World History*, (New York: Globe Book Co., 1969), p. 30.

Example 10.12   *Adjustment of rate to purpose and difficulty—skill inventory*

Directions: Read this selection carefully. Try to comprehend the author's point of view and remember the main ideas, details, and what might be implied by the author. (A selection with appropriate questions would follow.)

Read as rapidly as you can to understand the main points. The questions for the selection will deal with the main events of the selection. (A selection and appropriate questions would follow.)

Scan the following selection to answer the questions. (Appropriate questions would precede the selection.)

A skills chart can be developed for recording the instructional needs of students. Skills charts include a list of skills and a list of students' names. A check mark is placed under a skill by the name of a student who successfully achieves the skill. A glance at the chart will provide a clue as to which students need special help in developing a required skill. If most students need help with a particular skill, the teacher may plan a total class instructional session. If only certain students lack a skill, the teacher may set up a skill group, to help students who need it. Skill groups are temporary groups in that they are dissolved when the members have accomplished the skill. Perhaps a skills file (collection of materials, equipment, and supplies) will provide the needed practice activities for some students.

A sample record-keeping chart is provided in Example 10.13.

Example 10.13   *Sample skills record*

Skills	*Student Names*		
1. Parts of textbook			
2. Interpretation of maps, tables, charts, diagrams, etc.			
3. Specialized vocabulary			
4. Reference sources			
5. Special symbols/abbreviations			
6. Study methods			
7. Outlining/taking notes			
8. Flexibility of rate			

Key: Pupil Performance Code
I—needs introduction and teaching
R—needs review and reinforcement
S—satisfactory (regular instruction adequate)
M—has mastered (no more practice needed)

There are published, commercial inventories to gauge a student's reading levels. They are compilations of graded reading selections with questions prepared to test the reader's comprehension. These types of inventories are often administered by the special or remedial reading teacher to students identified as problem readers.

Informal Reading Inventories (I.R.I.)

Two widely-used inventories are:

1. Morton Botel, *Botel Reading Inventory*, Chicago: Follett Publishing, 1966. (For grades 1–12)
2. J. Nicholas Silvaroli, *The Classroom Reading Inventory*, 3rd ed., Dubuque, Iowa: Wm. C. Brown, 1976. (For grades 2–8)

The chief purpose of these inventories is to identify the frustration, instructional, and independent reading levels of the student. Such inventories are valuable in that they not only provide an overall estimate of the student's reading ability, but they make possible identification of the specific strengths and weaknesses of the reader. They are helpful in determining what books a student can read independently and how difficult an assigned reading can be if it is to be used as instructional material.

While it is time-consuming, it is possible for the teacher to construct and administer an informal reading inventory. The steps below are suggested:

1. Select a set of books (or other materials) used at various grade levels (as 7th, 8th, 9th, 10th, 11th, and 12th)—preferably a series used in the class.
2. From each book, select one passage to be used for oral reading and one passage to be used for silent reading. (200 words or more each.)
3. Make a copy of each of the passages from each book. (Later the student reads from the book. The teacher marks the errors on the copy.)
4. Make up approximately ten questions for each passage. The questions should be of various types, including:
   a. Main idea—Ask for the central theme of the selection.
   b. Detail—Ask for bits of information conveyed by the material.

    c.   Vocabulary—Ask for meanings of words used in the passage.

    d.   Sequence—Ask for a listing of events in order of their occurrence.

    e.   Inference—Ask for information that is implied but not directly stated in the material.

    f.   Cause and effect—Ask for related factors that establish a cause-effect relationship.

5. Direct the student to read the first passage orally. Mark and count his or her errors. (See the section on group reading inventories for the types of errors to count.) Then ask questions made up for the oral reading. Count the number of questions answered correctly.

    Direct the student to read the second passage silently. Ask him or her questions prepared for silent reading. Again, count the number of questions answered correctly.

6. Count the number of errors in oral reading. Subtract from the number of words in selection. Then divide by number of words in the selection:

$$\frac{Number\ of\ words\ correct}{Number\ of\ words\ in\ selection}$$

Total the number of correct answers to questions for both the oral and silent reading passages. Then divide by number of questions as:

$$\frac{Number\ of\ questions\ right}{Number\ of\ questions\ asked}$$

7. Read aloud to the student higher levels of material until you reach the highest reading level for which he or she can correctly answer 75 percent of the comprehension questions. (The highest level achieved indicates the student's probable *capacity*, or potential, reading level.)

The following chart will help the teacher in estimating the reading levels of the reader:

Level	Word Recognition		Comprehension
Independent	99%	and	90%
Instructional	95%	and	75%
Frustration	<90%	or	<50%
Capacity			75%

Again, it should be pointed out that the informal reading inventory provides only an estimate of a student's reading levels and the teacher must use his or her professional judgment in interpreting the results.

Second, reading at the instructional level can only be achieved if the reader receives instruction before and/or while reading selected materials at that level.

An alternative method of assessment that can provide information similar to that provided by the informal reading inventory is the cloze test procedure. This test is easy to construct, administer, and score. It takes much less time to administer than the informal reading inventory.

Cloze test procedure

Again, the student is asked to read selections of increasing levels of difficulty. The student is asked to supply words that have been deleted from the passage.

A sample passage that has been constructed is given in Example 10.14.

Sample cloze passage   **Example 10.14**

Rocks exposed to the atmosphere slowly change. Air, water, and materials (1) _from_ living things can react (2) _with_ minerals in rock to (3) _alter_ or even remove them.

(4) _Weathering_ is the process by (5) _which_ rocks change to soil. (6) _It_ may result from both (7) _chemical_ and physical action on (8) _rocks_.

In a common form (9) _____ chemical weathering, minerals containing (10) _____ are broken down. Iron (11) _____ to moisture and air (12) _____ a red-brown coating or (13) _____. The iron combines with (14) _____ and becomes a new (15) _____, iron oxide (rust). Similar (16) _____ occur in rocks exposed (17) _____ air and water. Some (18) _____ are more easily changed (19) _____ than others. In the (20) _____ of air and moisture, (21) _____, for instance, changes to (22) _____ minerals. Quartz, however is (23) _____ to chemical changes.

Physical (24) _____ acting on rocks cause (25) _____ *weathering*. In mechanical weathering, (26) _____ are broken down by (27) _____ forces as windblown sand, (28) _____ water, and temperature changes (29) _____ cause rocks to shrink (30) _____ expand.

Plants also weather (31) _____. Simple plants called lichens (32) _____ grow on unweathered rocks. (33) _____ the lichens weather the (34) _____, other types of plants (35) _____ themselves. Plants remove chemicals (36) _____ developing soil. Living and (37) _____ plants may also add (38) _____ such as acids to (39) _____. Besides their chemical effects, (40) _____ roots may act upon (41) _____ physically. Some plant roots (42) _____ work their way into (43) _____ and crevices and split (44) _____ apart. Plants also have (45) _____ great effect on soil (46) _____ it is formed. Soil

Example 10.14 (cont.)

(47) _____ might otherwise be carried (48) _____ by wind or water (49) _____ be held in place (50) _____ a dense mat of plant roots.

Answers:
1. from, 2. with, 3. alter, 4. Weathering, 5. which, 6. It, 7. chemical, 8. rocks, 9. of, 10. iron, 11. exposed, 12. develops, 13. rust, 14. oxygen, 15. substance, 16. changes, 17. to, 18. minerals, 19. chemically, 20. presence, 21. feldspar, 22. clay, 23. resistant, 24. forces, 25. mechanical, 26. rocks, 27. such, 28. moving, 29. that, 30. and, 31. rocks, 32. can, 33. As, 34. rocks, 35. establish, 36. from, 37. decaying, 38. chemicals, 39. rocks, 40. plant, 41. rocks, 42. can, 43. cracks, 44. rocks, 45. a, 46. after, 47. which, 48. away, 49. can, 50. by.

Source: Norman Abraham et al., *Interaction of Earth and Time*, 2nd ed., (Chicago: Rand McNally Co., 1976), pp. 264–65.

Following are the steps used for constructing, administering, and scoring the cloze test:

1. Select a set of materials typical of those used in your classroom. Select a passage of about 250 words. It should be one the students have not read previously.
2. Delete every fifth word until you have about fifty deletions. Replace the deleted words with blanks of uniform length. No words should be deleted in the first sentence.
3. Ask the student to fill in each blank with the exact word that has been deleted. Allow time to complete the test.
4. Count the number of correct responses. Do not count spelling mistakes as wrong answers; do not count synonyms as correct answers.
5. Convert the number of right responses into a percentage.

The following criteria may be used in determining levels:

Accuracy	*Reading Level*
57% or greater	Independent reading level
44–57%	Instructional reading level
Below 44%	Frustration level

A student who achieves a percentage of accuracy at or above the instructional level is asked to complete the next higher level cloze test until that student reaches his or her highest instructional level. The teacher can probably assign instructional reading of tested material to any student who makes a score of between 44 and 57 percent on that material. A score of 57 percent or better on any passage means the teacher can use the material from which the passage was taken for independent or instructional reading. A score of less than 44 percent accuracy on a passage would indicate that the material from which the passage was taken is probably not suitable for that particular student.

The cloze test is informal and provides only an approximation of a student's ability to read selected materials. Once again the teacher must be guided by his or her professional judgment in interpreting test scores.

It has been mentioned that careful teacher judgment must enter into decisions about a student's reading ability. In the classroom, the teacher has the opportunity to see each student perform each day and to become aware of the level and nature of each student's performance. Questions, such as the following, may be kept in mind as the alert teacher observes:

Observation Checklist

1. Does he or she approach the assignment with enthusiasm?
2. Does he or she apply an appropriate study method?
3. Can he or she find answers to questions of a literal type (main idea, details, sequence, etc.)?
4. Is he or she reading below the surface (answering interpretive and critical level questions)?
5. Can he or she ascertain the meanings of new or unfamiliar words? What word recognition skills are used?
6. Can he or she use locational skills in the book?
7. Can he or she use reference skills for various reference sources?
8. Is he or she reading at different rates for different materials and purposes?

Observations will be more directed if you keep a systematic record of observations. One of the values of such a record is that it provides information for planning instruction. Patterns of student development will become apparent over a period of days and weeks. Consistent and new needs will be noted. Growth of the student and other changes will be more evident.

When a student gives an oral report, or reads orally, the teacher has the opportunity to observe the following:

Oral report	*Oral reading*
pronunciation	methods of word attack
general vocabulary	word recognition problems
specialized vocabulary	rate of reading

sentence structures   phrasing
organization of ideas   attitude
interests   peer reactions

Observation may suggest a need for an individual interview with the student. In such a conference, a teacher can learn whether a student has successfully completed a given assignment and can assess attitudes toward reading, school, and self, as well as relations with other students. The uses a student has for reading may be divulged.

Self-assessment

Self-appraisal techniques can be used to help students evaluate their own strengths and weaknesses. Such techniques include:

1. *Discussion.* Self-assessment may focus upon a single topic, as word recognition, meaning vocabulary, comprehension, study skills, or problems in reading a particular textbook. With guiding questions from the teacher, the students can discuss, orally or in writing, their strengths and weaknesses in regard to the particular topic.
2. *Structured interview or conference.* After the student has written a reading autobiography (see page 358–361), such questions as the following may be asked:
    a. How do you figure out the pronunciation or meaning of an unknown word?
    b. What steps are you taking to develop your vocabulary?
    c. What do you do to get the main ideas from your reading?
    d. Do you use the same rate of reading in most of your assignments?
    e. What method of study do you use most?
    f. How do you organize your material to remember it?
    g. What special reference books have you used lately in the writing of a report?
    h. How do you handle graphic aids that appear in the reading material?
    i. How do you study for a test?
    j. What could you do to become an even better reader?
3. *Self-rating checklist.* A sample checklist is provided in Example 10.15. It deals with several broad areas. Similar checklists could be prepared that focus upon particular skills, such as reading to follow directions.

Self-rating checklist   **Example 10.15**

Name _____   Date _____

Subject _____

Please rate yourself on these items:

	Good	Average	Need Help
1. Pronouncing and knowing the meaning of most of the words in your content book	___	___	___
2. Using parts of textbooks	___	___	___
3. Using the dictionary	___	___	___
4. Using some plans to help increase vocabulary	___	___	___
5. Answering questions that call for critical thinking	___	___	___
6. Being flexible in reading rate	___	___	___
7. Knowing a good study method	___	___	___
8. Outlining, summarizing, and taking notes	___	___	___
9. Locating materials in books and reference sources	___	___	___
10. Writing a report	___	___	___
11. Following printed directions	___	___	___
12. Interpreting graphic aids	___	___	___
13. Remembering material	___	___	___
14. Test-taking	___	___	___

Attitude

A student's affective response to reading selections critically affects his or her becoming a reader. Therefore, some kind of measure of the student's attitudes toward reading experiences is an important aspect of the total assessment program. Reading takes many forms and means many different things to different students; a student might enjoy reading the sports page, but be bored or even dislike reading a library book to complete an English assignment. Whether or not a student likes "reading" then depends on what he or she is reading and for what purpose.

Therefore, perhaps the most valid measure of a student's attitude toward reading would be his or her responses to individual selections. Such a scale as the following one might be useful: A = *strongly agree;* B = *agree;* C = *disagree;* D = *strongly disagree.*

I enjoyed reading this selection.

A   B   C   D

This selection was boring.

A   B   C   D

This selection held my attention.

A   B   C   D

I disliked reading this selection.

A   B   C   D

Students will not be expected to respond positively to all their reading experiences, but if the majority of their responses indicate negative attitudes toward reading, something is amiss. For each student, a profile of scores may be kept as an ongoing assessment of his or her attitude toward reading.

To make a more comprehensive study of the student's reading, some reading authorities suggest the use of the reading autobiography—a developmental history of a student's reading experiences. Some accounts give details concerning the student's early reading experiences, when and how he or she was taught, range and variety of his or her reading, home background, and use of available resources. Other autobiographies reveal the writer's attitude, special reading interests, and perhaps reading difficulties. Sometimes they include the writer's ideas about ways to overcome the difficulties that he or she has recognized. Example 10.16 is a sample provided for consideration.

Example 10.16 *Reading autobiography*

	Yes	No	
1.	___	___	Did you learn to read before you came to school?
2.	___	___	Did any member of your family try to teach you to read?
3.	___	___	Did anyone often read aloud to you in your early preschool years?
4.	___	___	Do you remember the name of the first book you ever read?
5.	___	___	As a child, did you prefer books that were illustrated?
6.	___	___	Do you usually have something other than school work that you are currently reading?

7.   ___ ___   Do you read in bed?

8.   ___ ___   Do you reread a book you particularly enjoyed?

9.   ___ ___   Do you like to have the radio or record player on while you read?

10.   ___ ___   When you are reading a book in which you are particularly interested, do you often neglect other things?

11.   ___ ___   Do you ever read to younger children?

12.   ___ ___   Do you often find you have been reading without comprehending the meaning?

13.   ___ ___   Does your mother or father sometimes read aloud to the family?

14.   ___ ___   Does your family have group discussions of current events?

15.   ___ ___   Is more than one language spoken in your home?

16.   ___ ___   Do you read for pleasure during vacation time?

17.   ___ ___   Do you dislike English classes?

18.   ___ ___   Do you have a personal library of your own?

19.   ___ ___   Does your family subscribe to book clubs?

20.   ___ ___   Do you have and use a library card?

21.   ___ ___   Do you prefer reading the "digest" form of a novel in preference to the unabridged version?

22.   ___ ___   Do you read at the breakfast table?

23.   ___ ___   Do you agree with the girl who said, "Although I am in many clubs and engage in other activities, reading a good book is 'my first choice' "?

24.   ___ ___   When confined to bed with minor illnesses do you look forward to reading?

25.   ___ ___   Do you have a car available for your use?

26.   ___ ___   Do you ever read while riding in cars or buses?

27.   ___ ___   Do you read books or stories aloud with a friend?

28. How would you classify yourself as to reading speed (average reading speed for high school texts is around 250 wpm): ___Average reader, ___Slow reader, ___Fast reader?

29. Does reading make you sleepy? ___Yes ___No ___Sometimes.

30. Do the members of your family recommend books and articles for each other? ___Yes ___No ___Sometimes.

31. I go out approximately ___ evenings a week.

32. I spend ___ hours per week on extracurricular activities (clubs, sports, publications, etc.).

33. We have ___ television sets in our home.
    (Number of)

34. I (do) (do not) watch television more than I read for pleasure.

35. Writing original compositions (has) (has not) helped my interest in reading.

36. I have usually obtained (better) (worse) grades in English than in mathematics.

37. Circle the parts of the newspaper that you read:

    A.   Comics   C.   Sports   E.   Society

    B.   News items   D.   Editorials

Example 10.16 (cont.)

38. In my spare time I do the following most frequently (number 1 to 4 in order of frequency):
    Watch television
    Read
    Visit with friends
    Other

39. Circle the types of books and materials read aloud in your home:
    A. Juvenile literature   D. Current events
    B. Novels   E. None
    C. Short stories   F. Other (tell what kind)

40. In our home there are the following types of reading material:
    A. Hardback books consisting of (give number of)
       1. Approximately _____ novels, short stories, plays
       2. Approximately _____ essays and nonfiction other than science
       3. Approximately _____ scientific
       4. Approximately _____ others

41. I make use of our
    A. Public library _____ times a month.
    B. School library _____ times a week.

42. When I read for my own pleasure I choose mostly (check):
    A. Novels   D. Science fiction
    B. Short stories   E. Essays
    C. Comic books   F. Other (Name them)

43. Does the fact that you are expected to make a report on a book: _____ detract from your enjoyment of it, _____ deepen your understanding and enjoyment of it, _____ neither answer applies in all instances.

44. As far as your reading speed is concerned, do you: _____ read everything at about the same speed, _____ frequently "scan" certain types of reading material, or _____ change your speed with the kind of material and your purpose?

46. When a "pleasure" book fails to interest you after 25 pages or so, do you: _____ go ahead and finish it anyway, _____ stop reading it, _____ decide to read it at a later date?

47. Our family participated in reading aloud in the following ways:
    A. My _____ mother _____ father read to us at preschool age.
    B. My _____ mother _____ father have always read to us.
    C. My _____ mother _____ father never read to us.

48. How many schools have you attended since the first grade?

49. When I come across a word I don't know: I _____ look it up in the dictionary, _____ try to guess at its meaning from the context, _____ try to pronounce it by dividing it into syllables, _____ try to pronounce it by sounding it out, _____ skip over it. (Check more than one if they apply.)

50. Circle the following practices you follow when reading school work:
    A. Summarize material after you read it
    B. Raise questions before or when reading and then read to find the answers
    C. Underline key statements in your text during study
    D. Take notes for future reference: after reading a section _____, while reading _____

If these questions have called to your mind any comments you would like to make, please use the remaining space to do so. Any additions to this reading survey that you may be able to suggest would be greatly appreciated.

Source: Ruth Strang, *Diagnostic Teaching of Reading*, 2nd ed. (New York: McGraw Hill, 1969), pp. 82–85.

To supplement observation and attitude checklists, the teacher may present the stimulus known as *Incomplete Sentences*. In reading through the individual's responses, the teacher becomes aware of certain recurring types that suggest dominant trends. The sentences relating specifically to reading often give insight into the individual's attitude toward books and reading and reveal some of the difficulties he or she is having. Information of this kind, in conjunction with observation and formal and informal test results, can help the teacher to individualize the program of instruction.

"Incomplete sentences"   **Example 10.17**

Date _____   Grade or Subject _____   Name _____

1. When I have to read, I _____
2. To me, books _____
3. I like to read about _____
4. Comic books _____
5. I'd rather read than _____
6. I like to read when _____
7. Reading science _____
8. I'd read more if _____
9. Special help in reading _____
10. The last book I read _____
11. I read better than _____
12. I would like to read better than _____

Other attitude instruments include one prepared by Larry D. Kennedy and Ronald S. Halinski. It is a 70 item instrument, in which students respond to statements according to a four-point scale— Strongly Agree, Agree, Disagree, and Strongly Disagree. A copy of the instrument may be found in the *Journal of Reading* 18 (April 1975): 518–22 in the article entitled "Measuring Attitudes: An Extra Dimension." A second instrument is located in Thomas H. Estes, "A Scale to Measure Attitude Toward Reading," *Journal of Reading* 15 (November 1971): 135–38. Also see the following article: Kenneth L. Dulin and Robert D. Chester, "A Validated Study of the Estes Scale Attitude Scales," *Journal of Reading* 18 (October 1974): 56–59.

Interests   Interest is often the key that unlocks effort. Consequently, a study of students' reading and other interests is an important part of the teaching procedure. The dynamic force of interest should be fully used, so the teacher can plan ways to motivate the student and show how a subject is related to his or her personal life.

Studies have been conducted on the reading interests of students. One guide is *Books and the Teen-Age Reader* by G. Robert Carlsen, New York: Bantam Books, 1972. It is, of course, helpful to know the stages of interest development through which students frequently progress from early adolescence. However, the subject matter teacher is interested in more than a knowledge of the interests of students in general. The teacher needs to know the specific interests of a student in order to capitalize upon them in recommending materials.

One of the ways of studying a student's reading interests is through observation in daily classes. The teacher notes the books the student chooses to read, the degree of concentration and enjoyment with which he or she reads them, his or her eagerness to talk about them, and the desire to read more books of a like nature or books by the same author.

More detailed information about reading interests may be obtained from an interest inventory. An inventory should include both general interests and reading interests. A sample inventory is presented below in Example 10.18.

Example 10.18   *General and reading interests inventory*

Name: _____   Grade: _____   Age: _____

General Interests
 1. What do you like to do in your free time?
 2. What are your favorite TV shows?
 3. What are your favorite hobbies?
 4. What games or sports do you like best?
 5. What clubs or other groups do you belong to?
 6. Do you have any pets? If yes, what?
 7. What is your favorite type of movies?
 8. What is your favorite school subject?
 9. What is your most disliked school subject?
10. What kind of work do you want to do when you finish secondary school?
Reading
 1. How often do you go to the public library?
 2. What are the favorite books that you own?
 3. What things do you like to read about?
 4. Which comic books do you read?
 5. Which magazines do you read?
 6. What are some books you have liked?
 7. What part of the newspapers do you read most frequently?
 8. Do you like to read?

---

1. What type of standardized test measures general achievement in reading? (a) Survey (b) Diagnostic (c) Oral (d) Study skills.
2. What feature about a standardized test is assessed when the results on one form of a test are compared with results of an equivalent form of the test? (a) Validity (b) Reliability (c) Population (c) None of these.
3. What is expressing test scores in terms of position within a set of 100 scores called? (a) Grade equivalent (b) Percentile rank (c) Stanine (d) Median score.
4. What type of standardized reading test is S.R.A. Achievement Series: Work Study Skills? (a) Survey (b) Diagnostic (c) Oral (d) Study skills.
5. What would be the reading capacity or expectancy of a mid-year seventh grader who scores 90 on an intelligence test? (a) 4.6 (b) 6.9 (c) 5.2 (d) None of these.
6. What reliability coefficient should subtests have to be of much use? (a) Above .50 (b) Above .65 (c) Above .75 (c) .80.
7. What level is usually indicated by the score achieved on a standardized reading test? (a) Independent (b) Instructional (c) Frustration (d) Each of these.
8. If a student misses no more than one of ten words on a list of graded words, what level does this represent? (a) Independent (b) Instructional (c) Frustration (d) Capacity.
9. What classification may be given material on a group reading inventory that was read with a comprehension score of 50% or less? (a) Independent (b) Instructional (c) Frustration (d) Capacity.
10. For which skills common to all content areas can sample skill inventories be prepared? (a) Parts of a textbook (b) Reference sources (c) Specialized vocabulary (d) All of the above.
11. What is the chief purpose of an informal reading inventory? (a) Identifying reading levels. (b) Analyzing oral reading errors. (c) Providing an exact assessment of reading ability. (d) Both *a* and *b*.
12. Which is *not* a scoreable oral reading error on the IRI? (a) Dialect differences (b) Unknown words (c) Insertion of words (d) Reversals.
13. In using cloze test procedures as recommended in this text, which words are deleted in content material? (a) Every fifth (b) Every eighth (c) Every tenth (d) None of these.
14. What would be perhaps the most valid measure of a student's attitude toward reading? (a) Reaction to specific selections (b) A reading autobiography (c) "Incomplete sentences" (d) None of these.
15. What technique may be utilized in self-appraisal by students? (a) Discussion (b) Conference (c) Checklist (d) All of these.

Enrichment activities

1. Secure a copy (and manual) of a standardized reading test of each of these types: survey, diagnostic, oral, study skills. Study these tests and report on them to your peers. Use this outline for evaluation.

I. Test Overview
    A. Title
    B. Author(s)
    C. Publisher
    D. Date of publication—original, revised
        1. Manual
        2. Test
    E. Level and Forms
        1. Grade level
        2. Individual or group
        3. Number of forms available
    F. Administration Time
    G. Scoring—hand or machine scorable
    H. Cost
        1. Question booklets—consumable or not
        2. Answer sheets
        3. Manual

II. Evaluation of Subtests and Items
    A. Description of subtests
        1. Given meaningful name—describe test adequately.
        2. Is each subtest long enough to provide usable results?
        3. Is sequential development of each subtest logical and transition smooth?
    B. Author's purpose, reflected in selection of items
    C. Scoring ease and usability of tables
    D. Directions—clarity and level of language appropriate to grade level
    E. Design—format, currentness, printing, legibility, pictures
    F. Readability

III. Evaluation of Reliability and Validity
    A. Norming population
        1. Size
        2. Age, grade, sex
        3. Range of ability
        4. Socioeconomic level
        5. Date of administration
    B. Validity
        1. Content Validity
            a. Face validity
            b. Logical or sampling validity
        2. Empirical validity
            a. Concurrent
            b. Predictive

3. Construct validity
    a. Construct and theory of which construct is a part clearly defined
    b. Discriminant or convergent validity evidence
    c. Significant difference found in performance between groups that have varying degrees of this trait?
4. Does reported validity appear adequate in relation to author's stated purpose? Why or why not?

2. If feasible, observe the administration of a group-standardized diagnostic reading test to a group of secondary students.

*3. If feasible, administer a standardized reading rate test to a student and interpret the results.

4. Calculate the reading expectancy level, given the data:
    a. IQ of 80; mid-year (6.5) seventh grader
    b. IQ of 90; mid-year (10.5) eleventh grader
    c. IQ of 120; mid-year (8.5) ninth grader

*5. Administer the San Diego Quick Assessment to a student. Share your findings about reading level with peers.

*6. Prepare a group reading inventory, using content area reading materials. Administer your inventory to a student, record your results, and share the findings with the class.

7. Using a textbook of your choice, develop at least 10 sample questions on each of the book parts listed (If a particular book part is not included in your text, select examples from supplemental materials).

    a. Preface, Introduction, or Foreward
    b. Table of Contents
    c. Index
    d. Appendix
    e. Glossary
    f. Unit or Chapter Introduction and/or Summary

*8. Prepare a reading skills inventory for a content area textbook. Administer it to a student, record your results, and share the findings with the class.

*9. Secure a published IRI and administer it to a student. Report the results to the class.

*10. Prepare an IRI using content area reading materials. Administer it to a student; record the results, and share your findings with the class.

---

* These activities are designed for inservice teachers, student teachers, and practicum students.

*11. Prepare a cloze procedure test for a passage of content area reading material. Administer it to a student. Report the results to the class.

12. If feasible, visit a secondary school classroom. Use the observation checklist on page 355 to note the reading pattern of a student.

*13. Prepare a self-appraisal checklist of some aspect of reading (see sample on study skills, Example 10.10). Administer to a student and report your findings to the class.

*14. Administer a reading autobiography to a secondary school student. What helpful information may be gleaned from it?

*15. Use an "incomplete sentence" technique with a secondary school student. What helpful information may be gleaned from the answers?

*16. Administer an interest inventory to a student. What information may be utilized in the instructional program?

17. Prepare an interest check on one topic of study in your content area. If feasible, administer it to a student.

Selected references

Aukerman, Robert. *Reading in the Secondary School Classroom.* New York: McGraw-Hill, 1972. Chapter 5.

Blanton, William et al., *Reading Tests for the Secondary Grades.* Newark, Del.: International Reading Association, 1972.

Burmeister, Lou E. *Reading Strategies for Secondary School Teachers.* New York: Addison-Wesley, 1974. Chapters 1, 3, and 4.

Burron, Arnold and Amos Claybaugh. *Using Reading to Teach Subject Matter.* Columbus, Ohio: Charles E. Merrill, 1974. Chapters 2 and 3.

Dechant, Emerald. *Reading Improvement in the Secondary School.* Englewood Cliffs, N.J.: Prentice Hall, 1973. Chapter 11.

Dillner, Martha H. and Joanne P. Olson. *Personalizing Reading Instruction in Middle, Junior, and Senior High Schools: Utilizing a Competency Based Instructional System.* New York: Macmillan Co., 1977. Chapter 5.

Estes, Thomas and Joseph L. Vaughan. *Reading and Learning in Content Classrooms: Diagnostic and Instructional Strategies.* Boston: Allyn and Bacon, Inc., 1978.

Forgan, Harry W. and Charles T. Mangrum. *Teaching Content Area Reading Skills.* Columbus, Ohio: Charles E. Merrill, 1976. Modules 3 and 4.

Hafner, Lawrence E. *Developmental Reading in Middle and Secondary Schools.* Riverside, N.J.: Macmillan Co., 1977. Chapter 4.

Karlin, Robert. *Teaching Reading in High Schools: Selected Articles.* Indianapolis: Bobbs-Merrill, 1969. Chapter 4.

———— *Teaching Reading in High School.* Indianapolis: Bobbs-Merrill, 1964. Chapter 4.

McIntyre, Virgie. *Reading Strategies and Enrichment Activities for Grades 4–9.* Columbus, Ohio: Charles E. Merrill, 1977. Chapters 2 and 3.

Miller, Wilma. *Teaching Reading in the Secondary School.* Springfield, Ill.: Charles C. Thomas, 1974. Chapter 9.

Robinson, H. Alan. *Teaching Reading and Study Strategies.* Boston: Allyn and Bacon, 1975. Chapter 2.

Shepherd, David. *Comprehensive High School Reading Methods.* Columbus, Ohio: Charles E. Merrill, 1973. Chapter 2.

Smith, Richard J. and Thomas C. Barrett. *Teaching Reading in the Middle Grades.* Reading, Massachusetts: Addison-Wesley, 1974. Chapter 8.

Strang, Ruth. *Diagnostic Teaching of Reading.* 2nd ed. New York: McGraw-Hill, 1969. Chapters 3, 5, 6, and 7.

Viox, Ruth G. *Evaluating Reading and Study Skills in the Secondary Classroom.* Newark, Del.: International Reading Association, 1968.

11   Secondary school reading programs

Different types of secondary school reading programs are considered in this chapter. These include total-school reading programs, special "English" classes, special remedial reading classes, reading laboratories, and reading improvement classes. The total-school organization for reading is a much more comprehensive plan than the other plans discussed. Two or more of the less comprehensive plans are often initiated at the same time.

Any school reading program, regardless of the complexity, requires special planning. Responsibility for execution of the various aspects of the program must be assigned. Cooperation of staff members is essential. Inservice training for staff members is extremely important. Program goals and instructional techniques must be cooperatively determined by the involved personnel.

Purpose-setting questions

As you read this chapter, try to answer these questions:
1. What are necessary activities related to development of a total-school reading program?
2. In what two ways have English classes been utilized for reading instruction?
3. What are some techniques that should be used in working with remedial readers?
4. What are some skill areas considered in reading improvement classes?
5. What some some types of equipment which may be found in reading laboratories?
6. What responsibilities for reading instruction in secondary school

belong to the administrator, reading consultant, and special reading teacher?

As you read this chapter, check your understanding of these terms: **Key vocabulary**
controlled reader
corrective instruction
developmental instruction
diagnostic test
flexibility of rate
inservice training
Language Master

pacer
reading achievement test
reading consultant
reading laboratory
remedial instruction
remedial reader
special reading teacher
tachistoscope

A total-school reading program is one in which all school personnel cooperate and all students are offered reading instruction, according to their needs. Reading instruction is offered not only in special reading classes and clinical settings, but in content-area classes. The skills are taught as their use is required; therefore, the instruction is meaningful to the students because they see a direct application for it. Developmental instruction is offered to those who are progressing satisfactorily in the building of reading skills, and corrective and remedial instruction are offered to those who are experiencing difficulties. In such a program all aspects of reading are included: **Total-school programs**

1. Basic skills are taught.
2. Content area reading skills are taught.
3. Recreational reading is encouraged.
4. Remedial reading is offered.

Implementing a total-school reading program is a difficult, demanding assignment, but the energy invested in it is well spent. The process of implementation can be diagrammed as shown on page 370.

Figure 11.1 shows a sequence of activities through which a school's staff can move in developing a total-school reading program. The sequence shows movement from defining a reading philosophy to evaluating the program. Throughout the entire sequence, constant inservice training of one type or another is being offered to the staff involved in the program development. Suggestions offered during inservice activities will be most helpful if they can be implemented immediately. Therefore, the training sessions should be offered when a need for the particular information is current. Results of each step in the sequence provide input, which may affect subsequent inservice sessions, for the director(s) of the inservice training.

Figure 11.1   *Implementation of a school reading program*

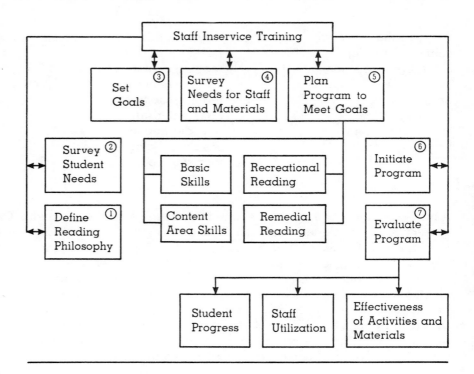

Staff inservice training   A first glance at this plan of implementation may result in the reaction that inservice training is being overemphasized. Careful consideration, however, will reveal that this is not the case. Many secondary teachers (in some schools, most of them) have little background knowledge concerning the nature of the reading act, reading skill needs of students, available formal tests of reading progress, informal measures of reading achievement, reading interests and tastes of adolescents, and other topics related to helping secondary students progress in reading. In addition to this lack of knowledge, some of the teachers feel hostile to the idea of teaching reading skills. They often fail to analyze the situation carefully enough to realize that helping their students read the subject matter with more understanding will help these students to learn subject matter concepts more effectively.

The first inservice training sessions should be designed to help the school's staff recognize the need for reading instruction in the school and the benefits to them as subject matter specialists if this need is adequately met. These sessions may involve selling the idea of a total-school program. Both teachers and administrators may need convincing, for many administrators have had no more background in the area of reading than have the subject matter specialists on the faculty. If the attempts to convince the staff are not effective, the chances of success for the program are greatly diminished. Inservice sessions should involve the entire school staff—administrators, faculty members from all departments, media specialist(s), and guidance personnel.

Subsequent inservice sessions may deal with topics such as:

1. Setting realistic program objectives.
2. Determining reading skill needs of students.
3. Locating and using appropriate materials for meeting student needs.
4. Techniques for teaching specific skills students need.
5. Teaching directed reading lessons in content areas.
6. Differentiating instruction in content area classes.
7. Fitting reading assignments in the content areas to the reading achievement of the students.
8. Using the library to full advantage.
9. Techniques of evaluating the program's effectiveness.

The inservice training may take a variety of forms, including:

1. Workshops in the school, conducted by the school's reading consultant or reading teacher.
2. Workshops in the school, conducted by an outside expert on the topic under consideration.
3. Attendance at reading conferences and conventions.
4. Demonstration lessons.
5. Faculty planning sessions (teachers working together to plan implementation of program in their special areas using the resources available in the school).
6. University courses.

Reading committee

Although staff members need to believe in the concept of a schoolwide program and need to be willing to cooperate in implementing the program, much planning can be done by a small staff group and submitted to the entire staff for input, endorsement, and implementation. This planning group is sometimes referred to as the reading committee. It should be composed of people with the ability and enthusiasm to offer effective guidance of the program. A good composition for such a committee might be: the principal, the reading consultant, all special reading teachers, a representative from each department, the media specialist, a guidance counselor, and perhaps a school board member or representative from a parent group (PTA or PTO). The principal may choose to act as chairman of the committee or may appoint a knowledgeable person such as the reading consultant to act in that capacity.

Defining reading philosophy

The reading committee may elicit ideas from the other members of the staff concerning the nature of reading, the reading abilities that are necessary for comprehending printed material in the respective subject areas, the importance of recreational reading, and other similar areas. These ideas should be integrated with carefully researched published materials. The committee may then produce a statement of the school's reading philosophy and share the results with the entire staff. Representative statements from such a document might include:

1. Reading is the process of getting meaning from printed symbols.
2. Secondary school students need reading instruction, although the type of instruction needed may differ from student to student.
3. Students need help in learning to read printed materials before they can read these materials to learn concepts.
4. Special reading skills are needed in order to read certain content area materials with understanding.

Surveying student needs

The idea of starting a total-school reading program may have come about because of low student scores on standardized reading achievement tests, or it may have come about because various faculty members detected reading deficiencies in their students. If test results inspired the effort, they may be used as a beginning for surveying students needs. Reading achievement tests generally reveal the student's accomplishments in broad areas of reading skills (comprehension, vocabulary, rate). If an achievement test in reading has not been previously administered, the reading committee will probably wish to choose an appropriate test and make arrangements for its administration. After broad areas of difficulty have been identified, the committee may wish to choose either standardized or informal diagnostic measures for administration in order to pinpoint specific skill difficulties. Measures of reading interests and attitudes toward reading may also be used at this time to help the staff clarify the needs of the students.

Setting goals

When embarking upon a new endeavor such as an all-school program, it is helpful to have some goals in mind. The reading committee may formulate a list of goals for the program and submit them to the rest of the faculty for input and approval. All faculty members need to feel that they have a part in deciding upon goals because these goals will have a great deal of influence over each teacher's classroom activities. Some goals that might be stated include:

1. All students will be offered an opportunity to develop and refine their basic reading skills through special reading classes.
2. All students will be helped to develop reading skills specific to particular content areas during the content area classes.
3. All students will be offered reading assignments that are appropriate to their reading achievement levels.
4. All students will be encouraged to read for recreation in a variety of interest areas.
5. All students will be given opportunities to utilize the resources of the school's media center.
6. All students who classify as remedial readers will be given special instruction by a qualified specialist.

Surveying needs for staff and materials

The reading committee can take the list of goals for the school's program and analyze the needs of the school relative to meeting them.

For example, the committee may discover that another qualified reading teacher will be needed if each student classified as a remedial reader is to receive special help. It may not be possible to meet such a need at mid-year, and the complete implementation of the remedial portion of the program may have to be postponed, but the program goal will at least clarify the need for specialized staff in the coming year.

If each student in the school is going to be offered an opportunity to develop and refine basic reading skills, the committee may find that rooms must be set aside for reading laboratories, staffed by reading teachers, and equipped with reading materials and equipment suitable for use by students reading on a wide variety of levels and needing help with a variety of different skills. Once again the commitee may find that complete implementation is not immediately possible, but a beginning can be made and future plans can include the needed changes.

Taking into account the amount of money available for implementing the program, the committee members may study catalogs of materials and equipment, preview or examine available items, and choose the items most needed for implementing the program. The committee may continue to preview promising materials even after the program goes into full operation, or the reading consultant and reading teachers may assume the responsibility at some time in the process. Naturally all staff members should be encouraged to suggest appropriate materials, especially those related closely to their disciplines.

Planning a program to meet goals   When the committee has obtained information about the skill needs of the students and the goals of the program, specific plans for a program can be made. Plans may center around the four major aspects of reading instruction—basic reading skills, content area reading skills, recreational reading, and remedial reading. Plans in one school were developed as shown in Example 11.1.

Example 11.1   *School reading plans*

Area One: Basic Reading Skills

The school's faculty had recognized the fact that all of the students in the school could improve their basic reading skills in some way. They wished to offer possibilities for improvement to accelerated readers (students reading above grade level) as well as average readers (students reading on grade level) and retarded readers (students reading below grade level). They realized that many students had the capacity to read much better than they were reading, even though they were reading at grade level or above, and that some students reading below grade level were making satisfactory progress when their capacity levels were taken into consideration.

To meet the basic skills needs of the students, the faculty decided to include in each ninth-grade student's schedule one semester of reading instruction. Since there were approximately 200 ninth graders in the school, about 100 students were assigned to reading classes each semester. A special reading teacher was designated to teach five classes of approximately 20 students each semester. Because the students within each class varied greatly in reading achievement and needs, the class was to be conducted as a laboratory with individual and small-group instruction, rather than whole-class instruction. The teacher would study test results for each student and plan an individual course of study for each one, based upon his or her current achievement level and needs. If several members of a class had similar needs, the teacher would plan small group sessions. Otherwise, the students would work independently with materials on appropriate reading levels and meet regularly with the teacher for teacher-pupil conferences concerning the assignments. During the conferences the teacher would sometimes give specific skill instruction, but conferences would also be used to help students choose reading materials from a pool of appropriate ones, to check on word recognition and comprehension skills, and to help students plan ways to share their reading experiences with their classmates.

On Friday of each week, five or more of the students would share with the rest of the class something that they had read. The sharing would take a number of forms: oral reading of episodes from a book, illustrations of scenes from a book, panel discussions presented by several students who had read the same book, skits presented by students who had read the same book, and many others.

The reading laboratory was to be arranged in the following way:

Sample reading laboratory Figure 11.2

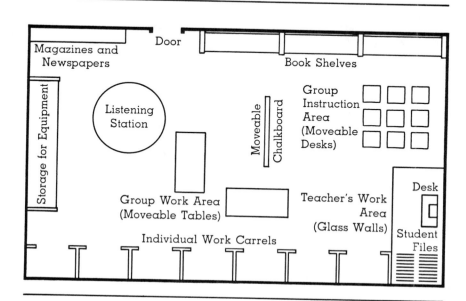

The room included ten carrels in which students could carry on individual work with a minimum of distraction, a listening station where up to eight students could listen to an audio presentation over headsets at the same time, two large tables at which small groups of students could work on common projects, a group instruction area in which up to 12 students could receive small group instruction from the teacher, and a glassed-in teacher's work area where the teacher could conduct individual conferences privately without having to leave the classroom totally unsupervised.

Plans were made to develop a second reading laboratory for students in the tenth, eleventh, and twelfth grades who were developmental readers but felt a desire to work to improve their basic reading skills and were willing to attend the laboratory during their regularly assigned study periods or free periods. This second laboratory had to be posponed until the second year of the program because another qualified reading teacher would be needed to provide specialized help for the students.

Area Two: Content Area Reading Skills
The reading committee identified reading skills that they felt could be developed through the content areas. Then they arranged for inservice training

Example 11.1 (cont.) sessions to help the content teachers learn to teach these skills in their subject areas. Each month of the year had a particular skill emphasis that was to be implemented in every subject area for which it was appropriate. The skill areas identified were vocabulary building, prefixes and suffixes, study methods, main ideas, following directions, locating information in textbooks, locating information in the library, developing flexibility of rate, sequence, context clues, drawing conclusions and making inferences, reading maps, reading tables, reading charts, reading graphs, detecting propangada, recognizing fact and and opinion, and detecting the author's motives or bias. During the first year, the faculty chose the following nine skills for emphasis: study methods, prefixes and suffixes, identifying main ideas, detecting sequence, using context clues, following directions, developing flexibility of rate, locating information in textbooks, and reading maps.

The content area teachers also learned how to teach directed reading lessons in their respective content classes. They learned to utilize study guides to direct the silent reading portions of the directed reading lessons.

The job of the media specialist was defined as helping the teachers locate appropriate materials for use in their subject areas. These materials were to include books, magazines, and pamphlets written on a variety of reading levels. The teacher then was to attempt to match the materials to the students' abilities.

The reading consultant was to be available to offer help to content area teachers in planning for the teaching of reading skills related to each content area. The consultant would be available to teach demonstration lessons in the content area classes when the content area teachers requested such help.

Area Three: Recreational Reading

All content area teachers were encouraged to make students aware of materials available for leisure-time reading in their respective disciplines. The English teachers decided to make available one day a week during their classes for recreational reading and the sharing of books and other materials read for pleasure. In addition, all students were to be encouraged to make use of the media center during their free periods.

A reading club was formed during the homeroom-club period. The reading consultant and special reading teacher would sponsor the club. Members would read books on areas of mutual interest and discuss the books with fellow club members.

Area Four: Remedial Reading

The faculty decided that all students reading two years or more below capacity level would be offered individual or small group (ten or fewer students) assistance by a qualified reading specialist. For ninth graders, this instruction would be in addition to the special reading class in basic skills and would be offered during the semester when the basic reading class was not scheduled. For tenth through twelfth graders, instruction would be offered two days a week during the study period. No student would be forced to enroll in the remedial course, but conferences would be held with students who needed help, and they would be invited to take part.

Initiating a total school program is a difficult undertaking. For this reason, some schools initiate such a program gradually. One possible method of gradual initiation might take place over a two-year period, as shown in Table 11.1.

Plan for initiating program

Table 11.1

	Basic Skills	Content Reading	Recreational Reading	Remedial Reading
1st year	9th grade developmental classes	Content teachers teach study methods; use DRA; emphasize vocabulary	Media center Reading clubs	9th grade remedial classes (voluntary)
2nd year	9th grade classes plus voluntary 10th–12th grade classes	Content teachers emphasize a reading skill each month	Media center English class time Reading clubs	9th–12th grade remedial classes (voluntary)

Another approach might be to initiate the program one or more grade levels at a time over a period of years.

A total-school reading program must be constantly evaluated in a variety of ways. Evaluation can be considered in three areas—student progress, staff utilization, and effectiveness of activities and materials.

Student progress Student progress can be evaluated through standardized and informal achievement tests, as well as teacher observation. Teacher observation may serve to help evaluate progress in areas which tests rarely cover. For example, students' attitudes toward, and interests in, reading can often be detected through observation, whereas tests may give no information about these areas. If progress has been unsatisfactory, reasons for this situation must be investigated.

Staff utilization The staff members will need to look at the functions that are being performed by different people and determine whether there is unwarranted overlap of responsibility, inadequate coverage of some area or areas by qualified personnel, or insufficient staff to handle the needs of the students in some areas (perhaps remedial reading). If any inadequacies are detected, the staff members will need to make plans to try to alleviate the problems in the future.

Effectiveness of activities and materials   Teachers can keep records of the activities and materials which seem to be most effective in meeting the objectives of the program. Use of ineffective activities and materials should be discontinued, and the advice of the reading consultant should be sought about other possible approaches to the students' problems.

Ongoing process   Evaluation of a program is an ongoing activity throughout the school year. It should not be considered to be only an end-of-school activity, although the end of the year is generally one good checkpoint for evaluation. Periodic evaluation sessions throughout the year can help keep teachers aware of the need for continuous assessment of progress toward program goals.

Needs assessment   When a school decides that it needs to examine its established reading programs with the possibility of making changes, a critical self-evaluation or "needs assessment" is necessary. Basically a "needs assessment" is an attempt to measure the gap between "what is" and "what should be." Such an evaluation overlaps program planning, implementation, and periodic check-ups by internal or external persons. It is presented below as an isolated phase only for ease of exposition. The following items suggest the components of a needs assessment.

1. Student Performance—What is the present reading level of students? What specific types of reading problems are the students having? What are the reading potentials of students? What may be the reasons for underachievement, if this exists? What reading attitudes and interests exist?
2. Personnel—Who are the personnel involved in the reading program, including classroom teachers and reading teachers? What are their training, experience, abilities? What other nonreading personnel are available (psychologists, speech and hearing therapists, guidance counselors, etc.)?
3. Present Reading Program—What are the location(s) of the reading classroom, reading laboratory, etc.? What basic pattern or type of reading program exists? What time is provided for reading instruction? What use is made of reading specialists? What inservice program in reading is provided for specialists and classroom teachers? What is the present reading evaluation program? What record-keeping patterns are maintained?
4. School plant—What are the size, location, and resources of

the school library? What reading resources and materials are available in the classrooms or elsewhere in the building?

5. Fiscal Resources—What money is available to the reading program from the local school budget? From other sources?

6. Professional Resources—What use is made of specialized clinics, reading centers, college and university departments, private reading specialists, and others? What consultant help is available from such sources as these?

Special "English" classes

In some schools, special sections of English are designated as classes for students who have reading difficulties. In these classes the students are taught reading skills by the English teacher instead of being taught grammar and composition skills.

Special sections of English

One problem with these programs has been that the students object to being placed in the special classes. Another common problem may be even more serious. Some English teachers have no training in teaching reading skills because their teacher preparation programs did not include the techniques of teaching reading. These teachers may lack the ability to identify the skill deficiencies of the students and to help students acquire these skills. These teachers often resent being asked to perform a function for which they lack sufficient training just because reading and English seem to others to be closely related. With reluctant students *and* reluctant teachers these classes are likely to be ineffective.

Many English teachers assigned to such special sections take the responsibility very seriously. They take reading courses from a nearby university, study professional literature, and attend conferences. Such teachers can do a great deal of good for their students, if they can find effective ways of motivating the students.

Special units in English

Some schools include reading units as a part of *all* English classes instead of designating certain classes as special English classes. For example, English teachers in a Minnesota junior high school taught students to use the SQ3R method when reading English, social studies, and science materials, using a special reward system. This instruction, although carried out in the English classes, was part of a total school reading program. Content teachers cooperated by reinforcing the use of the method in their classes.[1]

---

1. Paulette M. Gruber, "Junior High Boasts Super Stars," *Journal of Reading* 16 (May 1973): 600–3.

While such reading study skills as outlining, summarizing, and note-taking fit into the English curriculum fairly well and some interpretive and critical reading skills are given attention as literature is taught, the inclusion of special reading units in English classes alone should not be considered a comprehensive attack on the reading needs of the student population. English classes especially should not be the entire treatment of reading in the school if the English teachers have had no special training in identifying reading needs or teaching reading skills. Even if teachers know how to approach teaching the comprehension skills needed in literature study, it is unlikely that they will be equipped to handle a youngster with severe word recognition difficulties.

The three types of classes discussed next may be in the English department of some secondary schools. They may sometimes be offered as options to English classes, fulfilling the English requirements for graduation.

Special remedial reading classes

In some schools, students who are identified through testing procedures as remedial readers are assigned to special reading classes, whereas students who classify as corrective or developmental readers receive no outside help. Different schools define remedial readers in different ways. A common definition for a remedial reader is one who reads at a level two years behind where he or she should be reading.

Identifying remedial readers

Many teachers translate this definition into "a student who is reading two years below grade level." These teachers overlook the fact that not all students have the ability to read up to grade level and that some students who read two years below grade level are doing as well as can be expected for their capacity. Remedial readers should always be defined in terms of capacity level rather than in terms of grade placement level. If a large gap between capacity level and reading achievement level exists, there is a good chance for rapid student progress with adequate instruction. If the gap is small, little progress may result, even with excellent teaching, for the student is already performing at close to his potential.

Working with remedial readers

Ideally, remedial reading classes should be small and the work conducted in small groups and on a one-to-one basis. Each remedial reader will require much individual attention. Diagnostic tests must be given to each one to determine specific areas of strengths and weaknesses. Many of these tests are designed to be administered individually. After a student's weaknesses have been detected, a program to overcome these weaknesses that capitalizes upon the student's strengths must be developed. Several students with the same needs may be helped together, but students should not be forced into group activities that are not appropriate for their personal needs.

The students must be helped to recognize their specific reading needs and must understand how each activity used in the remedial work can help to overcome their difficulties. A teacher who develops good rapport with a student at the outset of the remedial instruction will find communicating with the student about his or her needs and about how to overcome these problems much easier than will a teacher who thinks only of lesson presentation and ignores the influence of the student's attitude toward the teacher and the instruction. When students recognize the goals they are working for, they are generally much more receptive to techniques designed to help them reach these goals.

In many cases, a remedial reader has never had success in reading activities. Since success is a powerful motivator, the remedial reading teacher should plan some activity for each session that is designed to allow the student to experience success. Progressing through the instruction in a series of small steps will make success more likely.

Remedial readers need to have indications of progress. Graphing their comprehension scores from week-to-week may help them to see that they are improving as they apply themselves to their reading activities. Keeping a record of books read and satisfactorily reported on to the teacher is another visible sign of progress.

Voluntary remedial reading classes seem to produce more impressive results than required ones. Resentment at being unwillingly placed in a remedial reading course may result in sullen, noncommunicative subjects who will resist all attempts of the reading teacher to help.

Students should probably also be offered credit for a remedial reading class. It is, after all, a skill development class in much the same sense that an English composition class or a speech class is. Students get credit for English composition and speech—why not remedial reading? The credit offered may serve as added incentive to some students to do well. At least, resentment will not be engendered by requiring them to work at a task they would not have chosen without credit.

Reading improvement classes

"Reading improvement classes" is a term often applied to developmental reading classes offered in the secondary school, although at times remedial programs, as described in the previous section, are also included under this title. In this section, only developmental classes will be considered.

Realizing that every reader has areas of reading in which he or she could improve if given the opportunity and assistance, many schools have initiated reading improvement classes for developmental readers. Developmental readers at the secondary level will generally have a good background in word recognition skills and general comprehension skills of a literal nature. In many cases, however, they will have much room for improvement in interpretive, critical, and creative reading skills as well as reading/study skills.

Evaluative instruments should be used to determine the skill profiles of the various members of a developmental reading class. Since these profiles will differ, grouping within the class and offering some individualized help will be necessary. Approaching any reading class with a "shotgun approach"—requiring the same activities of all students—wastes valuable instructional time and bores students who do not need help in the chosen skill.

Reading improvement classes often focus extensively upon developing rate with comprehension. Mechanical devices such as tachistoscopes, pacers, and controlled readers are often used, in addition to timed readings. Flexibility of rate is another topic commonly included in such programs. Students who have a firm foundation in basic word recognition and comprehension skills are ready for some emphasis on rate, but the basic skills should be emphasized first.

Recreational reading is also frequently emphasized in these classes. Time in class is often utilized for recreational reading activities, and teachers may use many motivational techniques to encourage reading for pleasure, both in class and outside of class.

Reading improvement classes can be slightly larger than remedial classes since the students generally require less one-to-one attention. In most programs, however, no more than twenty students are placed in a class of this type because of the diversity of needs that the teacher is trying to meet.

Some reading improvement classes are required; others are voluntary. Voluntary classes generally result in larger mean gains in reading achievement.

Some reading classes offer credit toward graduation; others do not. As in the case of remedial classes, it seems logical to offer some credit for the skill-developing reading class if credit is to be offered for English composition and speech, two other communication skills classes.

Reading laboratories   Many secondary schools have established reading laboratories for improving reading skills. Although reading improvement classes as described in the previous two sections can be housed in a reading laboratory, reading laboratories are not usually bound to class organization and the pupils work more independently than is the case in a typical class situation. Reading laboratories are generally equipped with a wide variety of materials and equipment designed to be used individually by students. The laboratory instructor administers diagnostic instruments and plans a special program for each student which the student can follow independently to overcome his or her weaknesses. Many of the available materials are self-scoring. Rate machines are usually available and sometimes other machines, such as Language Masters, are utilized. Programmed materials are valuable also. The laboratory instructor is available for helping students when needed.

Constant monitoring by the lab instructor of the students' activities and progress is important. If this is not done, a student can become locked into an unsuitable program that does not challenge enough or frustrates him or her.

Reading laboratory sessions may be required or voluntary, and attendance in the laboratory may be scheduled or offered at the convenience of the students. Each school must make decisions about these points based upon the needs of the student population and the available staff.

Combination programs

Some schools that do not have total-school reading programs utilize a combination of two or more of the other programs. A common combination is to offer both special remedial reading classes and reading improvement classes. Reading laboratories may house either remedial reading courses or reading improvement courses or both. The laboratories may be available for independent work by students while regular reading classes of one or both types are held elsewhere in the school or while special English classes or units are being utilized.

Responsibilities for reading instruction

This section cites the roles of three types of individuals within the secondary school who have a part to play in providing appropriate reading instruction: principal or administrator, reading consultant, and special reading teacher. (The role of the content area teacher has received attention in Chapter 1.)

Principal or administrator

A most significant prerequisite for a good secondary reading program is administrative direction. The administrator alone possesses the prestige and authority to carry through a sound reading program. He or she must encourage the staff and insure that the reading philosophy is implemented in logical and innovative ways. He or she needs to provide the impetus for defining the reading program's philosophy and must facilitate that philosophy by extending it to the entire school.

Example 11.2 presents an administrator's self-evaluation checklist. It suggests the responsibility of the administrator in the reading program.

Example 11.2   *Administrator's self-evaluation checklist*

(Please respond *yes* or *no* to these items)

General Goal Focusing

1. The teachers and I have in mind basic goals of the reading program. _____

2. The teachers and I keep in mind the interdependent instructional reading phases. _____

3. To keep knowledgeable about reading and students,
   a. I read books on the role of the administrator and reading. _____
   b. I take formal course work in reading and attend reading workshops and conferences. _____
   c. I visit often with outstanding reading teachers. _____
   d. I study the reading materials used in the school. _____
   e. I maintain a professional reading library. _____

4. The teachers and I have arrived at basic principles of reading instruction. _____

5. I help stimulate reading improvement opportunities by
   a. evaluating the present program with teachers. _____
   b. observing classrooms for reading instruction practices and noting such items as the following _____
      How are the students prepared for reading?
      How is the reading interpreted?
      How are skills/abilities extended?
      How are interests extended?
   c. providing for intervisitation demonstrations, videotaping. _____
   d. focusing upon reading topics of interest in faculty meetings, workshops, etc. _____

Resource Commitment

6. I make a real effort to reduce teacher-pupil ratio. _____

7. I try to meet and exceed requirements about library resources. _____

8. I try to involve parents, aides, and students in the reading program. _____

9. I make decisions about reading materials for school use only after tryouts on a limited scale and by following selection guidelines. _____

10. I recognize organization is a technique or a system—not a "method of instruction"—and that organization can only facilitate—or hinder—effective instruction. _____

Program Monitoring

11. The teachers and I maintain appropriate record forms for indicating reading progress of each student. _____
12. The teachers and I understand and use reading survey tests, diagnostic reading tests, informal reading inventories, and other assessment techniques. _____
13. The teachers and I have provided corrective/remedial services for appropriate students. _____
14. I am prepared to answer the questions about reading most frequently asked by parents and others. _____
15. The time allocated for reading instruction is sufficient to the task. _____
16. I attempt to designate space for a central resource center. _____
17. The teachers and I review results of our efforts to improve reading instruction. _____
18. I use the data from reviewing sessions to make needed changes.

Several points may be made to elaborate upon the preceding checklist. The administrator should consider important ultimate goals of a comprehensive reading program:

1. The student likes to read and has acquired an abiding interest in reading a wide variety of worthwhile material.
2. The student makes efficient use of skills to identify words and increase meaning vocabulary (understanding of words) through reading.
3. The student makes efficient use of skills needed to read informative (content) reading materials.
4. The student can understand literally; can interpret, evaluate, and react to printed ideas; and can organize and remember what he or she reads.
5. The student can adjust reading rates to the purpose and nature of the reading material.

As suggested by the preceding checklist, there are eight major functions of the administrator in the reading program:

1. Knowing about reading and students. Where knowledge needs to be supplemented, there are various avenues of learning. One avenue is reading of books (such as *Administering the School Reading Program* by Wayne Otto and Richard Smith, Boston: Houghton-Mifflin Co., 1970; and *Ad-*

ministrators and Reading by Theodore Carlson, New York: Harcourt Brace Jovanovich, 1972; and *Reading Problems: The Principal's Role* by Carl Smith, Newark, Del.: International Reading Association, 1969); other avenues are suggested in Example 11.2 (see 3b–3e). From such knowledge, the administrator will arrive at some basic principles or understandings about reading, such as: (a) reading is a complex act with many factors that must be considered; (b) reading depends upon the interpretation of the meaning of printed symbols—it is not just "decoding"; (c) there is no one correct way to teach reading—the teacher is the focal point; (d) learning to read is a continuing process; (e) reading and other language arts are closely interrelated; and (f) reading is an integral part of all content area instruction.

2. Stimulating improvement opportunities. This can be accomplished through the four procedures suggested in Example 11.2 (5a–5d). Reading topics of interest to many teachers—such as methods of grouping students, classroom analysis of reading needs, methods of improving comprehension and recall, methods of teaching word recognition skills, teaching study and research skills, methods of individualizing instruction in the various content areas, and planning a balanced reading program—certainly provide critical issues for consideration at faculty meetings, workshops, and conferences.

3. Enhancing teaching/learning environment. Three major contributions that can be made by the administrator involve items 6–8 in Example 11.2.

4. Selecting effective materials. Publishers and their representatives are in the business of making money; they produce material that they believe will sell well. Valid standards and procedures for selection of superior materials are needed to avoid ill-considered purchases. One of the residual results of the influx of federal money through various programs is storerooms filled with materials and devices that never should have been bought. The best way to avoid such problems is to pre-evaluate materials. Decisions to purchase should rarely be made by a single individual. Tentative decisions should be reached by a group that includes representatives who know (a) what the local resources are, (b) what alternatives are available, and (c) the opinions and preferences of the potential users. Final decisions should come only after tryouts on a limited scale.

Aids are available for material evaluation and selection. For example, see Kenneth Goodman, *Choosing Materials to*

Teach Reading, Detroit: Wayne State University Press, 1966. Also EPIE Reports Numbers 62, 63, 64 contain guides to instructional materials in the field of reading and contain analyses of commercial reading materials. These reports are available through EPIE Institute, 463 West Street, New York, New York 10014.

5. Creating appropriate organizational plans. In organizing for instruction, the administrator is aware of important guidelines: (a) there are vast differences among the instructional needs of students of similar age/grade placement, (b) organizational patterns should be flexible and altered as better ways are discovered, (c) more emphasis should be placed on methods of providing for individual differences by teachers than on methods of grouping, (d) and organization is a technique or system—not a "method of instruction"; therefore organization can only facilitate, or hinder, effective instruction.

6. Helping collect and interpret test data. Appropriate reading progress forms need to be maintained by the school in the student's cumulative folder. The administrator realizes that reading survey tests should show in a general way how well students are performing (they indicate the range of reading achievement in the class) while diagnostic reading tests locate specific strengths and weaknesses and possibly suggest causes. He or she is sensitive to the fact that the best tests to use are those for which the sample population used to standardize the test is like the class to be tested and that a test score on a standardized reading test frequently reflects the student's frustration level (where material is too advanced), rather than instructional level (level at which teaching may be effective) or independent reading level (where student can read on his or her own). The administrator also values informal reading inventories, informal skills checks, and interest inventories (See Chapter 3 for a detailed description of such assessment tools.).

7. Providing corrective/remedial services. The administrator (a) is sensitive to basic principles of corrective reading instruction; (b) helps identify students reading below capacity level; (c) focuses upon possible instructional weaknesses throughout the curriculum, such as failure to adjust content material to the student's reading levels and ineffective motivation for developing reading interests; (d) provides appropriate materials; and (e) wisely utilizes the reading specialist and the reading consultant for this specialized service.

8. Communicating about the reading program. The administrator should be aware of frequently posed questions and be prepared to answer them reasonably. How is reading taught in the school? Is my youngster reading at grade level? What can I do to help my child like reading? What about those machines? What can we parents do to help our poor reader? Does my child have dyslexia? Should I hire a tutor for my disabled reader? What special programs do you have for poor readers? How fast should my teenager be able to read?

Reading consultant   The reading consultant works with administrators and other school personnel to develop and coordinate the school-wide reading program. This person is freed from classroom teaching or instruction of special reading classes. He or she has a high degree of professional skill and knowledge, has had years of formal study in reading and related areas, has had several years of successful teaching experience, and meets certification qualifications as a special teacher of reading.

While the specific responsibilities of the reading consultant may vary somewhat from locale to locale, the following are typical:

1. Studies the population to be served—both students and teachers.
2. Assists principal/supervisor/administrator in planning a comprehensive reading program: (a) developmental, (b) correction/remediation, (c) content area reading and study skills, (d) development of interests and tastes in leisure reading.
3. Orients beginning teachers to philosophy, procedures, and materials for school reading program and keeps all school staff informed as to new developments in reading.
4. Evaluates the program through supervisory activities and research, making recommendations for changes as needed.
5. Provides inservice instruction, conducting workshops, seminars, conferences, and minilessons on such topics as readability formulas; informal reading inventories, constructing teaching or study guides, etc.
6. Evaluates and recommends reading materials.
7. Works as resource person with special cases where difficulty or complexity requires a high degree of professional competence.
8. Keeps the community informed as to purposes and progress of the reading program.

The reading specialist works directly with students. He or she has a graduate degree in reading or the equivalent, several years of teaching experience, and is certified as a reading specialist.

Again, while the specific responsibilities of the reading specialist may vary from locale to locale, the following ones are fairly typical:

1. Knows reading skills, formal and informal instruments for assessing reading (being able to administer and interpret them), and a variety of methods and materials for reading instruction.
2. Plans and teaches reading classes for average readers, accelerated readers, and disabled readers.
3. Works with paraprofessionals and parents who may assist with the reading program and keeps in touch with content area teachers whose students are in reading classes. Assists content area teachers in selecting instructional materials to meet the needs of students.
4. Assists the reading consultant as a demonstration teacher and resource person.

When the principal or administrator, reading consultant, and special reading teacher work with each other and with the content area teachers to produce a good reading program for a school, success for the program is likely. Each staff member needs to understand his or her own job and the jobs of his or her colleagues. This understanding can enhance cooperation.

---

1. What is true of a total-school reading program? (a) Basic skills are taught. (b) Content area skills are taught. (c) Remedial reading is offered. (d) All of the above.
2. If a total-school reading program is to be established, when should the school's reading philosophy be defined? (a) At the beginning of the planning period (b) At the end of the planning period (c) After the program has been implemented (d) At no time during the process.
3. If a total-school reading program is to be established, when should inservice training sessions be held? (a) Only at the beginning of the planning period (b) Only at the end of the planning period (c) Only after implementation of the program (d) Throughout the process of planning and implementation.
4. Who should be involved in inservice sessions? (a) Administrators (b) Faculty members from all departments (c) Media specialists (d) All of the above.

5. Which statement is true of a school reading committee? (a) It should be composed of only the school's reading teachers. (b) It should be composed of people who can offer effective guidance to the school's reading program. (c) It should never include an administrator. (d) It should never include faculty members from departments other than English.

6. Which statement is true of reading achievement tests? (a) They are of little use when planning a total-school reading program. (b) They generally pinpoint specific skill difficulties. (c) They generally reveal the student's accomplishments in broad areas of reading skills. (d) None of the above.

7. Which statement is true of recreational reading? (a) It is unimportant for inclusion in a school's reading program plans. (b) It can be encouraged through reading clubs. (c) It is not a concern of content area teachers. (d) None of the above.

8. What should evaluation of a total-school reading program include? (a) A measure of student progress. (b) Consideration of staff utilization (c) Consideration of the effectiveness of activities and materials (d) All of the above.

9. Which statement is true concerning evaluation of a total-school reading program? (a) It is an on-going process. (b) It cannot be reasonably carried out. (c) It should take place only at the end of the school year. (d) It should involve only the results of standardized tests.

10. Why are English teachers often chosen to teach reading in special English classes? (a) They are well-prepared to do so by their teacher-preparation programs. (b) Other faculty members perceive English and reading as being closely related. (c) Both *a* and *b* (d) Neither *a* nor *b*.

11. Which statement is true of reading instruction offered as special units in English classes? (a) It constitutes a comprehensive attack on the reading needs of the student population. (b) It is useless to most students. (c) It is useful for developing some types of reading skills. (d) None of the above.

12. How are remedial readers defined? (a) Students who are reading at levels two or more years behind where they should be reading. (b) Books for students reading below grade level. (c) Students who dislike reading. (d) None of the above.

13. What do remedial readers need? (a) Much individual attention (b) To see some evidence of progress (c) Both *a* and *b* (d) Neither *a* nor *b*.

14. Which statement is true of developmental readers at the secondary level? (a) They generally have a good background in word recognition skills. (b) They often need help with critical reading skills. (c) They often need help with reading study skills. (d) All of the above.

15. Which statement is true of reading laboratories? (a) They are generally set up to allow much independent work by the students. (b) They need to have a lab instructor present at all times. (c) Both *a* and *b*. (d) Neither *a* nor *b*.

16. Which personnel are primarily responsible for teaching reading classes *per se*? (a) Administrator (b) Reading consultant (c) Special reading teacher (d) None of the above.

1. List the duties which a member of a school reading committee might be expected to perform. Compare your list with the lists your classmates have developed. Discuss differences of opinion.

* 2. Report to the class on the provisions for reading instruction in your school.

* 3. Check with your principal and your fellow teachers about reading problems of students in your school. After identifying the two most common problems perceived by educators in your school, write up a plan for solving each of them. Share your findings and your plan.

* 4. List the personnel in your school who are concerned with reading instruction. Briefly describe the responsibilities of each one.

* 5. Draw a plan for a reading laboratory that would be adaptable to the needs of your school.

6. Make a list of reading skills that might be taught in a developmental reading class. Check the ones that could be taught by a content area teacher. Discuss your list with your classmates.

7. With a group of your classmates, design a total-school reading program. Include physical plant needs, materials and equipment needs, staff needs, organizational plans, and staff responsibilities.

* 8. Choose a reading program described in one of the periodicals in the "Selected References" and analyze the possibilities for utilization of all or part of the program in your own school.

* 9. Go over the administrator's checklist with a secondary school principal. Share his or her reactions to it with the group.

10. Interview a reading consultant and a special reading teacher. What are their functions and roles? Share your findings with the class.

Selected references

Artley, A. Sterl, ed. *Trends and Practices in Secondary School Reading.* Newark, Del.: International Reading Association, 1968. Chapter 3.

Aukerman, Robert. *Reading in the Secondary School Classroom.* New York: McGraw-Hill, 1972. Chapter 15.

Barth, Rodney J. "Remedial Reading Programs." *Journal of Reading* 17 (April 1974): 580–82.

Bennie, Frances. "Pupil Attitudes Toward Individually Prescribed Lab Program." *Journal of Reading* 17 (November 1973): 108–12.

Burmeister, Lou E. *Reading Strategies for Secondary School Teachers.* New York: Addison-Wesley, 1974. Chapter 12.

Criscuolo, Nicholas P. "Quality Reading Programs at Bargain Basement Prices." *Journal of Reading* 18 (November 1974): 127–30.

* These activities are designed for inservice teachers, student teachers, or practicum students.

Dawson, Mildred A., comp. *Developing High School Reading Programs.* Newark Del.: IRA, 1967.

Dechant, Emerald. *Reading Improvement in the Secondary School.* Englewood Cliffs, N.J.: Prentice-Hall, 1973. Chapter 5.

Duggins, James, comp. *Teaching Reading for Human Values in High School.* Columbus, Ohio: Charles E. Merrill, 1972. Chapter 10.

Earle, Richard A. and Richard Morley. "The Half-Open Classroom: Controlled Options in Reading." *Journal of Reading* 18, (November 1974): 131–35.

Gruber, Paulette M. "Junior High Boasts Super Stars." *Journal of Reading* 16 (May 1973): 600–03.

Gudaitis, Michael S. "A Reading Course Outline for the College Bound Student." *Journal of Reading* 19 (April 1976): 575–76.

Henry, Claire. "The Administration Helps Teachers Make the Difference." *Journal of Reading* 20 (March 1977): 508–12.

Hodges, Pauline. "Reading as an Elective in the English Program." *Journal of Reading* 18 (October 1974): 30–33.

International Reading Association. *Reading Instruction in Secondary Schools.* Newark, Del.: IRA, 1964. Chapters 1, 2, 4, 9.

Jeffers, Pearl B. "Guidelines for Junior High Reading Programs." *Journal of Reading* 15 (January 1972): 264–66.

Karlin, Robert. *Teaching Reading in High School: Selected Articles.* Indianapolis: Bobbs-Merrill, 1969. Chapter 14.

Kelly, Daniel J. "Program Designed for a Co-ed Reading Center." *Journal of Reading* 19 (November 1975): 121–24.

Kummer, Robert. "Reading as an Elective." *Journal of Reading* 19 (April 1976): 575–76.

McDonald, Thomas F. "An All School Secondary Reading Program." *Journal of Reading* (May 1971): pp. 553–58.

Peters, Charles W. "How to Get More Comprehensive Reading Programs at the Secondary Level." *Journal of Reading* 20, No. 6 (March 1977): 513–19.

Rauch, Sidney J. "Administrators' Guidelines for More Effective Reading Programs." *Journal of Reading* 17 (January 1974): 297–300.

Rossman, Jean F. "How One High School Set Up a Reading Program for 500 Students." *Journal of Reading* 20 (February 1977): 393–97.

Rutledge, Emma M. "What Principals Owe to Reading Teachers and Programs." *The Reading Teacher* 28 (May 1975): 748–49.

Sanacore, Joseph. "Enhancing the Reading Program: Administrative Considerations." *Journal of Reading* 18 (November 1974): 131–35.

——— "Evaluating Administration Performance in the School Reading Program." *Journal of Reading* 20 (January 1977): 312–16.

Schottenfield, Lorraine and Florence Maggie Lang. "Reading Resource Center: Programs and Personnel in Modular Scheduling." *Journal of Reading* (November 1973): 104–7.

Shepherd, David L. *Comprehensive High School Reading Methods.* Columbus, Ohio: Charles E. Merrill, 1973. Chapter 13.

Wood, Phyllis Anderson. "Judging the Value of a Reading Program." *Journal of Reading* 19 (May 1976): 618–20.

Post secondary reading programs

12

This chapter focuses upon post secondary reading programs. Specifically, the need for such programs, types of programs, approaches to organization, and approaches to instruction are considered.

As you read this chapter, try to answer these questions:
1. Why are post secondary reading programs needed?
2. What types of post secondary reading programs are offered at colleges and universities?
3. What are some approaches to organizing these programs?
4. What are some approaches to instruction used in these programs?

Purpose-setting questions

As you read this chapter, check your understanding of these terms:

controlled reading
  devices
developmental
  programs

open laboratory
  organization
reading accelerators

reading pacers
remedial programs
tachistoscopes

Key vocabulary

Need for such programs

Personnel of colleges and universities across the nation are becoming aware of a need to offer classes in reading improvement for their students. Students currently enrolled in programs of higher education exhibit reading difficulties ranging from lack of basic word recognition skills to inadequate ability to critically interpret material read. Students who do not have basic word recognition and comprehension problems frequently feel a need for instruction that will help increase their reading speeds.

393

Community college personnel, in particular, are realizing that their students have a definite need for reading assistance. One reason for the number of students in need of reading instruction at the community college level is the open-door admission policy. Students who may not be admitted to a four-year institution are allowed to enter community college programs. Many of these students plan to transfer to four-year institutions after they have completed a two-year program. The community college personnel have to attempt to assist high-risk students (students who are likely to fail or drop out of school) in meeting program requirements successfully. One way to meet these needs is to offer remedial courses in various areas, including reading. Since students who are not seriously remedial also tend to have reading skill needs, many community colleges also include offerings in developmental reading that are open to all students.

Professors sometimes lose sight of the fact that people continue to develop and refine reading skills as long as they live; therefore, they fail to see that college students who have a class concentrating on reading skills may be better able to handle reading assignments in all content areas. Due to this lack of understanding, developmental reading classes sometimes meet with opposition from professors who teach in other disciplines. Research studies have shown, however, that students who take reading courses often increase their grade-point averages significantly. The most obvious conclusion to draw from this information is that increased understanding of textbooks and outside readings has resulted in better grades. Since it is difficult to control all the variables affecting the students involved in the studies, this conclusion must be accepted only tentatively at present. Improved research designs with careful controls of variables may offer more definitive answers in the future. Reading programs in which students see themselves improving steadily may build self-concepts sufficiently to influence progress in some other subjects. This improved self-concept may be more influential in improving grade-point average than is the improvement in skills.

Administrators and professors who indicate that they have reservations about offering credit for a class designed to improve reading skills rarely hesitate to endorse English classes designed to improve composition skills or speech classes designed to improve public speaking techniques. Why is the development of one communication skill considered less important than the development of others? Careful consideration of this question should result in a positive view of a developmental reading class.

Four-year colleges and universities are also finding a need for teaching reading and study skills. The attrition rate is much greater among students who exhibit such difficulties than is desirable. To circumvent having students who fail to complete college programs, many institutions have initiated some type of reading improvement or study skills program.

Sometimes the reading and study skills programs offered by colleges and universities are augmented by guidance programs designed to build up the student's self-concept and help him or her cope with academic pressures. These adjunct programs are especially valuable to the students who tend to have low self-concepts and to expect failure rather than success.

College reading programs are generally designed to be either (1) developmental in nature, (2) remedial in nature, or (3) a combination of these two types of programs. The programs are generally administered by reading specialists, English department faculty, or guidance counselors. Sometimes graduate assistants are utilized as class instructors or tutors, under the supervision of a regular faculty member. Some of the programs are offered for credit, and others are not. Of those for which credit is given, the amount of credit usually varies from one to three hours. Courses offered for credit generally have better attendance and offer more incentive to the students to accomplish as much as they can. Some of the programs are strictly voluntary; others are required for either particular students or all entering students. Students who have low scores on entrance examinations are often required to enroll in a reading program. Students on academic probation are sometimes counselled to take reading programs to give them the skills necessary to make it possible for them to stay in school.

Types of programs

Developmental programs are generally designed to serve the students whose reading skills have developed normally in the past and who wish to further develop and refine reading skills in order to benefit more from their reading activities.

Developmental classes frequently feature group instruction, although some are individualized through assigning materials on different levels to different students and others make use of individual student contracts. The individualized programs often utilize a laboratory setting. These different approaches are discussed in the sections of this chapter on approaches to instruction and approaches to organization.

Skills that usually receive attention include study skills, vocabulary building, general comprehension, critical reading, appreciation, and rate. Some programs offer help with special reading problems in the content areas. In order to teach these skills, instructors make use of lectures, workbooks, and mechanical equipment.

Developmental programs

Lectures It is often beneficial to have some lectures on how to improve reading skills, even if the material is available in a textbook or workbook. Presentation of the information in lecture form is likely to elicit questions from the students, and the ensuing discussion is valuable to the class as a whole. In addition, some students are auditory learners and learn better those things to which they have listened. Lecture-demonstration combinations are especially effective in helping students acquire techniques for increasing rate of reading.

Workbooks/worktexts Most developmental reading programs make use of workbooks or worktexts either as the basic texts for the programs or as supplementary materials. Many programs use a number of different workbooks, assigning appropriate sections to individual students. Some important considerations concerning the choosing of workbooks for a class include the following:

1. Does the book include information about development of reading skills as well as exercises designed for practice of such skills? (If you intend to lecture on development of skills yourself, you may want only exercises. If the student is expected to learn some techniques of skill improvement through reading, the textbook should probably contain a balance of exercises and instructional material.)
2. Does the book cover all of the skill areas that you wish to cover in your class? (If you wish to use a basic text, you should choose one that covers all of the skill areas in which you are interested. If you are using the book as a supplement to other materials, check to be sure that the skills covered are ones for which you need further material.)
3. Are purposes indicated for each textbook assignment? (If not, you will need to provide purposes for the assignments to gain maximum benefit from the material.)
4. Are answers to the exercises included in the workbook? (If you wish the students to use the book independently, they should be.)
5. Are the reading selections ones that students consider interesting and relevant? (Lack of relevance of selections can result in decreased enthusiasm of the students for course activities.)
6. Does the book contain charts and/or graphs that are designed to help the student keep a record of his or her progress? (Such visible signs of progress serve as motivation for future effort. If the book does not include such aids, you may want to devise some for your students.)
7. Are the directions for the activities clear? (Vague directions may result in incorrect procedures being followed. As a result,

no learning may occur, or the students may learn an incorrect response.)

8. Is the workbook durable? (Students become understandably irritated by books that fall apart in the middle of a course.)

Some textbooks/worktexts available for use in a college reading program include:

Adams, W. Royce, *How to Read the Humanities*, Glenview, Ill.: Scott, Foresman, 1969.

———— *How to Read the Sciences*, Glenview, Ill.: Scott, Foresman, 1970.

Bamman, Henry A., Midori F. Hiyama, and Delbert L. Prescott, *World of Ideas: A Guide to Effective Reading*, San Francisco: Field Educational Publications, 1970.

———— *Free to Read: A Guide to Effective Reading*. San Francisco: Field Educational Publications, 1970.

Beringause, Arthur F. and Daniel K. Lowenthal, *The Range of College Reading*, Boston: Houghton Mifflin, 1967.

Brown, Charles M. and W. Royce Adams, *How to Read the Social Sciences*, Glenview, Ill.: Scott, Foresman, 1968.

Brown, James I., *Efficient Reading: Revised Form B*, Lexington, Mass.: D. C. Heath, 1976.

———— *Reading Power*, Lexington, Mass.: D. C. Heath, 1975.

Canavan, P. Joseph and William O. Heckman, *The Way to Reading Improvement*, Boston: Allyn and Bacon, 1966.

Cherington, Marie R., *Improving Reading Skills in College Subjects*, New York: Teachers College, Columbia University, 1961.

Gilbert, Doris W., *Breaking the Reading Barrier*, Englewood Cliffs, N.J.: Prentice-Hall, 1956.

Glock, Marvin D., *The Improvement of College Reading*, Boston: Houghton Mifflin, 1967.

Gray, Lee L., *Better and Faster Reading*, New York: Cambridge Book Company, 1970.

Jacobus, Lee A., *Improving College Reading*, New York: Harcourt Brace Jovanovich, 1972.

Jones, George L., Roy A. Morgan, and Edgar L. Petty, *Effective Reading for College Students*, New York: Appleton-Century-Crofts, 1968.

Leedy, Paul D., *Read with Speed and Precision*, New York: McGraw-Hill, 1963.

Merrill, Evelyne S., *The Power of the Word*, Cambridge, Mass.: Winthrop Publishers, 1973.

Pauk, Walter, *A Skill at a Time Series*, 10 skill booklets, Providence, R.I.: Jamestown Publishers, 1975.

Roe, Betty D. and Elinor P. Ross, *Developing Power in Reading*, Dubuque, Iowa: Kendall/Hunt Publishing Company, 1976.

Sherbourne, Julia Florence, *Toward Reading Comprehension*, Lexington, Mass.: D. C. Heath, 1977.

Spache, George D. and Paul C. Berg, *The Art of Efficient Reading*, New York: Macmillan Co., 1966.

Spargo, Edward, *The Now Student*, Providence, R.I.: Jamestown Publishers, 1971.

Spargo, Edward, ed., *Selections from the Black: College Reading Skills*, Providence, R.I.: Jamestown Publishers, 1970.

Stroud, James B., Robert B. Ammons, and Henry A. Bamman, *Improving Reading Ability*, New York: Appleton-Century-Crofts, 1970.

Mechanical equipment (hardware) Some people think that a reading program should be built entirely upon mechanical devices. Although mechanical devices definitely can contribute to a reading program, they are not essential to the development of a sound program. They seem to function primarily as motivational devices for the students.

Many types of hardware are utilized in reading programs. Some of them include (1) controlled reading devices, (2) tachistoscopes, (3) reading accelerators or pacers, and (4) tape recorders (often with listening stations).

Controlled reading devices are widely used in college reading programs. They include filmstrip projectors that project a reading selection onto a screen at varying rates, filmstrip viewers with built-in screens, and motion picture projectors that utilize special films.

Tachistoscopes are devices that expose letters, words, or phrases for selected periods of time (1 second, ½ second, etc.). They may be operated by hand, or they may be automatic. Simple ones may be made from cardboard or paper with slots cut out to expose only the printed material you wish the student to view. Tachistoscopic attachments are available for filmstrip projectors and can be utilized with special filmstrips.

Reading accelerators or pacers are each equipped with a movable bar that moves down a page of print. The bar can be set to move at varying speeds. The student attempts to stay ahead of the bar as he or she reads the material.

Tape recorders are often used to allow students to listen to instruction on how to improve reading skills. Commercial sets of tapes are available, or the teacher may construct his or her own tapes covering skills needed most by a particular group.

Controlled readers, tachistoscopes, and reading accelerators or pacers are ordinarily utilized to help students build reading speed. The printed material accompanying the controlled reading filmstrips is also designed to aid in vocabulary development and comprehension.

The tape recorder may be used in conjunction with any of the skills included in the program.

Since the various devices for increasing rate are adjustable to speeds appropriate for different individuals, they can contribute to individualization of a program. Group use of projected controlled reading materials, however, may cause teachers to neglect individual differences. The rate chosen may frustrate some students by being too fast and bore others with its slowness. Controlled reading devices in general can help individuals realize that it is possible for them to read faster. However, the skills so acquired must be transferred from reading with machine aid to reading without artificial assistance before the student will have truly acquired a useful reading technique.

Remedial programs

Remedial instruction is generally designed for those students who read two or more years below the level at which they could be expected to read with understanding. Some college programs, however, consider students who score below a certain percentile on a test of reading ability to be candidates for a remedial program, regardless of their capacities for learning.

Strictly remedial programs generally are implemented by a reading specialist, sometimes with the aid of graduate assistants. In most cases the student-teacher ratio for a remedial program is lower than that for a developmental program, and each student is given more individual attention by the instructor.

Diagnosis of needs for remedial readers is generally more extensive, two or more instruments being utilized instead of a single test, as is often true for a developmental program. Attitude, interest, and personality inventories are frequently used, and counseling personnel are often involved in the testing and advisement of the student.

Instructors strive to use high-interest, low-readability materials with remedial readers. Some of the materials listed as appropriate for use in the secondary school are also used for these college students, for some students have reading levels as low as ninth-grade or below. Care must be taken to avoid choosing materials obviously written for much younger readers.

Remedial students often enter reading programs with extremely poor self-concepts due to repeated failures in the past. Counseling, along with help in improving reading skills, may be needed for these students. They also have the need to see evidence of progress toward their goals. Therefore, their instruction must be carefully planned in order to allow them to successfully advance, step by step, through an orderly progression of instructional activities. Graphs of progress help to make their successes more visible, and being successful motivates them to further efforts.

Remedial programs are generally individualized as much as staffing will allow. To offer more individual and small group help than a single teacher can manage, schools often use tutors in addition to the regular instructor. The tutors may be graduate assistants or advanced students who donate their services, perhaps through membership in a service organization. The diagnosis and prescription for each remedial student is done by the regular faculty member. Then the faculty member shows each tutor how to conduct help-sessions with a specific student or a small group of students. Tutors are shown how to help their subjects use the printed materials and equipment prescribed in their individual programs, how to offer encouragement and reassurance, how to help the subjects correct poor reading habits, how to monitor attendance, and how to keep the faculty member apprised of changes in the subject's reading, whether these changes are positive or negative. While tutors work with individuals and small groups, the regular faculty member is free to offer intensive individual and small group help to students who have problems that the tutors are not qualified to handle. The instructor also must continuously monitor the activities of the tutors.

Remedial reading instruction needs to be as practical as possible. The students need to be able to see how it is going to help them cope with life in general and college in particular. Therefore, reading instructors would do well to confer with each student about his or her personal concerns and try to tailor the remedial program to reflect the perceived needs of the individual.

Remedial students often need instruction in basic word recognition and comprehension skills. Therefore, decoding skills, vocabulary building, and comprehension are generally stressed in remedial programs, whereas little attention is given to rate. The basic skills are necessary prerequisites to programs for increasing rate, but some attention may be given to developing flexibility of rate in a remedial program.

Combination programs

Many colleges and universities offer both developmental and remedial classes or offer an individualized laboratory-type class to fulfill both purposes. Frequently, high-risk students are required to enroll in remedial classes, whereas other students are free to elect developmental classes. In an individualized laboratory-type class, both remedial and developmental students may be enrolled simultaneously, and both would be offered individual diagnosis and prescription. This arrangement helps to eradicate the stigma placed on being in a strictly remedial class, but class size may not allow as much individual attention for each remedial student as is generally available when special remedial classes are formed. In such cases, too much independent, self-initiated work may be required of a student who is not highly self-directed.

Approaches to organization

The two main organizational approaches for college reading programs in institutions of higher learning are regular classrooms and open laboratories. There are, of course, many variations of these two arrangements.

Regular classroom organization

Reading programs in institutions of higher learning are frequently organized in the same way that classes in other subjects are—the student attends an assigned section of a class according to a regular schedule (one hour a day, three times a week, or a similar arrangement). Within each section, the instructor may offer whole-class instruction, small group instruction, individualized instruction, or a combination of these types of instruction. For example, the entire class might participate in a vocabulary building exercise, small groups might listen to appropriate instructional tapes at listening centers, and individuals might work independently with controlled readers or reading accelerators.

The size of the class may vary with the regular class organization, but the classes generally have between ten and thirty students. Strictly remedial classes tend to be smaller; developmental and combination classes larger. Many educators feel that twenty students is a good enrollment for a developmental class, but many classes have larger enrollments.

With a regular classroom organization the teacher may have more opportunity to become familiar with each of the students assigned to a section because each one will be with the same teacher for sustained periods of time at regular intervals. With a laboratory arrangement this frequently is not true. A student may attend the laboratory at irregular intervals when different laboratory instructors are in attendance.

Open laboratory

In open laboratory arrangements, the students generally meet in groups for diagnosis and orientation to the laboratory. Then each student is given an individual program of study that is pursued independently in the laboratory at his or her convenience. Sometimes the students are allowed to come into the laboratory and use the materials and equipment without undergoing diagnosis. In some programs, students are required to attend the laboratory for a specified number of hours during a quarter or semester. In others, the students attend only when they feel the need.

Most laboratory organizations have one or more laboratory instructors on duty during all hours when the laboratory is open to students. These instructors may be regular faculty or graduate assistants working under the supervision of regular faculty. The instructors may be responsible for monitoring the individual students' special programs, keeping track of hours spent by students, helping students with assignments, demonstrating materials and equipment, and evaluating progress through testing.

An open-lab arrangement offers students more flexibility in scheduling. They may spend large blocks of time in the laboratory when they feel they are accomplishing a great deal and may cease to work on days when they are pressured by other responsibilities (examinations in other courses, for example).

Because of the nature of the open-lab organization, the attendance in the laboratory at any given hour may vary from one student to thirty or more students, depending upon available facilities. Students may work together at some tasks (for instance, at listening stations), but most of them will work independently at their own paces with materials that fit their specific needs.

Combination approaches
It is possible to combine some of the aspects of the regular classroom organization and the open laboratory. An example from Tennessee Technological University will show how this combination can work. Students are assigned to regular sections of a class entitled "College Reading Improvement." The sections are scheduled for three hours a week. During the first two or three weeks the students meet with their regularly scheduled sections for diagnosis, introduction to the course, orientation to the laboratory materials and equipment, lectures on techniques for improving reading skills, and prescription of individualized programs. The rest of the quarter the students meet as a group only the first class meeting each week and spend the remainder of the required time in an open laboratory setting. A graduate assistant lab instructor is in attendance during all open-lab hours to help students as they pursue their programs and to keep track of attendance. In the regular class sessions, progress toward over-all program goals is monitored, and adjustments in assignments may be made.

Approaches to instruction
Approaches to instruction vary from primarily lecture classes to project packages to strictly individual assignments. Good programs have been developed with each of these instructional approaches.

Lecture classes
When lecture classes are utilized, lectures generally center around techniques for improving different types of reading skills. Many of the

classes could more exactly be called lecture-demonstration or lecture-discussion, since the teacher often demonstrates the techniques being described, and there is often class discussion following the presentation of information. These lectures are also often followed by practice sessions centering around the skill or skills currently under consideration. Some individualization is possible with this type of class by varying the level of difficulty of the practice materials being used.

Some instructors develop sets of materials concentrating upon different skills and refer to the different skill areas as projects. Students are either assigned certain projects or choose particular projects for concentration. Completion of a specific number of projects is often the determining factor in grading. The difficulty levels of material designated for the projects can be varied to fit the individual student's needs. Examples of projects used at one university are shown in Example 12.1.

Project packages

College reading improvement syllabus   **Example 12.1**

Text: *Developing Power in Reading* by Roe and Ross

Project Requirements
For a grade of C, three projects must be completed.
For a grade of B, one additional project must be completed.
For a grade of A, two additional projects must be completed.

A chart is to be kept that records the progress in each of the projects to be completed. This will be reviewed periodically by the student and the teacher. The student will be responsible for scheduling activities in order to complete the projects by the dates due.

Projects 1, 3, & 5 are required.
Not more than two intensive projects may be selected.
All exercises are to be kept in the student's folder until they have been checked.

Each student must attend the reading lab for 30 hours. Time spent in regularly scheduled classes as well as in open lab counts in this 30 hours. He or she should spend at least 3 hours in the lab each week to accomplish this goal. If the student finishes his or her work in less than 30 hours, he or she should use the remaining time to continue developing reading skills.

Students will meet in regular classes for the first scheduled class meeting *each week* (i.e. Monday for *MWF* classes; Tuesday for *TT* classes). The remaining portion of the required three hours must be spent in the open lab during any of the posted hours. These hours may be chosen at the student's convenience.

Example 12.1 (cont.)

Project 1: Vocabulary—required

Completion of the following activities and 80% score on quiz.

a.   Text Chapter II: Vocabulary. Read chapter and do exercises 1, 2, 3, 5, 7, 8, 9, 10, 11, 12, 13, 15, 16, 17, 18, 19, 20, 21, 22, 23, 24.

b.   The first 8 lessons of EDL programmed materials. (*Word Clues*)

Project 2: Intensive vocabulary

Completion of the following activities and 80% score on quiz.

a.   Completion of project 1

b.   Lessons 9 through 18 of EDL programmed materials (*Word Clues*)

c.   MN Tape 3 or Strang, Chapter 6 (answer *c*, *d*, and *e*)

d.   JKL Tape 6 or *How to Read the Humanities*, Chapter 4

e.   Text Chapter II: Vocabulary Exercises 4, 6, 14

Project 3: Rate with Comprehension—required

Completion of the following activities and 80% score on quiz.

a.   Do 8 controlled reader selections with average comprehension of not less than 70%. Try to increase speed at least one setting each week. Do one selection each week. (EDL)

b.   Any 12 McCall Crabbs activities (*Standard Test Lessons in Reading, Book E*)

c.   Use reading accelerator at least 10 minutes each week.

d.   Text Chapter VI: Rate. Read chapter and do all exercises.

e.   Text—Read (p. 147) 1 rate exercise each week, a total of 8 exercises. Record rate and comprehension scores according to directions in text.

Project 4: Intensive rate

Completion of the following activities and 80% on quiz.

a.   Completion of project 3

b.   Read 8 additional controlled reader selections. Do one selection each week. (EDL)

c.   Complete 12 additional McCall Crabbs exercises. (*Standard Test Lessons in Reading*)

d.   MN Tape 11 or Strang, Chapter 3 (answer *c*, *d*, and *e*)

e.   Read any 8 PDL practice book selections. Record rate and comprehension scores. Do one a week.

f.   Use reading accelerator at least 10 additional minutes per week. (Total of 20 minutes per week)

g.   Spargo, Chapter 7

Project 5: Comprehension—required

Completion of the following activities and 80% comprehension on quiz.

a.   Text Chapter III: Comprehension. Read chapter and do exercises 1; 2; 3; 4; 5; 6; 8; 10; 11; 12; 13 I, II, III; 14; 15; 16; 17 I, II, III, IV; 18.

b.   JKL Tape 7

Project 6: Intensive comprehension
Completion of the following projects with 80% comprehension on quiz.
a.   Completion of project 5
b.   Text Chapter III: Exercises 7; 9; 13 IV, V, VI; 17 V, VI, VII; 19; 20
c.   MN Tape 7 or Strang, Chapter 5 (answer c, d, and e)
d.   Spargo, Chapter 5
3.   MN Tape 9 or Strang, Chapter 4 (answer c, d, and e)

Project 7: Study Skills and Spelling
Completion of the following activities and a grade of at least 80% on a quiz covering text and Spargo.
a.   Text Chapter I: Study Skills and Spelling. Read chapter and do all exercises.
b.   MN Tape 24, or *How to Read the Humanities*, Chapter 12.
c.   Spargo, chapters 8, 22, 24, 25
d.   Choice of any 3 Spargo chapters: 9, 12, 13, 14, 16, or 20
e.   *Using an Index*—Complete any 4 exercises (10 questions in each exercise). See folder for answer sheets.

Project 8: Critical Reading
Completion of the following activities and score of 80% on quiz.
a.   Text Chapter IV: Critical Reading. Read chapter and do all exercises.
b.   JKL Tape 15 or *How to Read the Humanities*, Chapter 9
c.   MN Tape 13 or *How to Read the Social Studies*, Chapter 11

Project 9: Reading in Content Areas
Completion of the following activities and 80% achievement on quiz. Answer the questions at the end of each selection.
a.   Text Chapter V: Content Area Reading. Read chapter and do all the exercises.
b.   Do two selections in *Improving Reading Skills in College Subjects* by Cherington. Answer the questions at the end of the chapter on the answer form.
c.   Read introduction to *How to Read the Humanities*. Choose one chapter to read and do the exercises.
d.   Choose one area for concentrated study—science, humanities, or social studies. From this area choose three additional readings from *How to Read the Humanities*, *How to Read the Sciences*, or *How to Read the Social Sciences* and do any three accompanying exercises. Do not read any chapter you have already read for part of another project.
e.   MN tape 20 or Spargo, Chapters 15 and 16.

Project 10: Professional and Recreational Reading
Completion of the following activities and 80% achievement on test over content of the text.

Example 12.1 (cont.)

    a.   Text Chapter VII: Professional and Recreational Reading. Read chapter and do all exercises.

    b.   Do four selections in *Chapters*. Read each selection and answer the questions which follow.

Note: Tapes are *Listen and Read* Tapes
Strang = *Study Types of Reading Exercises: College Level*
Spargo = *The Now Student*
Source: Tennessee Technological University, Cookeville, Tennessee.

Students using project materials in Example 12.1 meet with instructors and cooperatively determine the projects they will work on during the quarter. Results of the *Nelson-Denny Reading Test* are considered as a help in deciding upon the most needed projects. Successful completion of five projects earns an *A* grade; four projects, a *B*, three projects, a *C*, and so on. Successful completion of the projects includes passing an end-of-project test for each one. Students contract to do specific projects, but no student is allowed to contract for less than three. A contract can be adjusted at any time during the quarter.

When students work under a project plan, they generally keep individual folders containing the work they have completed. Instructors may check these folders periodically to check on student progress. The project plan can be used in a regular classroom setting or in an open laboratory setting.

Strictly individual assignments

After diagnostic testing takes place, some instructors work out completely individual assignments for each student based upon the pattern of the individual student's strengths and weaknesses and his or her general level of performance. A wide variety of materials is necessary to carry out this type of program. Multilevel materials are important here, just as they are in a project plan. Some widely used materials include:

1. SRA *Reading Laboratories*, Science Research Associates.
2. *Word Clues* (programmed vocabulary materials), Educational Developmental Laboratories.
3. Controlled Reading Materials (filmstrips, workbooks, cassettes), Educational Developmental Laboratories.
4. *Listen-and-Read Program*, Educational Developmental Laboratories.
5. *McGraw-Hill Basic Skills System*, McGraw-Hill Book Company.
6. *Advanced Reading Program*, Perceptual Development Laboratories.
7. *Improving Your Study Skills Program*, Perceptual Development Laboratories.

Most college reading programs make use of some standardized tests to determine the skill needs of the students and the levels of materials to use with them. Many also administer a standardized test at the end of the program to allow the students to see how much progress they have made and/or to allow the faculty and administration to evaluate the effectiveness of the program. Some frequently used tests include the following:

1. *California Reading Test, Advanced* California Test Bureau, Grades 9–14.
2. *Cooperative English Tests: Reading,* Cooperative Test Division Educational Testing Service, Grades 9–14.
3. *Davis Reading Test,* Psychological Corporation, Grades 11–13.
4. *Diagnostic Reading Test: Survey Section,* Science Research Associates, Upper Level, Grades 7–13.
5. *Nelson-Denny Reading Test for High Schools and Colleges,* Houghton Mifflin.
6. *Reading Test McGraw-Hill Basic Skills Systems,* McGraw-Hill, Grades 11–14.
7. *Study Skills Test McGraw-Hill Basic Skills System,* McGraw-Hill, Grades 11–14.
8. *Survey of Study Skills and Attitudes,* Psychological Corporation, Grades 7–14.
9. *Vocabulary Test McGraw-Hill Basic Skills System,* McGraw-Hill, Grades 11–14.

The test used in a program should be chosen to fit the content of the program. Before a test is chosen, the manual should be studied carefully in order to determine whether or not the test will provide the needed information. (See Chapter 10, pages 324–325.)

One program in effect at a community college depends heavily upon use of a number of machines, including the multi-purpose Perceptoscope (Perceptual Development Laboratories) and Reading Accelerators (Science Research Associates). A variety of printed material is also available for use with the students. SRA *Reading Laboratories* and the *Reading for Understanding* kit are utilized with all students.

Students contract to complete certain projects in order to receive specific grades. Students work on project materials until they reach a 75 percent level of competence in each area. After the projects and associated materials have been explained to the students, they work independently on a suggested list of daily activities.

The program is conducted in a single large room, equipped with carrels and work tables. A single faculty member directs the program.

Program 2   In another community college reading program, the basic materials used in the program are the *McGraw-Hill Basic Skills System*. SRA *Reading Laboratories* and Reading Accelerators are also utilized. Students work independently at their own rates in materials on their own levels. Study carrels are utilized for individual work spaces. The students also use the facilities of the foreign language department for listening to tape recordings. Tapes are employed in the vocabulary building portion of the program to allow the students to hear both the pronunciations and meanings of the words.

    This program is directed by one faculty member. Fifteen to twenty students are in each section of the course.

Program 3   In a university setting a reading improvement course is taught through three lecture-discussion periods and two laboratory periods each week. Extensive attention is given to vocabulary development, interpretive reading, and critical reading. Faculty members and graduate assistants rotate in supervising the lecture-discussion classes. Lab periods are supervised by graduate or undergraduate students and consist exclusively of work with reading accelerators.

Self-test
1. Why do colleges and universities often offer reading courses? (a) To filter out undesirable students (b) To lower the attrition rate (c) To attract students who are academically gifted (d) None of the above.
2. Who may college reading programs may be administered by? (a) Reading specialists (b) English department faculty (c) Guidance counselors (d) All of the above.
3. Developmental reading programs are generally designed to serve which students? (a) Students who are uninterested in academic pursuits. (b) Students who are reading two or more years below the level at which they could be expected to read with understanding. (c) Both *a* and *b* (d) Neither *a* or *b*.
4. Which skills usually receive attention? (a) Phonics (b) General comprehension (c) Both *a* and *b* (d) Neither *a* and *b*.
5. Which statement should be true if you wish students to use a reading workbook independently? (a) The answers to the exercises should be included in the workbook. (b) The readability level of the workbook should be at least grade 16. (c) Both *a* and *b* (d) Neither *a* nor *b*.
6. What is true about charts and graphs for plotting student progress? (a) They are useless. (b) They should be available only to the instructor. (c) They serve as motivation for future effort on the part of the student. (d) None of the above.
7. What is true about mechanical devices (such as reading accelerators)? (a) They are essential to the development of a sound program. (b) They can

contribute nothing to a reading program. (c) They seem to function primarily as motivational devices for students. (d) None of the above.

8. What are filmstrip projectors that project a reading selection onto the screen at varying rates known as? (a) Controlled reading devices (b) Tachistoscopes (c) Reading pacers (d) None of the above.

9. What are devices that expose letters, words, or phrases for selected periods of time known as? (a) Controlled reading devices (b) Tachistoscopes (c) Reading pacers (d) None of the above.

10. Which statement is true of remedial readers? (a) They often enter reading programs with extremely poor self-concepts. (b) They may need counseling as well as help in improving reading skills. (c) They have the need to see evidence of progress toward their goals. (d) All of the above.

11. How can tutors be used in reading programs? (a) To demonstrate use of materials and equipment (b) To offer encouragement and reassurance (c) To help the students correct poor habits (d) All of the above.

12. Which statement is true of developmental reading classes? (a) They are generally larger than remedial classes. (b) They generally have 30 to 50 students in them. (c) Both *a* and *b* (d) Neither *a* nor *b*.

13. Which statement is true of reading laboratory instructors? (a) They need no special training or supervision. (b) They are always regular faculty members. (c) They are generally on duty during all hours when the lab is open to students. (d) None of the above.

14. Flexibility of scheduling is offered by which organization? (a) A regular classroom organization (b) An open-lab arrangement (c) Both of the above (d) Neither of the above.

15. Why are project packages often developed? (a) To concentrate upon different skill areas (b) To facilitate individualization through multi-level materials (c) Both *a* and *b* (d) Neither *a* nor *b*.

16. Which statement is true of standardized tests? (a) They are rarely used in college reading programs. (b) They are often used to determine the skill needs of students. (c) They are used to determine appropriate difficulty levels for reading materials assigned to students. (d) Both *b* and *c*.

Enrichment activities

1. Visit a college reading laboratory. Find out the following items:
   a. What materials are being used?
   b. What teaching approaches are being used?
   c. How are the programs staffed?
2. Poll a group of college students to find out the following items:
   a. How well do they feel they are able to handle reading assignments in their courses?
   b. Have they ever taken a reading improvement course? If they have, what kind of course was it?
   c. Do they feel a need for improving their reading skills? If they do, which skills?
   d. Does their college offer a course designed to meet their needs?

e. Would they consider enrolling in a college reading improvement course a wise use of a course elective? Why, or why not?

f. Would they enroll in a non-credit reading improvement course if one were available? Why, or why not?

Share your results with your classmates.

3. Analyze three of the workbook/worktexts listed on pages 397–398. Share your analyses of the usefulness of these books with your classmates.

4. Compare two of the college-level reading tests listed on pages 407. How do they differ? For what purposes would each one be most useful?

5. Develop a project package for some area in which college students often need help. Share your project with your classmates. Be ready to defend the content.

Selected references

Ahrendt, Kenneth M. *Community College Reading Programs.* Newark, Del.: International Reading Association, 1975.

Bergman, Irwin B. "Integrating Reading Skills with Content in a Two Year College." *Journal of Reading,* 20, No. 4 (January 1977): 327–29.

Burgess, Barbara A. et al. "Effect on Academic Achievement of a Voluntary University Reading Program. *Journal of Reading* 17 (May 1976): 644–46.

Evans, Howard M. and Eugene E. DuBois. "Community/Junior College Remedial Programs-Reflections." *Journal of Reading* 16 (October 1972): 42.

Fiddler, Jerry B. "Contemplative Reading: A Neglected Dimension of Flexibility." *Journal of Reading* 16 (May 1973): 622–26.

International Reading Association Committee. *College Adult Reading Instruction.* Perspectives in Reading No. 1. Newark, Del.: International Reading Association, 1964.

Kazmierski, Paul R. "Training Faculty for Junior College Reading Programs." Topic Paper No. 24. Los Angeles: Eric/Clearinghouse for Junior Colleges, May 1971. Pp. 2–4.

Littrell, J. Harvey. "Reducing Phonic Disability in Junior College." *Journal of Reading* 20, No. 2 (November 1976): 150–52.

Mayfield, Craig K. "Establishing a Reading and Study Skills Course for Law Students." *Journal of Reading* 20, No. 4 (January 1977): 285–87.

Newman, Loretta. "Community College Reading Facilities." Topic Paper No. 21. Los Angeles: Eric/Clearinghouse for Junior Colleges, 1971. Pp. 1–9.

Peck, Richard E. and Roy Brinkley. "College Reading Services for the Marginal Entrant." *Journal of Reading* 14 (October 1970): 19.

Price, Umberto, and Kay Wolfe. "Teacher Preparation of the Junior College Reading Teacher." *Junior College Reading Programs.* Newark, Del.: International Reading Association, 1967. Pp. 1–7.

Roe, Betty D. and Elinor P. Ross. "Keeping the Student in College." *The Tennessee Teacher* 40 (May 1973): 22.

Ross, Elinor P. and Betty D. Roe. "Collegians Contract for Reading." *Journal of Reading* 17 (October 1973): 40–43.

Ross, Elinor and Betty Roe. "Survey of College Reading Improvement Programs in Tennessee." *The Tennessee Reading Teacher* 1 (Fall 1973): 22–24.

Shepherd, James F. "The Future of Noncredit College Reading Courses." *Journal of Reading* 20, No. 6 (March 1977): 493–97.

Staiger, Ralph C. "Initiating the College or Adult Reading Program." In *Research and Evaluation in College Reading.* Ninth Yearbook National Reading Conference, Clemson, S.C.: NRC, 1960. P. 121.

Turner, Caroline S. et al. "The Effect of a Developmental Program on University Grades." *Journal of Reading* 17 (April 1974): 531–37.

Yuthas, Ladessa. "Student Tutors in a College Remedial Program." *Journal of Reading* 14 (January 1971): 231–34.

Appendices

These Appendices contain materials that, hopefully, the reader will find to be useful. If only one source were cited, it should be *The Reading Materials Handbook*, by Allen Berger and Hugo Hartig, Oshkosh, Wisc.: Academic Press, 1969. This is a guide to materials and sources for the improvement of reading at the secondary, college, and adult levels. It includes sections on:

> Reading Improvement Texts and Workbooks
> Reading Evaluation Materials
> Reading Improvement Devices and Programmed Materials
> Reading Reference Materials
> Periodicals in Reading
> Conference Proceedings and Yearbooks
> Sourcebooks in Reading Education
> Reading Research Publications

Appendix A. Additional Materials for Teaching Reading in Secondary (and Post-Secondary) Schools
1. Reading Improvement Workbooks
2. Some Paperbacks for Reading Improvement
3. Laboratories and Programmed Materials
4. Films and Filmstrips
5. Records and Tapes

Appendix B. Additional Materials for Supplementary Reading In Secondary Schools
1. High Interest, Low Readability Materials (Series)
2. Magazines
3. Newspapers

Appendix C. Sources of Free/Inexpensive Teaching Materials
Appendix D. Reading/Study Skills Tests
Appendix E. Publisher's Addresses
Appendix F. Answers to "Self-Tests"

Additional Materials for Teaching Reading in Secondary (and   **Appendix A**
Post-Secondary) Schools

1. Reading Improvement Workbooks

Adams, W. Royce, *Developing Reading Versatility.* Holt, Rinehart and Winston, 1973.

Adams, W. Royce, *Reading Through Listening.* Dickenson, 1972.

Bamman, Nordberg, and Nordberg. *Free to Choose: A Guide to Efficient Reading.* Field Educational Publications, 1970.

Bieda and Woodward. *Realizing Reading Potential.* Holt, Rinehart and Winston, 1971.

Braam and Sheldon. *Developing Efficient Reading.* Oxford University Press, 1959.

Canavan and King. *Developing Reading Skills.* Allyn and Bacon, 1968.

Carman and Adams. *Study Skills: A Student's Guide for Survival.* John Wiley, 1972.

Carter and McGinnis. *Reading: A Key to Academic Success.* William C. Brown, 1964.

Casty, Alan. *The Act of Reading.* Prentice-Hall, 1962.

Caughran and Mountain. *Reading Skillbooks.* American Book Co., 1962.

Christ, Frank L. *Study Reading College Textbooks.* Science Research Associates, 1967.

Cosper, Russell, and Griffin. *Towards Better Reading.* Appleton-Century-Crofts, 1967.

Dallman and Sheridan. *Better Reading In College.* Ronald Press, 1954.

Diederick et al. *Vocabulary for College, A, B, C, D.* Harcourt, Brace and World, 1967.

Deighton, Lee. *Vocabulary Development.* Macmillan Co.

Edwards and Silvaroli. *Reading Improvement Program.* William C. Brown, 1967.

Ehrlick, Murphy, and Pace. *College Developmental Reading.* The Free Press, 1968.

Fisher, Joseph. *Reading to Understand Science.* McGraw-Hill, 1970.

Gainsburg, Joseph, et al. *Advance Skills in Reading.* Macmillan Co., 1964.

Gilbert, Doris W. *Study in Depth.* Prentice-Hall, 1966.

Gibert, Doris W. *The Turning Point in Reading.* Prentice-Hall, 1969.

Guiler and Coleman. *Reading for Meaning Series.* J. B. Lippincott, 1970.

Harnadek, Anita E. *Critical Reading Improvement.* McGraw-Hill, 1969.

Heilman, Arthur. *Improve Your Reading Ability.* Charles E. Merrill, 1976.

Herber, Harold. *Go.* Scholastic Book Services, 1975.

Herber, Harold. *Success with Words.* Scholastic Book Services, 1964.

Herr, Selma. *Effective Reading for Adults.* 3rd ed. Charles E. Merrill, 1969.

Hill, Walter. *Basic Reading Power.* Wadsworth, 1970.

Hill, Walter. *Point: A Reading System.* Wadsworth, 1970.

Hill and Eller. *Analytical Reading.* Wadsworth, 1970.

Jennings and Stevenson. *Meaning from Context: Reading for Word Study.* Allyn and Bacon, 1971.

Joffee, Irwin L. *Developing Outlining Skills.* Wadsworth, 1972.

Judson, Horace. *The Techniques of Reading.* 3rd ed. Harcourt Brace Jovano-vich, 1972.

Kai and Kersteins. *Study-Reading for College Courses.* Macmillan Co., 1968.

Karlin, Robert. *Reading for Achievement.* Holt, Rinehart and Winston, 1969.

Klein, Marion H. *Dynamics of Comprehension: How to Learn from a College Textbook.* New Century Press, 1970.

Krantz and Kimmelman. *Focus on Reading.* Allyn and Bacon, 1970.

Leedy, Paul D. *Improve Your Reading.* McGraw-Hill, 1956.

Leedy, Paul D. *A Key to Better Reading.* McGraw-Hill, 1956.

Levine, Harold. *Vocabulary for High School Students.* Amsco School Publication, 1967.

Liddle, William. *Reading for Concepts.* McGraw-Hill, 1970.

McDonald and Simmy. *The Art of Good Reading.* Bobbs-Merrill, 1963.

Maxwell, Martha. *Skimming and Scanning Improvement.* McGraw-Hill, 1969.

Milan, Deanne K. *Modern College Reading.* Charles Scribner, 1971.

Miller, Lyle. *Developing Reading Efficiency.* 3rd ed. Burgess, 1972.

Miller, Lyle. *Increasing Reading Efficiency.* 3rd ed. Holt, Rinehart and Winston, 1970.

Millman and Pauk. *How to Take Tests.* McGraw-Hill, 1969.

Niles, Olive. *Tactics in Reading.* Scott, Foresman, 1967.

Norman, Maxwell. *Successful Reading.* Holt, Rinehart and Winston, 1968.

Norman, Maxwell. *How to Read and Study for Success in College.* Holt, Rinehart and Winston, 1971.

Oakman, Barbara. *Countdown to Successful Reading.* Appleton-Century-Crofts, 1971.

Patty and Ruhl. *The Need to Read.* Van Nostrand Reinhold, 1968.

Pauk, Walter. *Six-Way Paragraphs.* Jamestown Press, 1976.

Picket, Thomas. *Guide to Efficient Reading.* Burgess, 1969.

Rauch and Weinstein. *Mastering Reading Skills.* American Book, 1968.

Raygor, Alton. *Reading for Significant Facts.* McGraw-Hill, 1969.

Raygor, Alton. *Reading for the Main Idea.* McGraw-Hill, 1969.

Raygor and Schick. *Reading at Efficient Rates.* McGraw-Hill, 1970.

Reiter, Irene M. *The Reading Line.* Polaski Co., 1971.

Robinson, Francis P. *Effective Reading.* Harper & Row, 1962.

Roe and Ross. *Developing Power in Reading.* Kendall/Hunt, 1976.

Schafer, Robert. *Success in Reading.* Silver Burdett, 1967.

Schumacher et al. *Design for Good Reading.* Harcourt, Brace and World, 1969.

Sheldon and Braam. *Reading Improvement for Men and Women in Industry.* Educators Publishing Service, 1969.

Slater. Lo. *Why, What, How to Read: Different Skills for Different Reading* Random House, 1971.

Smith, Donald E. *Learning to Learn.* Harcourt, Brace and World, 1961.

Smith, Nila. *Better Reader Series.* Prentice-Hall, 1968.

Smith, Nila B. *Faster Reading Made Easy.* Popular Library, 1963.

Smith, Nila B. *Read Faster and Get More from Your Reading.* Prentice-Hall, 1957.

Spache and Berg. *The Art of Efficient Reading,* 2nd ed. Macmillan Co., 1966.

Spargo, Giroux, and Giroux (Eds.). *Voices from the Bottom: College Reading. Skills.* Jamestown Publishers, 1972.

Van Zandt, Eleanor, ed. *Pattern for Reading.* Scholastic Magazines, 1970.

Wainwright, Gordon. *Towards Efficiency in Reading.* Cambridge University Press, 1968.

Weinberg. *Troubleshooters II* Houghton-Mifflin, 1975.

Witty, Paul. *Reading Improvement Texts.* Science Research Associates, 1968.

2. Some paperbacks for reading improvement

Ehrlich, Ida. *Instant Vocabulary.* New York: Washington Square Press, 1968.

Funk, Wilfred. *25 Steps to Word Power.* Greenwich, Conn.: Fawcett Publishing, 1962.

Funk, Wilfred. *Words of Power.* New York: Pocket Books, 1953.

Funk, Wilfred and Norman Lewis. *30 Days to a More Powerful Vocabulary.* New York: Washington Square Press, 1942.

Goodman, Roger B. and David Lewin Lewis. *New Ways to Greater Word Power.* Dell Publishing Co., 1959.

Huff, Darrell. *Score.* New York: Ballantine Books. 1961.

Lewis, Norman. *How to Become a Better Reader.* New York: MacFadden Books, 1951.

Lewis, Norman. *Word Power Made Easy.* New York: Pocket Books, 1949.

Maddox, Harry. *How to Study.* Greenwich, Conn.: Fawcett Publications, 1963.

Morris, William. *It's Easy to Increase Your Vocabulary.* Garden City, N.Y.: Doubleday & Co., 1957.

Nurnberg, Maxwell and Morris Rosenblum. *All About Words.* New York: Signet, 1966.

Nurnberg, Maxwell and Morris Rosenblum. *How to Build a Better Vocabulary.* New York: Popular Library, 1961.

Pauk, Walter. *Reading for Success in College.* Oshkosh, Wisc.: Academic Press, 1968.

3. Laboratories and programmed materials

Bracken, Dorothy et al. *Galaxy Program.* Scott, Foresman, 1961.

Brown, James. *Programmed Vocabulary.* Appleton-Century-Crofts, 1964.

Buchanan, Cynthia D. *Programmed Reading for Adults.* Webster Division/ McGraw-Hill, 1966.

Coronet. *Coronet Learning Programs.* Coronet Film, 1970.

Feinstein, George. *Programmed College Vocabulary.* Prentice-Hall, 1969.

Grolier. *The Reading Attainment System.* Grolier Educational Corporation, 1970.

The Literature Sampler. Learning Materials, 1970.

Markle, Susan. *Words.* Science Research Associates, 1963.

Parker, Don. *Reading for Understanding.* Science Research Associates, 1970.

Parker, Don. *SRA Reading Laboratories.* Science Research Associates, 1960.

Parker, Don. *Vocabulab III.* Science Research Associates, 1970.

Staff of the Reading Laboratory. *Skill File.* The Reading Laboratory, 1966.

Stanton, Thomas. *Programmed Study Techniques.* American Guidance Service, 1964.

Steps to Better Reading. Harcourt, Brace and World 1970.

Taylor, Stanford. *EDL's Learning 100 and EDL Word Clues.* Educational Developmental Laboratories, 1969.

4. Films and filmstrips

Advanced Phrase Reading (set of six silent films). Ad-Ed Films.
Better Reading (Film, 13 min.). Encyclopaedia Britannica Films, Inc.
Build Your Vocabulary (Film, 14 min.). Coronet Films.
Cut Your Reading Time (Film, 15 min.). The Reading Laboratory.
Developing Effective Reading Study Skills (Sound Filmstrip). Bailey Films, Inc.
Developing Reading Maturity (Set of five films, 11 min. each). Coronet Films.
Harvard University College Reading Films (Set of 17 films). Harvard University
    Press.
How Effective is Your Reading? (Film, 11 min.). Coronet Films.
How to Read a Book (Film, 11 min.). Coronet Films.
How to Read Literature (Set of six filmstrips). Educational Audio-Visual Inc.
How Well Do You Read? (Film). Purdue University Audio-Visual Center.
Intermediate Phrase Reading (Set of six silent films). Av-Ed Films.
The Iowa Reading Films—High School Series (Set of 15 films). University of
    Iowa.
The Iowa Reading Films—College Series (Set of films). University of Iowa.
Learning to Study (Film, 14 min.). Encyclopaedia Britannica Films, Inc.
The Purdue Reading Films—College Level (Set of films). Purdue University
    Audio-Visual Center.
The Purdue Reading Films—High School Series (Set of films). Purdue Uni-
    versity Audio-Visual Center.
The Purdue Reading Films—Junior High School Series (Set of films). Purdue
    University Audio-Visual Center.
Reading Effectively (Film, 10 min.). University of Iowa, Bureau of Audio-
    Visual Instruction.
Reading Improvement Series (Set of five films, 11 min. each). Coronet Films.
Reading with a Purpose (Film, 11 min.). Coronet Films.
Study for Success (Set of eleven filmstrips). Eye Gate House, Inc.

5. Records and tapes

EDL Listen and Read Program (Set of 30 recordings). Educational Develop-
    ment Laboratories, Inc.
Imperial Junior High Aural Reading Lab (Set of 39 tapes). Imperial Produc-
    tions, Inc.
Reading Incentive Language Program Audio-Visual Kits. Bowmar.
Techniques in Reading Comprehension (Record). Educational Audio-Visual
    Inc.
The Understanding and Appreciation of the Novel (Record). Educational
    Audio-Visual Inc.
Vocabulary Improvement Series (Set of five records). National Council of
    Teachers of English.

Appendix B   *Additional Materials for Supplementary Reading in Secondary Schools*

1. High interest, low readability materials (series)

Addison Wesley: *Reading Development Series*
Allyn and Bacon: *Breakthrough*

American Guidance Service: *Coping With Series*
Bantam Books: *Bantam Perspective Series*
Barnell Loft: *Incredible Series*
Benefic Press: *Mystery Adventure Series; Challenger Books; Racing Wheels Readers; Space Science Fiction Series; Sports Mystery Series; Target Today.*
Berkeley Books: *Tempo Books*
Bowman: *Reading Incentive Series; Monster Books*
Children's Press: *". . . and Hereby Hangs the Tale" Series*
Davo: *Awareness Pictorial Books*
Dell, Laurel Leaf Library: *Mayflower Books; Yearling Books*
Doubleday and Co.: *Double Signal Books*
Ed-U Press: *Comics on Drugs, Sex, Venereal Disease and Birth Control*
Fearon: *Pacemaker Series*
Field Educational Publications: *Americans All; Checkered Flag Series; Deep Sea Adventure Series; Happenings; Kaleidoscope; Morgan Bay Mysteries; Reading Motivated Series*
Follett: *Interesting Reading Series*
Garrard: *Pleasure Reading Books, Target Books*
Globe Book Company: *American Folklore; Four Complete Teen-Age Novels; Insight and Outlook; and other titles*
Harper & Row: *American Adventure Series; Myths and Tales of Many Lands; Paperback Classics; Scope Reading*
Harr-Wagner: *Reading Motivated Series*
D.C. Heath: *Teen Age Tales*
Hertzberg New Method; *General Collection of Interesting Topics*
Holt, Rinehart and Winston: *Impact Series*
Houghton Mifflin: *Directions: Interact; New Riverside Literature Series; They Helped Make America*
Learning Research Associates: *Literature Sampler, Junior Edition*
Leswing Communications, Inc.: *Your Own Thing Series*
McGraw-Hill: *"What Job For Me?" Series*
Charles Merrill: *Mainstream Books*
National Association for the Deaf: *Classics for Low Level Readers*
New Dimensions in Education: *Name of the Game*
Noble and Noble: *Crossroads Series, Springboards, Falcon Classroom Library A and B*
Penguin Books: *Puffin Books*
Pyramid Publications: *Hi-Lo Books*
Rand McNally: *Voices*
Random House/Singer: *Alfred Hitchcock Mysteries; Aware; Challenger Books; Gateways; Green Interest Center; Blue Interest Center; Red Interest Center; Landmark Books; Landmark Giants; Pro Basketball Library; Punt, Pass and Kick*
Scholastic Book Services: *Action Libraries; Arrow Books; Biography; Black Literature Program; Contact; Dogs, Horses, Wildlife; Especially for Boys; Especially for Girls; Ethnic Reading; Fantasy; Favorites Old and New; Fun and Laughter; History; History Fiction; Making and Doing; Modern Stories; Mystery; Myths and Legends; People of Other Lands; Pleasure Reading Libraries I and II; Reluctant Reader Libraries; Science; Science and Fiction; Scope Play Series; Tab Books*

Science Research Associates: *An American Album; Countries and Cultures Kit; New Rochester Occupational Reading Series; Pilot Libraries IIb, IIc, IIIb; We Are Black; Manpower and Natural Resources*

Scott, Foresman: *Something Else; Action Reading Kits, Adapted Classics*

Silver Burdett: *Call Them Heroes*

Washington Square Press: *Archway Paperbacks*

Webster, *Everyreader Series; Reading for Concepts; Reading Incentive Series*

Xerox: *The Way It Was, Pilot Books*

2. Magazines

Action. Scholastic Magazines and Book Services, 50 West 44th Street, New York, N.Y. 10036

American Girl. Girl Scouts of America, 830 Third Av., New York, N.Y. 10022

Boy's Life. Boy Scouts of America, New Brunswick, N.J. 08901

Calling All Girls. Parent's Magazine Publications, Inc. Bergenfield, N.J. 07621

Cricket. Open Court Publishing Co., 1058 Eighth St., LaSalle, Ill. 61301

Current Events. American Education Publications, Education Center, Columbus, Ohio 43216

Current Science. American Education Publications, Education Center, Columbus, Ohio 43216

School Bulletin. School Service, National Geographic Society, Washington, D.C. 20036

Nature and Science. The Natural History Press, Garden City, N.Y. 11530.

Newsweek. Newsweek, Inc., 44 Madison Av., New York N.Y. 10022

Our Times. American Education Publications, Education Center, Columbus, Ohio 43216

Read. American Education Publications, Education Center, Columbus, Ohio, 43216

Reader's Digest. Reader's Digest Services, Pleasantville, N.Y. 10570

Scope. Scholastic Book Services, 904 Sylvan Av., Englewood Cliffs, N.J. 07632

Seventeen. 320 Park Ave., New York, N.Y. 10022

Sport. Sport Magazine, P.O. Box 5705, Whitestone, N.Y. 11357

Time. Time-Life, Inc., Time and Life Building, Rockefeller Center, New York, N.Y. 10001

Urban World. American Education Publications, Education Center, Columbus, Ohio 43216

World Traveler. 1537 35th St., N.W. Washington, D.C. 20007

3. Newspapers

Junior Review. Civic Education Services Inc., 1733 K St., Washington, D.C. 20036

Know Your World. American Education Publications, Education Center, Columbus, Ohio 43216 (Reading Level for Grades 2-3. Interest Level for Grades 5-12)

News for You. A and B Editions. Laubach Literary, Inc., Syracuse, N.Y. 13210 (Edition A: Reading Level for Grades 2-3. Interest Level for Grade 7-Adult. Edition B: Reading Level for Grades 3-4. Interest Level for Grade 7-Adult)

New York, New York. Random House, Inc., 201 E. 50th St., New York, N.Y. 10022 (Reading Level for Grades K-8. Interest Level for Grades 5-12)

The New York Times. Large Type Weekly. The New York Times Co., Times Square, New York, N.Y. 10036 (Reading Level for Adults. Interest Level for Adults)

You and Your World. American Education Publications, Education Center, Columbus, Ohio 43216 (Reading Level for Grades 3-5. Interest Level for Grades 9-12)

Sources of Free and Inexpensive Teaching Materials   **Appendix C**

Aubrey, Ruth H., ed. *Selected Free Materials for Classroom Teachers.* Palo Alto, Calif.: Fearon Publishers, 1965. Order from: Fearon Publishers, Inc., 2165 Park Blvd., Palo Alto, Calif. 94306.

Educational Service Bureau of Dow Jones and Co., Inc. *List of Materials Available to Secondary School Instructors.* Princeton, N.J.: Dow Jones & Co., 1970–71. Order from: B. A. Schuler, Educational Service Bureau, Dow Jones and Co., Inc., Princeton, N.J. 08540.

Horkheimer, Mary Foley and John W. Deffor, eds. *Educators Guide to Free Films,* 30th ed. Randolph, Wisc.: Educators Progress Service, 1970. Order from: Educators Progress Service, Inc., Randolph, Wisc. 53956

Horkheimer, Mary Foley and John W. Deffor. *Educators Guide to Free Filmstrips,* 22nd annual ed. Randolph, Wisc.: Educators Progress Service, 1970. Order from: Educators Progress Service, Inc., Randolph, Wisc. 53956.

Jackson, Joe L., ed. *Free and Inexpensive Learning Materials,* 15th biennial ed. Nashville, Tenn.: Division of Surveys and Field Services, George Peabody College for Teachers, 1970. Order from: George Peabody College for Teachers, Division of Surveys and Field Services, Nashville, Tenn.

Marshall, Jane N., ed. *Free and Inexpensive Pictures, Pamphlets and Packets for Air/Space Age Education,* 6th ed. Washington, D.C.: National Aerospace Education Council, 1966. Order from: National Aerospace Education Council, 806 15th St., N.W., Washington, D.C. 20005.

O'Hara, Frederic J., ed. *Over 2,000 Free Publications, Yours for the Asking.* New York: New American Library, 1968. (A Signet Reference Book) Order from: New American Library, Inc., P.O. Box 2310, Grand Central Station. New York, N.Y. 10017. (Note: This compilation places substantial reliance upon bulletins, pamphlets and documents produced by the U.S. Government Printing Office. Rather than being strictly free as one would infer from the title, most of them have a cost of 5 to 25 cents.)

Salisbury, Gordon. *Catalog of Free Teaching Materials.* Riverside, Calif.: Rubidoux Printing Co., 1970. Order from: Catalog of Free Teaching Materials, P.O. Box 1075, Ventura, Calif. 93001.

Sources of Free Teaching Aids. Order from: Bruce Miller Publications, Box 369, Riverside, Calif. 92502.

Sources of Teaching Materials. Order from: Catherine Williams, Ohio University Press, Columbus, Ohio 43210.

Wagner, Guy and Dorlan Mork. *Free Learning Materials for Classroom Use.* (An annotated list of sources with suggestions for obtaining, evaluating, classifying and using.) Cedar Falls, Iowa: Extension Service, State College of Iowa, 1967. Order from: The Extension Service, State College of Iowa, Cedar Falls, Iowa.

Wittich, Walter A. and Raymond H. Suttles, eds. *Educators Guide to Free Tapes, Scripts, Transcriptions*. Randolph, Wisc.: Educators Progress Service, 1970. Order from: Educators Progress Service, Randolph, Wisc. 53956.

Other supplemental materials for the classroom are available from such sources as the following:

California Redwood Association, 617 Montgomery St., San Francisco, Calif. 94111.

Forest Service, U.S. Department of Agriculture, Washington, D.C. 20250.

Bureau of Mines, U.S. Department of the Interior, 4800 Forbes Ave., Pittsburgh, Pa. 15213.

Bureau of Reclamation, U.S. Department of the Interior, Washington, D.C. 20240.

Pendleton Woolen Mills, Home Economics Department, 218 S.W. Jefferson St., Portland, Ore. 97201.

U.S. Atomic Energy Commission, Technical Information, Oak Ridge, Tenn. 37830

John Hancock Mutual Life Ins. Co., 200 Berkeley St., Boston, Mass. 02117

Fort Ticonderoga Education Services, Attention: Mrs. Thomas Lape, Box 390 Ticonderoga, N.Y. 12883

Tennessee Valley Authority, Information Office, Knoxville, Tenn. 37902

Japan National Tourist Organization, 333 N. Michigan Av., Chicago, Ill. 60601

Appendix D   *Reading/Study Skills Tests*

Survey

1. *Burnett Reading Series: Survey Test*. N.Y.: Scholastic Testing Service, 1970. Grades 7–13. Tests vocabulary, comprehension, rate and accuracy.
2. *California Achievement Tests: Reading*. Monterey, Calif.: California Test Bureau, McGraw-Hill, 1970. Grades 6–12. Tests vocabulary, study skills, comprehension in different types of materials.
3. *Comprehensive Tests of Basic Skills: Reading*. Monterey, Calif.: California Test Bureau, McGraw-Hill, 1969. Grades 6–12. Tests vocabulary, comprehension, study skills.
4. *Cooperative English Tests: Reading Section*. Princeton, N.J.: Educational Testing Service, 1960. Grades 9–14. Tests vocabulary, comprehension, speed of comprehension.
5. *Davis Reading Test*. N.Y.: Psychological Corporation, 1961. Grades 8–13. Tests level and speed of comprehension.
6. *Durrell Listening-Reading Series*. N.Y.: Harcourt Brace Jovanovich, 1969–70. Grades 1–9. Tests vocabulary listening and reading, paragraph listening and reading.
7. *Gates-MacGinitie Reading Tests*. Survey E&F. N.Y.: Teachers College Press, Columbia University, 1970. Grades 7–12. Tests speed and accuracy, vocabulary, comprehension.

8. *Iowa Silent Reading Tests.* N.Y.: Harcourt Brace Jovanovich, 1973. Grades 6–12. Tests vocabulary, comprehension, locating information, skimming and scanning, reading efficiency.

9. *Metropolitan Achievement Tests: Reading.* Advanced, N.Y.: Harcourt Brace Jovanovich, 1970. Grades 7–9. Tests vocabulary, comprehension.

10. *Nelson-Denny Reading Test.* Hopewell, N.J.: Houghton-Mifflin, 1973. Grades 9–16. Tests vocabulary, comprehension, rate.

11. *Reading Test: McGraw-Hill Basic Skills System.* N.Y.: McGraw-Hill, 1970. Grades 1–14. Tests rate, flexibility, retention, skimming and scanning, comprehension.

12. *Sequential Tests of Educational Progress. (STEP), Series II.* Princeton, N.J.: Educational Testing Service, 1969. Grades 4–14. Tests comprehension.

13. *SRA, Achievement Series.* Multilevel Edition. Chicago: Science Research Associates, 1963. Grades 1–9. Tests comprehension, vocabulary, work-study skills (references and charts).

14. *Stanford Achievement Tests: Advanced Paragraph Meaning: High School Reading.* N.Y.: Harcourt Brace Jovanovich, 1966. Grades 7–12. Tests comprehension.

15. *Traxler High School Reading Test—Revised.* Indianapolis: Bobbs-Merrill, 1967. Grades 9–12. Tests comprehension, rate.

16. *Traxler Silent Reading Test.* Indianapolis: Bobbs-Merrill, 1969. Grades 7–10. Tests rate, vocabulary, comprehension.

Diagnostic Tests

1. *Botel Reading Inventory.* Chicago: Follett Educational Corporation, 1970. Grades 1–12. Tests (Group test except for word recognition) phonics, word opposites, reading and listening.

2. *Classroom Reading Inventory.* Dubuque, Iowa: William C. Brown, 1969. Grades 2–8. Tests (Individual test except for spelling) word recognition, independent, instructional and frustration reading levels; hearing capacity level.

3. *Diagnostic Reading Tests.* Mountain Home, N.C.: Committee on Diagnostic Reading Tests, 1963. Grades 7–13. Tests vocabulary, comprehension (silent and auditory), rate, word attack.

4. *Durrell Analysis of Reading Difficulty.* N.Y.: Harcourt Brace Jovanovich, 1955. Grades 1–6. Tests oral and silent reading; listening; word recognition and analysis; naming, identifying and matching letters; visual memory of words; sounds of words and letters; spelling; handwriting.

5. *Dvorak-Van Wagenen Diagnostic Examination of Silent Reading Abilities.* Minneapolis: Van Wagenen Psychological Educational Laboratories, 1939–54. Grades 4–16. Tests rate, perception of relations, vocabulary, information, details, central thought, inferences, interpretation, reading for ideas.

6. *Gates-McKillop Reading Diagnostic Tests.* N.Y.: Teachers College Press, Columbia University, 1962. Grades 1–8. Tests oral reading, word recognition, phrase recognition, syllabication, letter names and sounds, visual and auditory blending, spelling (28 score in all).

7. *Pupil Placement Tests.* Hopewell, N.J.: Houghton Mifflin Company, 1970. Grades 1–9. Tests word recognition, oral sight reading, timed silent reading, listening subtests. To determine independent, instructional frustration and potential reading levels.

8. *Reading Miscue Inventory.* N.Y.: The Macmillan Company, 1972. Grades (all levels). Tests psycholinguistically; analyzes why miscues are made as reader extracts meaning; qualitative as well as quantitative analysis.

9. *Roswell-Chall Diagnostic Reading Test of Word Analysis Skills.* N.Y.: Essay Press, 1959. Grades 2–6. Tests consonant and vowel sounds and combination, syllabication.

10. *Silent Reading Diagnostic Tests.* Chicago: Lyons and Carnahan, 1970. Grades 2–6. Tests words in isolation and in context, visual structural analysis, syllabication, word synthesis, beginning and ending sounds, vowel and consonant sounds.

11. *Spache Diagnostic Reading Scales.* Monterey, Calif.: California Test Bureau/McGraw-Hill, 1963. Grades 1–8 (retarded readers). Tests word recognition, oral and silent reading, phonics.

12. *Stanford Diagnostic Reading Test.* N.Y.: Harcourt Brace Jovanovich, 1973. Grades 4.5–8.5. Tests comprehension (literal and inferential) vocabulary, syllabication, auditory skills, phonic analysis, rate.

13. *Standard Reading Inventory,* Klamath Falls, Oregon: Klamath Printing Company, 1966. Grades 1–7. Tests recognition vocabulary, oral reading accuracy, oral and silent reading comprehension and speed, listening.

14. *Sucher-Alfred Reading Placement Inventory.* Provo, Utah: Brigham Young University Press, 1971. Grades 1–9. Tests word recognition and paragraph comprehension, screening for placement.

Oral

1. *Gilmore Oral Reading Test.* N.Y.: Harcourt Brace Jovanovich, 1968. Grades 1–8. Tests accuracy, comprehension, rate of oral reading.

2. *Gray Oral Reading Test.* Indianapolis: Bobbs-Merrill, 1963. Grades 1–6. Tests oral reading.

Study skills

1. *Iowa Every-Pupil Tests of Basic Skills.* Test B. Hopewell, N.J.: Houghton-Mifflin, 1947. Grades 3–9. Tests (group test) map reading, use of references, use of index, use of dictionary, graphing.

2. *Iowa Tests of Educational Development.* Chicago: Science Research Associates, 1942–61. Test 5: Ability to interpret reading materials in the social studies. Test 6: Ability to interpret reading materials in the natural sciences. Test 7: Ability to interpret reading materials in literature. Test 9: Use of source of information.

Other tests

1. *ANPA Foundation Newspaper Test.* Cooperative Tests and Services, 1969. Grades 7–16. Tests newspaper reading ability.

2. *California Phonics Survey.* Monterey, Calif.: California Test Bureau/McGraw-Hill, 1963. Grades 7–16. Tests (group test) vowel and consonant

confusions, reversals, configuration, endings, negatives-opposites-sight words, rigidity.

3. *Reader Rater with Self-Scoring Profile*. Better Reading Program, 1965. Grades 10–12. Tests (individual test) speed; comprehension; reading habits; reading for details, inferences and main ideas; adjusting speed; summarizing, skimming, recall of information; speeded and unspeeded vocabulary.

4. *Reader's Inventory*. N.Y.: Educational Development Laboratories, 1963. Grades 9–16. Tests (group Test) reading interests, attitudes, habits, visual conditions, background, expectation in reading.

5. *Reading Versatility Test*. N.Y.: Educational Developmental Laboratories, 1968. Grades 5–16. Tests (group test) rate, comprehension, skimming, scanning.

6. *Survey of Study Habits and Attitudes*. N.Y.: Psychological Corporation, 1967. Grades 7–14. Tests (group test) efficiency, promptness, attitudes towards teachers, co-educational objectives.

7. *Tests of General Educational Development*. Washington, D.C.: American Council on Education, 1944–70. Grades 9–16. Test 2: Interpretation of reading materials in the natural sciences. Test 3: Interpretation of reading materials in the social studies. Test 4: Interpretation of literary materials. (Used for candidates for high school equivalency certificates. Special editions for the blind and partially sighted.)

8. *Watson-Glaser Critical Thinking Appraisal*. N.Y.: Harcourt Brace Jovanovich, 1964. Grades 9–16+. Tests (group test) inference, recognition of assumptions, deductions, interpretation, evaluation of arguments.

Publisher's Addresses   **Appendix E**

Abelard-Schuman, Ltd. *See* Intext Press

Abingdon Press, 201 Eighth Avenue, Nashville, Tenn. 37203

Academic Press, Inc., subsidiary of Harcourt Brace Jovanovich, Inc., 757 Third Avenue, New York, N.Y. 10003

Addison-Wesley Publishing Co., 2725 Sand Hill Road, Menlo Park, Calif. 94025

Allyn and Bacon, Inc., Rockleigh Industrial Park, Rockleigh, N.J. 07647

American Book Co., 450 West 33rd Street, New York, N.Y. 10001

American Council on Education, 1 Dupont Circle, Washington, D.C. 20036

American Education Publishers, Inc., Education Center, Columbus, Ohio 43216

American Guidance Service, Inc., Publishers Bldg., Circle Pine, Minn. 55014

American Library Association, 50 East Huron Street, Chicago, Ill. 60611

American School Publication (AMSCO), 315 Hudson Street, New York, N.Y. 10013

Ann Arbor Publishers, 611 Church Street, Ann Arbor, Mich. 48104

Appleton-Century-Crofts. *See* Meredith Corp.

Association for Childhood Education International, 3615 Wisconsin Avenue, N.W., Washington, D.C. 20016

Audio-Visual Research Co., 1317 Eighth Street, S.E., Waseca, Minn. 56093

Av-Ed Films, 7934 Santa Monica Boulevard, Hollywood, Calif. 90046

Avon Books, 959 Eighth Avenue, New York, N.Y. 10019

Bailey Films, Inc., 6509 DeLongpre Avenue, Hollywood, Calif. 90028

Baldridge Reading Instruction Materials, Inc., Box 439, Greenwich, Conn. 06830

Bantam Books, 666 Fifth Avenue, New York, N.Y. 10019

Barnell Loft, Ltd., 958 Church Street, Baldwin, N.Y. 11510

Clarence L. Barnhart, Inc., Box 250, Bronxville, N.Y. 10708

Basic Books, Inc., 404 Park Avenue South, New York, N.Y. 10016

Beckley-Cardy Co. *See* Benefic Press

Behavioral Research Laboratories, Box 577, Palo Alto, Calif. 94302

Bell and Howell Co., Audio Visual Products Division, 7100 McCormick Road, Chicago, Ill. 60645

Benefic Press, 10300 West Roosevelt Road, Westchester, Ill. 60153

Berkley Publishing Corp. *See* G. P. Putnam's

Better Reading Program, Inc., 230 East Ohio Street, Chicago, Ill. 60611

Bobbs-Merrill Co., 4300 West 62nd Street, Indianapolis, Ind. 46268

Book Lab Inc., 1449 37th Street Brooklyn N. Y. 11218

Borg-Warner Educational Systems, 7450 North Natchez Avenue, Niles, Ill. 60648

R. R. Bowker Co., 1180 Avenue of the Americas, New York, N.Y. 10036

Bowmar Publishing Co., 622 Rodier Drive, Glendale, Calif. 91201

Milton Bradley Co., Springfield, Mass. 01101

Brigham Young University Press, 205 University Press Building, Provo, Utah 84602

Wm. C. Brown Co., 2460 Kerper Boulevard, Dubuque, Iowa 52003

Brown University Press, 129 Waterman Street, Providence, R.I. 02912

Burgess Publishing Co., 7108 Ohms Lane, Minneapolis, Minn. 55435

California Test Bureau/McGraw-Hill, Del Monte Research Park, Monterey, Calif. 93940

Cambridge Book Co. Inc. (Division of N.Y. Times Media Co.), 488 Madison Avenue, New York, N.Y. 10022

Cambridge University Press, 32 East 57th Street, New York, N.Y. 10022

Career Institute, 555 East Lange Street, Mundelein, Ill. 60060

Cenco Educational Aids, 2600 South Kostner Avenue, Chicago, Ill. 60623

Center for Applied Linguistics, 1611 North Kent Street, Arlington, Va. 22209

Center for Applied Research in Education, Inc., 521 Fifth Avenue, New York, N.Y. 10017

Chandler Publishing Co., 124 Spear Street, San Francisco, Calif. 94105

Childcraft Education Corp., 150 East 58th Street, New York, N.Y. 10022

Chilton Book Co., Chilton Way, Radnor, Penn. 19089

Citation Press, 50 West 44th Street, New York, N.Y. 10036

College Skills Center, 101. West 31st Street, New York, N.Y. 10001

Committee on Diagnostic Reading Tests, Mountain Home, N.C. 28758

Communicad, Box 541, Wilton, Conn. 06897

Consulting Psychologists Press, 577 College Avenue, Palo Alto, Calif. 94306

Continental Press, Inc., 520 East Bainbridge Street, Elizabethtown, Penn. 17022

Coronet Instructional Media, 65 East South Water Street, Chicago, Ill. 60601

Coward-McCann and Geoghegan, 200 Madison Avenue, New York, N.Y. 10016

Craig Corporation, 921 West Artesia Boulevard, Compton, Calif. 90020

Croft Educational Services, 100 Garfield Avenue, New London, Conn. 06320

Thomas Y. Crowell, 201 Park Avenue South, New York, N.Y. 10003

Curriculum Associates, 94 Bridge Street, Chapel Hill Park, Newton, Mass. 02158

Curtis Publishing Co., Independence Square, Philadelphia, Pa. 19105

Davco Publishers, 5425 Fargo, Skokie, Ill. 60076

John Day Co. *See* Intext Press

Delacorte Press. *See* Dial Press

Dell Publishing Co., 245 East 47th Street, New York, N.Y. 10017

Developmental Learning Materials, 7440 Natchez Avenue, Niles, Ill. 60648

Dexter and Westbrook, Ltd., 958 Church Street, Baldwin, N.Y. 11510

Dial/Delacorte Press, 245 East 47th Street, New York, N.Y. 10017

Dickenson Publishing Co., 16250 Venture Blvd., Encino, Calif. 91436

Docent Corporation, 430 Manville Road, Pleasantville, N.Y. 10570

Dodd, Mead and Co., Inc., 79 Madison Avenue, New York, N.Y. 10016

Doubleday and Co., Inc., 277 Park Avenue, New York, N.Y. 10017

Dreier Educational Systems, Inc., 320 Raritan Avenue, Highland Park, N.J. 08904

E. P. Dutton and Co., 201 Park Avenue South, New York, N.Y. 10003

The Economy Co., Box 25308, 1901 West Walnut Street, Oklahoma City, Okla. 73125

Educational Aids, 845 Wisteria Drive, Fremont, Calif. 94538

Educational Audio-Visual, Inc., 29 Marble Avenue, Pleasantville, N.Y. 10570

Educational Developmental Laboratories, Inc., a Division of McGraw-Hill, 1221 Avenue of the Americas, New York, N.Y. 10020

Educational and Industrial Testing Service, Box 7234, San Diego, Calif. 92107

Educational Progress, P.O Box 45663, Tulsa, Okla. 74145

Educational Service, Inc., Box 219, Stevensville, Mich. 49127

Educational Teaching Aids, 159 West Kinzie Street, Chicago, Ill. 60610

Educational Testing Service, Princeton, N.J. 08540

Educators Publishing Service, 75 Moulton Street, Cambridge, Mass. 02138

Ed-U Press, (Educational Press Association of America), Glassboro State College, Glassboro, New Jersey 08028

Encyclopaedia Britannica Educational Corp., 425 North Michigan Avenue, Chicago, Ill. 60611

ERIC Clearinghouse on Reading and Communications Skills, 11 Kenyon Road, Urbana, Ill. 61801

ERIC Clearinghouse on Tests, Educational Testing Service, Princeton, N.J. 08540

Essay Press, Box 5, Planetarium Station, New York, N.Y. 10024

Eye Gate House, Inc., 146–01 Archer Avenue, Jamaica, N.Y. 11435

Exposition Press, Inc., 50 Jericho Turnpike, Jericho, N.Y. 11753

Fearon Publishers, 6 Davis Drive, Belmont, Calif. 94002

Field Educational Publications, Inc., 2400 Hanover Street, Palo Alto, Calif. 94304

Field Enterprises Educational Corp., Merchandise Mart Plaza, Chicago, Ill. 60654

Follett Educational Corp., 1010 West Washington Boulevard, Chicago, Ill. 60607

Four Winds Press, a Division of Scholastic Magazine, 50 West 44 Street, New York, N.Y. 10035

Free Press. *See* Macmillan Publishing Co.

Funk and Wagnalls, Inc., 53 East 77th Street, New York, N.Y. 10021

Gable Academies, 770 Miller Road, Miami, Fla. 33155

Garrard Publishing Co., 1607 North Market Street, Champaign, Ill. 61820

Ginn and Co., a Division of Xerox, 191 Spring Street, Lexington, Mass. 02173

General Learning Corp., 250 James Street, Morristown, N.J. 07960

George Peabody College for Teachers, Nashville, Tenn. 37203

Globe Book Co., 175 Fifth Avenue, New York, N.Y. 10010

Golden Gate Junior Books, a Division of Children's Press, 8344 Melrose Avenue, Los Angeles, Calif. 90009

Golden Press. See Western Publishing Co.

Grolier Educational Corp., 845 Third Avenue, New York, N.Y. 10022

Grossett and Dunlap, 51 Madison Avenue, New York, N.Y. 10010

Grune and Stratton, Inc., 381 Park Avenue South, New York, N.Y. 10016

Gryphon Press, 220 Montgomery Street, Highland Park, N.J. 08904

E. M. Hale and Co., 1201 South Hastings Way, Eau Claire, Wis. 54701

Hammond, Inc., 515 Valley Street, Maplewood, N.J. 07040

Harcourt Brace Jovanovich, 757 Third Avenue, New York, N.Y. 10017

Harper and Row, Inc., 10 East 53rd Street, New York, N.Y. 10022

Harr-Wagner. See Field Educational Publications

Harvard University Press, 79 Garden Street, Cambridge, Mass. 02138

Harvey House, Inc., 5 South Buckout Street, Irvington-on-Hudson, N.Y. 10533

Hastings House, Inc., 10 East 40 Street, New York, N.Y. 10016

D. C. Heath & Co., 125 Spring Street, Lexington, Mass. 02173

Hoffman Information Systems, 4423 Arden Drive, El Monte, Calif. 91734

Holiday House, Inc., 18 East 56th Street, New York, N.Y. 10022

Holt, Rinehart and Winston, Inc., 383 Madison Avenue, New York, N.Y. 10017

The Horn Book, Inc., 585 Boylston Street, Boston, Mass. 02116

Houghton Mifflin Co., Pennington-Hopewell Road, Hopewell, N.J. 08525

Imperial International Learning Corp., Box 548, Kankakee, Ill. 60901

Initial Teaching Alphabet Publications, 6 East Third Street, New York, N.Y. 10017

Instructional Communications Technology, Inc., Huntington, N.Y. 11743

Instructional Objectives Exchange, Box 24095, Los Angeles, Calif. 90024

The Instructo Corp., Cedar Hollow & Matthews Road, Paoli, Pa. 19301

International Reading Association, 800 Barksdale Road, Newark, Del. 19711

Intext Press, 257 Park Avenue South, New York, N.Y. 10010

Jamestown Publishers, Box 6743, Providence, R.I. 02904

John Hopkins Press, Baltimore, Md. 21218

Charles A. Jones Publishing Co., a Division of Wadsworth Publishing Co., Inc., 4 Village Green, Worthington, Ohio 43085

Jones-Kenilworth Co., 8801 Ambassador Drive, Dallas, Texas 75247

Judy Publishing Co., Box 5270, Main Post Office, Chicago, Ill. 60680

Kendall/Hunt Publishing Co., 2460 Kerper Blvd., Dubuque, Iowa 52001

Kenworthy Educational Service, Inc., Box 3031, 138 Allen Street, Buffalo, N.Y. 14205

Keystone View Co., 2212 East 12th Street, Davenport, Iowa 52803

Kinsbury. See Remedial Education Press

Klamath Printing Co., 320 Lowell Street, Klamath Falls, Or. 97601

Alfred A. Knopf, a subsidiary of Random House, Inc., 201 East 50th Street, New York, N.Y. 10022

Laidlaw Bros., a Division of Doubleday and Co., 30 Chatham Road, Summit, N.J. 09701

Language Research Associates, 175 East Delaware Place, Chicago, Ill. 60611

Learn, Inc., 21 East Euclid Avenue, Haddonfield, N.J. 08033

Learning Materials, Inc. 100 East Ohio St., Chicago, Ill. 60611

Learning Research Associates, 1501 Broadway, New York, N.Y. 10036

Learning Through Seeing, Inc., Box 268, LTS Building, Sunland, Calif. 91040

Lerner Publication Co., 241 First Avenue North, Minneapolis, Minn. 55401

Leswing Communications, Inc., 750 Adrian Way, San Rafael, Calif. 94907

J. B. Lippincott Co., East Washington Square, Philadelphia, Pa. 19105

Little, Brown, and Co., 34 Beacon Street, Boston, Mass. 02106

Love Publishing Co., 6635 East Villanova Place, Denver, Colo. 80222

Lothrop, Lee and Shepard Co., Inc., 105 Madison Avenue, New York, N.Y. 10016

The Macmillan Publishing Co., 866 Third Avenue, New York N.Y. 10022

Macrae Smith Co., 225 South 15th Street, Philadelphia, Pa. 19102

Maico Hearing Instruments, 7375 Bush Lake Road, Minneapolis, Minn. 55435

McCormick-Mathers Publishing Co., 450 West 33rd Street, New York, N.Y. 10001

McGraw-Hill Book Co., 1221 Avenue of the Americas, New York, N.Y. 10020

David McKay Co., Inc., 750 Third Avenue, New York, N.Y. 10017

Melmont Publishers, 1224 West Van Buren, Chicago, Ill. 60607

Meredith Corp., 440 Park Avenue South, New York, N.Y. 10016

Charles E. Merrill Publishing Co., 1300 Alum Creek Drive, Columbus, Ohio 43216

Julian Messner, Inc., 1 West 39th Street, New York, N.Y. 10036

Michigan State University Press, Box 550, East Lansing, Mich. 48823

The Mills Center, Inc., 1512 East Broward Boulevard, Fort Lauderdale, Fla. 33301

MIT Press, 28 Carleton Street, Cambridge, Mass. 02142

Modern Curriculum Press, Inc., 1390 Prospect Road, Cleveland, Ohio 44136

William Morrow and Co., 105 Madison Avenue, New York, N.Y. 10016

C. V. Mosby Co., a subsidiary of the Times Mirror Co., 11830 Westline Industrial Drive, St. Louis, Mo. 63141

National Assessment Office, Room 201A, Huron Towers, 222 Fuller Road, Ann Arbor, Mich. 48105

National Association for the Deaf, 814 Thayer Avenue, Silver Springs, Md. 20910

National Council of Teachers of English, 1111 Kenyon Road, Urbana, Ill. 67801

Thomas Nelson and Sons, Ltd., 36 Park Street, London W1Y, England

Thomas Nelson, Inc., 407 Seventh Avenue South, Nashville, Tenn. 37203

C. M. Nevins Printing Co., Pittsburgh, Pa.

New Century. *See* Meredith Corp.

New Dimensions in Education, 160 Dupont Street, Plainview, N.Y. 11803

Noble and Noble Publishers, 1 Dag Hammerskjold Plaza, New York, N.Y. 10017

Odyssey Press, Ltd., 300 East 42nd Street, New York, N.Y. 10017

Ohio State University Press, Hitchcock Hall, Room 316, 2070 Neil Avenue, Columbus, Ohio 43210

Open Court Publishing Co., Box 599, La Salle, Ill. 61301

The Orton Society, Inc., 8415 Bellona Lane, Suite 204, Towson, Md. 21204

F. A. Owen Publishing Co., 7 Bank Street, Dansville, N.Y. 14437

Oxford University Press, 417 Fifth Avenue, New York, N.Y. 10016

Parents Magazine Press, 52 Vanderbilt Avenue, New York, N.Y. 10017

Parker Publishing Co., a subsidiary of Prentice-Hall, Inc., West Nyack, N.Y. 10994

F. E. Peacock Publications, Inc., 401 W. Irving Park Road, Itasca, Ill. 60143

Penguin Books, Inc., 7110 Ambassador Road, Baltimore, Md. 21207

Perceptual Development Laboratories, Box 1911, Big Springs, Texas 79720

Personnel Press, 191 Spring Street, Lexington, Mass. 02173

Plays, Inc., Publishers, 8 Arlington Street, Boston, Mass. 02116

Popular Library (Unit of CBS), 600 Third Avenue, New York, N.Y. 10011

Prentice-Hall, Inc., Englewood Cliffs, N.J. 07632

The Psychological Corp., 757 Third Avenue, New York, N.Y. 10017

Psychological Test Specialists, Box 1441, Missoula, Mont. 59801

Psychotechnics, Inc., 1900 Pickwick Avenue, Glenview, Ill. 60025

Purdue University Audio-Visual Center, Lafayette, Ind. 47901

G. P. Putnam's Sons, 200 Madison Avenue, New York, N.Y. 10016

Pyramid Books, 919 Third Avenue, New York, N.Y. 10022

Rand McNally and Co., Box 7600, Chicago, Ill. 60680

Random House, 201 East 50th Street, New York, N.Y. 10022

Reader's Digest Services, Inc., Educational Division, Pleasantville, N.Y. 10570

The Reading Institute of Boston, 116 Newbury Street, Boston, Mass. 02116

Reading Is Fun-Damental, Smithsonian Institute, Washington, D.C. 20560

The Reading Laboratory, Inc., 55 Day Street, South Norwalk, Conn. 06854

Remedial Education Press, Kingsbury Center, 2138 Bancroft Place N.W., Washington, D.C. 20008

Right to Read, 400 Maryland Avenue S.W., Washington, D.C. 20202

The Ronald Press Co., 79 Madison Avenue, New York, N.Y. 10016

Scarecrow Press, Inc., a subsidiary of Grolier, Inc., 53 Liberty Street, Box 656, Metuchen, N.J. 08840

Scholastic Magazines and Book Services, 50 West 44 Street, New York, N.Y. 10036

Scholastic Magazines and Book Services, 50 West 44th Street, New York, N.Y.

Science Research Associates, Inc., 259 East Erie Street, Chicago, Ill. 60611

Scott Education Division, 35 Lower Westfield Road, Holyoke, Mass. 01040

Scott, Foresman and Co., 1900 East Lake Avenue, Glenview, Ill. 60025

William R. Scott, Inc., 333 Sixth Avenue, New York, N.Y. 10014

Charles Scribner's Sons, 597 Fifth Avenue, New York, N.Y. 10017

The Seabury Press, 815 Second Avenue, New York, N.Y. 10017

Selected Academic Readings, 630 Fifth Avenue, New York, N.Y. 10017

Silver Burdett Division, General Learning Corp., 250 James Street, Morristown, N.J. 07960

Simon and Schuster, Inc., 630 Fifth Avenue, New York, N.Y. 10020

L. W. Singer, Inc., a Division of Random House, 201 East 50th Street, New York, N.Y. 10022

Slosson Educational Publications, 140 Pine Street, East Aurora, N.Y. 14052

Society for Visual Education, Inc., 1345 Diversey Parkway, Chicago, Ill. 60614

Special Child Publications, 4635 Union Bay Place N.E., Seattle, Wash. 98105

Spoken Arts, Inc., 310 North Avenue, New Rochelle, N.Y. 10801

Steck-Vaughn Co., Box 2028, Austin, Texas 78767

Stoelting Co., 1350 South Kostner Avenue, Chicago, Ill. 60623

Syracuse University Press, Box 8, University Station, Syracuse, N.Y. 13210

Teachers College Press, Columbia University, 1234 Amsterdam Avenue, New York, N.Y. 10027

Teachers Publishing, a Division of Macmillan Publishing, Inc., 100 F Brown Street, Riverside, N.J. 08075

Teaching Resources Corp., 100 Boylston Street, Boston, Mass. 02116

Teaching Technology Corp., 2103 Green Spring Drive, Timonium, Md. 21093

Charles C. Thomas, Publisher, 301 East Lawrence Avenue, Springfield, Ill. 62717

Titmus Optical Vision Testers, 1312 West 7th Street, Piscataway, N.J. 08854

U.S. Government Printing Office, Division of Public Documents, Washington, D.C. 20402

University of Chicago Press, 1130 South Langley Avenue, Chicago, Ill. 60628

University of Illinois Press, Urbana, Ill. 61801

University of Iowa, Bureau of Audio-Visual Instruction, Iowa City, Iowa 52240

University of Minnesota Press, 2037 University Avenue S.E., Minneapolis, Minn. 55455

University Park Press, Chamber of Commerce Building, Baltimore, Md. 21202

The Vanguard Press, Inc., 424 Madison Avenue, New York, N.Y. 10017

Van Nostrand Reinhold, (Division of Litton), 450 W. 33rd Street, New York, N.Y. 10001

Van Wagenen Psychological Educational Laboratories, 1729 Irvin Ave. S. Minneapolis, Minn. 55403

The Viking Press, Inc., 625 Madison Avenue, New York, N.Y. 10022

Wadsworth, 10 Davis Drive, Belmont, California 94002

J. Weston Walach, P.O. Box 658, Portland, Maine 04104

Henry Z. Walck, Inc., 750 Third Avenue, New York, N.Y. 10017

Frederick Warne and Co., 101 Fifth Avenue, New York, N.Y. 10003

Washington Square Press, Inc., a Division of Simon and Schuster, 630 Fifth Avenue, New York, N.Y. 10020

Franklin Watts, Inc., 845 Third Avenue, New York, N.Y. 10022

Wayne State University Press, 5980 Cass Avenue, Detroit, Mich. 48202

Webster Division of McGraw-Hill Book Co., 1221 Avenue of the Americas, New York, N.Y. 10020

Weekly Reader, 245 Longhill Road, Middletown, Conn. 06457

Western Psychological Services, Box 775, Beverly Hills, Calif. 90213

Western Publishing Co., 850 Third Avenue, New York, N.Y. 10022

Westinghouse Learning Corp., Box 30, Iowa City, Iowa 52240

The Westminster Press, Witherspoon Building, Philadelphia, Pa. 19107

Albert Whitman and Co., 560 West Lake Street, Chicago, Ill. 60606

John Wiley & Sons, Inc. 605 Third Avenue, New York, N.Y. 10016

Williams and Wilkins Co., 428 East Preston Street, Baltimore, Md. 21202

H. W. Wilson Co., 950 University Avenue, Bronx, N.Y. 10452

Winston Press, 25 Grove Terrace, Minneapolis, Minn. 55403

Winter Haven Lions Research Foundation, Inc., Box 112, Winter Haven, Fla. 33880

Workshop Center for Open Education, 6 Shepard Hall, City College of New York, Convent Avenue and 140 Street, New York, N.Y. 10031

World Publishing Co., 280 Park Avenue, New York, N.Y. 10017
Xerox Education Publications, Education Center, Columbus, Ohio 43216
Richard L. Zweig Associates, 20800 Beach Boulevard, Huntington Beach, Calif.
   92648

Appendix F: *Answers to "Self Tests"*

Chapter 1

1.	d	5.	c
2.	c	6.	b
3.	d	7.	a
4.	c	8.	d

Chapter 2

1.	a	8.	a
2.	b	9.	c
3.	a	10.	d
4.	b	11.	a
5.	d	12.	b
6.	d	13.	a
7.	c	14.	d

Chapter 3

1.	b	7.	d
2.	d	8.	a
3.	a	9.	b
4.	a	10.	d
5.	d	11.	a
6.	b	12.	b

Chapter 4

1.	b	14.	a
2.	c	15.	a
3.	a	16.	a
4.	c	17.	a
5.	a	18.	b
6.	d	19.	a
7.	d	20.	a
8.	b	21.	b
9.	a	22.	c
10.	c	23.	b
11.	d	24.	a
12.	b	25.	b
13.	c	26.	d

Chapter 5

1.	c	7.	b
2.	c	8.	a
3.	a	9.	d
4.	b	10.	a
5.	b	11.	d
6.	c		

Chapter 6

1.	b	8.	d
2.	a	9.	c
3.	b	10.	a
4.	c	11.	c
5.	a	12.	b
6.	b	13.	d
7.	c	14.	c

Chapter 7

1.	a	10.	b
2.	d	11.	a
3.	b	12.	b
4.	d	13.	b
5.	d	14.	d
6.	c	15.	c
7.	a	16.	c
8.	c	17.	d
9.	c		

Chapter 8

1.	a	8.	b
2.	d	9.	c
3.	c	10.	c
4.	a	11.	b
5.	a	12.	a
6.	b	13.	d
7.	d	14.	c

Chapter 9A

1.	d	9.	b
2.	b	10.	c
3.	d	11.	a
4.	c	12.	b
5.	d	13.	a
6.	c	14.	b
7.	d	15.	c
8.	d		

Chapter 9B

1.	c	6.	c
2.	b	7.	d
3.	c	8.	d
4.	a	9	b
5.	c	10.	d

Chapter 10

1.	a	9.	d
2.	b	10.	d
3.	b	11.	d
4.	d	12.	a
5.	c	13.	a
6.	c	14.	a
7.	a	15.	d
8.	c		

Chapter 11

1.	d	9.	a
2.	a	10.	b
3.	d	11.	c
4.	d	12.	a
5.	b	13.	c
6.	c	14.	d
7.	b	15.	c
8.	d	16.	c

Chapter 12

1.	b	9.	b
2.	d	10.	d
3.	d	11.	d
4.	b	12.	a
5.	a	13.	c
6.	c	14.	b
7.	c	15.	c
8.	a	16.	d

Index

Ability (achievement) grouping, 49–50
Accelerating (rate) devices, 398–99
Activities:
    categorization, 117
    connectives, 132–33
    details, 149–50
    dictionary, 107–08
    fiction, 272–73
    figurative expression, 138–39
    following directions, 195–97
    foreign languages, 277–78
    interpretive level, 159–60
    literal level, 157–59
    main ideas, 148–49
    newspapers/magazines, 249–51
    sight words, 84–86
    structural analysis, 96–97
    syllabication, 99–100
    mathematics, terms in, 265–66
    types of literature, 271–72
    writing patterns
        for driver education, 308–09, 309–10
        for science, 257–58, 259, 261–62
        for social studies, 241–42, 244, 245–46
Affective dimension of comprehension,
    165–66
Affixes, 93–97
Analogies, 123–24
Aptitude (intelligence) tests, 331–33
Art, 316–18
Assessment, informal,
    of attitudes and interests, 357–61
    of comprehension, 337–40, 351–55
    of oral reading, 340–41, 352
    of sight vocabulary, 335–37
    of study skills, 341–51
    of word analysis skills, 88–89, 92;
        102–04, 106–07
Assumptions, faulty, 12–13
Astigmatism, 21
Attitudes, inventory of, 357–61

Auditory perception, 26
Autobiography, reading, 358–61

Book features, 188–90
Business education, 297–300

Card catalog, use of, 185–88
Categorization, 116–17
Cause/effect
    study guide, 260
    writing pattern
        for driver education, 308–09
        for science, 259–61
        for social studies, 240–42
Charts and diagrams, 206–07
Checklist
    for basic comprehension skills, 169–70
    for content reading skills, 278–79
    of factors related to reading, 20
    for word and sentence skills, 139–40
    for vision problems, 22–24
Chronological events:
    writing pattern for social science,
        243–44
Classification:
    writing pattern for science, 254–55
Classroom groupings, 49–53
Cloze test:
    directions for, 354
    procedure, 353
College reading program:
    materials for, 397–98
    open laboratory, 401–02
    organization of, 401–02
    syllabus, 403–06
Comparison/contrast:
    writing pattern for social science,
        244–46
Composition/grammar, 275

Compound words, 97–98
Comprehension:
  creative, 164
  critical, 160–64
  interpretive, 159–60
  literal, 156–59
  skills, 169–70
Concept development, 115–116
Connectives, 130–133
Content materials:
  abilities/skills needed in, 229–230
  compared with narrative materials,
    223–25
  concepts, 225
  graphic aids in, 228
  interest of, 228
  organizational styles in, 227
  rates for reading, 228
  readability, 227
  vocabulary, 226
Context analysis
  assessment of, 88–89
  instruction in, 89–91
  types of, 88
Creative thinking, 164
Critical reading, 160–64

Daily reading needs, 6
Developmental program, post
    secondary, 395–99
Diagnostic reading tests, 329–30
Dialects, 33–35
Dictionary:
  simplified, 109
  skills pretest, 106–107
Directed reading approach (DRA):
  examples of, 63–65, 65–68, 292
  features of, 61–63
Disability in reading, causes of, 20–37
Disabled readers, description of, 17–20
Drama, 274
Driver education, 307–16

Encyclopedia, teaching use of, 190–92
English (Language Arts), 270–75
Evaluative thinking, 160–64
EVOKER, 177
Expectancy reading level, 332–33
Experiment:
  writing pattern, for science, 255–56
Explanation of a process:
  writing pattern, for science, 256–58
Explanatory pattern, mathematics, 267
Eye-movements, 25

Fiction, 272–74
Figurative language, 138–39

Films/filmstrips, Appendix A, 416
Flexibility of reading rate, 209–13
Foreign languages, 277–78
Free/inexpensive teaching materials,
    Appendix C, 419–20
Frustration reading level, 340
Fry readability graph, 48

Goals, setting of, 372–73
Graded word list, 335–37
Grade equivalent, 325
Graphic aids, 197–08
Grouping, 49–53
Group reading inventory, (GRI) 337–41

Health (*see* Science), 253–64
Hearing, 25–26
High interest, low readability materials,
    Appendix B, 416–18
Home economics, 300–05
Home environment, 35–36

Incomplete sentence stimulus, 361
Individualized reading, 276–77
Industrial arts, 293–97
Inflectional endings, 93
Informal reading inventory (IRI), 351–53
Informal inventories:
  dictionary skills, 106–07
  phonics, 102–04
  structural analysis, 92
Informal skills checks, 341–51
Instructional reading level, 340
Integration of reading and content
    instruction, 233–34
Intelligence tests, 28–29, 331–32
Interests, reading, 8–9
Interest inventory, 362
Interpretive reading, 159–60
Inventory, skills, 341–51

Key words, 147–48

Laboratories and programmed
    materials, Appendix A, 415
Language experience materials, 72–73
Lessons:
  DRA, 61–68
  newspaper, 251–52
Levels of reading, 155–64
Library (trade) books:
  art, 317–18
  driver education, 315–16
  home economics, 304–05
  industrial arts, 297

mathematics, 269–70
music, 320
physical education, 307
Library skills, 185–88
Listening comprehension tests, 332–33
Literal thinking, 156–59
Literature, 271–75
Location of information:
in informational books, 188–90
in libraries, 185–88
in reference books, 190–92

Main ideas:
writing pattern for social sciences,
147–50, 242–43
Magazines/newspapers, Appendix B,
418–19
Maps, 197–00
Materials:
free/inexpensive, Appendix C, 419–20
supplementary reading, Appendix B,
416–19
teaching reading, Appendix A, 413–1
Mathematics
additional skills, 269
high interest material, 269–70
words/symbols, 264–66
writing patterns, 266–69
Mechanical equipment (hardware),
398–99
Motivation, 10
Multilevel textbooks, 68–70
Music, 318–20

Needs assessment, 378–79
Newspapers/magazines, 248–53
Norm - referenced tests, 324–35
Notetaking, 183–85

Observation, 355–56
Oral errors, marking of, 341
Oral tests, 330
Organizational skills
notetaking, 183–85
outlining, 179–82
summarizing, 182–83
Outlining, 179–82

PANORAMA, 178–79
Paragraph:
main ideas in, 147–49
structures, 150–54
Percentile ranks, 325
Periodical aids, 77
Phonics:
generalizations, 104–05

inventory, 102–04
terms, 101–02
Physical education, 305–07
Poetry, 274
Post-secondary reading programs
description of, 407–08
need for, 393–95
Prefixes and suffixes (*see* Affixes)
Preview guide, 145–46
Principal/administrator, 383–88
Problems:
writing pattern for
mathematics, 266–67
science, 261–62
Propaganda techniques, 162–63
Publishers' addresses, Appendix E,
423–30
Punctuation, 137–38

Questions and answers:
writing pattern for social science,
246–47

Readability
factors that influence, 45
formlas, 46
studies, 43–44
Reading
achievement
data about, 2–6
survey tests, 327–28
for appreciation, 6–10
autobiography, 358–61
committee, 371–72
consultant, 388
expectancy formula, 332–33
to follow directions, 194–97
improvement classes, 381–82
interests, 8–9
inventories, samples of, 92, 102–04,
106–07, 341–51
laboratories, 282–83
levels, 340
phases, 11–12
philosophy, 372
potential, determination of, 332–33
programs, 407–08
tests, kinds of, 324
Reading rate
adjustment, 209
factors affecting, 210
flexibility exercises, 213
machines, 211–12
skimming and scanning, 212–13
timed readings, 212
Reading–study skills, 174
Reading/study skills tests, Appendix D,
420–23

REAP, 178
Reciprocal Questioning (Re Quest), 165
Records/tapes, Appendix A, 416
Recreational reading, 6–10
Reference books, use of, 190–92
Reliability, 324–25
Remedial reading classes:
   college level, 399–00
   secondary level, 380–81
Report writing, 192–94
Retention, 213–15
Rewriting materials, 70–72

San Diego quick assessment, 335–36
Scanning, 212–13
Science:
   additional skills, 262-63
   resource books/magazines, 263–64
   style and vocabulary, 253–54
   writing patterns, 254–62
Selecting standardized tests, 333–35
Selection aids for materials, 76–77
Self-appraisal, 356–57
Self-concept, 31–33
Sentence:
   meaning, 136–139
   patterns, 136
Sight vocabulary, 82–84
Skill inventories:
   graphics, 343–45
   outlining/taking notes, 349–50
   rate flexibility, 350
   special symbols, formulas, 347–49
   study methods, 349
   using parts of a textbook, 342–43
   using reference material, 345–46
   vocabulary, 346–47
Skimming, 212–13
Social sciences:
   additional skills, 247–48
   vocabulary and organization, 238–40
   writing patterns, 240–47
Special English classes, 379–80
Special reading teacher, 389
SQ3R, 176
SQRQCQ, 177–78
Staff inservice training, 370–71
Standardized reading tests, 324–35
Stanines, 325–26
Statement of facts:
   writing pattern for science, 258–59
Structural analysis:
   activities to develop skill of, 96–97
   affixes/roots, 93–96
   compound words, 97–98
   inflectional endings, 93
   inventory of, 92
   syllabication/accent, 98–101

Structured overviews, 59–61, 129
Study guides, 54–58
Study methods, 175–79
Study skills tests, 330
Summarizing, 182–83
Supplementary reading materials,
   Appendix B, 416–19
Survey tests, 327–28
Syllabication/accent, 98–101
Symptoms:
   of auditory difficulties, 26
   of emotional maladjustment, 30
   of general health, 27
   of visual difficulties, 22–24
Syntax, 136–38

Tables, 205
Technical vocabularies, 226
Tests:
   college reading level, 407
   diagnostic, 329–30
   oral, 330
   reliability of, 324–25
   survey, 326–28
   of study skills, 330
   validity of, 324
Test-taking, 215–16
Textbooks, alternatives to, 68–72
Transformations, 137

Unit teaching:
   features of, 73–75
   health, 75
   literature, 75–76

Validity, 324
Vision problems, 21–22
Visual perception, defined, 25
Visual screening instruments, 24
Visualizing, 166–67
Vocabulary:
   assessment, 120–21
   discussion sessions, 133–34
   program, 118–20
   study guide, 129–30
Vocational materials
   following directions, 287–88
   interpreting graphics, 288–91
   low readability materials, 292–93
   reading of, 291–92
   technical vocabulary, 287
   writing patterns for, 285–86
Vowels:
   digraphs, 102
   diphthongs, 102

Whole selections, 154–55
Wide reading, 135
Word:
    attributes, 125–28
    changes, 122
    puzzles, 125–26
Word recognition:
    and context clues, 87–91
    and dictionaries, 106–09
    and sight words, 82–86

    phonics analysis in, 101–06
    structural analysis in, 91–101
Workbooks, Appendix A, 413–15
Writing patterns:
    driver education, 308–10
    English, 272–74
    mathematics, 266–69
    science, 254–62
    social sciences, 240–47
    vocational materials, 285